Wissenschaftliche Untersuchungen
zum Neuen Testament · 2. Reihe

Herausgeber / Editor
Jörg Frey (Zürich)

Mitherausgeber / Associate Editors
Friedrich Avemarie (Marburg)
Markus Bockmuehl (Oxford)
Hans-Josef Klauck (Chicago, IL)

297

Jason Maston

Divine and Human Agency in Second Temple Judaism and Paul

A Comparative Study

WIPF & STOCK · Eugene, Oregon

Wipf and Stock Publishers
199 W 8th Ave, Suite 3
Eugene, OR 97401

Divine and Human Agency in Second Temple Judaism and Paul
A Comparative Study
By Maston, Jason
Copyright©2010 Mohr Siebeck
ISBN 13: 978-1-5326-4255-5
Publication date 10/19/2017
Previously published by Mohr Siebeck, 2010

This licensed edition published by special permission
of Mohr Siebeck GmbH & Co. KG

Preface

This study is a slightly revised version of my PhD thesis accepted by Durham University in 2009. I thank, first, Prof Dr Jörg Frey and Prof Dr Friedrich Avemarie for recommending the study for acceptance into this series. The editorial staff at Mohr Siebeck led by Dr Henning Ziebritzki have been very efficient and helpful throughout the publication process. Ted Yoder of TSY Music saved me many hours of work by typesetting the book.

Several persons have contributed to the completion of this study. Professors John Barclay, J. Louis Martyn, and George H. van Kooten kindly shared pre-published material. Professor Barclay and Dr Simon Gathercole examined the thesis and pressed me for more precision at points. I would like to thank Dr Andrew Clarke for the opportunity to participate in the New Testament department at Aberdeen.

Professor Francis Watson guided the research with patience and grace at every stage. From our first conversation until our last, he always encouraged me and showed real interest in my ideas and conclusions. This study and my development as a scholar owe more to our conversations than this word of thanks can convey.

My fellow PhD companions made this journey more enjoyable. Drs Preston Sprinkle and Kyle Wells offered advice on several points. Two in particular gave more than I could have expected. Dr Ben Blackwell kindly opened his home to me during my trips to Durham. Dr Jonathan Worthington, a participate with me in the Durham Diaspora, was always willing to listen to my rambling thoughts and graciously gave his time to read the thesis.

Obviously, none of these are responsible for any remaining errors.

Above all, my wife Erin, deserves the most thanks, and I dedicate this study to her. You have sacrificed much in the pursuit of my dreams. Thank you for being a model of grace and love. You have created the perfect home for our children. Your reward will be great in the day of our Lord Jesus Christ.

Jason Maston
August 2010

Table of Contents

Preface V

Introduction 1

   A. Divine and Human Agency in Recent Discussion 1
   B. The Jewish Schools, Human Action, and Fate 10
   C. The Argument of This Study 18

Chapter 1: Obedience and the Law of Life in Sirach 22

   A. Identifying the Alternative Theologies 22
   B. The Establishment of the Human Agent 26
      1. Life through Torah Observance 30
         a. Wisdom and Torah in Sirach 31
         b. The Creator, His Commandments, and Human Obedience 34
         c. Obedience, Fear of God and Faith 48
         d. Atonement and Sin 53
         e. Summary 57
      2. The Human Ability to Obey 58
         a. Wisdom as the Result of Endurance 59
         b. Freedom and Providence 64
   C. Judgment as the Re-Action of God 66
      1. Patience and Mercy 67
      2. The Criterion of Divine Judgment 69
      3. Summary 73
   D. Conclusion 73

Chapter 2: God's Gracious Acts of Deliverance
              in the *Hodayot* 75

   A. Background Issues 75

B. Divine Saving Acts and Human Obedience	80
1. The Creaturely Limitations of Humanity	81
a. The Material Weakness of Humanity	83
b. The Moral Weakness of Humanity	87
c. The Problem of Being a Creature	88
d. Summary	94
2. Divine Action as the Basis for Human Action	94
a. Predestination	97
b. The Gift of Knowledge	113
c. Purification from Sin	117
d. The *Hodayot* as Covenantal Nomism?	119
e. Summary	121
C. Conclusion	122

Chapter 3: Sin, the Spirit, and Human Obedience in Romans 7–8 124

A. Paul's Critique of the Two-Ways Theology (7.7–25)	127
1 The Death of the ἐγώ	133
a. The Law and Life	133
b. Moral Optimism	136
2. Sin's Takeover of Human Capacity	140
a. The Concept of Sin	141
b. Sin's Destructive Reign	144
3. Conclusion	152
B. Obedience Accomplished Through the Spirit (8.1–13)	153
1. The Christological Modification	154
2. The Establishment of Human Ability	158
C. Conclusion	170

Conclusion 175

Bibliography 181

Index of Ancient Sources	199
Index of Modern Authors	213
Index of Subjects	217

Introduction

A. Divine and Human Agency in Recent Discussion

With the publication of *Paul and Palestinian Judaism* in 1977, Sanders began what has been described as a "Copernican revolution."[1] Prior to this work, NT scholars generally portrayed Judaism as crass legalism. Each individual attempted to meticulously keep the law, and each lived in perpetual fear of falling short at the Judgment by a mere one evil deed. Those who did manage to keep the law more often than not boasted egotistically before God. They demanded that God honour them, for they had successfully kept the law. Rejecting this Judaism as a false religion, NT scholars found in Paul true religion, and they read Paul as an opponent of this version of Judaism. The apostle of Christ came triumphantly to man's rescue with his proclamation of righteousness by faith alone. He showed that salvation was wholly the work of God. Here the apostle and his former religion are set in the sharpest contrast, and the dividing issue is the divine-human relationship. On whom does salvation depend – God or man? This version of Judaism and Paul is what Sanders found in the scholarship prior to his volume.[2]

Against this view of Judaism and the apostle's relationship to it, Sanders argued that Judaism was not "works-righteous legalism." He proposed instead "covenantal nomism" as the pattern of religion for Judaism.[3] Salvation was by God's grace, not human deeds. God graciously chose Israel as his people, gave to them the covenant, and this act determined that "all Israelites have a share in the world to come" (*Sanh.* 10.1 [Danby]). Obedience became, then, not the way into salvation, but the means to maintaining salvation. It was the response of any faithful covenant member. Obedience to the law belongs within the covenant relationship and was never far from God's grace. In Sanders' own words, "[C]ovenantal nomism is the view that one's place in God's plan is established on the basis of the covenant and that the covenant requires as the proper response of man his obedience to its commandments, while providing means of atonement for transgression" (75; cf. 236; 422).

---

[1] Hagner, "Paul and Judaism," 75.

[2] Sanders, *Paul and Palestinian Judaism*, 33–59. Parenthetical references in the following are to Sanders, *Paul and Palestinian Judaism*.

[3] In addition to Sanders' *Paul and Palestinian Judaism*, see also his "Covenant" and *Judaism*, 262–78. Sanders' view of Judaism was not new, as he notes (*Paul and Palestinian Judaism*, 4–7) with reference to Montefiore (*Judaism and St. Paul*), Schechter (*Aspects of Rabbinic Theology*), Moore (*Judaism*) and Davies (*Paul and Rabbinic Judaism*).

With this drastically different perspective on Second Temple Judaism, Sanders attempted a different reading of Paul. The opposition between grace/faith and works that so many earlier generations of scholars found in Paul simply could not be there. Instead, Paul's problem with the law was not that it required doing, but because it was not Christ. Paul held that salvation was by Christ alone, and this meant that salvation could not be through the law. Sanders argued,

> *Since* salvation is only in Christ, *therefore* all other ways toward salvation are wrong, and attempting to follow them has results which are the reverse of what is desired. What is wrong with following the law is not the effort itself, but the fact that the observer of the law is not seeking the righteousness which is given by God through the coming of Christ (Rom. 10.2–4). Effort itself is not the sin; the sin is aiming towards *any* goal but being found 'in Christ' (Phil. 3.9). (482; emphasis original)

While agreeing with other Jews about the goal, namely righteousness, Paul claims that the only true "righteousness" is that found by faith in Christ. He, therefore, rejects the righteousness of the law not because it requires obedience, but because "such a means leads to the wrong end (righteousness based on the law); and the end itself is wrong, since it is not salvation in Christ" (551). Paul also denies the salvific value of the Jewish covenant and claims instead that those who have faith in Christ are Abraham's descendants. In his rejection of the covenant and the election and grace implied by it, "it is thus not first of all against the *means* of being properly religious which are appropriate to Judaism that Paul polemicizes ('by works of the Law'), but against the prior fundamentals of Judaism" (551; emphasis original). *"What Paul founds wrong in Judaism,"* Sanders famously claimed is that *"it is not Christianity"* (552; emphasis original).

In his later work, *Paul, Judaism and the Law*, Sanders maintained this contrast between Christ and the Torah as fundamental to Paul's theology and rejection of the law. He also brought in an emphasis on the relationship between Jews and Gentiles. Sanders argues that especially in Galatians, but also in Romans Paul does not oppose faith or works themselves but the refusal to accept Gentiles apart from law observance.[4] The issue is about membership into the people of God. This is "the actual subject of the dispute" between Paul and the Christian missionaries in Galatia, not "the theological issue of grace and merit."[5] The theological content is not dismissed entirely. It is rather interpreted as a contrast between Christ and the law, and the sociological argument is elevated to equal status.

Despite setting the law in opposition to Christ, Sanders maintained that the pattern of religion was fundamentally the same: salvation is by grace and one remains in the sphere of salvation through obedience. The point at which

---

[4] Sanders, *Law*, 18–20, 47, 155.
[5] Sanders, *Law*, 19.

A. Divine and Human Agency in Recent Discussion

many find Paul and Judaism to diverge irreconcilably, namely grace and works, Sanders claimed instead that "Paul is in agreement with Palestinian Judaism" (*Paul and Palestinian Judaism*, 542). He continues, "There are two aspects of the relationship between grace and works: *salvation is by grace but judgment is according to works; works are the condition of remaining 'in', but they do not earn salvation*" (543; emphasis original). Although Paul and Judaism shared this similar view, Sanders held that Paul's thought should not be described as "covenantal nomism." Paul's thought revolved around participatory categories, and covenantal nomism could not capture these ideas (514).[6] Despite Paul thinking in fundamentally different categories, the relationship between "getting in" and "staying in" was basically the same. No substantial differences can be detected in the patterns.

Sanders' two volumes, especially *Paul and Palestinian Judaism*, have decisively altered the direction of Pauline research. Within four years, Dunn had dubbed the possibilities opened by Sanders' work the "New Perspective on Paul."[7] In this lecture of the same title, Dunn began to develop an understanding of Paul built firmly on Sanders' picture of Judaism. Dunn was unimpressed by Sanders' interpretation of Paul, though, so he sought to understand Paul within Sanders' Judaism.[8] Dunn thus agreed with Sanders that Judaism did not think salvation was by works. Recognising the importance of Paul's antithesis between "faith in Christ" and "works of the law," Dunn argued that the latter phrase should not be generalised to any human deed. It is rather a contextually specific phrase referring to the key distinguishing markers of the Jewish people: circumcision, food laws, and Sabbath regulations, or covenantal nomism when bound too close to Israel's national identity.[9] While Dunn's subsequent works have clarified how he understands this phrase, he argues consistently that the phrase has nothing to do with legalistic works-righteousness.[10] It cannot mean this simply because Judaism believed that salvation was by grace not works.

---

[6] He discusses Paul's participation ideas in *Paul and Palestinian Judaism*, 453–72, 502–08.

[7] Dunn, "New Perspective." This article was originally given as a lecture in 1981 and published in 1982. Page references are to the reprint in *The New Perspective on Paul*.

[8] Dunn, "New Perspective," 93–95. Commenting on Sanders' Paul, Dunn writes, "But this presentation of Paul is only a little better than the one rejected. There remains something very odd in Paul's attitude to his ancestral faith. The Lutheran Paul has been replaced by an idiosyncratic Paul who in arbitrary and irrational manner turns his face against the glory and greatness of Judaism's covenant theology and abandons Judaism simply because it is not Christianity" (93).

[9] Dunn, "New Perspective," 101; idem, "Works of the Law," 117.

[10] Dunn writes, "'[W]orks of the law' characterize the whole mind set of 'covenantal nomism'—this is, the conviction that status within the covenant (= righteousness) is maintained by doing what the law requires ('works of the law'). Circumcision and food laws in particular come into play simply (!) because they provided the key test cases for most Jews of Paul's time" ("Yet Once More," 208). See also idem, *Theology of Paul*, 358; "New Perspective on Paul: Whence, Whither, and How," 22–26.

Whereas Sanders set Christ and the Torah in opposition to one another as the distinction between Paul and Judaism, Dunn found this contrast in Paul's claim that Gentiles can be among God's people without Jewish identity markers and the exclusivity of Judaism.[11] Paul's gospel opened the way for Gentiles to be saved apart from observance of the Jewish Torah. They could come to faith in Christ as Gentiles. The antithesis between justification by faith or works of the law encapsulates Paul's attempt to establish that salvation is possible outside the confines of Jewish exclusiveness.[12] While the antithesis might have something to say about the individual's standing before God, it is primarily about the ecclesiological relationship between Jews and Gentiles as the one people of God.[13] Paul's problem with his fellow Jews, then, is not that they prioritise human action over divine action, but that they limit the scope of salvation.

In contrast to those who found Paul's soteriology to be radically different from Judaism, Dunn contends that one finds in Paul's thought the same basic relationship between grace and obedience that one finds in Judaism. Against Sanders Dunn argues that covenantal nomism is an accurate description of Paul's soteriology. He agrees with Hooker, who writes, "In many ways, the pattern which Sanders insists is the basis of Palestinian Judaism fits exactly the Pauline pattern of Christian experience: God's saving grace evokes man's answering obedience."[14] What Paul objects to is not "covenantal nomism" itself, but a form of covenantal nomism that ties the covenant and the law too closely to Israel's ethnic and national identity.[15] Once removed from this nationalistic context, Paul is quite comfortable with the pattern.

While some scholars opposed Sanders' interpretation of Judaism,[16] for the most part Sanders' view was warmly embraced and would come to be simply taken for granted by much of subsequent scholarship. Studies by Garlington and Yinger sought to support Sanders' interpretation of the Jewish texts. Garlington explores the relationship between faith and obedience in the "apocryphal" texts.[17] He contends that the two are not in opposition, but expressions of one another. The Jewish person did not obey in order to attain salvation since this was already given by grace through the covenant and election. Obedience has the precise function that Sanders claimed for it, namely, as the response of

---

[11] Dunn, "New Perspective," 104; idem, "Noch einmal," 411.

[12] See Dunn's interpretation of Galatians 2.15–16 in his *Galatians*, 132–41. Cf. Wright, "Paul of History," 71: "[W]e must see justification by faith as a polemical doctrine, whose target is not the usual Lutheran one of 'nomism' or *'Menschenwerke'*, but the Pauline one of Jewish national pride."

[13] See Dunn, "Justice of God;" idem, "Paul and Justification by Faith," 365–69.

[14] Hooker, "Paul and 'Covenantal Nomism'," 157. Cited by Dunn, *Theology of Paul*, 632n.29.

[15] Dunn, "Theology of Galatians."

[16] See Carson, *Divine Sovereignty*, 86–95; Seifrid, *Justification by Faith*.

[17] Garlington, *'Obedience of Faith'*.

A. Divine and Human Agency in Recent Discussion

the covenant member to God's grace. Based on his analysis of the uses of the phrase "judgment by deeds" in the Jewish texts, Yinger concludes that obedience did not earn salvation. Rather it was the evidence of one's faithfulness to God.[18] Both studies maintain that salvation according to the Jewish texts discussed is by God's grace.

Although giving broad support to Sanders' interpretation of Judaism, many scholars have rejected his interpretation of Paul, and they have busied themselves with the task of making sense of Paul against the backdrop of a non-legalistic Judaism. The two works just noted fall squarely in this category. Both seek to demonstrate the continuity between Paul and Judaism on the relationship between obedience and salvation. Yinger argues that there is no conflict between justification by faith and judgment according to works in Paul because faith and works are simply not in opposition. Garlington and Yinger explicitly maintain that Paul's pattern of religion is identical to covenantal nomism.[19] Although the taxonomy "covenantal nomism" itself may not be entirely accurate, Yinger maintains that "the fundamental structure of grace and works, election and obedience, salvation and judgment, remains the same" even though "the role of the Spirit in enabling obedience, while not absent in Judaism, is certainly heightened significantly in Paul." He continues, "Salvation . . . is given by God's grace; *and* it is contingent upon continuance in the faith and obedience which are required by that relationship."[20]

The important work by Engberg-Pedersen begins from the premise that Sanders is correct about Judaism and that the "New Perspective" is accurate about the basic problem that Paul had with other Jews.[21] The details of Engberg-Pedersen's study need not detain us, for the primary reason to note him here is his refusal to discuss Paul's statements about divine acts. This refusal stems from his claims about what constitutes "real options" for the post-Enlightenment person. Paul's ethics, as well as those of the Stoics, are still valid options, but theological claims, while important for Paul, must be bracketed out and ultimately ignored.[22] Engberg-Pedersen does not deny that Paul makes statements about divine action nor that these claims may have been important for Paul himself. For example, while noting Paul's "participation" ideas ex-

---

[18] Yinger, *Judgment*, 285–86.
[19] Garlington, *'Obedience of Faith'*, 264–65; Yinger, *Judgment*, 288–90.
[20] Yinger, *Judgment*, 289 (emphasis original).
[21] Engberg-Pedersen, *Paul and the Stoics*, 14–16.
[22] "[T]he present work cannot at all get off the ground unless one takes the historical-critical, 'naturalistic' perspective wholly seriously. One must bracket completely, at least initially, any 'theological' interest one may have in aligning oneself with Paul's own perspective, which is definitely a 'theological' one that begins, logically, 'from above' in ideas about God and his acts. One must part company with Paul and give up reading him merely from within. Instead, one must read the whole of Paul—including his 'theological' ideas—coolly from the outside" (Engberg-Pedersen, *Paul and the Stoics*, 2).

pressed in Romans 8.1–13, they are quickly set aside because they do not help the modern interpreter to understand why the Christ event can result in sinless living.[23] Statements about divine action (that is, the Christ event) are passed over in favour of statements about how the believer perceives himself or herself.

The outcome of Engberg-Pedersen's hermeneutical claims is that one can talk seriously only about Paul's statements about human understanding.[24] In his interpretation of Paul's ethics and anthropology, the issue of divine and human agency stands out not because he explicitly discusses the issue, but because of the dismissal of the problem. He has attempted to clarify his understanding of divine and human agency in subsequent studies, but in both one finds an emphasis on the human agent and one senses in fact hesitancy toward the subject itself.[25]

Two decades after Sanders' volume, Marshall described the "New Perspective on Paul" as "the new orthodoxy."[26] Scholars in general have been content with Sanders' picture of Jewish soteriology, and while disagreeing with his interpretation of Paul, they have often claimed that the basic pattern that one finds in Judaism is also found in Paul. This brief survey has highlighted the general rejection by recent scholars of the Pauline contrast between faith and works of the law as indicating fundamentally different means to salvation, an interpretation of Paul's antithesis that earlier scholars simply took for granted. Against this "traditional" reading of Paul's antithesis, these scholars have claimed that everyone agreed that salvation was by grace not works. To put this claim in the language of this study: salvation is accomplished through divine action not human action. The outcome of Sanders' portrayal of Judaism and the development of the New Perspective on Paul is a general claim that Paul and Judaism agreed on the relationship between divine and human action. While the relationship between certain aspects of a "soteriological" pattern or a "pattern of religion," such as justification by faith and judgment by works, remains unclear, these items do not indicate alternative means to salvation. This is so because faith and works were never in conflict. This claim, which is based on Sanders' portrayal of Judaism and the "ethnic" interpretation of Paul's antithesis, has become the

---

[23] Engberg-Pedersen, *Paul and the Stoics*, 248–52.

[24] Engberg-Pedersen denies that one must choose between Paul's apocalyptic statements about God and his philosophical statements about humanity ("Response," 106), but the only "real option for us" remains his statements about human understanding.

[25] Engberg-Pedersen, "Self-Sufficiency and Power;" idem, "Material Spirit." In the latter article on Romans 8.1–13, he interprets the *pneuma* not as the divine Spirit, but as a constituent part of the human being. Where others have found divine action, he has explained it away.

[26] Marshall, "Salvation, Grace and Works," 340. Many scholars have been stressing the diversity of the "New Perspective," and it is mistaken to think of it as a "school." There are nevertheless key points that hold a group of scholars together under the umbrella "New Perspective." These would include (an uncritical) following of Sanders' view of Judaism and generally an opposition to a "Lutheran" interpretation of Paul and justification by faith. See Westerholm, *Perspectives*, 250–57.

trump card against any attempt to find in Paul's debate with Judaism different understandings of how God and humans interact. This is nowhere clearer than in the works of Engberg-Pedersen.

In his review of Watson's *Paul and the Hermeneutics of Faith*, Engberg-Pedersen claims that Sanders and the New Perspective on Paul have demonstrated that Paul's antithesis between faith and works of the law is not "between unconditionality (divine agency or saving action) and conditionality (human 'salvific' action)" but "is fundamentally an ethnic one."[27] Watson argues that Paul's antithesis derives from his interpretation of the soteriological patterns found in the Torah.[28] One view arises from Leviticus 18.5 and makes life contingent on law observance. The other view originates from Genesis 15.6 (and Hab 2.4), which describes the unconditional nature of God's promise. Whereas other Jews highlighted Abraham's obedience to God's will as the reason he is declared righteous, Paul centres the story on God's unilateral promise. This interpretative claim, according to Watson, is Paul's antithesis, and at the heart of this antithesis are two alternative means to salvation. The one is based on human obedience to the Torah, and the other is oriented toward what God has done in Christ. Paul's antithesis, according to Watson, is primarily about the ways in which the divine and human agents interact, and in this sense, it is set over against the "ethnic" interpretation advocated by Dunn, Wright, and others.[29] Watson seeks to reintroduce into the interpretation of Paul's antithesis a "vertical" aspect and to read the antithesis as less directly about the Jew-Gentile problem. Paul's claims about the unconditional divine saving act have consequences for how Jews and Gentiles relate within the church, but the antithesis is not fundamentally about this issue.[30]

In Watson's view, the contrast between the unconditional nature of God's saving act and human obedience set forth in Paul's antithesis between faith in Christ and works of the law is not the sum total of Paul's view on divine and human agency. Abraham is not simply a passive recipient of divine grace. Rather, the divine saving act calls for a response in faith and obedience.[31] The two phrases "faith in Christ" and "works of the law," Watson argues, refer to communal ways of living and, therefore, human agency.[32] Each way, however, has a different focus since the former is directed toward what God did in Christ

---

[27] Engberg-Pedersen, "Lutheran Paul?" 457.
[28] Watson, *Paul and the Hermeneutics of Faith*, 39, 76; idem, "Constructing an Antithesis," 101–02.
[29] Watson, *Paul and the Hermeneutics of Faith*, 218.
[30] Watson shows how the antithesis functions within an ecclesiological setting in his revised *Paul, Judaism, and the Gentiles*. He argues that the antithesis has the social function of limiting the scope of salvation to the "Christian" community, which is formed of both Jews and Gentiles, rather than the "Jewish" community (121–21; 212).
[31] Watson, *Paul and the Hermeneutics of Faith*, 192, 218.
[32] Watson, *Paul, Judaism, and the Gentiles*², 121–25, 129.

and the latter is oriented toward what humans do.³³ In Paul's view, Watson contends, divine and human agency are not set in opposition, but in comparison with some of his fellow Jews, Paul does indeed prioritise divine action.³⁴

Watson's argument that the Pauline antithesis is about the divine-human relationship runs against the grain of recent studies that have claimed the antithesis is solely or fundamentally about how Gentiles can be considered equal members of the one people of God. Additionally, his argument that Paul's theology prioritised divine action in a manner not seen in some other Jewish texts directly opposes claims that Paul and Judaism agreed on the relationship between works and grace. These claims about Paul's view of the divine-human relationship are what Engberg-Pedersen objects to when he asserts that Paul's antithesis is "fundamentally an ethnic one." His critique of Watson assumes that the arguments made in favour of the New Perspective over the last three decades are accurate and beyond question.³⁵ Moreover, the "ethnic" interpretation is set against any explicit "theological" reading of the grace/works contrast.³⁶ All Paul's talk about grace, faith, and works of the law amounts simply to an attempt to get Gentiles into the people of God. The language means nothing more than this. As the title to Engberg-Pedersen's review implies, "Once More a Lutheran Paul?", any interpretation that resembles the old perspective and thus raises even the slightest possibility that Paul has something to say about how God and humans, both Jews and Gentiles, relate in the salvation process, is to be rejected outright. The New Perspective has taught us this, at least in Engberg-Pedersen's view.³⁷

Engberg-Pedersen advances a second reason that talk about divine and human agency in Paul is invalid: it introduces an "either/or-*dichotomy*" between divine and human action that no one in the ancient world made.³⁸ Here along with Watson's work, Martyn's interpretation of Paul is subjected to criticism. Martyn contends that at the heart of Paul's gospel is a claim about God's apocalyptic act in Christ to liberate humanity from the grasp of Sin and the Flesh.³⁹ Here God himself has invaded the human realm to resolve the human dilemma

---

[33] Watson, *Paul, Judaism, and the Gentiles*², 125–27, 129.

[34] Watson, *Paul, Judaism, and the Gentiles*², 15–19.

[35] Engberg-Pedersen does briefly discuss Romans 4.16 as support for the ethnic interpretation ("Lutheran Paul?" 457–58). His conclusion that Paul's point is only that faith makes salvation available to all never actually addresses the issue that Paul writes about divine initiative and human response. The relationship between these two aspects is simply ignored.

[36] Here the charge that the New Perspective amounts to a sociological study does have some validity. See Matlock, "Almost Cultural Studies;" Byrne, "Interpreting Romans Theologically," 230–32.

[37] While Engberg-Pedersen claims that Watson is wrong to prioritise divine action, Hays criticises Watson for underemphasising divine action in his interpretation of πίστις Χριστοῦ as "faith in Christ" ("Paul's Hermeneutics," 129–30).

[38] Engberg-Pedersen, "Response," 109.

[39] Martyn, *Galatians*, 97–105, 349.

created by Sin and the Flesh. Against the power of the Flesh, God sends his Spirit. The Christian community is swept up into this cosmic battle between the Flesh and the Spirit as each battles the other for the loyalty of the community. Believers are not passive agents, unable to act in accordance with one power or the other. Rather, they are "soldiers."[40] Even in points of exhortation, according to Martyn, the focus remains on God's acts of deliverance through his Son and in the Spirit. Paul's gospel prioritises divine action.[41]

In Engberg-Pedersen's view, the emphasis placed on divine action by Martyn and Watson fundamentally misconstrues Paul because it introduces a mode of thinking that has its origins in post-ancient debates. He writes, "[T]he idea of a clear and radical contrast between a way to salvation that is 'unconditional', in the sense that it is exclusively an expression of divine agency, and a way that is 'conditional' in the sense that it also involves human agency" is a contrast that "has no footing at all in the ancient texts themselves."[42] The proposed distinction that Watson, Martyn, and others identify is simply the creation of modern minds. "There just is not such a distinction to be found anywhere, neither phenomenologically nor in the ancient texts themselves. It is a later, distinctly theological construct, made in order to contrast the one true 'faith' from all other types of (ir)religion, which are so many forms of humanly based idolatry."[43] Here the creation of the distinction is given a polemical thrust since the contrast arose as an attempt in modern times to defend "the one true 'faith'" (presumably he means Christianity) from all pretenders. As he contends in another essay, "It is possible, therefore, that the question of specifically divine and human agency understood in this theological sense is a fundamentally post-ancient one. Perhaps the distinction will turn out not to have any real grip in an ancient analysis of action but rather to have served as a weapon in a more recent battle between 'religion' and 'humanism', Christianity and philosophy."[44] The very question of divine and human agency has been ruled beyond the pale by Engberg-Pedersen because it belongs to a different time and a different debate. Thus, not only is it not found in Paul's letters because he is concerned with ethnic issues (as the New Perspective has demonstrated), but one should not even expect it to be there because he simply could not have thought about it (since no one in the ancient world did).

This final quote comes from Engberg-Pedersen's contribution to the volume *Divine and Human Agency in Paul and His Cultural Environment* edited by Barclay and Gathercole. This claim sits awkwardly in a volume devoted to the very subject of divine and human agency in the ancient world. While recognis-

---

[40] Martyn, *Galatians*, 529–32; cf. idem, *Theological Issues*, 251–66.
[41] Martyn, *Galatians*, 271.
[42] Engberg-Pedersen, "Lutheran Paul?" 452.
[43] Engberg-Pedersen, "Lutheran Paul?" 456.
[44] Engberg-Pedersen, "Self-sufficiency and Power," 116; cf. 127.

ing the difficulty of speaking about this subject, the essayists in this volume are generally quite comfortable exploring how various sources explained the interaction between God and humanity. No thought is given to the possibility that the very issue, especially in this either/or format, is invalid. They find in the Jewish texts a variety of attempts to explain the relationship between divine and human actions. Engberg-Pedersen's claim, therefore, sits uneasily in a volume that finds the issue in the ancient texts.[45] It presses the question of whether the entire project was misguided from the outset.

Engberg-Pedersen's claims appear to be significant challenges to those interpretations that have sought to find in Paul's letters contrasting salvific patterns based on either divine initiative or human obedience. Nevertheless, the assumption that the New Perspective interpretation is right must be tested against the sources themselves rather than assumed. Here Josephus' description of the Jewish schools is very informative. Josephus' texts indicate that the claim that Judaism maintained that salvation was always by grace (divine action) not obedience (human action) is not entirely accurate. Also, the assertion that no one discussed the issue of divine and human agency is contradicted by Josephus.

B. The Jewish Schools, Human Action, and Fate

Josephus often mentions men who belong to the leading Jewish groups of the Second Temple Period, but only on three occasions does he describe the theological positions of the groups (*J.W.* 2.119–166; *Ant.* 13.171–173; 18.11–25). While in two of the accounts he lists several differences between the three groups, the only issue that appears in all three accounts is the relationship between fate and human freedom, the issue of divine and human agency. Although Josephus considered his description in *War* 2.119–166 to be the definitive statement (cf. *Ant.* 13.173; 18.11), it is more useful for our purposes to begin with *Antiquities* 13.171–173.

Although following the narrative of 1 Maccabees in this section of *Antiquities,* Josephus interjects this comment about the Jewish schools:[46]

Now at this time were three schools among the Jews, which thought differently about human actions [περὶ τῶν ἀνθρωπίνων πραγμάτων διαφόρως]; the first of these were called Pharisees, the second Sadducees, and the third Essenes. The Pharisees, for their part, say that certain events, but not all, are the work of fate [εἱμαρμένης]; with others it depends on ourselves [τινὰ δ' ἐφ' ἑαυτοῖς ὑπάρχειν] whether they shall take place or not. The sect of the Essenes, how-

---

[45] Indeed, his discussion of Epictetus and Paul presumes that ancient thinkers did discuss and attempt to work out how divine and human agency related. He never relates this to his claim that the topic is a modern one, though.

[46] The reason Josephus puts this passage here is debated. See Sievers who argues that the passage was introduced secondarily into the text ("Josephus, First Maccabees, Sparta, The Three Haireseis").

ever, declares fate the mistress of all things [πάντων τὴν εἱμαρμένην κυρίαν] and says that nothing befalls men unless it be in accordance with her decree. But the Sadducees do away with fate, believing that it is nothing and that human actions are not achieved in accordance with her decree, but that all things lie within our power [ἅπαντα δὲ ἐφ' ἡμῖν αὐτοῖς κεῖσθαι], so that we ourselves are responsible for our well-being, while we suffer misfortune through our own thoughtlessness [ὡς καὶ τῶν ἀγαθῶν αἰτίους ἡμᾶς γινομένους καὶ τὰ χείρω παρὰ τὴν ἡμετέραν ἀβουλίαν λαμβάνοντας]. (*Ant.* 13.171–73 [Marcus, LCL])

The main topic of this comment is how the Jewish schools (αἱρέσεις) understand the issue of "human actions," and particularly how each understands the relationship between human actions and divine sovereignty ("fate"). Although aware of other differences between the schools, Josephus here distinguishes them based solely on their views of fate and responsibility. Boccaccini rightly comments, "[I]t is important to see how the major ancient historian of Jewish thought took exactly the problem of the relationship between human and divine agency as the criterion for identifying the Jewish 'schools of thought' of his time, more than any halakhic controversy. The emphasis on theological and philosophical issues is not (only) a modern obsession of Christian scholars."[47]

Josephus' language is drawn from philosophical debates, and his presentation of the Jewish schools mirrors other summary statements about different views taken by the Greek philosophical schools.[48] His presentation has caused many debates, most of which centre around the issue of whether Josephus intended his readers to identify individual Jewish sects with individual philosophical schools.[49] Josephus' language is too vague to go much beyond superficial generalities. More likely, he portrays the Jewish schools through common philosophical patterns simply in order to give his readers a point of contact. He assumes his readers will be familiar with the philosophical debates and the manner in which one can briefly relay those positions, so he adopts this pattern in order to relay to his readers something about the leading Jewish groups of that period. More importantly, for our purposes, his use of these standard patterns indicates that one need not be a philosopher to have an interest in the subject of divine and human agency.

Josephus plots the three schools along a single line. The Essenes and Sadducees correspond to the extremes, with the Pharisees representing something of a compromise. The Essenes, according to Josephus, attribute everything to

---

[47] Boccaccini, "Inner-Jewish Debate," 15. Cf. Moore, *Judaism*, 1:456.

[48] See Mason, *Flavius Josephus*, 132–52; idem, "Josephus' Pharisees." See Winston, *Wisdom of Solomon*, 46–58, for a survey of Jewish and Greco-Roman perspectives on freedom and determinism.

[49] These issues include his use of εἱμαρμένη (is it being used in a philosophical or popular sense? how does it relate to God and Jewish ideas about providence?), the intent behind identifying the "schools" as "philosophies," and the historical accuracy of his description. On the first issue, see Moore, "Fate and Free Will;" Martin, "Josephus' Use of *Heimarmene*;" Mason, *Flavius Josephus*, 132–42, 383–98. On the second see Saldarini, *Pharisees*, 123–27; Mason, *Flavius Josephus*, 125–28. On the third see Maier, *freier Wille*.

fate. They view God's sovereignty as absolute and uncompromising. The Essenes on this view eliminate the human agent entirely by making him or her a passive character acted upon by fate but never acting with or against it. The position is theological determinism in its fullest expression. The Sadducees, on the other end, deny the reality of fate and attribute every action to the human agent alone. They do not deny the existence of God – such a notion would make little sense in an ancient Jewish (or Greco-Roman) context (cf. *J.W.* 2.165 [see below]). They reject rather the notion that God is the ultimate cause behind what a human does. The prospect of blessing belongs to those who do good, while misfortune is the outcome for those who are careless. Apparently, they deny fate because they wish to maintain human accountability. The Sadducean view comes close to human autonomy. The Pharisees hold the middle ground between these two extremes. They deny neither human nor divine agency, and neither do they allow one more control. In their view, according to Josephus, they attribute some actions to fate, but others to humans. Despite recognising both agents, they do not fall outside of Josephus' single trajectory. They do not view God and humans working together. Instead, they limit each to certain tasks. God does this; humans do that.

In this account of the Jewish schools, Josephus has selected only one issue by which to introduce them: the relationship between fate and human freedom. He presents the schools similarly to the Hellenistic philosophical schools of which his readers would probably have been aware. By plotting the schools along a single line, Josephus depicts the divine-human relationship in antithetical terms. The two agents do not cooperate, but when one acts the other does not. This antithetical framework appears in the other two school passages also, although Josephus does hint at the possibility that there are other frameworks in which to relate the two agents.

The school passage in *War* 2.119–166 is the longest because of Josephus' lengthy description of the Essenes (§§119–161). When he finally comes to the Pharisees and Sadducees (§§162–166), he very quickly lays out the differences between them regarding the issues of fate, immortality of the soul, and their mannerisms toward "members" and outsiders. Due to this last comment, the Pharisees are presented in a good light, although they are still overshadowed by the glowing review of the Essenes. This alerts the interpreter to be aware that Josephus has a rhetorical purpose in view as he writes. He is not striving for historical objectivism, although he is describing the schools' views in a manner that he considers accurate.

He writes:

Of the two-first named schools, the Pharisees, who are considered the most accurate interpreters of the laws, and hold the position of the leading sect, attribute everything to Fate and to God [εἱμαρμένῃ τε καὶ θεῷ προσάπτουσι πάντα]; they hold that to act rightly or otherwise rests, indeed, for the most part with men, but that in each action Fate co-operates [καὶ τὸ μὲν πράττειν τὰ δίκαια καὶ μὴ κατὰ τὸ πλεῖστον ἐπὶ τοῖς ἀνθρώποις κεῖσθαι βοηθεῖν δὲ

B. The Jewish Schools, Human Action, and Fate

εἰς ἕκαστον καὶ τὴν εἱμαρμένην].... The Sadducees, the second of the orders, do away with Fate altogether [τὴν μὲν εἱμαρμένην παντάπασιν ἀναιροῦσιν], and remove God beyond, not merely the commission, but the very sight, of evil. They maintain that man has the free choice of good or evil, and that it rests with each man's will whether he follows the one or the other [φασὶν δ' ἐπ' ἀνθρώπων ἐκλογῇ τό τε καλὸν καὶ τὸ κακὸν προκεῖσθαι καὶ κατὰ γνώμην ἑκάστου τούτων ἑκατέρῳ προσιέναι]. (*J.W.* 2.162–165 [Thackeray, LCL])

Josephus uses some of the same language here that he uses also in *Antiquities* 13.171–173. He places the issue of fate at the beginning of his account thereby bringing the focus of the reader onto this topic.[50] He had not mentioned the Essene position on fate in his review of them, which further highlights the importance of this topic for his contrast between the Pharisees and Sadducees.

Concerning the Pharisees, Josephus explains that they hold both fate and human freedom. On the one hand, the Pharisees are comfortable ascribing to God and fate an absolute sovereignty. "Everything" (πάντα) has its origin in God and fate. On the other, they maintain that humans are ultimately responsible for their deeds. Humans possess within themselves the capacity to choose between good and evil. The Sadducees represent the contrasting position. They not only claim that God neither sees nor does any evil, they also cast out the very idea of fate.[51]

The account of the Sadducean position here is virtually identical to the one in *Antiquities* 13.173. Josephus makes clear that they approach "fate" and God differently. They deny the existence of the former, while only limiting the purview of the latter. By rejecting fate, "they deny the 'executive' aspect of God's nature, his involvement in the world."[52] This distinction between fate and God confirms the assumption made in the interpretation of *Antiquities* 13.173 that the Sadducees are only rejecting the concept of fate not God himself. Their disavowal of fate leaves ethical behaviour solely in the hands of humans. Again, Josephus presents their view in antithetical terms, and it is a form of human autonomy.

The description of the Pharisees, though, contains more complexity. In *Antiquities* 13.172–173, the Pharisees hold the middle position between the other two schools.[53] In *War* 2.162–165, Josephus only works with two schools so he

---

[50] The two participles δοκοῦντες and ἀπάγοντες, according to Mason, "are strictly preliminary to the main issue in 2:162ff., which now comes clearly into view, namely: the Pharisee's position on εἱμαρμένη and voluntary action." He continues, "By isolating the main verb (προσάπτουσι), we have also found the central issue in the comparison (μέν ... δέ.) between Pharisees and Sadducees in §§162–165. The two schools differ about whether 'fate' is a factor in human life" (*Flavius Josephus*, 132).

[51] Baumbach draws a false distinction between "the question of predestination and free will" and "a Jewish problem of a soteriological sort" ("Sadducees in Josephus," 175).

[52] Mason, *Flavius Josephus*, 137n.62.

[53] For discussion see Mason, *Flavius Josephus*, 203–07. His conclusion is that the difference stems from Josephus' vagueness when discussing the divine-human relationship (p.205).

presents the Pharisees as the opposite perspective of the Sadducees. Whereas in Antiquities 13.172 only some things (τινὰ καὶ οὐ πάντα) are attributed to fate and some (τινά) to human action, in *War* 2.162 everything (πάντα) originates from fate. The change in the Pharisaic view is due to rhetorical pressures. Josephus needs the Pharisees to contrast the Sadducees in *War* 2.162–163, and in *Antiquities* 13.172–173, that role can be filled by the Essenes. Based on this alteration in the accounts, Mason contends that it "shows how little he wishes to be seen as the pedantic sort of philosopher. Broad strokes, changeable as needed for presentational reasons, suffice."[54]

This apparent change, however, relies too heavily on single words and downplays the consistency that does appear in both texts. Mason himself rightly notes that Josephus' language in both passages is vague and imprecise,[55] and this should caution the interpreter against overemphasising the exact language used. In fact, "everything" (πάντα) in *War* 2.162 is immediately modified by the point that the Pharisees think the act of doing good or evil arises from the human agent. By overplaying the potential difference between "all" and "some," Mason has actually missed the one new point that may affect substantially how one defines the Pharisaic position. The new point is that fate "helps" (βοηθεῖν) the human in what he or she does.[56] How exactly fate assists humans is not made clear, but at the least it suggests that divine and human agency are not viewed by the Pharisees, according to Josephus, as always in opposition. Whereas in *Antiquities* 13.172, Josephus holds fate and human action apart in his description of the Pharisees, here in *War* 2.162 he brings them together. The ultimate agency of the human is in some fashion dependent upon the actions of fate. If this is something of what Josephus intended with his statement in *War* 2, then it also indicates that Josephus can work with different models of the divine-human relationship. As discussed below, the oppositional model, which is what Josephus presented in *Antiquities* 13.171–173, is not the sole method by which to explain the interaction between God and humans. Josephus' more precise, although not extremely helpful statement about the Pharisees in *War* 2.162–163 introduces another possible way to relate the two agents.

In summary, according to *War* 2.162–165 a fundamental dividing issue between the philosophical schools (cf. §§119; 166) is their respective understandings of the interaction between fate and humanity. The Pharisees are the polar opposites of the Sadducees not because they ascribe "everything" to fate and the Sadducees ascribe nothing, but because the former believe in fate and the latter deny it. The issue that divides these two schools is whether the divine

---

[54] Mason, "Josephus' Pharisees," 59; cf. idem, *Flavius Josephus*, 205.

[55] Mason, *Flavius Josephus*, 205.

[56] Thackeray's translation of βοηθεῖν as "co-operates" is probably too specific. The term has the general idea of assisting or helping, while "co-operates" implies more direct involvement than Josephus probably intends.

agent acts at all. The positions ascribed to the two schools in both *Antiquities* 13.171–173 and *War* 2.162–165 are basically the same, although Josephus has opened up the possibility that the oppositional perspective taken in *Antiquities* 13.171–173 is not the only model of which he is aware. In both passages, though, the Pharisees find room for both fate and human volition, but the Sadducees have space only for the human.

It is clear from these two passages that Josephus considered the issue of divine and human agency to be a clear dividing line between the three leading Jewish philosophical schools. In the third school passage (*Ant.* 18.11–25), Josephus states the position taken by the Pharisees, hints at the view of the Essenes, and ignores the Sadducean understanding.[57] The text of this school passage is difficult and many textual variants have been introduced.[58] The precise meaning does not need to be resolved since the overall idea can be determined, and it has much in common with the description of the Pharisees in *War* 2.162–163.

Josephus does not attempt to place the schools on a single line as he had done in *Antiquities* 13.171–173, and no direct comparison between the schools on the issue of divine and human agency is intended. The Pharisees, Josephus records, attribute everything to fate, while at the same time not taking away human volition. This relationship between fate and ability is traced back to God himself who saw fit that the two should cooperate in the doing of virtue or vice (*Ant.* 18.13). The statement does not add much more to one's understanding than the account in *War* 2.162–163. This statement in *Antiquities* 18.13 may be an attempt to fill out more precisely how the Pharisees, in Josephus' understanding of them, came to the conclusion that "in each action Fate cooperates (βοηθεῖν)," but any clarification has not been attained. Regarding the Essenes, Josephus remarks that they ascribe all things to God (§18). If this statement is intended as a reference to their view of fate and divine sovereignty, then it is no different from what is related about the Essenes in *Antiquities* 13.172.

In conclusion to this discussion of Josephus' portrayal of the Jewish schools, the following points should be noted. First, these passages reveal that the issue of divine and human agency was being discussed in the ancient world. The topic, even in the antithetical framework, is not a modern issue introduced solely to justify one faith position over others. Moreover, it is not simply an issue hidden away from the public and dealt with only in philosophical debates. Josephus assumes that his readers, who were probably not all trained philosophers, will be familiar with the topic and that they will wonder how the Jewish schools view the subject. Additionally, Josephus reveals that he himself took a position on the matter (*Ant.* 16.398). All this indicates that the topic was important even in the ancient world.

---

[57] He also mentions a fourth philosophy, lead by Judas the Galilean (§§23–24), which holds the same theological positions as the Pharisees but differ on the issue of freedom.

[58] See Thackeray, "On Josephus' Statement;" Mason, *Flavius Josephus*, 294–97.

Second, unless one regards the school passages as fictitious, they reveal a scope of opinions about divine and human agency among ancient Jews.[59] The Judaism with which Josephus was familiar was not monolithic in its view on this subject. To be certain, the groups did unite around certain concepts, such as the Temple and the authority of the Mosaic Torah. Nevertheless, the agreement that these items were foundational to Jewish identity does not mean that each group held the same opinion about them. What made one Jewish in the Second Temple Period was not that they held a certain "orthodox" or "common" view about the Torah, the Temple, or Israel, but that they believed these items were fundamental to their identity.[60] Josephus witnesses to this diversity, and he does so regarding the topic of divine and human agency. Not everyone viewed halakhic the same, and we should not expect everyone to view the divine-human relationship the same.

Finally, Josephus has constructed the school passages and inserted them into his narratives at a certain point to serve his rhetorical goals. In both *War* 2.119–66 and *Antiquities* 18.11–25, he sets forth the schools of the Essenes, Pharisees, and Sadducees as alternatives to the "fourth philosophy," which is credited with being the cause of the revolution against the Romans.[61] These schools are portrayed as "ancient" (*Ant.* 18.11). The role of the account in *Antiquities* 13.171–173 is not entirely clear. Taking note of Josephus' own rhetorical aims in constructing and inserting these passages does not mean that he has simply concocted the descriptions. Rather, it makes the reader aware that Josephus may not have related the intricate details of any group's view. Josephus has adopted in each case standard methods of relating philosophical discussion. This method is given to sharp contrasts in order to help the reader see clearly the differences between the schools. Almost inevitably, the reproduction of the schools' views will be given to simplicity and reductionism, along with the fact that the author formulates the schools' views in his own way. The possibility must be kept open that the views taken are more refined than Josephus indicates.

A word about terminology is necessary at this point. Engberg-Pedersen's objection that the issue of divine-human agency is a modern one arises in part from how he construes the issue. He portrays the issue solely as an either/or dichotomy: to speak of one agent necessitates that the other reside into the background. This formulation can be seen at work in several theological debates

---

[59] See Mason, *Flavius Josephus*, 384–98, for a discussion of the secondary literature dealing with the historical accuracy of the school passages. See Beall, *Josephus' Description of the Essenes*, 34–130, for the parallels between Josephus' account and the Dead Sea Scrolls.

[60] Cf. Dunn, *Partings of the Ways*, 18–36; Wright, *New Testament*, 215–338. Neither Dunn nor Wright, however, takes full account of the diversity of Judaism. On diversity, see Boccaccini, "History of Judaism."

[61] See Weissenberger, "Die jüdischen ‚Philosophenschulen' bei Josephus," for the differences between *J.W.* 2.117–66 and *Ant.* 18.1–25.

throughout the centuries.⁶² Engberg-Pedersen is right to react against this formulation, but he does not offer any other models in which to relate divine and human action. Fortunately, Barclay fills this gap when he articulates three different frameworks in which to understand the relationship.⁶³

1) *Competitive.* The divine and human agents are individual actors, and their actions are mutually exclusive. The identity of the human agent is attained at the expense of the divine. Divine sovereignty negates any human action, rendering the human a puppet. Even when the divine and human seek to accomplish the same task, their actions are independent of one another.⁶⁴ "Divine sovereignty and human freedom are thus mutually exclusive; human freedom must be understood as freedom from God" (6). This pattern can be represented by a straight line with God at one end and the human at the other. The more emphasis one places on God's actions, the further one moves from the human and vice versa.

2) *Kinship.* Rather than being contrastive, divine and human agency are bound up together in this model. The human agent participates in divine action because humanity operates within the same sphere as God as an extension of God. While some differences between the two agents can be made, when observing them acting no distinctions can be drawn. "[H]uman beings participate in the nature of God, and might even be described as 'fragments' of God: what makes them most effective as human agents is what they share with God" (7). This model is similar to pantheism.

3) *Non-contrastive transcendence.* Here both divine sovereignty and human freedom are affirmed but not as contrastive principles nor at the expense of each agent's own identity. Divine sovereignty distinguishes God from humans and indicates that God operates outside the realm of the human agent. Humans are real agents who act from their own freedom. Yet, human agency is grounded in divine sovereignty rather than constrained by it. "The two agencies thus stand in direct, and not inverse proportion: the more the human agent is operative, the more (not the less) may be attributed to God" (7).

These three models provide a way forward in the discussion that avoids both the claim that no one in the ancient world was discussing divine and human agency as well as the modern tendency toward playing divine and human

---

⁶² For example, the debate between Erasmus and Luther over the freedom of the will operates with this oppositional framework. More recently Open Theism begins from the assumption that humans possess free will and this necessitates that God cannot know the future. If he did, then there would be no free will. See Pinnock et al., *Openness of God.*

⁶³ Barclay, "Introduction," 6–7. Parenthetical references in the following are to Barclay, "Introduction."

⁶⁴ Barclay writes, "Even where God is regarded as the originator of the causal chain, the human respondents act from their own self-initiated wills, since the integrity of that will can be maintained only if it is in some respects or at some points independent of the direct creative will of God" ("Introduction," 6).

agency off against one another. The models should remain viable possibilities for each text of the ancient world, including the possibility that an author conceives of the divine-human relationship in contrastive terms. At the same time, one should not force an author into any of these models. Some authors introduce other agents, such as Belial or the power of Sin, alongside the divine and human, and this third group of agents will invariably change the relationship between the divine and human agents. Moreover, it is possible that an author works with one model at a particular point and for some reason switches to another model at a different point.

A philosophical issue should also be briefly noted. The axiom that "ought" implies "can" serves as the basis for much of current thought about human ability. It is assumed true in the study, for example, of VanLandingham.[65] Exhortations made by Paul or other authors are addressed to agents who possess the moral capacity to keep the commandments. Anything less cheapens human agency. While such an assumption contributes to the current obsession with human autonomy, it was not universally held to be true in the ancient world.[66] The point here is only to suggest that one must keep open the possibility that an author does not work from the same starting points that contemporary ethical theory does.

Josephus' description of the Jewish schools as dividing over the issue of divine and human agency indicates that it was a prevailing topic of concern for that time. When studying the Jewish sources of the Second Temple period, therefore, one should expect to find something about divine and human agency. Obviously not every text will deal with the subject, but neither should one be quick to explain away potential statements on the topic. Additionally, diversity should be allowed. Josephus himself indicates that Judaism was not monolithic. There is no reason to force the texts to hold the same position, and reductionism must be avoided. If two Jewish texts contradict each other, then that should be allowed. If the Josephus material is taken seriously, then the possibility is opened that scholars can investigate the topic of divine and human agency in the ancient Jewish (and Greco-Roman) texts. This is what this thesis proposes to do.

C. The Argument of This Study

Josephus' spectrum will be mirrored in the contrasting positions set forth in Sirach and the *Hodayot*. The argument in this study is not that Josephus was

---

[65] VanLandingham, *Judgment and Justification*, 113–14.

[66] It will be argued below that Ben Sira does hold this axiom, but the *Hodayot* and Paul reject it.

historically accurate (or inaccurate) in his statements about the three schools.⁶⁷ Ben Sira has often been considered as a forerunner to the Sadducees, and the *Hodayot* may descend from the Essenes if one accepts the traditional view that the Dead Sea Scrolls were the collection of the Essenes or a splinter group of the Essenes. Neither theory is necessary for the argument here. What is observed by comparing Ben Sira and the *Hodayot* is that Josephus' claim that Jewish groups held different views of the divine-human relationship is valid.

Ben Sira represents Josephus' Sadducean position which stresses the human agent. The issue of divine and human agency is brought out by several debate passages. In these passages, Ben Sira engages views that demote or eliminate the human agent by either claiming that God has determined whether a human obeys or disobeys or denying the judgment and thereby making obedience irrelevant. Ben Sira seeks throughout his teaching to establish the human agent as a valid member within the divine-human relationship. Even more than that, he argues for the primacy of the human agent.

Ben Sira constructs his understanding of the divine-human relationship on the two-ways model, which he finds in Deuteronomy 30.15–20. This tradition, as developed by Ben Sira, indicates that law observance brings life and that humans have the moral capacity to obey. This pattern centres on the human agent. The divine agent is not eliminated, but he is assigned a particular place. For Ben Sira the divine agent appears at creation when he empowers the human to obey and at the time of judgment, which is when he acknowledges the human's actions and gives either "life" or "death." According to the two-ways tradition as Ben Sira develops it, the divine and human agents operate independently and at very specific points. Neither agent acts at the same time. The human does not need God's assistance to be obedient to the law. Law observance is straightforward because the human knows the difference between good and evil. With this well structured scheme, Ben Sira confronts teachings that he considers deceptive and fundamentally wrong because they emphasise the divine agent and misunderstand the crucial role played by the human agent.

In sharp contrast to this perspective, the *Hodayot* stresses the role played by the divine agent. The *Hodayot* comes very close to Josephus' Essenes who attributed all things to God or fate. It constantly highlights the individual's sinfulness and frailty, and what emerges from the overwhelmingly depressive anthropology is a critique of the human as a creature. This pessimistic anthropology is equally matched by statements about the marvellous grace and mercy of God. These statements highlight the act of predestination, the giving of knowledge, and the purification of the sinner. Each is attributed to God and especially to his spirit as the means through which God resolves the human's problem. Salvation itself rests solely in the hands of God.

---

⁶⁷ See Maier, *freier Wille*, for a defence of Josephus based on Ben Sira (the Saducean position), the *Psalms of Solomon* (the Pharisaical position), and 1QS 3–4 (the Essene view).

Yet the human agent is not merely the passive receiver of these great deeds. The hymnists portray the divine acts as empowering. What emerges from the *Hodayot* is not a denial of human agency, but a restored human agent empowered and continuously sustained by a gracious divine agent. Through the spirit of knowledge, the human is enabled to observe God's commandments and avoid sin because he possesses the spirit of holiness. Obedience becomes a possibility and indeed a reality precisely because God is always at work in the human.

The stress placed on the divine agent in the *Hodayot*, therefore, contrasts sharply with Ben Sira's emphasis on the human agent. The two positions stand opposed to one another. Taking account of this diversity that Josephus claimed existed and the *Hodayot* and Ben Sira reveal, the possibility becomes stronger that Paul can fit within the Jewish diversity. Josephus' statements also suggest that one should expect Paul to have an opinion on the matter. It would be rather odd indeed for Paul, the former Pharisee (Phil 3.5), to ignore completely the topic. A starting point for an analysis of Paul's view could be the antithesis between justification by πίστις Χριστοῦ or works of the law, but as will be shown the debate over this phrase is at a stalemate. A way forward, and one that allows for more than a superficial summary of Pauline texts and ideas, is through a careful study of a single text. Suitable for this purpose is Romans 7.7–8.13. Here Paul engages Jewish positions on the possibility for and necessity of obedience.

In Romans 7.7–25, it will be argued, Paul portrays the ἐγώ as the human agent of the two-ways tradition. The law, which is unto life, is given to the human who thinks that he possesses the moral capacity to obey. Against this view, Paul introduces another agent – the power of Sin – who enslaves the human and causes him or her to produce evil, the very thing he or she tried to avoid. Having exposed what Paul thought to be the serious flaw in the two-ways pattern, he turns in Romans 8.1–13 to describe how obedience becomes a possibility. God delivers the human from Sin's grasp through the death of his own Son, and he imparts his Spirit as the empowering agent. Paul's own approach resembles the *Hodayot*. Both prioritise divine action and set forth the Spirit as the means through which humans obey. The Spirit enables obedience, which brings about, according to Paul, the fulfilment of the righteous requirement of the law.

Pauline scholarship for the last three decades has been driven by Sanders' portrayal of the role of grace and obedience in Second Temple Judaism and the implications of this for Paul's interaction with Jewish traditions. The last decade has seen a serious attempt to reconsider the grounds of Sanders' argument about covenant, grace, and obedience in Judaism.[68] This study par-

---

[68] See Das, *Paul, the Law*; Gathercole, *Where is Boasting?*; Watson, *Paul and the Hermeneutics of Faith*; VanLandingham, *Judgment and Justification*; and Sprinkle, *Life and Law*.

ticipates in this discussion. Ben Sira and the *Hodayot* played crucial roles in Sanders' argument, but no full-length study of either text has been made since Sanders' study. While each has been called on at various points, this has been in the service of asking other questions, such as the meaning of judgment by works or the relationship between faith and obedience. This study fills that gap by asking the broader and more fundamental question about how each author understands the issue of divine and human agency. This study also attempts to find a place for Paul within the Jewish spectrum. Paul's understanding is not radically opposed to all forms of Judaism. Rather, it will be made clear that Paul is firmly at home in a Jewish debate. He engages with his fellow Jews, subjecting every idea to his understanding of God's act in Christ.

This study will begin with Ben Sira before turning to the *Hodayot*. With the spectrum firmly established, Paul's view as it emerges from Romans 7–8 will be set into this spectrum.

Volume 1 of *Justification and Variegated Nomism* edited by Carson et al. is a thorough revaluation of the Jewish texts, but reaction to it has been mixed.

Chapter 1

Obedience and the Law of Life in Sirach

The Sadducean position according to Josephus attributed everything to the human agent, and this position is found in Sirach. Writing around the beginning of the second century BCE, Ben Sira seeks to amalgamate the wisdom and Torah traditions. He presents himself as a sage and an interpreter of Israel's sacred writings. As a sage, his primary interest lies in teaching others how to live in a manner that honours God. The twin themes that hold his teaching together are, therefore, fear the Lord and obey the commandments.

This chapter explores how Ben Sira develops his understanding of the divine-human relationship throughout his work. The problem of divine and human agency is forced on him by some alternative theologies that deny any role to the human agent. Against these views, Ben Sira adopts the two-ways tradition as the basic paradigm for the interaction between the divine and human agents. This scheme centres on the human agent, who possesses the moral capacity to obey the commandments. These commandments are found in the Mosaic Torah, which was given by God as the means to life. The divine agent's role is limited particularly to the act of judgment, which is a time when God gives "life" or "death" based on one's obedience or disobedience. Even in this act, the focus of Ben Sira's thought remains on the human agent.

A. Identifying the Alternative Theologies

In a series of passages built around an Ancient Near Eastern debate formula, Ben Sira encapsulates the opinions of others. In this debate formula, authors use direct speech to introduce the views they oppose.[1] The formula, as Ben Sira has it, is "relatively fixed" according to Crenshaw: "(1) the prohibition-formula *'al-tō'mar*, (2) the direct quotation, and (3) the refutation introduced by *kî*."[2] The expression is infrequent in previous Israelite wisdom texts (Prov 20.22;

---

[1] As other Ancient Near Eastern examples, Crenshaw cites Ani (*ANET*, 420), Amen-emopet (*ANET*, 413), and 'Onchsheshonqy ("Problem of Theodicy," 48–49).

[2] "Problem of Theodicy," 51. The corresponding Greek is μὴ εἴπῃς and γάρ.

A. Identifying the Alternative Theologies

24.29; Qoh 7.10, 13).[3] By contrast, according to Crenshaw, Ben Sira employs the formula nine times.[4]

Do not depend on your wealth,
  And *do not say*, "It is in my power."[5]
Do not walk after your heart and eyes
  To go after treasures of evil.
Do not say, "Who can comprehend my power?"
  For YHWH seeks the persecuted.
Do not say, "I have sinned and what has happened to me: nothing at all."
  For God himself is slow to anger.[6]
They will not be forgiven;
  Do not be so confident to add sin upon sin.
And you say, "His mercy is great.
  He will forgive the multitude of my sins."
For mercy and wrath are from him
  Upon sinners rests his wrath. (5.1–6)

Do not say, "What is my need,
  And what good is now from this for me?"
Do not say, "I am sufficient.
  And what evil will now come from this?"
For it is easy before the Lord in the day of death
  To repay man according to his ways. (11.23–24, 26 [Greek])[7]

Do not say, "From God (comes) my sin."
  For that which he hates, he does not do.
Do not say, "He caused me to stumble."
  For he has no need of violent men. (15.11, 12)

Do not say, "I am hidden from the Lord.
  And in the high place, who will remember me?
Among all the people, I am not known;
  And what is my soul in the totality of the spirits of the sons of Adam?" (16.17)

When supplemented with other statements using a modified form of the formula or direct speech found throughout Sirach (e.g. 7.9; 11.18–19; 23.17–18; 39.12–35), a coherent picture of these alternative views begins to emerge.

---

[3] The reason Crenshaw includes Qoh 7.13 is unclear since the complete formula is provided in v.10. Crenshaw notes that Prov 20.22; 24.29 "both differ from the usual debate-formula in that they do not employ the particle *kî*" ("Problem of Theodicy," 49n.5).

[4] The phrase is identified with italics. The versification of Sirach is problematic. The numbering follows Ziegler's *Sapientia Iesu Filii Sirach*, unless discussion is of the Hebrew text in which case the numbering follows Beentjes, *Book of Ben Sira*.

[5] The Hebrew phrase is יש לאל ידי, which is an idiom that appears only twice in the OT, Gen 31.29 and Mic 2.1. The Greek reads αὐτάρκη μοί ἐστιν ("I am sufficient"), which is the same phrase found in 11.24. These two texts (5.1–6; 11.23–24) are linked then in both wording and themes.

[6] After this line the Hebrew adds, "*Do not say*, 'YHWH is merciful, and all my sins will be wiped out.'"

[7] The Hebrew of 11.21–22 is damaged: אל תאמר [........].[כי עש] כי חפצי ומה עתה יעזב לי
אל תאמר דיי [..].י א[...]ה א[...] יהי עלי

In these passages, Ben Sira depicts alternative understandings of the activity of God in this world and the implications these theologies have for ethics. Ben Sira addresses two different views of God. The first view maintains that God is remote from the world and will neither judge humans for their sins nor reward them for obedience (5.1–8; 7.8–9; 11.17–19; 16.17–22; 20.16; 23.17–21). The second view presents an overbearing God who determines every action, including sin, in the world (15.11–20). In each case, these rival understandings of God are used to avoid obeying the divine will as revealed in the Mosaic Law. For the first perspective, God's distance means one can sin because he will not respond. The second outlook maintains that humans are not responsible for their moral failures because they do not control their own actions.

The first theological position builds its ethics around its view of a distant God. Sirach 16.17–22 develops at length the theology and ethics of this view. These people begin with the assumption that God pays no attention to them. They are lowly creatures, "hidden from God," and insignificant in comparison to the multitude of other people (v.17). The speaker next draws out the implications of this logic for ethics.[8] The people think that God does not concern himself with their actions, especially the sins committed in secret (vv.20–21).[9] So long as they are not caught in their sin, they do not need to fear punishment. As a vivid picture of this logic, Ben Sira describes the adulterer who confidently relies on the darkness to shield his sinful act from others and God (23.18). They further reason that God is unaware of just acts (16.22). Obedience is pointless then because God does not know when one does good works.[10] Their thinking is similar to that of the fool who thinks he never receives a reward for his good works (20.16). Even if God is made aware of these acts or their sins, though, they have no reason to fear because his "decree" (חק), his judgment of human action, lies somewhere in the distant future (16.22).[11] Their thinking might even suggest that they doubt a judgment on human action by God.

The opponents are clearly confident in their wealth. Twice Ben Sira describes them boastfully claiming, "I am sufficient" (5.1; 11.24 [Greek]). They have no needs and can gain nothing from obedience to God (11.23). Their wealth encourages them to presume nothing evil can happen to them (11.24; cf. 11.19 [Heb 17]). Relying on their wealth and power (5.1, 3), they boldly declare their sin and the lack of action on God's part (v.4). Because of the inactivity of God, they see no reason to stop sinning. Even if God decides to act, these people are

---

[8] Verses 18–19 are a parenthetical comment made by Ben Sira (cf. Di Lella in Skehan/Di Lella, *Wisdom of Ben Sira*, 275; Gilbert, "God, Sin and Mercy," 123–24; contra Argall, *1 Enoch and Sirach*, 231).

[9] This interpretation follows the Hebrew text. The Greek text, which picks up some hints from Ben Sira's parenthetical comment, discusses the extent to which humans can know about God's actions.

[10] Skehan/Di Lella, *Wisdom of Ben Sira*, 275.

[11] Schnabel, *Law and Wisdom*, 36.

certain that he will forgive them. Their God is merciful and full of forgiveness. He will certainly overlook their sins (v.6). As extra protection, they rely on the multitude of their sacrifices (7.9). If God decided to judge, he would ignore their sins because their sacrifices will appease his anger. These people think that sacrifice will overcome their lack of obedience. The great mercy of God and their meagre obedience evidenced by sacrificing will account for their lack of righteousness.[12]

The second theological position advocated a deterministic view of God's actions in the world. The proponents of this position maintain that God actively directs the events of the world and of each human. In two similar statements, they blame God for their moral failures: "From God (comes) my sin," and "He caused me to stumble" (15.11a, 12a). God controlled their actions and caused them to sin. They do not deny that their deeds are immoral, but they refuse to take responsibility for them.[13] In fact, one cannot accuse them of disobedience, for ultimately the responsibility lies with God. They are not agents, but puppets on a string moved about as God wills. Because of this view of God, these people escape responsibility for their actions and need not fear punishment from God.

Although promoting different views of God, these two positions agree that obedience is unnecessary. They openly acknowledge that their actions are sinful, but they see no reason to change their current actions. Although God made wisdom available and he revealed his will in the Torah, these previous acts by God do not compel them to respond with obedience. Further, the prospect that God will reward or punish them does not motivate them to be obedient. Actually, they are certain that God will not reward or punish them. They find no benefit in obedience.

Using these direct speech statements as guidelines, one can begin to see the theological tendencies against which Ben Sira set himself. Based on his analysis of the "do not say" statements, Crenshaw concludes that the underlying problem is "theodicy."[14] The focus, then, is on the divine agent and his apparent failure to judge. Crenshaw writes, "Sirach enlists the debate-form to refute antagonists who used the delay in retribution as an excuse to multiply transgressions."[15] Based on the fact that God has not acted, these adversaries

---

[12] Cf. Crenshaw's summary: "In essence they argue that God's boundless mercy bestows upon his devotees license to sin, that his blessings in material wealth give security, that his power robs man of the freedom to act decisively to avoid sinful conduct, and that his blindness makes evil profitable, especially when the perfidious deed can be concealed from human eyes as well" ("Problem of Theodicy," 47).

[13] Gilbert, "God, Sin and Mercy," 119.

[14] Crenshaw, "Problem of Theodicy," 51.

[15] Crenshaw, "Problem of Theodicy," 51.

find little reason to think that God is concerned with their obedience, and since disobedience has proven profitable, they will pursue that route.

Crenshaw is certainly correct that Ben Sira opposes any notion that humans should act disobediently because of God's (apparent) lack of involvement in the affairs of humanity. However, it is doubtful that the issue addressed in these passages is the problem of theodicy. Theodicy, at least in its most common usage, is an attempt to defend God's goodness and justice in spite of the prosperity of the wicked and the suffering of the righteous.[16] The problem of theodicy is fundamentally a problem with God. While Ben Sira attacks the opponents' understandings of God, he does this because their views result in a massive misunderstanding of the human. This is particularly clear in 15.11–20. Beginning with the problem of God, Ben Sira turns to a defence of human freedom. This is certainly not the issue of theodicy.[17] Crenshaw's conclusion draws attention to the wrong agent, for the issue in the "do not say" passages is not how and when God will act, but that these other positions have eliminated the human agent. The human agent has become negotiable because there is no fear of judgment. They have declared obedience meaningless, and Ben Sira will not stand for this. Even in the "do not say" passages that describe the delay in retribution (5.1–8), the purpose is not to defend God's patience but to challenge the conclusion that obedience is irrelevant in light of God's patience and mercy.

The issue in these passages is precisely the problem of divine and human agency. These alternative views use their understandings of God to eliminate the human agent, and Ben Sira seeks to establish the human agent. In order to accomplish this task, Ben Sira employs the two-ways paradigm. In this paradigm, as is explained below, law observance is the means to life and blessing. As Ben Sira develops this pattern, the human agent becomes the focal point of the divine-human relationship.

B. The Establishment of the Human Agent

In contrast to the alternative theological positions, Ben Sira seeks to establish the human as the crucial element within the discussion. He finds in the two-ways paradigm the teaching that human action is the means to divine blessing. Ac-

---

[16] Crenshaw defines theodicy as "the attempt to defend divine justice in the face of aberrant phenomena that appear to indicate the deity's indifference or hostility toward virtuous people" (ABD s.v. "Theodicy" [6:444]). Examples of "theodicy" include Ps 10 [LXX 9] and Habakkuk. Crenshaw uses the term "theodicy" too freely, however. For example, Eve's response in the garden is theodicy (Gen 3.13), as well as Jonah's questions about God's justice when he offers forgiveness to Nineveh (4.1–11). Theodicy comes to apply to "the problem of evil" regardless of the connections with divine justice or the suffering of the righteous. To be useful, a more refined application of the term "theodicy" is required.

[17] Cf. Leisen, *Full of Praise*, 236n.127.

B. The Establishment of the Human Agent

cording to this paradigm, which, for Jewish authors, is rooted in Deuteronomy 30.15–20, God sets before the human agent "life and death" as the two possible outcomes of law observance. The human possesses the moral capacity to obey, and he or she must choose which path to follow. Obedience brings covenantal blessing, while disobedience results in death. The two-ways scheme provides a well-structured pattern focused on the human agent. Each of the two agents, God and the human, act at the appropriate time and in a specific order.[18]

In Ben Sira's work, this paradigm is most clearly laid out in 15.11–20.[19] In this text, he directly engages the other theological positions (vv.11–12), and he states clearly in vv.14–20 his position, which is developed in other places throughout the book (cf. especially 16.17–17.24).

> God created (the) man from the beginning,[20] and he gave him into the hand of his inclination [ויתנהו ביד יצרו; καὶ ἀφῆκεν αὐτὸν ἐν χειρὶ διαβουλίου αὐτοῦ]. If you choose [אם תחפץ], you may keep the commandment, and you will understand to do his will.[21] Poured out before you are fire and water: for whichever you choose [תחפץ], stretch out your hand. Before a man are life and death, and whichever he chooses [יחפץ] will be given to him. The wisdom of the Lord is in abundance. He is strong in power and sees all. The eyes of God see his works and he observes all of man's actions. He does not command a man to sin nor cause men of falsehood to dream. (15.14–20)

He describes the creation of the human agent through the lens of Deuteronomy 30.15–20 in order to establish that the individual, not fate, is responsible for his or her destiny. "Life and death" are placed before the individual (v.17a), and he or she can choose which path to take (vv.15–17). God does not interfere with the human's decision (v.14), but at some point in the future, he will judge the individual based on his or her deeds. In this passage, Ben Sira presents the classic Jewish argument for human freedom in the form of the two-ways tradition.

Two key points should be noted about Ben Sira's use of this paradigm. First, the law is directly connected with life, and the way to acquiring this life offered by the law is through obedience. In 15.11–20 law observance leads to "life." Ben Sira takes the pair "life and death" (v.17) from Moses' exhortation to Israel in Deuteronomy 30.15–20. Moses declares that he has set before the Israelites "life and death," and if they so choose, they can live (vv.15, 19). Life and death represent two alternative outcomes for human existence, and they are defined

---

[18] On the origins and use of this paradigm, see Nickelsburg, *Resurrection*, 144–65; Kraft, "Early Developments." These discussions revolve primarily around later texts, and surprisingly little is said about Deuteronomy 30.15–20 or Sirach 15.14–17.

[19] These verses have been significantly altered in the transmission process. See Liesen, *Full of Praise*, 236–38, who argues that the expansions introduce an eschatological aspect. Reiterer contends for Hebrew A as original at points ("immateriellen Ebenen der Schöpfung," 111–16)

[20] Hebrew A adds: "and he put him into the hand of the one who would snatch him."

[21] Hebrew A adds: "If you trust in him, you will even live." Cf. the Greek: "and to act faithfully is a matter of choice [πίστιν ποιῆσαι εὐδοκίας]."

in this-worldly terms. Life entails receiving the covenantal blessings of a long life and enjoyment within the Promised Land (vv.19–20; cf. 28.1–14). Death by contrast is physical death and exile (30.18; cf. 28.15–68). The means to either destiny is determined solely by the human's response to the commandments. Moses tells Israel that if they will "obey the commandments . . . then you will live, multiply, and YHWH your God will bless you in the land" (30.16). If they disobey, then they "will certainly perish" and will not live long in the land (vv.17–18). In this passage from Deuteronomy, which functions as a summary of the entire book, Moses clearly outlines two paths for Israel's future, and these two paths are marked by how one responds to the law. Ben Sira picks up this two-way imagery and adopts it as his basic understanding of the divine-human relationship. When he lists the pairing of "life and death" in Sirach 15.17, he is recalling Moses' exhortation to the people, and he, like Moses, makes the human's destiny dependent on law observance.

The second key point of Ben Sira's conception of the divine-human relationship is that humans have the moral capacity to observe the commandments. Foundational to the sapiential and legal traditions that Ben Sira follows is the assumption that a human can obey the commandments.[22] The "ought" of God's will implies a "can" on the human's part. The human capacity to know the difference between good and evil (cf. 17.7) indicates for Ben Sira that humans have the ability to do good. In 15.14–17 he argues strongly for the individual's freedom to determine his or her own destiny through obedience to the Torah. Against the view that God dictates what humans will do (vv.11–12), Ben Sira claims that after creating the human agent God "has given him into the hand of his inclination" (ויתנהו ביד יצרו) (v.14). The noun יצר first appears in the biblical narrative in the flood account (Gen 6.5; 8.21).[23] There it has a negative connotation and refers to humanity's preference for evil over the ways of God. Ben Sira transforms the meaning of this term, though, by removing it from the flood narrative and placing it within the context of creation.[24] God gives the inclination, and therefore it cannot be predisposed toward evil. The inclination must be neutral otherwise he concedes to his opponents that God is responsible for their moral shortcomings. The יצר is for Ben Sira "a neutral capacity which enables people to choose morally."[25] Within this debate context, this divinely imparted ability highlights "man's autonomy and power of decision."[26]

---

[22] The wisdom text 4Q418 126.1–10, however, stresses God's sovereignty over human beings (see Harrington, "Wisdom at Qumran," 149–51).

[23] I am following here Levison, *Portraits of Adam*, 34–35.

[24] He may have been motivated by the use of the verb יצר in Genesis 2.7, 8, 19. See Aitken, "Divine Will," 289–90, for the connections with creation.

[25] Levison, *Portraits of Adam*, 35.

[26] Murphy, "Yēṣer in the Qumran Literature," 337.

B. The Establishment of the Human Agent

Ben Sira also accentuates human ability through the verb חפץ. If one desires, he or she can keep the commandments (15.15) or select between "fire and water" (v.16) or "life and death" (v.17). The point of repeating this verb is to emphasise that God has created humans with the moral capacity to choose their own destiny.[27] Verse 15 is significant because it clearly states that humans can observe the law. Verse 17 indicates that the human's destiny is ultimately at stake.[28] Whether the individual decides to obey or disobey the law determines whether he or she receives life or death. The failure to be obedient lies with the human who actively chooses to reject the commandments and the life offered by them. Nothing prevents the individual from observing the commandment except one's own decision to disobey.

Ben Sira also conveys his optimistic view of human agency by claiming that God does not interfere in the human's autonomous decision. Ben Sira writes that God "has given (the) man into the hand of his inclination" (15.14). The idea is that God has set the human before the two paths – life and death – and the individual can determine for himself or herself from his or her own will because he or she possesses the necessary competence which path to take. God will not interfere. The human is autonomous. Martyn captures the idea well when he describes the actions taken by the divine and human agents as separate steps. God acts first by creating the human, and then he removes himself from the scene. The human act is a distinctly separate, independent step in the process. God's action, Martyn argues, is limited to the initial, creative moment, and he "neither interfere[s] in the human agent's subsequent autonomous choice nor tak[es] measures to improve that agent's formation."[29] God's self-limiting action protects him from the charge that he is responsible for sin, and it also ensures that the human agent is responsible for his or her own decision. This divine limiting presents a unique situation in that the human stands alone before the two alternative paths. The decision for life or death ultimately belongs to the human.

These two points arise directly from the two-ways pattern. An additional point for Ben Sira's understanding of the divine-human relationship that is not clearly stated in 15.11–20 is the idea that God will eventually judge humans according to their deeds. Although leaving the human to his or her own devices, God carefully observes all that each human does (vv.18–19). At the appropriate

---

[27] "Ben Sira employs the verb "to choose," Heb[rew] ḥps, three times in as many verses, thus emphasizing that human beings enjoy personal freedom in deciding whether or not to observe the Law (v 15) and in choosing life or death (v 17)" (Skehan/Di Lella, *Wisdom of Ben Sira*, 272).

[28] Ben Sira has no eschatological connotations, so "life" and "death" refer to this-worldly destinies. Life includes wealth, peace, long life, peaceful death, and honour after one's death by the continual praise of one's name. Death is the opposite and culminates in a violent death. The person is either forgotten or remembered as a fool. See Collins, "Root of Immortality."

[29] Martyn, "Epilogue," 176.

time, he re-enters the scene in order to reward or punish the individual. In this paradigm, God re-acts to what each individual does. Although judgment is not mentioned directly in 15.11–20, it is vitally important to Ben Sira. It is mentioned in almost all the other debate passages and appears throughout the work.

These three aspects (life attained through law observance; human moral capacity; divine judgment) form Ben Sira's view of the divine-human relationship. This relationship revolves around the human agent's decision whether to obey or disobey. Although God begins the process by giving humans freedom and the covenant, these actions are intended to bring about human obedience. Similarly, divine judgment focuses on what the human has done. God's actions are important not because of what they reveal about his nature, but because of how they affect human obedience. This chapter explores how Ben Sira develops these three aspects in order to establish the human agent as the central figure in the divine-human relationship.

1. Life through Torah Observance

Numerous statements can be found in Sirach which suggest a relationship between obedience and life, disobedience and death. In his exposition on honouring one's parents, he repeatedly claims that honour, glory, or long days will be the outcome of one's obedience (3.1–16). The obedient person is assured of a peaceful death (2.3). Ben Sira instructs his students that if they will care for the orphan and widow then they "will be like a son of the Most High and he will love you more than your mother" (4.10). Those who remain steadfast will not be abandoned, and if someone trusts in God, he will give assistance (2.2–3, 6). The person who remains faithful will not lose his or her reward (v.8). Those who devote themselves to studying the Torah and acquiring wisdom will serve kings (8.8; 39.4), and future generations will remember their names and teachings (39.9–11; cf. 41.11–13). A prime example of this is the "Praise of the Fathers" (44–50). The representatives are not chosen at random; rather, Ben Sira mentions those who are worthy of remembrance because of their obedience to God's will, particularly the Torah. For example, Enoch walked with God and avoided death (44.16; cf. Gen 5.24),[30] and because he stood against the rebellious people, Caleb is given strength to capture a hill (Sir 46.7–10). Their names live on perpetually because of their obedience, and now they serve as motivation to Ben Sira's students to be obedient.

---

[30] Skehan disputes the authenticity of the Enoch saying (*Wisdom of Ben Sira*, 499; cf. Mack, *Wisdom and the Hebrew Epic*, 199–200). The textual evidence is evenly split (ms B and Greek have it; Masada and Syriac do not), but Skehan's argument that the statement should be excluded because Enoch became popular in Jewish traditions is weak. If the line was inserted by a supporter of Enoch, then surely this person would have embellished the statement more. As it stands, the verse comes straight from the scriptural account. Moreover, if Ben Sira is debating an "Enochic" group, as many scholars claim, then by mentioning Enoch first he claims Enoch as a supporter of his movement.

Wisdom's blessings are acquired through discipline and testing (4.17–18). If a person goes astray, though, Wisdom rejects him or her and gives the person over to destruction (v.19). Obedience to the commandments is the alternative to corruption and death (28.6). Indeed, the sinner will suffer greatly (7.17; 9.11), and a violent death awaits him or her as the punishment of God (7.31). Those who commit adultery will be humiliated in public and punished for their sin (23.21–27).

Ben Sira's ultimate goal in writing is to instruct his students in how to acquire wisdom (24.34; 50.27–29; cf. Prologue). The way to wisdom, he maintains, is through obedience, particularly observance of the Torah. The first imperative of the book is to keep the commandments: "If you desire wisdom, keep the commandments, and the Lord will provide it to you" (1.26).[31] This statement sets forth straightforwardly the fundamental role of obedience. The human must obey the law in order to attain wisdom, and the keeping of the law is observed by God who acknowledges the obedience by imparting wisdom.

The precise relationship between obedience and blessing, however, is unclear from these statements. These statements need to be placed within a broader context in order to understand the relationship. It will be argued in this section that the divine-human relationship is modelled after the Creator-creation relationship. This relationship is based on God's commands. God gives orders, and creation obeys. As part of this analysis, Ben Sira's understanding of "covenant" will be addressed in response to Sanders' argument that the establishment of the covenant was an act of grace. After establishing the link between Torah observance and blessing, the arguments that the divine-human relationship is built around "fear of God" or "faith" will be evaluated, as well as the claim that the possibility of atonement means that God's mercy is the ultimate determining factor in the relationship.

a. Wisdom and Torah in Sirach

Before describing how Ben Sira related divine action to human action, it is necessary to clarify the role of the Torah in his thinking. Of the scriptures, Ben Sira's writing style is closest to Proverbs, and most scholars situate him firmly within the wisdom tradition. Many scholars consider him to be influenced by Job and Qoheleth, perhaps even directly responding to the latter.[32] Torah traditions have also greatly influenced Ben Sira's thinking, and his attention to Israel's history is considered by some scholars to be a new element in the wisdom tradition.[33] The issue that needs to be resolved, for our purpose, is whether

---

[31] On vv.11–30 see Di Lella, "Fear of the Lord as Wisdom." He points out the influence of Deuteronomy on Ben Sira's thoughts.

[32] So Hengel, *Judaism and Hellenism*, 1:141, 143.

[33] So Murphy, *Tree of Life*, 76–78; Jacob, "Wisdom and Religion," 255. See, however, Whybray, "Ben Sira and History," who questions this claim.

his ethical exhortations are derived primarily from the wisdom tradition or if the Torah's commandments are foundational to his ethics.

While some scholars maintain that Ben Sira's ethics are overwhelmingly dominated by the outlook of the sapiential tradition not the Torah, the division between these two sources downplays Ben Sira's attempt to wed the two. In his account of Wisdom's decent, he concludes boldly, "This is the book of the covenant of the Most High God, the law which Moses commanded us as an inheritance for the gathering of Jacob" (24.23). Wisdom traditions are undeniably joined with the Torah, and it is probably even appropriate to speak of "identification."[34] He encourages his students not only to fear the Lord, which is the most fundamental expression of piety in the wisdom tradition (see Prov 1.7; Qoh 12.13), but also to "keep the commandments" (Sir 1.26). Wisdom is identified as the fear of the Lord and the doing of the law (19.20).

The link between wisdom, life, and Torah also comes through the concept of "instruction, discipline" (מוסר/παιδεία). "Instruction" belongs to the world of wisdom, and it is from here that Ben Sira develops his initial understanding of it. However, as is typical of most of his thinking, he connects it with the Torah. The relationship between the three concepts (discipline, Torah, and wisdom) is evident in 24.25–29. Following the identification of pre-temporal Wisdom with the Torah (v.23), Ben Sira describes the Torah as a bountiful river that provides nourishment.[35] The Torah overflows with "wisdom" (v.25) and "knowledge" (v.26), and "instruction" flows freely from its banks (v.27). These three terms all belong to the wisdom tradition, but Ben Sira uses them to describe the contents of the Torah. The abrupt switch back to wisdom in vv.28–29 shows the connection between Wisdom and Torah for Ben Sira. He can shift easily and effortlessly between the two categories.

In several statements, the Torah provides the basis for Ben Sira's exhortations.[36] Obedience to the commandments is the alternative to corruption and death (28.6). The Torah also governs one's interaction with his or her neighbours (28.7; cf. 19.17). One should give to the poor because of the commandment (29.9; cf. vv.1, 11). The greatest sin is not disobedience to the sages' instructions, but rejecting the Torah (41.8; cf. 19.24). 3.1–16 is an extended reflection on the commandment to honour one's parents (cf. Exod 20.12; Deut 5.16).[37] The answer to Ben Sira's request for help controlling his tongue and thoughts mixes wisdom and Torah motifs as the solution (Sir 22.27–23.6).

---

[34] Schnabel, *Law and Wisdom*, 69–79, 90–91. Boccaccini argues that wisdom and the Torah are not identical because wisdom is eternal while the Torah is historical (*Middle Judaism*, 81, 89). While this is correct, after the giving of the Torah wisdom is identified as the Torah.

[35] The six mentioned rivers (Pishon, Tigris, Euphrates, Jordan, Nile, and Gihon) were important throughout Israel's history. See Sheppard, *Wisdom*, 69–71.

[36] Schnabel, *Law and Wisdom*, 46–9. He discusses 19.17; 21.11; 23.23; 28.6–7; 29.9; 32.14–33.6; 35.1–7; 37.7–15; and 41.5.

[37] Contra Sanders, "Sacred Canopies," 123–24, who ignores v.6 when he says that Ben Sira does not mention the promise of long life.

B. The Establishment of the Human Agent

He calls his students to listen to his instruction (παιδεία), which sets the tone for a discussion of wisdom ideas (23.7).[38] In the middle of the section, Ben Sira comments on the person who utters the divine name while swearing falsely (23.9–10). Although using different terminology, the instruction arises from the third commandment (Exod 20.7; Deut 5.11), and a person familiar with the Torah would not miss the connection.[39] Similarly, in his comments on adultery (Sir 23.16–27), which replies to the problem of one's thoughts (vv.2–6), he focuses on disobedience to the Torah. The adulteress is guilty first of all because she disobeyed the law of the Most High (v.23). Ben Sira does not accuse the adulteress of failing to obey a maxim from the sages.[40] Further, the woman's disobedience to the law functions as a teaching moment. As Ben Sira explains in the conclusion to the section, the woman's children will realise that nothing is greater than fearing God and keeping his commandments (v.27). This statement forms an inclusio with v.23, which began the discussion of the woman's punishment, and highlights the importance of obedience to the law.

Collins contends that Ben Sira's ethical instructions come primarily from the sapiential tradition, while Nickelsburg points out that the form is derived from this tradition not a legal one.[41] Identifying exact sources for Ben Sira's teaching, however, is difficult since the content of Proverbs and other wisdom sources matches the instructions found in the Mosaic Torah. Both address the basic ethical actions of life and often with the same language. Ben Sira's historical position in Judea prior to the conflict with Hellenism explains the lack of references to the so-called Jewish identity markers (circumcision, Sabbath, and food laws).[42] In addition, his interest in the cult shows an awareness of traditions that cannot be assigned to sapiential traditions (7.29–31; 35.1–12).

---

[38] The Greek has the title "Instructions on the Tongue" (παιδεία στόματος) prior to 23.7. This title fits well the content of this section even if it appears in the middle of the pericope (contra Skehan/Di Lella, *Wisdom of Ben Sira*, 322).

[39] Cf. Di Lella, "Ben Sira's Doctrine," 241.

[40] Collins argues that Ben Sira's primary interest is the tradition against adultery, not the specific details of the law because he does not follow the injunction to put the adulterers to death (cf. Lev 20.10; Deut 22.22–24) (*Jewish Wisdom*, 70). Di Lella appeals to later Rabbinic tradition to explain why Ben Sira does not impose the death penalty (Skehan/Di Lella, *Wisdom of Ben Sira*, 325). The Rabbinic evidence, however, is too late to provide the reason for Ben Sira's position.

[41] Collins, *Jewish Wisdom*, 62; Nickelsburg, "Torah and the Deuteronomic Scheme," 230.

[42] It is perplexing when Collins claims that Ben Sira "ignores certain sections of the Law, particularly the cultic and dietary laws of Leviticus" (*Jewish Wisdom*, 57). Ben Sira is well versed in the cultic practices (see Perdue, *Wisdom and Cult*, 188–260), and his praise of Simon the High Priest reveals his respect for Israel's cultic practices (51.1–12). In several places, he encourages his students to sacrifice (e.g. 35.4–11). The charge that Ben Sira ignored the dietary laws is equally unfounded (contra Gammie, "Sage in Sirach," 360–61). Sirach 31.16 refers to table etiquette, and the audience in 32.1 ("they") is not necessarily Gentiles (Mattila, "Ben Sira and the Stoics," 491n.74).

Ben Sira's own search for wisdom began in the temple (51.14). His wedding of the two traditions cautions one from attempting to identify specific backgrounds when the two traditions are themselves so similar. The issue of form is not important since it does not indicate from where one derives authority for the particular instructions in a book.

Burkes claims that the Torah was not vital to Ben Sira's ethics because he tells his students to gain wisdom through the teaching of the elders (6.32–35; cf. 8.8–9).[43] She fails to note, though, that the content of the elders' discussions is the Torah itself (6.37; 37.12; cf. 9.15 [Greek]).[44] The sages, then, do not represent authority in themselves, but their authority comes through the source of their discussions. The instruction to seek wisdom through the sages' reflections on the Torah summarises the very task that Ben Sira has set for himself, as his grandson recognised (Prologue 7–14).

Ben Sira's appropriation of the wisdom and Torah traditions is complex. The strict distinction between wisdom and law proposed by some scholars, however, does not adequately explain Ben Sira's practice. He seeks to make clear that the two sacred traditions speak with a unified voice. The manner in which Ben Sira brings the law and wisdom together makes it appropriate to speak of one attaining life through law observance.

b. The Creator, His Commandments, and Human Obedience

According to Sanders, Ben Sira's exhortations to Torah observance must be understood within the covenant context. He enlists Sirach as one of his examples of covenantal nomism. He begins his analysis of Sirach by arguing that Ben Sira held a traditional (that is, Rabbinical) view of Israel's election.[45] Israel's place of prominence is noted in 17.1–14. Ben Sira appears at first to be reflecting on all of humanity, but part way through the poem he turns to Israel and her encounter with God at Mt. Sinai (vv.11–14; cf. Exod 19.16–19).[46] Among all the nations, God has chosen Israel for himself (Sir 17.17), which, developing from Deuteronomy 32.8–9, is a clear statement of Israel's election.[47] In 24.1–23 Ben Sira highlights Israel's special election by describing Wisdom's decision to make her dwelling place in Israel.[48] Wisdom is specifically identi-

---

[43] Burkes, "Wisdom and Law," 259.

[44] Collins suggests that Ben Sira presents two different sources for wisdom in 6.34–37 (*Jewish Wisdom*, 56). The two options are not presented as alternatives in these verses, though, and this solution conveniently ignores the verses which state that the elders discuss the Torah.

[45] Sanders, *Paul and Palestinian Judaism*, 329–33. Parenthetical references in the following are to Sanders, *Paul and Palestinian Judaism*.

[46] Wischmeyer identifies v.12 as "[e]ine klassische Formulierung des Bundesnomismus" ("Theologie und Anthropologie," 23).

[47] Cf. Hos 2.19–20; *Jub.* 15.31.

[48] The claim that Israel alone possesses the wisdom that the world sought is often read as a polemic against Hellenism (see Hengel, *Judaism and Hellenism*, 1.138–39, 160–62; Skehan/Di Lella, *The Wisdom of Ben Sira*, 77; Crenshaw, "Sirach," 625–26). Ben Sira's opposition to Hel-

fied as "the book of the covenant of the Most High God, the law which Moses commanded us as an inheritance for the gathering of Jacob" (v.23). The equation of wisdom and the Torah, Sanders notes, serves as a sign of Israel's election, and this connection between wisdom and the Torah is the "theme" of the book (332; emphasis removed).

Sanders is undoubtedly correct that the connection between wisdom and the Torah is crucial for Ben Sira, even if he overstates it by calling it the "theme." The election of Israel also is assumed throughout and stated at points, but it is questionable how significant election and the covenant (as understood by Sanders) are for Ben Sira's conception of the divine-human relationship. Sanders himself seems to recognise this problem when he writes, "What Ben Sirach has to say about the fate of the individual is not thematically connected with his traditional picture of the salvation of Israel at the time of the Lord's coming" (332). Because Ben Sira's eschatological hopes only apply to Israel as a nation and not the individual (36/33.1–22), "the question of the election has no soteriological consequences" (333).[49] The connection between election, the covenant, and salvation that Sanders finds in the rabbinical literature, the Dead Sea Scrolls, and other texts and is fundamental to covenantal nomism is radically broken in Ben Sira. Concerning the relationship between obedience and

---

lenism was the standard position for most of the twentieth century. Tcherikover classically claimed, "Ben Sira fought against the spirit of Greek civilization all his life, for he understood the danger threatening Judaism from Hellenism" (*Hellenistic Civilization*, 144; cf. Siebeneck, "May Their Bones Return to Life!" 411; Tennant, "Teaching of Ecclesiasticus and Wisdom," 208; Di Lella, "Conservative and Progressive Theology," 141; Garlington, *'Obedience of Faith'*, 15–19; Blenkinsopp, *Wisdom and Law in the Old Testament*, 163; deSilva "The Wisdom of Ben Sira," 435–38). This proposed background has been challenged. There is little evidence that Hellenism was perceived as a threat to Jewish tradition and lifestyle before the Maccabean era (Goldstein, "Jewish Acceptance and Rejection of Hellenism;" Aitken, "Biblical Interpretation"). In the space of a few years, the situation changed, and some Jews began to attack certain aspects of the Hellenistic lifestyle. Other parts of Hellenism were openly embraced not only in Alexandria, but also in Jerusalem itself (Collins, *Jewish Wisdom*, 32–33 [with reference to Ben Sira]; Perdue, *Sword and the Stylus*, 259–65). More scholars are arguing that Ben Sira's opposition is not Hellenism but apocalyptic strands of Second Temple Judaism (see Boccaccini, *Middle Judaism*, 77–81; Wright, "Fear the Lord and Honor the Priest;" Martin, "Ben Sira," Prockter, "Torah as a Fence;" Argall, *1 Enoch and Sirach*).

[49] The authenticity of this prayer for deliverance from the nations has been questioned by Collins because it does not fit Ben Sira's historical timeframe and the eschatological fervour is unparalleled in the rest of the work (*Jewish Wisdom*, 110–11). However, Ben Sira may well have been favourable to Seleucid rule over against other rulers but still desired for Israel to govern itself. He chooses the best of the available options, while pleading with God to remove any foreign rulers. Also, Ben Sira's plea for an eschatological future is for the nation not the individual. He, therefore, is in complete agreement with the prophets who spoke of Israel's future as a nation but without direct concern for the individual in the future (cf. Ezek 37.1–14). There is no contradiction between longing for Israel as a nation to have a glorious future, but not thinking that all individuals of Israel will participate in that future.

disobedience and the covenant in the rabbinic literature and Qumran, Sanders argues,

> The distribution of reward and punishment does not, in rabbinic literature, become the basis of salvation; rather, the covenant is the main factor in salvation, while a man is punished or rewarded for his deeds within the covenant. Similarly in Qumran, one is punished for transgressions of the ordinances of the covenant and rewarded for adherence, but saved by being in the covenant itself. (297)

Individual salvation in Ben Sira's this-worldly perspective, however, is not dependent on election but is determined by whether one is among the righteous or wicked, which is determined by "whether or not he more or less satisfactorily keeps the commandments of the covenant" (333; cf. 346). Individual salvation is, Sanders concludes, ultimately determined by obedience. The difference between Ben Sira and the Rabbis and Qumran is stark. To be certain, the relationship between obedience and blessing should not be construed as "works-righteous legalism in the pejorative sense, in which a man arrogantly thinks that his good deeds establish a claim on God" (345). Nevertheless, it remains the case, as Sanders notes, that the individual's hope of blessing rests on his or her obedience to the commandments.

Having separated the covenant and election from divine blessing, the structure of covenantal nomism collapses. The individual, which is Ben Sira's primary focus, no longer relates to God based on some prior divine act of grace. Now he or she relates based on whether or not the law is obeyed. One might still argue that, despite Ben Sira's interest in the individual human, the establishment of the covenant was initiated by God and this, therefore, indicates that the divine-human relationship is founded on unmerited grace. The individual Israelite's obedient response, then, is no the means to acquire life and blessing. Obedience would have the same function as it has in the rabbinic literature, namely, the means to remaining within the covenant. The pattern of covenantal nomism would remain intact. Yet, not only does Sanders seem to acknowledge that this account of the function of obedience is problematic when applied to Ben Sira, it also presumes that Ben Sira thought the covenant was initiated and established by God, as covenantal nomism claims.

In Sanders' understanding, the covenant signifies an act of divine electing grace. The establishment of the covenant relationship is always prior to the demand for obedience, as the very phrase "covenantal nomism" indicates. While the covenant cannot be divorced from the commandments and expectation for obedience, the focus remains on the divine agent who acts prior to any human action.[50] Sanders identified several statements in the rabbinic literature that recounted God establishing the covenant prior to giving the commandments

---

[50] See Watson, *Paul and the Hermeneutics of Faith*, 8–13.

B. The Establishment of the Human Agent

and Israel accepting and obeying those commandments.[51] Ben Sira's story of Wisdom's descent and identification with the Torah even lends itself to this interpretation (24.1–23). Here in no uncertain terms Israel is declared to possess the wisdom that the world sought, and this is given as an act of divine grace.[52] Yet, this single account of Israel's election in 24.1–23 must be set within the broader context of Ben Sira's concept of the covenant relationship. Such prioritising of the divine agent in giving the covenant (1) does not represent Ben Sira's description of how one enters into a covenant relationship with God, and (2) it hides the fact that, in the case of the Mosaic covenant, the covenant relationship consists of the giving and obeying of commandments.

When not overlaid with supposed rabbinical understandings of how one comes to be in a covenantal relationship with God (by grace), Ben Sira's own perspective about how one enters into a covenantal relationship with God appears differently. He gives priority to the human act of obedience. Regardless of its genre, the point of the "Praise to the Fathers" is clear: those obedient to God are rewarded for their actions.[53] Ben Sira first identifies Noah as a righteous and blameless man, who endured during a period of wrath and is responsible for the continuation of the human race (44.17). He received an eternal "sign" (אות) or "covenants" (διαθῆκαι) to signify that God would not wipe out humanity (v.18). While Ben Sira does not state that Noah was chosen to be the survivor of the human race because of his righteousness, within the context he probably intends one to draw that conclusion.[54]

Ben Sira is more explicit when he describes Abraham as one who

> kept the commandments (מצות) of the Most High, and entered into a covenant (ברית) with him. In his flesh, he cut a statute (חק), and when he was tested, he was found faithful. Therefore, he gave an oath to him:[55] to bless the nations by his seed, to multiply him as the dust of the earth,[56] to raise high his seed like the stars, to give them an inheritance from sea to sea and from the River to the ends of the earth. (44.20–21)

In v.20b Ben Sira clearly has in mind Genesis 17, which records God's establishment of the covenant with Abraham and the command to circumcise. The opening verses summarise the remainder of the chapter (vv.1–2). Further, they highlight the close connection between covenant and obedience. Verses 3–14

---

[51] Sanders, *Paul and Palestinian Judaism*, 85–87, citing, e.g., *m. Bek.* 2:2; *Mekilta Baḥodesh* 5; 6.

[52] "[B]en Sira's myth of Wisdom is the story of how God's freely given, innervating, vivifying goodness has been made present in the Torah. It is the story of grace told from the perspective of eternity" (Nickelsburg, *Jewish Literature*, 58).

[53] Brown, "God and Men in Israel's History."

[54] Cf. VanLandingham, *Judgment and Justification*, 36.

[55] This line is translated from the Greek. The Hebrew is damaged at the centre of the line, but appears to convey the same idea: על כן בש[..]עה הקים לו.

[56] This line and the next have dropped out of the Hebrew. If the line began with a ל (as both v.21b, d), then it is, most likely, a case of homoioarcton.

outline the covenant obligations for the two parties beginning with God's. He will make Abraham's descendants into a mighty, numerous nation and will provide them with a dwelling place (vv.3–8). Abraham, for his part, will be obedient to God's commands, especially the command to circumcise. His descendents will observe this statute perpetually as a sign of the covenant (vv.9–14). The order in which the covenant is described as well as the obligations placed on Abraham and his descendents shows that the author of Genesis does not think the covenant is given based on Abraham's obedience.

Ben Sira moves away from Genesis 17 in his next comment on the testing of Abraham (Sir 44.20d). Here he draws on a common early Jewish theme found initially in Genesis 22. The most well known example is probably *Jubilees*, which divides Abraham's life into ten (actually nine) tests (17.17; 19.8).[57] Ben Sira likely only has in mind the sacrifice of Isaac (Gen 22.1–19), which is the only point in Abraham's life that Genesis calls a test (v.1).[58]

Ben Sira continues in Sirach 44.21 by recalling the Abrahamic blessing found initially in Genesis 12.1–3 (cf. 15.1–21). Genesis 22 may provide the example for how Ben Sira orders his recounting of the events. After God tested Abraham, he blesses Abraham and his descendants because (כִּי) he did not withhold Isaac (22.16). Similarly, Ben Sira follows the order of Genesis: Abraham was tested, he remained faithful, and God blessed him for it. The blessing given to Abraham is the outcome of his obedience to the test.

Despite the formal similarities between Sirach and its source in Genesis, Ben Sira makes several interpretative moves in this short statement that shift the focus from God's establishment of the covenant to Abraham's obedience as the reason for the covenant. First, he focuses on Abraham's obedience to God's will.[59] The opening line sets the tone for the rest of the section. Ben Sira describes Abraham as obedient to the "commandment," which is probably a reference to the Mosaic Torah (Sir 44.20). While he probably does not envision Abraham possessing a copy of the law, he nevertheless thinks that Abraham was obedient to it.[60] Abraham's obedience is also highlighted when Ben Sira makes him the subject of the verbs in v.20. Particularly interesting is the claim that Abraham entered (בָּא) into a covenant with God (v.20b). In Genesis 12.1–3, 15.1–17, and 17.1–14, God is the one who approaches Abraham about enter-

---

[57] The author says that Sarah's death was the tenth test (19.8), but he only lists seven in 17.17. The sacrifice of Isaac is the eighth. For a discussion of this motif in *Jubilees*, see Watson, *Paul and the Hermeneutics of Faith*, 222–36.

[58] The singular וּבְנִסּוּי (πειρασμῷ) in Sir 44.20 probably refers to one event.

[59] de Roo, "God's Covenant with the Fathers," 195.

[60] Ben Sira never clarifies how Abraham could be obedient to the Torah, which he normally describes as the book of the law given to Moses. Perhaps he thinks that Abraham was obedient to the Torah because of the connection between wisdom and the Torah (cf. 24.1–23) or because of the connection between the Torah and creation (cf. 17.1–14).

ing into a covenant relationship. Ben Sira could be making the simple observation that Abraham was in a covenant relationship with God, but in light of his focus on Abraham's actions in Sirach 44.20, he could intend more. Abraham's obedience to the law led to the establishment of the covenant relationship, and one could then say that the covenant was initiated by Abraham not God.[61]

Second, in 44.20d Ben Sira combines Genesis 22.1–14 (testing) and 15.6 (faithfulness).[62] Joining these two texts is not unique since other early Jewish authors did so also (cf. 1 Macc 2.52), but the implications that result from the combination are significant. By combining the two, Ben Sira identifies Abraham's obedience to the command to sacrifice Isaac as faithfulness. In Genesis 15.6, however, Abraham's faith is in response to God's promise, and there is no mention of any obedience. In fact, the covenant ceremony described in vv.9–21 is unilateral. Stipulations are placed on God, but nothing is said about Abraham's actions. Ben Sira interprets "faith" so that it means obedience to God's commands rather than trust in God's promise.

Ben Sira's third significant hermeneutical move concerns his understanding of the point at which God makes his oath. Ben Sira places the establishment of the covenant and the testing of Abraham prior to his explanation of the "oath." He is most likely following Genesis 22 as noted previously. In adopting the pattern of Genesis 22, though, he overlooks the promises made previously to Abraham in 12.1–3 and 15.1–21. By placing the promises prior to any obedience on Abraham's part, the author of Genesis draws to one's attention the action of God. By ignoring these two texts, though, Ben Sira highlights Abraham's actions as the reason for his special relationship with God. If in Sirach 44.21 Ben Sira is not simply following the order of Genesis 22 but has in mind Genesis 12.1–6 and 15.1–6, the contrast between the actions of Abraham and God becomes even sharper. By rearranging these events, Ben Sira places the emphasis on Abraham's actions rather than God's. Regardless of which texts Ben Sira intends to summarise in Sirach 44.21, the conjunction עַל כֵּן (διὰ τοῦτο) suggests a logical relationship in which the following statement (in this case the blessings) is dependent on the preceding statement (here, the obedience). The blessing is the outcome of Abraham's obedience rather than an unconditional divine gift.

---

[61] Some later traditions provide more specific reasons for why God chooses Abraham: *Apoc. Abr.* 8.1–6: because he rejected idolatry; *L.A.B.* 6.11: Abraham refuses to help build the tower of Babel (for discussion of these and others, see Evans, "Abraham in the Dead Sea Scrolls," 149–58; VanLandingham, *Judgment and Justification*, 23–35).

[62] Genesis 15.6: "And he [Abram] believed (וְהֶאֱמִן) God, and it was credited to him as righteousness." 22.1: "And after these things, God tested (נִסָּה) Abraham."

By focusing exclusively on Abraham's obedience, Ben Sira makes a theological claim about the relationship between obedience and the covenant.[63] The structure of covenantal nomism, in fact, is reversed. The first act is taken by the human, and God's action is secondary and a response to the human. God neither enters into an unconditional covenantal relationship with Abraham nor initiates it; rather, the covenant relationship is God's acknowledgement of Abraham's obedience.

Ben Sira's praise of Phinehas for his zealous action on behalf of the people when they rebelled follows a similar pattern as the other examples mentioned (45.23–24; cf. Num 25.6–13; Ps 106.28–31). In response to what he did, he was awarded a "covenant of peace" (Sir 45.24).[64] The conjunction לכן (διὰ τοῦτο) in v.24 signifies that the covenant was established in response to Phinehas' action. Ben Sira simply follows the description of events in Numbers 25.6–13 and even uses the same language. Nevertheless, Phinehas receives the covenant because of his act to purify Israel.

Another example is Ben Sira's comments on David. He begins by recounting David's magnificent works during his childhood and his battles with the Philistines (47.1–7). He commends David for his musical talent and the order he introduced to Israel's worship (vv.8–10). Finally, he notes that the Lord overlooked David's sin and gave him a covenant (v.11). One could argue that the establishment of the covenant is based on divine initiative and is not given in response to David's obedience. Two points should be noted, however. First, Ben Sira stresses David's exceptional obedience. His transgression is mentioned only in passing. Second, David's sin does not affect Ben Sira's understanding of him or his children.[65] He does not attribute the split in the kingdom to David's transgression but to the foolishness of Solomon, Rehoboam, and Jeroboam (vv.19–25). In fact, David's love for God assures that his line will never be destroyed despite the actions of his children (v.22). The mention of David's transgression is not intended to indicate that the covenant was established by

---

[63] On the similarities between *Jubilees* and Ben Sira, Garlington states, "There is, then, a general agreement between this book and Ben Sira that the ratification of the 'covenant in his flesh' was subsequent to a prior obedience" (*'Obedience of Faith'*, 39). This order of events, however, does not cause him to question the assumption that the covenant was established by grace without any reference to obedience. Contrast VanLandingham's discussion of *Jubilees* in *Judgment and Justification*, 23–26.

[64] חק ברית שלום becomes διαθήκη εἰρήνης. Schwemer comments, "Hier vereinfacht der Enkel zu διαθήκη εἰρήνης, weil διαθήκη für ihn beides, חק und ברית, ausdrückt" ("Zum Verhältnis von Diatheke und Nomos," 78). Skehan offers an alternative in his translation: "Therefore on him again God conferred the right, in a covenant of friendship, to provide for the sanctuary" (*Wisdom of Ben Sira*, 508). The grandson may have reduced the two words because he was familiar with Num 25.12, which has only בְּרִיתִי שָׁלוֹם. (διαθήκη εἰρήνης).

[65] Contrast 2 Samuel 12.13–14.

B. The Establishment of the Human Agent

God's grace. Ben Sira is simply retelling the key points of David's life. Even the example of David, therefore, continues the pattern observed throughout the rest of the poem: obedience leads to divine blessing, and the concept of the covenant for Ben Sira does not begin with God's gracious election.

The situation with the Mosaic covenant is more complex, but ultimately Ben Sira's understanding of this covenant emphasises the human act of obedience not divine initiation. Unlike his accounts of Abraham, Phinehas, and David, Ben Sira does not state that Israel received the covenant because of their obedience. Rather, the giving of the covenant is portrayed as a gracious event in which God elects Israel as his people (24.1–23).[66] When actually reflecting on this covenant, however, Ben Sira's interest is not in why Israel received it, but the content of it, namely the commandments, and the expectation that comes with it. Ben Sira centres his thoughts around the Mosaic covenant, because it, unlike any of the other covenants, tells a person how to relate to God. At the climax of the tale of Wisdom, wisdom is identified not solely as the covenant, but as "the book of the covenant of the Most High God, the law that Moses commanded us" (v.23). The Mosaic covenant is the commandments.[67]

In the first creation hymn (16.26–17.32), the Mosaic covenant is clearly identified as the commandments. Recounting how God as Creator rules over all creation, Ben Sira comes to the creation of Israel. He does not begin with Abraham's election or the deliverance from Egypt. His view of the beginning of Israel coincides with the moment the people stand at the base of Mt. Sinai (17.11–14; cf. Exod 19.16–19). Here Israel is created by God and selected as his people (v.17). In this event, Israel enters into a covenantal relationship with God when he gives them "the law of life" (17.11b). This law is further identified as an "eternal covenant," and when giving this covenant God "revealed his decrees" (v.12).[68] The giving of the Torah is the creation of a relationship that can be described as a covenant. This text clearly indicates that the Torah is foundational to Israel's relationship with God, and defined as "the law of life," the Torah is the source of life for any who obey its commandments. There is no two-stage idea of God establishing a covenant relationship with Israel and then giving the commandments and the expectation for obedience. Watson argues correctly,

---

[66] Nickelsburg misses the point of Sirach 24 when he says that Ben Sira is not concerned with Moses receiving the Torah as an historical event, but with the "ahistorical interpretation that sees the Mosaic Torah as the repository of heavenly wisdom, which is then expounded by the sages" (*Ancient Judaism and Christian Origins*, 39; cf. Nickelsburg with Kraft, "Introduction," 21).

[67] Note the parallelism between "commandments" and "the covenant of the Most High" in 28.7. There is no difference for the covenant is the commandments.

[68] Reiterer ("Interpretation of the Wisdom Tradition," 225) argues that the "eternal covenant" refers to Genesis 17, but this ignores the clear allusions to Exod 19.16–19 in Sir 17.13.

What is significant, however, is not the usage of the term *diathēkē* but the assumption that the giving and observing of commandments is fundamental to God's relationship to Israel. This giving and observing of commandments is not here [in 17.11–14] set within a *prior* "covenant" characterized by pure divine electing grace.[69]

When describing God as allotting the law or establishing the covenant, the purpose is not to declare that this act is done out of divine mercy. Rather, by crediting God with the giving of the Torah, Ben Sira underscores the divine origin of the commandments. The commandments must be obeyed because God himself gave them.

Ben Sira's emphasis on the obligation found in the Mosaic covenant is not a case of misunderstanding the covenant. The covenant structure itself highlights the requirement for obedience.[70] Moses' plea for the people to obey in Deuteronomy 30.15–20, for Ben Sira, functions as the hermeneutical guide for how the rest of the Torah should be read. Those places that link blessing and obedience in this reading strategy stand out. Indeed, the previous covenants between God and an individual are read through this understanding of the Mosaic covenant. Whereas Paul argues that the covenant with Abraham was initiated and sustained by divine grace (Gal 3; Rom 4), Ben Sira finds Abraham's obedience to God's commandments as the reason for the covenant. The different readings of Ben Sira and Paul stem from their hermeneutical starting points.[71] Finding in Habakkuk 2.4 the principle that righteousness comes through faith (Gal 3.11; Rom 1.17), Paul confirms this in the Abraham narrative (Gen 15.6; Gal 3; Rom 4) and therefore rejects the reading strategy found in Ben Sira and other Second Temple texts. Because Paul will not discard the Torah as divine revelation, he is forced to remarkable interpretations of those parts that seem to oppose his interpretation (cf. Rom 10.5–8; Deut 30.11–14). Ben Sira, by contrast, employs Deuteronomy 30.15–20 as his guide to reading the Torah, and this leads him to focus on the acts of Abraham rather than God. The significant acts of divine intervention, such as the Exodus, mentioned at the beginning of Deuteronomy (4.20) are ignored by Ben Sira. Israel's blessings, for Ben Sira, are the outcome of their faithfulness to the commandments, not the result of God's invading mercy nor his fulfilment of the promises to the Patriarchs (contrast Deut 1.8; 9.27). In Ben Sira's view, each individual must reconfirm the covenant, and God's goodness to previous generations is the result of their obedience and

---

[69] Watson, *Paul and the Hermeneutics of Faith*, 9–10 (emphasis original).

[70] Freedman and Miano compare the Mosaic covenant with the Hittite suzerainty treaties. In these treaties, "[t]he covenantal relationship is dependent on the behavior of the vassal and can only be maintained if the vassal complies with the terms of the arrangement" ("People of the New Covenant," 7–8).

[71] See especially Watson, *Paul and the Hermeneutics of Faith*.

B. The Establishment of the Human Agent

does not carry over to later generations. Both authors exploit the text of Deuteronomy and the Torah based on their hermeneutical starting points, and the different starting points explain the radical outcomes of their readings.

The failure by much of contemporary scholarship to recognise the different hermeneutical starting points results in a systemic misreading of Paul and Second Temple Judaism. The two are conflated with the result that both are distorted. This failure to acknowledge the different starting points even affects readings of Deuteronomy. Many scholars attempt to read Deuteronomy through Paul's (prophetic?) lens without acknowledging that they have begun with this hermeneutical presupposition.[72] Yet, Paul's reading strategy results in a drastic rewriting of part of Deuteronomy and an explicit rejection of other parts of the Torah (see Lev 18.5 in Gal 3.12; Rom 10.5). No less, adopting Ben Sira's pattern requires one to ignore key elements of the Torah. An objective reading of Deuteronomy is not possible, but recognising these fundamentally different hermeneutical starting points will, at the least, force one to acknowledge those points in Deuteronomy or the Torah as a whole that do not actually fit one's perspective. This is exactly what Paul and Ben Sira do.

Whereas Sanders argued that the divine-human relationship was grounded in God's electing grace, Ben Sira maintains that the divine-human relationship revolves around the giving and observing of the commandments. Ben Sira's perspective, in fact, gives more attention to the actions of the human agent than those of God. A covenantal relationship, as Ben Sira formulates it, is often depicted as God's acknowledgement of human obedience. All this indicates that covenantal nomism is not the correct framework in which to interpret Ben Sira's statements that correlate obedience and blessing and disobedience and cursing. The proper context must account for the central point that God is one who gives commandments and the human agent is one who should obey them. In Sirach this context is the Creator-creation relationship. In several passages, Ben Sira reflects on the works of God and how they consistently obey his command. The divine-human relationship, or more specifically the Israel-God relationship, is a subset of the created order, and the giving of the covenant with its commandments is the specific form of how the Creator relates to those who are endowed with his image. While there are significant differences between humans and the rest of creation, they relate to God in the same manner as all of creation: through obedience to his commandments.[73]

The pattern of God giving commandments and his creatures obeying them can be observed in the relationship between God and Wisdom, the first of his creations. Wisdom roamed freely throughout the heavens, and she sought on earth a people among whom she could reside (Sir 24.3–7). God chose Israel

---

[72] Take, for example, Block, "Grace of Torah;" Barker, *Grace in Deuteronomy*.

[73] On the function and meaning of creation theology in Sirach, see Perdue, *Wisdom and Creation*, 248–90.

for her, and at his command, she took up residence within Israel: "Then the Creator of all things commanded me and the Creator caused me to rest in my tent. He said, 'In Jacob you will settle and in Israel you will obtain an inheritance'" (v.8). Despite her eternal nature, she finds her resting place in Israel's cult where she serves the Lord (vv.9–10). Wisdom interacts with her Maker by observing his commandments. God is portrayed as one who gives commandments. From the outset, then, God's interaction with his creation is portrayed as the giving and observing of commandments.

Similar to his depiction of Wisdom's interaction with God, Ben Sira reflects on creation's obedience to God's commands in the three creation hymns. In the third creation hymn (42.15–43.33), Ben Sira describes how different parts of creation obey their Maker's instructions. He opens the hymn with the statement "By his word are the works of the Lord, and the creatures do his will" (42.15). The second half of this statement summarises the content of the latter part of the hymn (43.1–26). The sun continues on its path because of the Lord's word (43.5). The stars are assigned their positions in the sky by the word of the Lord, and they give light to the night sky without tiring (v.10). The snow, wind, and other astronomical occurrences come from his commands (vv.13–22). In the second creation hymn (39.12–35), Ben Sira describes how God uses various aspects of creation as a means of divine judgment on the wicked or redemption for the righteous. Referring to the crossing of the Red Sea (Exod 14.21–30), Ben Sira says that the waters parted because God commanded them (Sir 39.17). This salvific event occurred at the "word" of the Lord, the very command issued "from his mouth." Based on this event, Ben Sira concludes that the purpose of the Lord is always accomplished, and no one can limit his saving power (v.18). Some winds, along with fire, hail, famine, and other pestilences, are forms of divine judgment, and they were created to calm the wrath of their Maker (39.28–29). Even some animals were created to inflict punishment on ungodly people (v.30). These various means of punishment eagerly wait for and then accomplish the Lord's commands. They never fail to complete their assigned task (v.31). The first creation hymn also reflects on God's control over the celestial beings. He placed them in the sky according to his will, and they do not waver from their assigned tasks (16.26–27). "They never disobey his word" (v.28), Ben Sira claims. These three hymns reference God's control over creation as a reason to praise him. The celestial beings and weather events diligently serve their Creator and accomplish the tasks for which they were created. Their relationship is formed around the commands given by God.

The theme of creation's obedience to God is common in Second Temple Judaism.[74] God is worthy of praise because he controls creation (*Pss. Sol.* 18.10–

---

[74] Most of the examples provided by Garlington (*'Obedience of Faith'*, 59n.259) describe the consistency of the created order (i.e., the ability to calculate the number of days in a year because of the regular movement of the sun and moon) but do not directly connect this with God's command over these phenomena.

12; 1QH^a 20.6–14), and this characteristic of his power distinguishes him from idols (Bar 3.33–35; Let Jer 60–65). Baruch appeals to God's control over all of creation as the reason for him to sustain human life (*2 Bar.* 24.4–9) and ultimately to bring an end to wickedness (v.19). The consistent obedience of creation contrasts with the inconsistency of humankind, who is not today what it will be tomorrow (vv.15–16).[75] In several instances, other authors use the idea to contrast the obedience of the non-human creation with the disobedience of some humans and the obedience of others. In the Two-Spirits Treatise, God's control over creation is paralleled to his act of placing within humans two spirits and ultimately his decision concerning who will be in the lot of the Prince of Lights and the Angel of Darkness (1QS 3.15–21). The closest parallel to Ben Sira's use of this motif is *1 Enoch* 5. Enoch utilises the consistent obedience of creation to chastise the disobedient for their neglect of the commandments and to encourage the obedient that God will bless them. The difference between the non-human part of creation and the human part is the possibility that humans can revolt against their Maker. This is precisely the same link that Ben Sira establishes between the heavenly beings and humans in Sirach 16.26–17.14.

The first creation hymn brings this pattern of the Creator-creation relationship into direct contact with the divine-human relationship. Having briefly claimed that God established the boundaries for all the heavenly beings and that they always serve him (16.26–28), Ben Sira proceeds to explain the place of humanity within the broader created order. He reflects directly on the creation accounts in Genesis (17.1–10), while offering his own distinctive interpretations of key aspects. Although being in the image of God (Sir 17.3; cf. Gen 1.27–28), humanity is a subset within the created order, and the divine-human relationship is simply an expression of the Creator-creation relationship. Consistent throughout the discussion on each category of creation is the claim that each part relates to God through obedience to the commands he gives. Humanity differs from the rest of the created order because it possesses knowledge of good and evil, is endowed with freedom, and thus the possibility exists that individuals might rebel against God.

In the description of humanity, the key characteristics of the two-ways paradigm can be detected. First, Ben Sira identifies the Torah as "the law of life" (17.11b) and the "eternal covenant" (v.12a). The parallelism between "covenant" and "law" indicates that obedience to the law is not simply the means to remaining within a previously established covenantal relationship. Torah observance is the means to life. Even if a covenant of grace was established prior to any human action, it is the case, for Ben Sira, that one's enjoyment of life is contingent solely on one's obedience. This emerges, in this poem, at the conclusion when Ben Sira describes how God observes all human action. He sees both those who do evil (v.20) and those who do good (v.22). What matters

---

[75] Cf. *2 Bar.* 48.1–24; 54.3.

at the time of judgment is not ethnicity, but obedience: "Afterward [God] will rise up and repay them. He will give back their recompense upon their heads" (v.23). The divine act is a response to the human's obedience or disobedience to the commandments found in the Torah (cf. v.14).

Second, in 17.1–14 Ben Sira focuses particularly on God revealing to humans what is expected of them.[76] Along with giving to humans "discretion and tongue and eyes, ears and a mind for thinking" (v.6), God also "filled them with knowledge and understanding and showed to them good and evil" (v.7).[77] Ben Sira differs significantly from Genesis in explaining how humans came to know the difference between good and evil. According to Genesis 2–3, Adam and Eve learned the difference between good and evil only after they ate from "the tree of the knowledge of good and evil" (2.17; 3.1–13). This slight, but significant interpretative move brings Ben Sira's view in line with Moses' claim that by giving the people the law he had set before them good and evil (Deut 30.15).[78] Again, Deuteronomy functions as the hermeneutical key to interpreting the rest of the Torah. As the poem in Sirach 17.1–14 continues, Ben Sira claims that "knowledge" and the "law of life" are revealed (vv.11–12). He summarises the divine demand as "beware of all evil. He gave commandment to each of them concerning his neighbour" (v.14; cf. 27.30–28.7). For Ben Sira it is fundamental that God himself made the moral categories of good and evil known and not that humans learned them because of the serpent's deception (cf. Gen 3.13). By revealing good and evil, humans have a clear understanding of what is expected from them. The failure to do good cannot be attributed to a lack of understanding. Moreover, in Ben Sira's view possession of knowledge implies that one can keep the commandments.[79] Obedience is possible because humans know what is expected of them.[80]

Third, the divine decision to leave the human to his or her own will is not as apparent in 17.1–24 as it is in 15.14, but the poem does describe God's judgment of human action. Contrary to those who deny the judgment (16.17–23), Ben Sira holds that God sees everything done by each person (17.15–22). Only "after" the human obeys or transgresses the commandments (17.20, 22), does God respond: "Afterward [μετὰ ταῦτα] he will rise up and repay them. He will

---

[76] Sheppard notes that in vv.6–10 especially Ben Sira "surrounds the statement in phrase upon phrase of free and copious embellishment in celebration of mankind's intellectual capacity" (*Wisdom as a Hermeneutical Construct*, 79).

[77] Cf. the fragmentary 4Q504 8.4–5, which describes God as giving Adam "intelligence and knowledge" when he was created. Much of this fragment mirrors Sirach 17.1–10.

[78] Cf. Schökel, "The Vision of Man," 239.

[79] Kaiser, "Der Mensch als Geschöpf Gottes," 10–12.

[80] On the basis of 17.1–4, Levison remarks that "human beings are ephemeral and sinful, in contrast to the celestial creature" (*Portraits of Adam in Early Judaism*, 37). Nothing indicates that humans are "sinful," but the gift of knowledge does indicate that they possess the ability to be sinful unlike the celestial beings.

give back their recompense upon their heads" (v.23). The divine act of judgment is a re-action to what humans do from their own free will.

In 17.1–14 Ben Sira places Israel's special relationship with God within the broader context of humanity's and the rest of creation's relationship with God. In claiming that Israel relates to God in the same manner as all other humans, he has not eliminated the unique relationship that Israel possesses with her God. Israel's legal, covenantal traditions rather have been placed into the wider context of a creation theology. Creation theology typifies wisdom theology,[81] and by combining the Torah with creation, Ben Sira gives creation theology a specific focus on Israel. Ben Sira perceives no tension between these two traditional types of theology.[82] A reason that there is no fundamental tension is because both have the same pattern for the divine-human relationship: God gives commandments and creation follows them.

Although created in the image of God and given dominance over other creatures, humans belong to the same created order as Wisdom, the stars, and the animals. The divine-human relationship is a subcategory of the Creator-creation relationship, and the former takes its structure from the latter. Humans, like the rest of creation, are to obey God. God has given to humans knowledge of good and evil and revealed specifically to Israel the covenant that contains the law that Moses commanded to them (17.11–14; 24.23; 45.5). This covenant pattern forms the basis of the relationship. Ben Sira undoubtedly thinks of God as loving, merciful, gracious, but whenever he sets out to describe how any aspect of creation interacts with God, he argues that the interaction is based on the commandments given by God. The entire cosmos exemplifies an ordered harmony centred on God as the one who issues commandments.

The Creator-creation relationship revolves around God giving commandments and creation obeying them. The divine-human relationship, as a subset of the Creator-creation relationship, likewise is built around God giving commandments and the human observing them. This correlation between the divine-human relationship and the Creator-creation has significant implications for how one understands the relationship between obedience and blessing, disobedience and cursing that was observed at the beginning of this section. It is not the case that obedience is merely the response of the faithful human to God's prior grace. Nor is it the case that obedience is simply the means to maintaining a life already possessed. Rather, obedience is the means to attaining life and blessing. Ben Sira exhorts his students to observe the law because he thinks that this is the only means to life. His nomism has not collapsed into perverse legalism in which one arrogantly demands blessing from God, as Sanders rightly noted, but it remains the case that Ben Sira contends that life comes through keeping the

---

[81] Zimmerli, "Place and Limit of the Wisdom." Cf. Hermisson, "Observations on the Creation Theology in Wisdom."

[82] Wischmeyer, "Theologie und Anthropologie," 23–24.

law. This is, in Ben Sira's view, God's ordained method by which one should acquire the blessings of life.[83]

Against his opposition, Ben Sira argued that God set life and death before the human agent in the form of the Torah (15.17; 17.11). The human's obedience to the commandments is the means to possessing life and blessings. This was the first point in the two-ways pattern, and it has been seen in other parts of Sirach. Numerous statements indicate a connection between law observance and life, but it is the broader context of the Creator-creation relationship that defines how obedience relates to life. In this relationship, God is portrayed as one who gives commandments and creation obeys them. For Ben Sira, the divine-human relationship is modelled after the Creator-creation relationship, and the roles of God and humans remain the same. God gives commandments, and humans should obey them. The one who obeys will be given life and blessing, while those who disobey will be punished.

c. Obedience, Fear of God, and Faith

In the discussion of covenant and Sanders' claim that Ben Sira employs covenantal nomism, it was observed that this focus on a divine act of grace is misplaced. The giving of the covenant does not establish a relationship centred on divine acts of mercy. Rather than looking to the divine agent as the primary actor, Ben Sira points to the human agent and his or her obedience to the commandments. Obedience is, as argued above, the means to life and blessing. Whereas Sanders sought to orient the divine-human relationship around God's acts of mercy, others have attempted to sever the link between obedience and life by arguing that the relationship is founded, for the human's part, on a prior, internal basis. As important as law observance is, it comes in second place behind the inner dispositions and attitudes that form the true heart of the relationship and the basis for life.[84] Obedience to the law is the visual evidence of one's belief in God and, in some views, as the means to maintaining life in the covenant. Either way, life is acquired through another means than obedience to the law. In recent scholarship, two characteristics in particular have been highlighted: fear of the Lord and faith.[85]

Schnabel maintains that one's obedience to the law arises from an inner dependence on God, which is expressed by the phrase "fear of the Lord." The

---

[83] Alexander ("Torah and Salvation in Tannaitic Literature," 271–72) and Watson (*Paul and the Hermeneutics of Faith*, 12–13) question Sanders' assumption that a relationship based on grace is superior to one based on Torah observance.

[84] These human actions are usually thought to be in response to something God already did to establish the relationship (e.g., the covenant).

[85] One could add "hope," "love," or "humility" (the last stressed by Sanders, *Paul and Palestinian Judaism*, 345), but these receive less attention from Ben Sira. Nonetheless, the comments made about "fear of God" and "faith" would apply also to these attitudes.

close relationship between the two concepts is revealed in several verses where they appear in parallel lines. For example:

Consider diligently in the fear of the Most High and in his commandments and meditate continually. (6.37)

The one who fears YHWH will do this, and the one who grasps the Torah will understand her [wisdom]. (15.1)

The fear of YHWH is all wisdom, and in all wisdom, there is the doing of the law. Better is the fearful who lacks intelligence, than the one abounding in intelligence who also transgresses the law. (19.20, 24)

The one who observes the law prevails over his thoughts, and fulfilment of the fear of the Lord is wisdom. (21.11)

According to Schnabel, the order of the parallelism, which is determined by the context, clarifies the relationship between fearing the Lord and keeping the commandments. If the context focuses on "a fundamental or 'inner' viewpoint," then fear of the Lord appears first, and the mention of the law "appears to be a concretization" (6.37; 15.1; 23.27; 37.12; 39.1). When the Torah appears first, the emphasis is on accomplishing certain actions, and the thought process moves from the "concrete to the more comprehensive realm" (1.26–27; 9.15–16; 21.11; 32.14–16; 32.24–33.1). Based on this scheme, Schnabel concludes that the fear of the Lord is the foundation for obedience to the law. The fact that fearing God is not lost in keeping the commandments, he further notes, "makes sure that the keeping of the law is not a routine performance or accomplishment but a result of one's personal commitment and confidence in God who makes the obedience to his law possible (cf. 15,13)."[86] According to this perspective, then, fear of the Lord refers to the disposition or character of a person, while obedience to the law defines how one lives. Further, fear of the Lord establishes a personal relationship with God so that one's obedience flows from that prior relationship.

Garlington focuses on the role of "faith" in the divine-human relationship. Employing Sanders' distinction between getting in and staying in, he argues that one responds to God's gracious election by believing in him. Just as grace is the divine action on which the relationship with Israel is founded, faith is the human action that serves as the basis for the relationship. One's faith manifests itself in obedience to the Torah; that is, obedience is the outward expression of one's inner faith in God. Two quotes will make clear his position. First, commenting on the relationship between faith and fear of God in 1.14, he states, "[F]aith, which is the gift of God, is both temporally and logically prior to obedience." Second, commenting in 2.6, he writes, "The accent is on human activity: one must do as well as believe. This is the obedience which proceeds from

---

[86] Schnabel, *Law and Wisdom*, 45. Cf. von Rad who thinks that Ben Sira needed the law to define and elucidate the meaning of fearing God (*Wisdom in Israel*, 244–45).

faith and complements faith."[87] Although obedience functions as the means for remaining in the covenant, it is not abstracted from faith. At times the linear relationship resides into the background, so that faith becomes obedience (see 4.15–16). These instances, according to Garlington, highlight the active nature of faith.[88] Generally speaking, however, Ben Sira views obedience as the evidence of one's faith.

Despite these claims, several points show that one's obedience does not arise from one of these internal perspectives and that they do not form the foundation of the divine-human relationship. Three comments will be made about fear of the Lord followed by some observations about faith.

First, although Schnabel's analysis does clarify the relationship in some of the texts (e.g., 1.26–27; 2.15–16), it does not adequately explain all of them. The priority of the fear of the Lord is not found in some of the texts. In 9.15–16 the statements imply no dependent relationship. There is no conceptual difference between conversing about the law and making one's glory the fear of the Lord. Fearing God is only a "more comprehensive realm" (Schnabel's phrase) if one imposes a distinction between the two expressions. In 15.1 no movement from a prior, internal attitude to physical manifestation of that perspective is evident. The previous verses depict one's actions (14.20–27), and 15.1b continues describing one's actions. Fear of the Lord can only be an internal disposition if one ignores the focus on obedience in the section and has decided previously that obedience to the law is an external expression of a prior commitment. Likewise, in 23.27, Ben Sira does not distinguish between the two ideas nor does he suggest that fearing God is more important than keeping the law.[89] The context actually implies that the two concepts are the same. The adulterer fails to fear God (v.19), and the adulteress neglects the Torah (v.23). Further, v.27 concludes Ben Sira's reflections on the outcome of adultery, which arise from his prayer for deliverance from sexual temptation (23.2–6). The prayer may contain hints that a character change is needed toward sin, but the answer focuses on actual obedience not a change of character or disposition toward God. One final text worth noting is 32.24–33.3 (35.28–36.4 Greek), where Ben Sira describes what will happen to the one who observes the commandments.

The one who obeys the Torah watches his soul, and the one who trusts in YHWH will not be ashamed. Evil will not befall the one who fears YHWH, for when tested he will turn and

---

[87] Garlington, *'Obedience of Faith'*, 20, 23 (respectively).
[88] Garlington, *'Obedience of Faith'*, 27.
[89] "And those who remain will know that nothing is more prominent than fear of the Lord and nothing sweeter than to devote oneself to the commandments of the Lord."

be saved. The one who hates the Torah will not be wise, and is tossed about like a boat in a storm.⁹⁰ A man who is insightful understands the word, and the Torah is for him as trustworthy as the Urim.⁹¹

The main subject is clearly one's attitude toward the law, which is mentioned three times.⁹² Six descriptions are given of the nature of the one who follows the law. The one who fears YHWH is the same as the wise person, the faithful one, and the intelligent person. These descriptions are synonymous expressions intended to encompass the entire being. Priority is not placed on one action over the other. There is no conceptual difference between the character traits.

Second, claiming that the fear of the Lord provides the basis for obedience overlooks Ben Sira's statements that define the fear of the Lord as an action to be accomplished. In an exposition on the fear of the Lord in 1.11–30, Ben Sira claims,

You who desire wisdom keep the commandments, and the Lord will supply her to you. The fear of the Lord is wisdom and discipline, and his desire is fidelity and meekness. Do not disobey the fear of the Lord, and do not come to him with a double heart. (vv.26–28)

Fear of God is identified as wisdom, and the means to attaining wisdom is through obedience to the commandments. It is, in fact, the fear of the Lord that one disobeys. Boccaccini succinctly states, "Being pious, loving God, and fearing God represent one thing: obeying the law."⁹³ In his last biographical statement, Ben Sira claims that those who follow his instructions will be wise and equal to all "because [כי] the fear of YHWH is life" or, according to the Greek, "his path" (50.29). Those who fear God avoid sin (15.13; contrast 23.19), and when they do sin, they repent (21.6) and offer sacrifices to God (7.31). The fear of the Lord is not merely a mental assessment or disposition; rather, it is obedience to the will of God.

Finally, one should observe how the fear of the Lord and the law are related by the authors of Deuteronomy and Proverbs, the two texts from which Ben Sira primarily draws his understanding of the fear of the Lord. Neither of these texts makes the fear of the Lord the basis for obedience. In Deuteronomy the fear of the Lord is a covenantal concept linked with obedience to the Torah, which is found in a written text. Moses instructs the future leaders of Israel to read the law publicly every seventh year "so that [the people] may hear and learn in order that they may fear YHWH their God and obey by doing (לעשות) all the words of this Torah" and so that their children, who were not present

---

⁹⁰ This line is Skehan's translation based on the Greek and Hebrew texts (*Wisdom of Ben Sira*, 393, 395).

⁹¹ The last line is based on the Greek text because Hebrew ms B (33.3b) is damaged (ותורתו [......]ק [..]ש).

⁹² On this text see Liesen, "A Common Background."

⁹³ Boccaccini, *Middle Judaism*, 84.

when Moses gave the law, will also learn to fear the Lord (Deut 31.12–13). When a new king comes to power, a copy of the law is to be written, and he shall study it all his life "in order that he may learn to fear YHWH his God and to keep all the words of this Torah and its decrees to do them" (17.18–19). A programmatic statement of the Deuteronomic perspective is 10.12–13:

> Now, Israel, what does YHWH your God require from you? Except to fear YHWH your God, to walk in all his ways, to love him, to serve YHWH your God with all your heart and with all your soul (and) to obey the commandments of YHWH and his decrees which I am commanding you today for your good.[94]

This text brings together key ethical phrases found throughout Deuteronomy in order to underscore the necessity for obedience to the law, particularly the law Moses is currently delivering to the people just before they enter the Promised Land. There is no movement from an inward attitude to an outer expression in these phrases. Moses' comment is intended to motivate the Israelites to obey the Torah. Aside from one mention of fearing God, it is always connected with obedience to the Torah.[95] Fear of the Lord does not establish one's relationship nor refer to a personal relationship with God that then provides the basis for one's obedience.

The sages responsible for Proverbs often stress the practical side of the fear of the Lord. The one who fears the Lord obeys his commands (Prov 23.17; 24.21 LXX), which means avoiding evil (3.7; 8.13; 16.6) and living an upright life (14.2). Those who desire knowledge choose to fear the Lord (1.29). The sages highlight the obedience aspect of the fear of the Lord by placing it in parallelism with various terms for wisdom (cf. 1.7; 9.10; 15.33), which is a practical concept. Wisdom is not simply the acquiring of book knowledge, but rather it is living in conformity to the teaching of the sages. The sages' instructions are even equal to the fear of YHWH (compare 13.14 with 14.27). The postscript to Qoheleth equates fear of God and obedience to the commandment as the single (זֶה) duty of a human (12.13). Even if fear of the Lord is an internal attitude that is expressed through obedience, the sages never describe it as forming the foundation of one's relationship with God. For these sages, the fear of the Lord refers to obedience to the "divine will."[96]

The relationship between faith and obedience proposed by Garlington is simply not evident in the text. First, faith is never said to be a gift from God. It is a human action that is generated by one's own desire for God. Second, Ben Sira does not establish a linear relationship between faith and obedience. In 2.6

---

[94] See also 4.10; 5.29; 6.2, 24; 8.6; 13.4.

[95] Amalek attacked the stragglers because "he did not fear God" (25.18; cf. Exod 17.8–17). This is the only occurrence of fearing God in Deuteronomy that does not have the covenantal name YHWH.

[96] Von Rad, *Wisdom in Israel*, 66, 243–45. By defining the "divine will" as the teaching of the sages (244), von Rad detects a difference between Ben Sira and his predecessors, since for Ben Sira the divine will is found in the Torah (245).

"trust" (πίστευσον) is one of nine imperatives found in vv.1–6. Nothing in these verses suggests that faith precedes any of the other commands or serves as the grounds for motivating one to be obedient. Third, faith is not based on some prior divine action; rather, one trusts that God will help in the future: "Believe in him, and he will help you" (2.6). Throughout chapter 2 faith in God is forward looking (vv.8, 10, 13), and in other places Ben Sira encourages one to trust God because he will act on one's behalf (11.21; cf. 32.24).[97] Faith in God looks to what he will do for a person not backwards to what he might have done.

Rather than being the basis for one's obedience, fear of God and faith are ways of obeying the law. One final point is worth noting about both of these perspectives. They maintain that a relationship with God founded on human obedience is inappropriate, fundamentally wrong, and a weaker form of religion. Without one of these inner dispositions as the foundation of the relationship, personal obedience can become simply routine or, worse, one's perspective can slip into the mindset that "salvation" is achieved by obedience rather than through divine grace. The underlying assumption is that these attitudes are the correct and proper human responses to God. Ben Sira's exhortations to obedience, then, must be put in a linear relationship to the attitudes that truly form the divine-human relationship. Elevating faith or the fear of the Lord above the other commands, however, is an attempt – either consciously or unconsciously – to conform Ben Sira to a (traditional) Pauline perspective. Ben Sira's own emphasis on obedience to the law is lost. Rather than imposing a paradigm on Ben Sira, one must first allow him to define his view of how the divine-human relationship works without judging its value.

In summary: Fear of the Lord and faith do not form the basis of the divine-human relationship. Further, obedience is not the outward expression of these inner attitudes. The relationship is the opposite: obedience to the law is expressed through fearing God and believing in him.

d. Atonement and Sin

Whereas some have sought to distance the connection between obedience and blessing by focusing on prior, internal human attitudes that reveal themselves in obedience, others have sought to lessen the importance of obedience by pointing to the need for forgiveness. Human sinfulness and the possibility for repentance and atonement signal, for Gowan, that Ben Sira did not "operate with a strictly merit-based theology."[98] Sanders argues that atonement points

---

[97] On the secular level, Ben Sira encourages one to trust in his neighbour when he is poor so that when the neighbour becomes wealthy they might rejoice together (22.23).

[98] Gowan, "Wisdom," 238. For an overview of Ben Sira's thoughts on repentance and forgiveness, see Murphy, "Sin, Repentance, and Forgiveness," 265–69.

away from the human agent and to the divine. It is ultimately not the human's imperfect obedience that brings life but God's undeserving mercy, which is offered despite the human's sin. Ben Sira is acutely aware of the moral shortcomings of humanity (8.5; 19.16). Unlike those who forsake God's law (41.8), the occasional sinner is not hopelessly condemned to suffer an excruciating death or to come under the curses of God. Avoidance of sin is ideal, but when one sins, atonement and forgiveness are available. The possibility for forgiveness suggests, then, that the divine-human relationship is founded on God's mercy which is given in spite of the human's sin. Ultimately, life and blessing are acquired not by law observance, but by God's grace.

Certainly, there is an appeal to God to have mercy, forgive, and forget the sinner's transgressions. The basis on which God acts in this manner, however, is not his limitless mercy, but the human's return to the Torah. The solution to imperfection and sin is not an appeal for mercy, but obedience to the commandments. Performing acts of atonement indicates to God that the human's desire is to be faithful to the commandments, and because one has obeyed, God is willing to forgive past transgressions. God forgives because the human obeys. Atonement, for Ben Sira, is an act of obedience to the Torah.[99]

Traditional methods of atonement, such as repentance (17.25) and praying for forgiveness (21.1; cf. 28.2), are encouraged. Ben Sira stresses also almsgiving (3.30; 7.10; 12.3; 29.1; 35.4) and honouring one's parents (3.3, 14–15a). Ben Sira's view of the sacrificial system is disputed.[100] Büchler argued that Ben Sira does not specifically mention the sin or guilt offerings, and he often exhorts one to pray rather than sacrifice (cf. 7.8–10; 21.1; 28.2).[101] Büchler assumes that because prayer brings forgiveness Ben Sira does not think the person should also sacrifice. This assumption must be questioned since Ben Sira encourages other means of atonement along with prayer. Prayer does not cancel the need to forgive one's neighbour (28.2), and it does not stand in opposition to almsgiving or honouring one's parents, which are the two means of atonement most often mentioned by Ben Sira. Ben Sira advocates several methods of atonement that neither compete with nor cancel out one another. Ben Sira also denounces those who abuse the sacrificial system by assuming that God will forgive them if they give abundantly (7.8–9; 34.21–24; 35.15). Attacking this view would not be necessary if he thought the sacrificial system was irrelevant.[102] Büchler's argument is simply biased against the sacrificial system.

---

[99] Boccaccini comments: "The idea that a person's merits can somehow compensate for inevitable transgressions in the eyes of God is stated here for the first time in the history of Jewish thought.... [T]he 'righteous' person is the person whose inevitable transgressions are compensated for by a multitude of good deeds" (*Middle Judaism*, 117–18).

[100] See Perdue, *Wisdom and Cult*, 188–211.

[101] Büchler, "Ben Sira's Conception of Sin and Atonement," 14: 57–58 (on prayer and sacrifice); 61–83; esp. 61, 66, 74–75 (on the sin and guilt offerings); cf. Sanders, *Paul and Palestinian Judaism*, 339; Crenshaw, "Restraint of Reason," 217.

[102] Cf. Sanders, *Paul and Palestinian Judaism*, 339.

B. The Establishment of the Human Agent

In his statements on almsgiving and honouring one's parents, Ben Sira describes the one who does these acts as observing the law. By performing these atoning acts, one is not appealing solely to God's mercy as the source of forgiveness. By doing these atoning acts, one fulfils the commandments, so that obedience cancels disobedience. The two statements about honouring one's parents (3.3, 14–15a) form an inclusio around an exposition on the fifth commandment (3.1–16):

The one who honours his father atones (ἐξιλάσκεται) for sin. (v.3)

Kindness (צדקת) to a father will not be forgotten, and it will be firmly planted in place of sins. In your day of distress, it will be remembered for you. (vv.14–15a)[103]

Throughout the passage, Ben Sira interprets the two aspects of the fifth commandment: the command to honour parents and the reward (or promise) of long life in the land that results from obedience (Exod 20.12; Deut 5.16).[104] He explains that the command takes different forms: honour (vv.3, 8), respect (v.6), service (v.7), help (v.12a), and patience (v.13) are positive expressions of the command, while glorifying one's self at the expense of a parent (vv.10–11) and grieving (v.12b) or forsaking (v.16) one's parents evidence one's failure to obey. The reward for obedience is joy in one's own children (v.5a), one's prayers being heard by God (v.5b), and a father's blessing which provides security (vv.8b–9a). Ben Sira generalises the reward of life in the land to simply "long life" (v.6). Disobedience brings the opposite consequences: no stability (v.9b), lack of glory (vv.10, 11b), and the curse of the Lord (v.16). The rewards (or punishments) are the outcome of one's obedience (or disobedience) to the commandment.

The two comments on obedience to the fifth commandment resulting in atonement follow this same pattern (vv.3, 14–15a). Atonement for disobedience is given to someone who honours his or her parents. Obedience to the law brings forgiveness.[105] "The day of distress" in v.15 could refer to any point of trouble, but more likely Ben Sira is thinking about a point of divine judgment when God calls a person to account for his or her actions. Obedience to the law is remembered by God and functions as atonement in place of one's transgressions when God judges. The difficult clause in v.14b also supports the idea that one's obedience counts in place of one's sin. The NRSV renders v.14b as "will be credited (προσανοικοδομηθήσεται) to you against your sins." Sanders rightly criticises this translation of the rare verb, which is unsupported by

---

[103] צדקת (ms A, C) is ἐλεημοσύνη. "Forgotten" (תשכה/ἐπιλησθήσεται) follows Hebrew ms C and Greek; ms A has תמחה. The modifier "distress" comes from ms A and Greek.

[104] Deuteronomy does divide the reward into two aspects: prolonged life and a good life in the land. This development may provide the scriptural impetus for Ben Sira's interpretation of the fifth commandment.

[105] This point is stressed by Box/Oesterley, "Sirach," 1.324–25; cf. Oesterley, *Ecclesiasticus*, 19; Boccaccini, *Middle Judaism*, 116.

the Hebrew.[106] Nevertheless, he too quickly dismisses the idea that one's obedience stands in place of one's disobedience. Verse 14b sets one's obedience directly against one's sins. Moreover, this clause comes between two positive statements about God remembering one's obedience (vv.14a, 15a). The implication is that obedience is remembered instead of disobedience.

Ben Sira contributes to the growing tradition that almsgiving is an atoning act of righteousness done in obedience to the law.[107] The first mention of alms or charity appears in his interpretation of the fifth commandment (3.14). One means of fulfilling the commandment is by being charitable to one's father, which brings forgiveness of sin. This concept is developed further in 29.1–20, where Ben Sira offers advice on loaning money. Providing monetary assistance to a neighbour is a means of keeping the commandments (v.1). One's willingness to lend money, however, should not be limited only to those who can repay. Alms should be given without hesitancy to those in need (v.8), and one should "help the poor for the commandment's sake" (v.9; cf. Deut 15.7–11). Providing alms is like storing up a treasure and is accomplished in accordance with the commandments (Sir 29.11–12a; cf. Tobit 4.9–10). Further, almsgiving provides a means of security against disaster (Sir 29.12–13; cf. 12.3; 40.17, 24). A helpful analogy is Tobit 14.10–11. Tobit explains to his children that Ahikar escaped death because he gave alms, while Nadab was imprisoned for his evil ways. Almsgiving is also stated as a means of fulfilling the commandments in Sirach 35.4, which appears in a section on the sacrifices (vv.1–12). In the first paragraph, Ben Sira outlines various actions that function like sacrifices (vv.1–5). Almsgiving is equal to offering a "thank offering."

Elsewhere almsgiving is said to count in one's favour against one's sin: "Water extinguishes a flaming fire, so almsgiving atones (תכפר/ἐξιλάσεται) for sin" (3.30).[108] Almsgiving functions like obedience to one's parents and sacrifices since all accomplish the same task, namely, atonement. Almsgiving is also mentioned in 17.22, where Ben Sira says it is valuable before God. The juxtaposition of this statement with divine knowledge of human sin in the previous verse (v.20) and the divine judgment of humans in the next two verses suggests that alms counters one's sin before God.[109] When God judges one's works, he takes account of one's sin or one's almsgiving and repentance (v.24) and rewards or punishes in accordance.

---

[106] Sanders, *Paul and Palestinian Judaism*, 338n.24. Sanders, as well as most commentators, follows ms A (ותמור חטאת היא תנתע [the margin has תנטע for תנתע]). Box/Oesterley translate, "And as a substitute for sins it shall be firmly planted" ("Sirach," 1.325, following the margin). Cf. Schechter/Taylor, *Wisdom of Ben Sira*, xv: "But it shall be planted instead of sin."

[107] Almsgiving and atonement appear together in the LXX of Prov 15.27 (cf. 16.6) and Dan 4.27 (MT 24). Ben Sira's comments echo similar ones found in Tobit (third or second century BCE); see 4.10; 12.8–9; 14.10–11. Of the books in the LXX, only Tobit mentions almsgiving more than Sirach (Fitzmyer, *Tobit*, 103).

[108] Cf. Tobit 12.9: "For almsgiving delivers from death, and it will cleanse all sin."

[109] Verse 21 is a later addition.

Both honouring one's parents and almsgiving are obedience to the commandments and means of atonement. Ben Sira is an early witness to the idea that one's obedience to the law, particularly through almsgiving, brings atonement. One must be careful, however, to neither over-interpret nor under-interpret Ben Sira's claim. One over-interprets the statements when it is claimed that the Jewish person lived in fear that he or she might not amass enough good works to overcome one's sinful deeds. For Ben Sira God does not count one's deeds so that life (or a peaceful death) hangs in the balance. Rather, God judges the totality of one's life: did the person live according to the law, which includes making atonement when one fails? Others under-interpret the statements by avoiding the straightforward equation between obedience to the law and atonement.[110] Appeals are made to divine mercy as the means for accounting for human sin, or some point out that Ben Sira expects a person to repent.[111] While sin affects one's standing before God and the possibility of life or death, Ben Sira maintains that sin and the possibility of atonement do not alter the pattern of the divine-human relationship. Law observance ultimately determines whether one enjoys a blessed life or dies a miserable death. Mercy is not the sole cause of forgiveness, and repentance does not replace other acts of atonement. Sin is accounted for by human obedience to the law. The means to life remains the same, namely, obedience to the law.

e. Summary

This section has analysed the first characteristic of the two-ways paradigm: the connection between life and law observance. The "law of life" is given to Israel (17.11; 45.5) and before each individual God sets "life and death" (15.17). Against Sanders' claim that obedience to the commandments is subsequent to the establishment of the covenant, it was argued that God enters into a covenantal relationship as a response to the person's obedience. Moreover, Sanders misunderstood the primary conceptual background for the relationship between obedience and life. This context is the Creator-creation relationship. According to Ben Sira's description, this relationship revolves around God giving commandments and creatures, whether angels, the sun, or humans, obeying those commandments. Obedience to the commandments sits at the centre of the relationship since the human task is to keep them. While some have attempted to circumvent the centrality of obedience by highlighting either "internal" attitudes or God's merciful forgiveness, these were seen to actually be expressions of or responses to law observance. Ben Sira defines everything about the divine-human relationship in terms of obedience to the commandments.

---

[110] Moore reduces Tobit 12.9 to a "proverb," which ultimately escapes the implications of Tobit's statement (*Tobit*, 270).

[111] Snaith, *Ecclesiasticus*, 20–21; Sanders, *Paul and Palestinian Judaism*, 334; 421.

All one must do in order to acquire life and blessing from God is observe the commandments.

2. The Human Ability to Obey

The second key aspect of Ben Sira's conception of the divine-human relationship follows naturally from the link made between life and law observance. Ben Sira maintains that humans are morally capable of obeying the commandments. In 15.14–17 he uses the combination of יצר and חפץ to make this point. Humans are created morally neutral, and they are capable of choosing between life and death (v.17) and of keeping the commandments if they desire (v.15). With the knowledge of the law, the human can decide based on his or her own will power whether to take the path leading to life or the one unto death. Nothing prevents the individual from obeying except his or her own deliberate refusal to obey. The optimistic portrayal of human ability is also found in 17.1–14. Ben Sira claims that God himself gave knowledge, and this divine act makes humans culpable for their actions. The underlying assumption is that because the individual is responsible for the outcome he or she must be capable of controlling that outcome. For Ben Sira the divine act of giving the law implies that the recipient is capable of keeping it. Life and blessing can be attained through obedience because the knowledge of what is necessary to acquire life is clearly known.

In contrast to what will be noted about the *Hodayot* and Paul, Ben Sira does not think the human needs God's assistance to obey the law. In fact, Ben Sira claims the precise opposite: Not only is divine assistance not needed, God actually withdraws his presence from the scene. After setting the human before the alternative paths of life and death, God leaves the individual to his or her own will (15.14). God himself does not interfere in the human's autonomous choice. Whereas the opponents argued that God determined human action, Ben Sira claims that God is not responsible for the disobedience of any individual because God is not actively working in the human's life. He is a passive observer (vv.18–20). The act of obedience is an independent, secondary step. Only because God is removed (temporarily) from the scene can the human be held responsible for his or her transgression. This divine decision to separate from the human creates the possibility for the human to obey. God's holiness is protected and human obedience is made important.

Many of Ben Sira's statements simply presume that his students are capable of obeying his instructions. 15.14–20 and 17.1–14 are exceptions since in these passages Ben Sira actually attempts to justify this assumption. Despite the lack of formal argument for this view, one can detect its influence elsewhere. Particularly relevant here are several passages in which Ben Sira personifies Wisdom as God's agent (4.11–20; 6.18–37; 14.20–15.10). In these poems, Ben

B. *The Establishment of the Human Agent*

Sira personifies "wisdom" as a beautiful female who should be pursued with all one's energy. Two important points run throughout each poem. First, each poem describes humans successfully keeping the law apart from divine assistance. Second, Wisdom, as God's agent and the mediator of his presence, avails her benefits only to those who have endured her trials. This second point further supports the argument that life and blessing are attained through obedience.

a. *Wisdom as the Result of Endurance*

In 4.11–19 Ben Sira explains the blessings received by those who pursue and acquire wisdom. The passage opens with some general observations about the one who desires Wisdom. He or she sits under Wisdom's tutelage and rises early looking for her (vv.11–12). Once one finds wisdom, he should never let go (v.13). One willingly serves and obeys her (vv.14–15), and as a result will enjoy her benefits, which include "glory" (v.13), security, and the ability to "judge the nations [אמת/ἔθνη]" (v.15).[112] In these instructions, Ben Sira makes blessing contingent on obedience. One must remain faithful to Wisdom by being obedient (v.16), and the result is all the wonderful treasures that Wisdom has to offer.

In vv.17–19 Ben Sira goes on to describe the testing one must endure in order to acquire Wisdom.[113]

For I will go with him, making myself strange [נכר],[114] and I will test him with temptations. I will bring fear and timidity on him, and I will torture him with my discipline [παιδείᾳ] until his heart is filled with me.[115] I will turn and lead him, and I will reveal to him my secrets. If he wanders away, I will forsake him, and will deliver him over to the destroyers.

The idea of the Lord's people being tested is not unique, but the method employed by Wisdom differs remarkably from the Lord's.[116] When he tested his people in the wilderness, he continued to meet their needs (cf. Deut 8.2–3), and no trickery was involved. Wisdom, by contrast, tests her pursuer by concealing her identity from him. While the verb נכר can simply mean that one's appearance is changed so that others are unable to identity the person (Job 2.12; Lam 4.8), in other instances it describes one who alters his or her appearance in order to deceive someone. Rebekah covered Jacob in animal skin in order to mislead Isaac (Gen 27.23). Similarly, Jeroboam's wife tried to trick Ahijah by disguis-

---

[112] The Hebrew could be interpreted as "judge with truth." For a defence of the Greek translation as the correct translation of the Hebrew, see Skehan/Di Lella, *Wisdom of Ben Sira*, 172; and Garlington, *'Obedience of Faith'*, 27.

[113] The text of vv.17–19 is complicated. The translation combines parts of the Greek and Hebrew texts based on the reconstruction of Skehan/Di Lella, *Wisdom of Ben Sira*, 170. The Hebrew uses first person throughout while the Greek has third person.

[114] נכר becomes διεστραμμένως ("perverse paths") in the Greek.

[115] The Greek reads: "until she believes in him."

[116] Contra Calduch-Benages, "Trial Motif," 142.

ing herself (1 Kings 14.5–6). In light of the testing imagery, Ben Sira probably intends the latter meaning.[117] Wisdom hides her presence from her disciple in order that she might entice him to abandon her. The nominal form of this word (נָכְרִי) is the name given by the ancient sages to the Foolish Woman, who seeks to trap the simple (Prov 2.16; 5.20; 6.24; 7.5). By using this root, Ben Sira may be suggesting that Lady Wisdom appears to her pursuer as the Foolish Woman in order to test him. The sentence "I will torture him with my discipline" (Sir 4.17d) likely means that Wisdom, acting as the Foolish Woman, continuously presents her pursuer with opportunities and reasons to disobey. The stringent commands of Wisdom appear burdensome and unnecessary in light of the pleasures offered by the Foolish Woman.

The testing motif highlights the crucial role of obedience, and this is confirmed by the contrast between the two individuals in vv.18–19. Only those who remain obedient receive Wisdom's benefits. Those who are led astray by Wisdom's trickery are cast aside.[118] Wisdom's relationship with any individual revolves around that person's obedience. This pattern of interaction suggests that the divine-human relationship is similar, for Wisdom is God's representative agent.

Along with this idea of blessing being acquired through obedience, one should also note that Wisdom's assistance is not required in order for one to obey her demands. The entire poem functions as an implied exhortation, and it assumes that the exhortation can be fulfilled. Ben Sira, in fact, is so confident in an individual's ability to obey that he even describes Wisdom as working against the human. Wisdom's presence at the beginning is no benefit to the human and may actually have adverse affects. When Wisdom finally reveals herself to the obedient, she comes with blessings and not to assist the human to obey. Implied throughout the poem is that the human can be obedient apart from God and even in spite of Wisdom's trials.

The lengthy poem in 6.18–37 details how one chooses "discipline" (παιδεία) in order to acquire wisdom (v.18). Ben Sira uses two images, agriculture and hunting (imprisonment in the Greek), to convey how one attains discipline. These images emphasise the trial and labour required to become disciplined and acquire wisdom. The poem teaches that Wisdom comes only through constant discipline, and this includes careful reflection on and observance of the Torah.[119]

---

[117] Calduch-Benages underestimates the significance of the verb נכר when he states, "Wisdom transforms herself in a veiled, but very near presence that takes care of the disciple" ("Trial Motif," 142).

[118] Di Lella comments, "[I]f one refuses discipline and chastisement and the pain of trial (v 17a-d), one will never achieve genuine Wisdom (in the Heb[rew] sense of the word) but will be left devoid of any real sense of meaning in life (v 19)" (Skehan/Di Lella, *Wisdom of Ben Sira*, 173).

[119] Cf. Di Lella, "Meaning of Wisdom," 140–41.

B. The Establishment of the Human Agent

Like a farmer labouring in the field, one must toil and become disciplined in order to reap the benefits of Wisdom (vv.19–22). The effort put forth is minimal compared to the benefits given by Wisdom (cf. 51.27). This is only the path for those who accept discipline. Like a farmer who removes a rock from his field, those who reject discipline cast aside Wisdom (6.20–21). Unlike the farmer, however, who removes the rock in order to cultivate the field, the undisciplined cast away the item that they need the most. In the mind of the foolish, undisciplined person, the burden of Wisdom's discipline outweighs the benefits she makes available to those who toil.

The second stanza employs the image of hunting to describe one's desire to capture Wisdom (vv.23–31). Ben Sira exhorts his students to place themselves in Wisdom's net and become her prey (vv.24–25).[120] The image conveys the sense that Wisdom's ways appear as a trap for those who desire her discipline. The image frightens the weak-hearted and assures that only those who truly desire Wisdom will pursue her. This idea is even stronger in the Greek, which uses the image of imprisonment. The human must give up all his or her privileges to Wisdom. One becomes like a prisoner, taken captive by a foreign ruler. The subjection, however, is voluntary and for the time being difficult. Verses 26–28 mix into the hunting image themes associated with the Love Story (*Liebesgeschichte*).[121] The human is portrayed as a suitor pursuing his beloved (vv.26–27). Once he has hold of her, he must not let go. The hunter has captured his prey, and now, like a new bride, Wisdom gives herself to her suitor. "For at last you will find her rest, and she will turn into delight for you" (v.28). Wisdom now becomes a delight to her capturers, and the fetters, which seemed like bondage (v.24), now provide protection (vv.29–30). Just as hunting for animals requires patience and discipline and the pursuit of love takes endurance, one's attempt to capture Wisdom requires the same.

In the final stanza (vv.32–37), the pursuit of discipline is connected with Torah observance.[122] Students should attach themselves to wise men who discourse about the Torah (cf. 9.15; 37.12). Presumably, Ben Sira has in mind teachers like himself (33.16–18) who discuss not only the interpretation of the ancient Scriptures but, more importantly, how one obeys the commandments. He concludes this section by commanding his students to devote themselves to the Torah: "Consider diligently in the fear of the Most High and in his com-

---

[120] Skehan/Di Lella suggest that the hunting imagery alternates between Wisdom and humans. At first Wisdom is the hunter (vv.24–25), and then the image switches so that humans become the hunter (vv.26–27). At the final stage, Wisdom becomes the hunter again (vv.28–31) (*Wisdom of Ben Sira*, 194). While Wisdom is portrayed as the hunter with a net, Ben Sira instructs his students to place themselves within the net. The focus is not on Wisdom actively pursuing a prey but the human doing everything possible to make sure he is captured.

[121] Argall, *1 Enoch and Sirach*, 61–62. Argall, however, does not connect the two images together.

[122] Boccaccini, *Middle Judaism*, 94.

mandments and meditate continually. Then he will inform your heart and will give you wisdom as you desire" (6.37).[123] The ultimate and most important means for acquiring Wisdom is through Torah observance. This verse indicates clearly the conditional relationship between law observance and blessing. God acknowledges the obedience of the human by giving to the human what he or she desired.

As with 4.11–20, this poem teaches that the one who desires wisdom must embrace hard work and endure a period during which Wisdom's benefits are not evident. Ben Sira's focus throughout the poem is on the human agent actively pursuing life and wisdom. The metaphors used highlight the difficultly involved in acquiring wisdom, and they all emphasise the active pursuit required by the human. Obedience is the means to attaining wisdom, which is then given by God. Wisdom's presence is, therefore, a blessing attained through obedience. This indicates that Wisdom's assistance is not needed in order to obey the commandments. There is no suggestion that the human will fail because of some moral incapacity or hindrance from an external being. The human possesses the power to obey and endure the difficult paths that lead to wisdom.

In the third poem, Ben Sira again mixes the images of hunting and love to explain the human pursuit of wisdom (14.20–15.10). He first describes the one who desires Wisdom. He pursues her like a hunter and sets traps for her (14.22), and he camps near her place of residence (vv.23–27). The person progressively moves closer to Wisdom until he resides under her protection and is able to avoid the blazing sun. Finally, the person dwells inside Wisdom's own home. Wisdom, for her part, "comes like a mother to him and like a young bride, she welcomes him" (15.2). She satisfies with "bread of understanding" and "water of wisdom" (v.3). She provides support and exalts the one who relies on her (vv.4–5) and rewards her pursuer with the greatest of all rewards, "an everlasting name" (v.6).

Contrary to Boccaccini, this poem does not describe "a contemporary and simultaneous movement" of Wisdom and her pursuer toward one another.[124] Rather, it describes a sequential process in which a lover strives after his beloved until he has won her over. Much like the lover of the Song of Songs, the one who desires Wisdom pursuers her. Similar to the beloved of the Song, Wisdom receives her suitor and imparts joy and provision to him. Wisdom must be sought first before she gives her benefits. The only way to Wisdom is through obedience to the law, and Wisdom herself is the reward for those who keep the commandments.

---

[123] The Greek reads slightly different: "Ponder the ordinances [προστάγμασιν] of the Lord and study always his commandments." Skehan/Di Lella follow the Greek (*Wisdom of Ben Sira*, 196).

[124] Boccaccini, *Middle Judaism*, 87.

B. The Establishment of the Human Agent

The crucial point for understanding the poem comes at the very centre: "For the one who fears the Lord will do this (זאת), and the one who grasps the Torah will come to her" (15.1). The referent of זאת is not clear. It could point back to what has been described in 14.20–27. Alternatively, it could refer to the next line about Torah observance (15.1b). Either way, Ben Sira's poem about the pursuit of wisdom culminates in obedience to the Torah. As Webster points out, the erotic images in these verses elicit emotions that are then directed toward the Torah.[125] Again, this poem contains an implicit exhortation to pursue wisdom with all one's focus since this is the way to life and blessing. Ben Sira also assumes that the human can obey the law apart from God's intervention. Wisdom arrives on the scene only after the human has successfully obeyed.

These three poems are linked both in terminology and in thought. Each portrays the human pursuit for wisdom and blessing through obedience. As with his statements elsewhere, Ben Sira describes blessing as contingent upon obedience. Contrary to the claims of Sanders, Garlington, and others, life is not freely given through the covenant. Rather, it is attained through persistent obedience to Wisdom's demands.

Each poem also relates how the human is capable of obeying apart from divine assistance. In each section, Wisdom's assistance comes only after the human has endured her tests and faithfully pursued her. The lack of divine assistance does not indicate that Ben Sira's understanding of the divine-human relationship is legalistic in the pejorative sense. Yet, there is, contrary to Garlington's claim, a "notion of unaided self-achievement" portrayed in these passages and others.[126] The idea of "unaided self-achievement" does not have to be understood in a negative Pauline/Reformation sense, however. The unassisted obedience of the human does not result in boasting before God,[127] but it is nonetheless the case that Ben Sira thinks the human can obey apart from divine intervention.[128] This indeed is fundamental to his theology.[129]

This separation between God and Wisdom and the human is crucial for Ben Sira for two reasons. First, it protects the human agent's autonomy. God does not influence the human in his or her decision whether to choose life or death. The alternative view's claim that God dictates human action, therefore, is rejected. Second, it keeps the focus on the human agent. Whereas Ben Sira's opponents seek to eliminate the human agent, he establishes the primacy of the human agent by arguing that God removes himself.

---

[125] Webster, "Sophia," 71–72.

[126] Garlington, 'Obedience of Faith', 30.

[127] Sanders, Paul and Palestinian Judaism, 345.

[128] Gowan, "Wisdom," 221; Martyn, "Epilogue," 176. The idea of divine assistance is added by later scribes. In the Lucian recension (GII) and ms 672, 17.21 is added: "But the Lord, being gracious and knowing their form, neither abandoned them nor forsook from sparing them."

[129] 24.22 ("those who work with me [ἐν ἐμοί] will not sin") does not contradict this conclusion, since the argument here is not that there is no element of divine assistance, but rather that there is a time when God offers no aid.

b. Freedom and Providence

Despite his claim that humans are free to determine their own destinies, one should not conclude that Ben Sira views God as anxiously looking at humans wondering what they will do next. Nor should one conclude that God has simply left creation to run itself and he has no interest in what humans do. This was the position taken by Ben Sira's opponents (16.17, 20–22), and he strongly rejects it. In Ben Sira's view, God remains the sovereign Creator. Nothing is hidden from God's sight (15.18–19; 17.15, 19–20; 23.19) since his knowledge extends from before creation and continues unabated (23.20). God's sovereign hand is visibly seen in the ruling governments (10.4–5; cf. Prov 21.1), and, as will be discussed below, at some point he will judge each individual for his or her sins. God himself distinguished between the days when he declared some holy and some common and between humans when he blessed some and cursed others (36/33.7–15). In this text is the teaching about the duality of the world. "All the works of the Most High," Ben Sira claims, "come in pairs, one the opposite of the other" (v.15; cf. 42.24).[130] Ben Sira's belief in the ultimate sovereignty of God is, in the view of many scholars, difficult to reconcile with his claims about human freedom. It is possible that Ben Sira was simply confused or, as some scholars contend, gave different answers to different problems as the situation necessitated without realising that the answers were contradictory.[131] Such a conclusion, however, denies to Ben Sira the ability to be a complex thinker as well as overlooks the traditional nature of Ben Sira's claims.[132]

The traditional nature of Ben Sira's statements should not be missed. One is hard pressed to find any Jewish source of the Second Temple period that denies to God knowledge of future events or that declines to him ultimate control over the world. While some authors, however, did deny human freedom (cf. 1QS 3–4), the wisdom tradition did not view God's sovereignty as impinging on human freedom. Prior sages taught that God not only sees the actions of both the evil and the good (Prov 15.3), but also that he created everything, including "the wicked for the day of trouble" (16.4). This specific divine action, however, does not mean that God created a specific group of people designated as "the wicked." Rather, the wicked are those who have been arrogant (v.5), prideful, and generally reject wisdom. The sages behind Proverbs see no conflict between claiming that God determines the lot (v.33), directs the king (21.1), or

---

[130] See Winter, "Teaching of the 'Two Ways';" Wischmeyer, "Gut und Böse."

[131] So Maier, *freier Wille*, 98–115; Collins, *Jewish Wisdom*, 83.

[132] Ben Sira's views on freedom and providence are often paralleled with Stoic thought, and there remains a divide among scholars regarding the extent of Stoic influence on him. See Winston, "Theodicy in Ben Sira and Stoic Philosophy;" Wicke-Reuter, *Göttliche Providenz und menschliche Verantwortung*; idem, "Ben Sira und die frühe Stoa;" Mattila, "Ben Sira and the Stoics."

C. Judgment as the Re-Action of God

provides "the answer of the tongue" (16.1) and the exhortation "to watch over mouth and tongue is to keep one's soul from distresses" (21.23). Fundamental to the sapiential worldview is the possibility for humans to act according to their own will and the assumption that God remains in control of the world. The ordered nature of creation is what reveals God's control, and the goal of wisdom instruction is to teach a person how to cohere one's life with this order. This background provides the context within which Ben Sira thinks about the relationship between God's providence and human free will.

Ben Sira's teaching on the duality of creation should be read within this context (Sir 36/33.7–15). The passage affirms that God can move individuals as he pleases (v.13), but Ben Sira's general view is that God does not interfere with individual decisions.[133] The passage is not a blanket statement of divine determination of every human being or activity. Ben Sira rather relates the general teaching that God remains in control of his creation. The principle of opposites (v.14) testifies to the order of creation and should not be taken as a statement that God created two opposite groups of humans whose destinies are eternally fixed.[134] Similarly, the potter image in v.13 indicates that God has ultimate control over creation, but, as in Jeremiah 18.1–11, the image is not necessarily deterministic.[135] Ben Sira's reflections on God's sovereignty are presented in a specific form that is in some ways new, but the actual content and teaching of the passage is the same as one finds in other sapiential passages. God's will (רצון) does not ultimately determine human destiny, but neither does human freedom negate God's foreknowledge and providence.[136]

To summarise: the two-ways paradigm laid out in 15.14–17 has thus far proven to be an accurate summary of Ben Sira's understanding of the divine-human relationship. Ben Sira correlates law observance with life so that life and blessing are ultimately dependent on obedience not divine initiative or an unconditional act of God's grace. His statements about life and obedience are best understood within the framework of the Creator-creation relationship, not Sanders' pattern of covenantal nomism. For Ben Sira, a covenantal relationship with God is itself a blessing given by God in response to obedience to the Torah. Ben Sira has also claimed either explicitly or implicitly in several passages that humans can obey the Torah. The three passages in 4.11–20, 6.18–37,

---

[133] Di Lella suggests that Ben Sira's language in 33.12 may allude to key events in Israel's history when the Lord intervened on behalf of his people (Skehan/Di Lella, *Wisdom of Ben Sira*, 400–01; cf. Perdue, *Wisdom and Creation*, 274). The language, though, is too vague for the precise identifications he makes.

[134] Sauer remarks that the polarity is "eine einfache Feststellung der Tatsachen" (*Jesus Sirach*, 233–34).

[135] Contra Collins, *Jewish Wisdom*, 83; von Rad, *Wisdom in Israel*, 266–68.

[136] Aitken, "Divine Will," 297–98.

and 14.20–15.10 develop the theme of the human pursuit for wisdom. One aspect that connects these passages is the description of humans obeying without Wisdom's assistance and even in spite of Wisdom's trickery. For Ben Sira the human simply has no need for God to intervene to correct some inherent problem or to enable one to obey.

While Ben Sira sought to distance the human from God, he does not eliminate God entirely from the scene. The next section looks at how Ben Sira describes the judgment of God. The act of judgment is, for Ben Sira, God's most important act, since in this act God re-enters the drama and gives blessings or curses based solely on what each individual has done.

C. Judgment as the Re-Action of God

Although God's initial act of giving the law establishes the basic structures of the divine-human relationship, the final act of God dominates Ben Sira's thinking about God. The giving of the law sets in motion a chain of events in which the human must choose to either obey or disobey and the outcome of the human's decision determines how God will respond. The judgment is God's second major act. Here he re-enters the scene in order to judge the individual based on his or her deeds.[137]

Ben Sira's view of judgment is forged out of his debate with his opponents. If God decides to judge, the other positions think that they have nothing to worry about because God's default position toward humans is mercy. "His mercy is great" is their rallying call (5.6). Mercy assures them that forgiveness is available for all their sins. They focus on God and his attributes as the key to understanding how God will judge humans. Against this view, however, Ben Sira claims that God's mercy and wrath are equally balanced. God has no default position toward humanity. Rather than focusing on God's character at the judgment, Ben Sira makes judgment revolve around the human agent. God's decision whether to bless or punish is a re-action to whether the individual obeyed or disobeyed. As with all of Ben Sira's thought, the focus even of his view of the divine act of judgment is on the human agent.

Ben Sira's understanding of the method by which God judges can be summarised: God evaluates a person's deeds and rewards or punishes based solely on what a person has done. God's default position is neither mercy nor wrath,

---

[137] Because Ben Sira has no notion of an eternal life or death, the judgment he speaks about should not be confused with the Final Judgment anticipated in some other Jewish and Christian sources. God's judgment, according to Ben Sira, typically takes place in one's lifetime, although it might be delayed until after one's death. In this latter case, it is determined by how one's name is remembered (41.11–13; Sanders, "Wisdom, Theodicy, Death," 270–73).

since whether he shows mercy or wrath is determined entirely by an individual's obedience.[138]

1. Patience and Mercy

Whereas the other views hold that the delay in retribution is evidence that God is uninterested in what humans do, Ben Sira argues that the delay shows God to be patient.[139] Following the lead of his scriptures, he says that God is "slow to anger" (5.4b). The terminology comes from the often-repeated creed found first in Exodus 34.6. Moses has requested to see God's glory, and from his position behind the rock, he hears the claim that God is merciful, slow to anger, forgiving but still one who punishes sin. Ben Sira fully embraces the idea that God is patient and allows time for a person to repent of his or her sins (17.15–29). God's patience is for the benefit of humanity (18.11–12).

God's patience should not be understood as non-action. First, history proves that God calls people to account for their actions. Ben Sira recalls God's judgment of Sodom, the removal of the Canaanites from the Promised Land, and the punishment of the wilderness generation (16.6–10). History also provides examples of those who trusted in God and were not disappointed (2.10). Second, the delay in judgment supports Ben Sira's non-eschatological understanding of reward and punishment. The moment of death serves as the final and most important point at which God reveals his view of a person's actions. The person who suffers greatly or dies young is being punished by God. God rewards the obedient with a peaceful death. Ben Sira, therefore, warns his readers not to rely on current perspectives since the truth about a person will be revealed at his or her death.

Ben Sira's understanding about the timing of divine judgment is not controlled by his view of divine patience. He exhorts, "Remember retribution does not delay" (7.16b). In 5.7 he claims, "For suddenly [God] will go forth cursing." Even the rich should not trust in their money since death can come at any point (11.18–19; cf. 9.12) or worse they could lose their wealth to the poor (11.21).

---

[138] On the relationship between mercy and judgment, see Kamell 'The Soteriology of James', 29–41, who reaches very similar conclusions.

[139] This topic is typically approached in terms of the development of the wisdom tradition. According to Collins, Job and Ecclesiastes maintain that the suffering of the righteous and the success of the wicked causes a significant problem for divine judgment. Ben Sira, therefore, attempts to maintain the goodness of God in spite of these developments in the wisdom tradition (*Jewish Wisdom*, 13–14). Von Rad claims that Ben Sira simply ignores the arguments of these other sages (*Wisdom in Israel*, 238). Burkes thinks God's apparent lack of concern regarding suffering was a cause of "anxiety" for Ben Sira (*God, Self, and Death*, 91). He reinterpreted certain features of divine judgment to account for the issue, and he neither regresses to the simplistic view of Proverbs nor accepts the position of Job or Qoheleth (90–98). While this issue is important for one's understanding of how Israel's wisdom tradition developed, it extends beyond the discussion here.

The prayer of the humble rises quickly to the Lord, and like a warrior, he will not delay or be patient when executing judgment (35.21–22).[140] An example of this is when God delivered Israel from Assyria. In response to the prayers of the people, the Lord acted quickly by sending Isaiah to provide instructions (48.20). Both divine redemption and judgment are found in this single event. The delay in judgment upon which the alternative theologies relied is not the only pattern for how God interacts with humans. Divine judgment can come at any moment and without any warning. Ben Sira, therefore, concludes his work with an exhortation to obedience, which serves as a summary of the entire message of the work. Each person should continue in obedience, and God will reward the person when he deems it appropriate (51.30). The importance of proper timing is emphasised through the repetition of καιρός in both halves of the verse.[141]

Closely related to the idea of God as patient is also the notion that God is merciful (cf. 18.11).[142] The alternative positions claim that if God decides to judge he will show mercy. They unyieldingly claim, "Great is his mercy. He will forgive the multitude of my sins" (5.6). They confidently rely on God's mercy and forgiveness so that they have no need to worry about the outcome of the judgment. God will find in their favour because of his mercy. They maintain that God's default position toward humans is mercy.

Ben Sira, by contrast, claims God has no default position toward humans. If only one "stiff-necked" (מקשה ערף) person remained, God would not overlook this person's transgressions. Rather, he would punish the person (16.11). This verse clearly shows that God's default position toward the sinner is not mercy. In his discussions of judgment, Ben Sira maintains an equal balance between mercy and wrath:

For mercy and wrath are from him. (5.6c)

For mercy and wrath are with him; and he remits and forgives, but his wrath rests on the wicked. As his mercy is great, so also is his wrath; He judges each according to one's deeds. (16.11c–12)[143]

Mercy and wrath stand parallel to each other and neither dominates the other. God's interactions with humans are controlled by neither his mercy (grace or love) nor his wrath.

The balance between these attributes does not remain forever since God will eventually judge each person. The evaluation of a person's deeds deter-

---

[140] Cf. 27.28 where Ben Sira says that vengeance waits like a lion for the proud.

[141] Gathercole, *Where is Boasting?* 38.

[142] See Beentjes, "God's Mercy," for the textual problems surrounding the term "mercy" in the Hebrew text.

[143] This translation follows the Hebrew. Skehan (*Wisdom of Ben Sira*, 270) prefers the Greek for the second half of 16.11d ("and pours out his wrath") because the Hebrew is too similar to 5.6d. Either way the meaning is the same.

mines whether God shows mercy or wrath. In 16.12–13 Ben Sira places wrath and mercy in balance, states that God will judge according to deeds, and then explains that the sinner will not escape and the godly will be rewarded. God's undetermined position gives way at the judgment of one's deeds. It is only after the judgment that one receives mercy or wrath. In 17.29 Ben Sira writes, "How great is the mercy of the Lord and (his) atonement to those who turn to him." Mercy and atonement are given only to those who repent of their transgressions. Although patience is shown to all, it is given especially to those who accept God's discipline (18.14). The wicked fall under the wrath of God, while the righteous receive mercy.

Sanders is, therefore, incorrect to claim that "the heart of Ben Sirach's religion" is "confidence in God's justice tempered by confidence in his mercy: pragmatic nomism modified by the assurance of compassion."[144] The mercy of God does not lessen his justice or his wrath. Similarly, Yinger is incorrect when he claims that "the divine recompense according to deeds is superseded for the penitent by mercy and forgiveness."[145] Judgment by works does not cease to operate because the person repents. Repentance and subsequent obedience are acknowledged by God so that the person is no longer deserving of punishment. The righteous person looked to God's mercy as his reward for obedience. The justice of God assures that mercy is given to those who deserve it, while wrath to those who warrant it. God does not overlook the sins of the wise because he is merciful, but because the wise atone for their sins through the various means supplied by God. Seifrid's conclusion about mercy in the *Psalms of Solomon* is applicable to Ben Sira also: mercy does not "express deliverance *in spite of* justice, but deliverance *as justice* rendered by God."[146] Divine mercy is the reward given to the obedient. The interpretation put forth by Sanders and Yinger is, in fact, closer to the perspective of the alternative theologies than to Ben Sira.

2. *The Criterion of Divine Judgment*

If God decided to judge humanity for their sins, the alternative theologies relied on their sacrifices to appease God's wrath. Ben Sira rejects their claim: "The Most High is not pleased with the offerings of the ungodly, nor because of many sacrifices does he atone for sins" (34.23). As he explains, sacrifices are only valid when accompanied by obedience (35.1–12). Divine judgment is not based on one's ability to slaughter an animal but on one's success in keeping the law.

Scholars agree that, in his perspective on divine judgment, Ben Sira adopts the commonly held "doctrine of retribution" as the basic paradigm by which

---

[144] Sanders, *Paul and Palestinian Judaism*, 334; cf. 345.

[145] Yinger, *Judgment*, 42.

[146] Seifrid, *Justification by Faith*, 131 (emphasis original).

God judges humans.[147] This view can be summarised: the person who obeys God's will, as expressed particularly in the Torah, will be rewarded with "life" (security, peaceful death, everlasting name, etc.); the one who commits evil and rejects the Torah will be punished and experience "death" (tribulation, short life and painful death, dishonoured name, etc).[148] The concept of retribution arises from the basic principle that God judges a person based on one's actions. Thus, Ben Sira writes that the Lord will "reward a person according to his ways" (11.26).[149] This widely held idea is particularly important for Ben Sira as he seeks to counter the alternative views, which is probably why four of the five instances of this statement are made in the context of his disputes with the other positions (11.26; 16.12–14; 17.23).[150] Against the claims of the wicked (11.23–24), Ben Sira reminds one that material possessions provide no security at the time of judgment. Even if judgment tarries until one's death, God will expose the person's deeds (v.26). The righteous, therefore, should continue in their obedient ways with the certainty that God will reward them (vv.21–22) and punish the wicked. 16.12–14 provides the grounds on which God condemns the previous examples listed in vv.5–10. God did not arbitrarily judge in the past, for those he condemned were sinners. He evaluated their actions and rewarded them accordingly. Although God can show mercy, it is only given to those who deserve it. The sinner will not go unpunished just as the godly person's obedience does not go unnoticed. 17.24 appears in the middle of Ben Sira's appeal for the wicked to turn from their sins (vv.15–29). Their evil ways are not hidden from God, as they think (16.17), which means they cannot escape judgment. Punishment can be avoided if they will repent and abandon their evil ways. Giving alms will replace their evil deeds before God (17.22). The prospect of judgment according to works serves, then, as motivation for repentance.

The idea of judgment by works appears regularly outside of the debate passages.[151] Writing about the one who seeks to honour himself, Ben Sira says, "The Lord will reveal your secrets, and in the midst of the assembly, he will overthrow you" (1.30). About the righteous person, he writes, "Do good to the just, and reward will be yours, if not from him, from the Lord" (12.2).[152] These two verses establish two different ways in which God interacts with humans, and the deciding factor is what each person does. The first person exalts

---

[147] "The idea is built into the very structure of many of ben Sira's proverbs, which describe the consequences of one's conduct" (Nickelsburg, *Jewish Literature*, 60).

[148] Cf. Skehan/Di Lella, *Wisdom of Ben Sira*, 83.

[149] ἀποδοῦναι ἀνθρώπῳ κατὰ τὰς ὁδοὺς αὐτοῦ.

[150] The other instance is 35.24.

[151] See the list of verses in Hengel, *Judaism and Hellenism*, 2.93n.238; and Skehan/Di Lella, *Wisdom of Ben Sira*, Index of subjects s.v. "Deuteronomic Theology: doctrine of retribution."

[152] Translation by Skehan, *Wisdom of Ben Sira*, 242.

C. Judgment as the Re-Action of God 71

himself, while the second shows goodness to someone else. The one receives punishment, and the other is rewarded. In both cases, God evaluates one's actions and then renders a judgment. Ben Sira exhorts those who fear God to not sway but to remain faithful. If they stumble, they could fall and lose their reward (2.7–8). The possibility of reward functions in 2.7–9 as a motivation for obedience. In contrast to the righteous, God will punish the sinner because of their lack of trust (2.12–14). The one who does evil will have evil returned to him (7.1–3; cf. 13.1; 27.25–29; 28.1), and the one who embraces a prostitute will be caught (9.3–9).[153] The one who cares for the outcast of society will be as a son to God (4.10). The final statement of the book highlights the importance of this theme: the human does his or her duty, and God rewards for it (51.30). Although this is only a small sampling of the verses that describe the judgment, it is clear that the criterion of judgment is one's deeds.

The idea of judgment by works is enhanced through the image of a treasury and the counting of good versus evil deeds. Ben Sira warns, "Do not commit a sin twice since you will not go unpunished for one" (7.8). Although the comment could be overstated for rhetorical effect, Ben Sira could actually think that one sin could be the difference between life and death. He notes later that God keeps account of one's sins (28.1). Whereas humans are supposed to keep the Torah, God keeps track of when they break his commandments. Ben Sira uses the image of a treasury as a motivation for obedience. Giving alms is considered making a deposit in a holding so that in the face of disaster one will be delivered (29.12). One's treasure is one's obedience to the commandments, and obedience is more valuable than gold (v.11). Charity to one's father counts in place of one's sin (3.14). This image could suggest a strict counting of deeds where one's obedience replaces one's sin before God and tips the scales in one's favour.[154]

One should not conclude from these verses, however, that judgment amounts to a single deed. The singularity of sin in 7.8 contrasts with the multiple gifts the sinner intends to offer as the means of repentance in v.9. By explaining that God keeps track of one's sins (28.1), Ben Sira is pointing out that nothing the human does escapes God's notice and that judgment will happen someday. The treasure image does not necessarily mean that each action done by a human either contributes to the chest or removes something. The image is only used in a positive sense: the obedient person contributes to a treasury, which brings a reward. Ben Sira never says that the wicked contribute to a treasury nor does

---

[153] In some of these statements, judgment is not attributed directly to God (cf. 7.1–3). Instead, Ben Sira describes a cause and effect scheme. One could conclude that the outcome is not a form of divine punishment, but, most likely, Ben Sira would see God as working behind the punishments.

[154] Box/Oesterley comment, "The good deed is written down in God's book and therefore cannot be blotted out" ("Sirach," 1.325; cf. Skehan/Di Lella, *Wisdom of Ben Sira*, 156).

he claim that the righteous deduct something from the treasury when they sin. The lack of a negative application of this image is significant for understanding what it means. The image underscores the importance of obedience and encourages one to continue being obedient. One's status as righteous or wicked does not hang in the balance waiting for the moment of judgment. Life or death is the result of God's judgment, but the individual Israelite can be certain of the outcome.

Throughout Sirach the criterion of judgment remains consistent. One's status as a member of Israel does not factor into Ben Sira's understanding of judgment. As Sanders notes, the only criterion that matters when determining if a person has "salvation" is whether one is among the wicked or the righteous, which is determined entirely by one's obedience to God's will.[155] Further, one's mental disposition toward the law does not factor into the judgment.[156] Ben Sira assumes that the person who loves the law will obey it (2.16). The judgment evaluates what a person actually does, not what one claims to think or believe.

Sanders, however, is wrong when, in explaining the relationship between mercy and justice, he describes the judgment asymmetrically: "the usual formulation is that God punishes the wicked *for their deeds*, while bestowing *mercy on the righteous*."[157] This subtle shift alters the entire paradigm and introduces God's action into the issue. The wicked are judged based on *their* actions, but for the righteous judgment is dependent on *God's* actions. Regardless of the applicability of this formulation to other Jewish texts, it misunderstands Ben Sira's claim. Ben Sira views divine judgment in symmetrical terms: both the wicked and righteous are judged according to deeds. The wicked are judged and punished because they disobey; the righteous are judged and rewarded because they obey.

At the judgment, according to Ben Sira, God does not evaluate one's desire or attempt to keep the law. Nor does God count how many bulls and goats one killed. He looks solely at one's obedience to the law. The question asked at the judgment is, did this person keep the law? The difference between the wicked and the righteous is not an attitude toward the law, but actual observance of the law. The wicked refuse to obey the law and reject it as the means to life. The righteous embrace the law, obey it fully, which includes atoning for one's sins, and accept it as the means to life and God's favour. The wicked are punished, while the righteous are rewarded.

---

[155] Sanders, *Paul and Palestinian Judaism*, 333.
[156] Contra Yinger, *Judgment*, 285
[157] Sanders, *Paul and Palestinian Judaism*, 420 (emphasis original).

3. Summary

Ben Sira's understanding of judgment, while derived from his scriptures, is forged out of conflict. These other positions, in their own ways, deny that God will call humans to account for their deeds. Their understanding of judgment revolves around God's actions, not humanity's. Ben Sira, however, will have none of this, for it is the reality of judgment that reveals the necessity for obedience to the commandments. In his view of the judgment, Ben Sira's focus is ultimately on the human agent and what he or she does. When God judges he looks at whether the human has obeyed or disobeyed. The delay in retribution only indicates that God is patient, and his default position toward humans is not mercy. Mercy and wrath are equally balanced, and whether God shows one or the other depends solely on whether the individual has obeyed or disobeyed. The criterion of judgment is one's deeds. Within Ben Sira's perspective on the divine-human relationship, the judgment is not important because God does it, but because the obedient are vindicated and the disobedient punished. The judgment is ultimately about the human agent.

D. Conclusion

Of Josephus' three schools, Ben Sira provides a clear example of the Sadducean view. Neither Ben Sira nor the Sadducees denied the existence of God, but both believed that God had empowered human beings to keep the Torah and determine for themselves their own individual destinies. This view, in the case of Ben Sira, is defended against other views, which deny the prospect of judgment or presume on God's grace. The problem with these views, for Ben Sira, is that they overemphasise divine action. In contrast to these views, Ben Sira argues that the divine-human relationship revolves around the human agent and whether he or she obeys the Torah. He adopts the two-ways tradition (15.14–17), which he finds in Moses' appeal to Israel (Deut 30.15–20). In this pattern, the human is empowered to obey and Torah observance leads to divine blessing. For Ben Sira, Moses' statement indicates that the human's destiny is determined by his or her obedience to the Torah, not God's grace.

Sanders presented Sirach as an example of covenantal nomism. He did not deny the emphasis placed on obedience by Ben Sira. Instead, as covenantal nomism makes clear, he contended that obedience was the response of the faithful Israelite to the prior grace of God. This covenantal context, however, is the wrong framework for Ben Sira's demand for obedience. Ben Sira understands the divine-human relationship as a subset of the Creator-creation relationship. Just as the latter is based on the creature's obedience to God's commands, so the former is also. The human is distinguished from the rest of creation because he or she possesses freedom and can disobey God's will. By viewing the divine-human relationship within the sphere of the Creator-creation relationship and with this claim that human's possess freedom, Ben Sira centres his thought on the human agent and his or her obedience.

In his reaction to the alternative views' overemphasis on God, Ben Sira does not deny that God acts. He rather depicts God as reacting to the human's obedience or disobedience. God is merciful, but he is equally wrathful. How he responds to the individual is determined entirely by whether a person has kept the Torah. The single criterion of the judgment is indeed obedience. God's mercy is not given to any Israelite, but only to the faithful. Sanders' interpretation of Sirach, along with Garlington's and Yinger's, turns out to ascribe to Ben Sira the very view that he sought to disprove.

Ben Sira provides one end of the spectrum of Jewish views offered in the Second Temple Period. His focus on the human agent contrasts sharply with the *Hodayot's* attention to divine action, as the next chapter will show.

Chapter 2

God's Gracious Acts of Deliverance in the Hodayot

Ben Sira argued robustly that law observance is the means to life and blessing. The divine-human relationship revolves around what each individual does. He matches Josephus' claim that the Sadducees ascribe everything to human action not "fate" (εἱμαρμένη). On the other end of the spectrum, for Josephus, stand the Essenes, who attribute everything to "fate." This chapter investigates the *Hodayot* as a representative of an Essene-like position. The hymns contained in this document consistently point to God's saving acts. The human is a sinner created from perishable material, and when left to his or her own devices, the sinner will always disobey. God, however, has predestined some to salvation, and he brings the sinner from a state of condemnation to salvation. To bring the human into the realm of salvation, God imparts his spirit of knowledge and holiness. Led by this spirit, the human is enabled, despite his continuing sinful condition, to obey God's will. The focus throughout the hymns is God's gracious acts of deliverance. While the hymnists maintain that humans must be obedient, this obedience is based on God's prior and continuing acts. The possibility for human action is created by God himself when he delivers the human from his frail, sinful creaturely condition.

After addressing some introductory issues regarding the *Hodayot* material, this chapter will analyse how the hymnists set human action in relation to divine action. Attention will be drawn to the pessimistic anthropology and how God resolves this problem through various means, all of which are associated with the spirit. These divine saving acts enable obedience. The hymnists develop a clear understanding of the divine-human relationship that prioritises God's actions, while creating the possibility for human action. Because the spirit works through the human to produce obedience, it is not an independent, secondary act. The human is an active agent, but one led by the spirit given by God. Throughout the *Hodayot*, the claim is made that God works to bring about salvation and everything that is necessary to attain it.

A. Background Issues

Research on the Dead Sea Scrolls has passed through several stages, and scholarship now finds itself re-evaluating many of the early claims made about the scrolls and the community behind them. Regarding the *Hodayot,* a general sense of excitement surrounded this work in the initial years after its discovery.[1] Several studies devoted to individual columns appeared within a decade of its discovery. The *Hodayot* was attributed to the "Teacher of Righteousness," who was identified as the "founder" of the sectarian group residing at Qumran, and it was assigned a key role in how scholars assessed the theology of the community.[2] As study of the Dead Sea Scrolls has become more complex and the assured results and assumptions of previous scholarship have been questioned, the conclusions drawn by previous scholarship about the *Hodayot* have not gone unchallenged. Before turning to the theological statements about God and humanity, it is necessary to comment briefly on several background issues that are relevant to the *Hodayot.*

Among the vast number of scrolls discovered in the caves near Khirbet Qumran, eight copies of the *Hodayot* were found. The first scroll, 1QH^a, is the fullest copy, and it has served as the basic unit of comparison for other scrolls. Additionally, six copies were found in cave 4 and another one in cave 1.[3] Although these other scrolls are in poor condition, their remains overlap significantly with 1QH^a, only rarely presenting a different wording.[4] 4QH^a is the only scroll that contains any material of significant length not found in 1QH^a.[5] While the material has assisted in filling some gaps in 1QH^a and confirmed the original order of 1QH^a, these additional scrolls have not assisted greatly in resolving any of the background issues surrounding the *Hodayot.* Schullers' sober assessment is worth repeating:

> Although some quite small pieces can prove to be very significant (particularly for reconstructing the arrangement and extent of an individual manuscript) what we can learn from the 4Q manuscripts is limited. For the most part, they do not allow us to recover major portions of text missing in 1QH^a, nor do they readily answer many or most of our questions about the origin, authorship and purpose of this collection.[6]

---

[1] E.g., the studies by Baumgarten and Mansoor, "Studies in the New *Hodayot,*" and Mansoor, "Studies in the *Hodayot.*" Also Mowinckel. "Some Remarks on *Hodayot* 39.5–20;" Silberman, "Language and Structure."

[2] The connection with the Teacher of Righteousness was suggested by Sukenik in his publication of the scroll (*Dead Sea Scrolls,* 39). It has become the standard view.

[3] The other scrolls are 1QH^b (1Q35) and 4QH^{a-f} (4Q427–432). For a brief history of the publication of this material, see Schuller, "Hodayot," 69–71.

[4] Schuller, "Hodayot," 87–88, 131, 181–82, 203, 212–13; idem, "Some Contributions of the Cave Four Manuscripts." In some instances, 1QH^a has been corrected to match readings found in the 4QH scrolls (see Schuller, "Hodayot," 182, 213).

[5] 4QH^a 8.i.13–21; 8.ii.8–9. See Schuller, "Hodayot," 86; idem, "Cave 4 Hodayot Manuscripts," 148.

[6] Schuller, "Cave 4 Hodayot Manuscripts," 140.

A. Background Issues

In terms of the issues being addressed in this chapter, the 4QH scrolls neither create nor resolve any problems. This study will focus primarily on 1QH^a and utilise the other *Hodayot* scrolls to fill lacunae where appropriate.

The question that has dominated study of the *Hodayot* most concerns the original authorship. From the earliest days, some part of the *Hodayot* has been attributed to the "Teacher of Righteousness." This obscure figure, who is infrequently mentioned, is considered to have been the "founder" of the community and to have initiated its separation from the Temple and perhaps society in general.[7] The precise dates of this figure are disputed, and it is not clear that he ever resided at Qumran itself.[8] Of course, all this presumes that the scrolls belong to a community that lived at Qumran.[9]

---

[7] Knibb, "Teacher of Righteousness," 918–21;" Stegemann, *Library of Qumran*, 147–52; Charlesworth, *Pesharim*, 30–40; Eshel, *Dead Sea Scrolls*, 29–61.

[8] This person has traditionally been dated to around 150 BCE, which is the traditional date for the foundation of the Qumran community (Stegemann, *Library of Qumran*, 147–48; Charlesworth, *Pesharim*, 30–36). Others have argued that he lived at the beginning of the first century BCE (Wise, "Dating the Teacher of Righteousness").

[9] The relationship between Khirbet Qumran, the caves, and the Dead Sea Scrolls is problematic. The archaeological evidence favours the conclusion that a group lived at the site roughly between the end of the second century/beginning of the first century BCE until about 68 CE when the Romans took control. Attempts to identify the remains as a Roman style villa or a fortress are unconvincing. For the archaeological details and secondary literature, see Magness, "Qumran Archaeology," 1.47–77; idem, *The Archaeology of Qumran*. While not denying the existence of a group at Qumran, some scholars suggest that there is no or a limited relationship between the site and the scrolls. Wise, Abegg, and Cook in *The Dead Sea Scrolls*, 32–33, argue that those who used the scrolls and finally hid them in the caves are not the same group that composed them. The scrolls were placed in the caves by the *sicarii* around the time of the Jewish revolt. Closer to the more traditional understanding of the relationship between the caves and the site, Stegemann suggests that the scrolls were placed by the community (the Essenes) on the brink of war with Rome ("The Qumran Essenes;" idem, *Library of Qumran*). This explains the lack of trails between the site and the caves, since the caves were not used for storage during the community's existence.

Our knowledge of the group's existence prior to settling at Qumran is scanty. The majority position connects the Qumran community with the Essenes (see Charlesworth, *Pesharim*, 55–58; for a critique, see Talmon, "Qumran Studies," 11–14). The "Groningen Hypothesis" developed by García Martínez and van der Woude maintains that the community split from an existing apocalyptic group that originated in the third century BC ("'Groningen' Hypothesis"). Boccaccini identifies this prior group with Enoch Judaism (*Beyond the Essene Hypothesis*). Others argue that the Essenes and subsequently the Qumran community arose around the time of the Maccabean uprising. The traditional position maintains that the Qumran community split from the larger Essene community, most likely because of disputes concerning the priesthood (Charlesworth, *Pesharim*, 27–44). The hypothesis of disputes over the priesthood has been challenged, however (see Collins, "Origin of the Qumran Community," 159–67). Alternatively, the community gathered at Qumran may have been a special group of Essenes, those devoted to a more secluded life-style, or the "headquarters" of the larger group (Stegemann, *Library of Qumran*, 147–52). On the historical problems, see now Eshel, *Dead Sea Scrolls*, and the essays edited by Boccaccini, *Enoch and Qumran Origins*.

Although initially scholars tended to ascribe all of the *Hodayot* to the "Teacher of Righteousness," scholars began to refine the criteria by which one could determine the authorship of individual hymns.[10] Eventually the hymns were divided into two groups: the "Community Hymns" and the "Teacher Hymns."[11] This has been the standard position since the 1960s, and the cave 4 material seems to support the division of the hymns since some scrolls have only the "Teacher Hymns" or the "Community Hymns."[12] This division of the *Hodayot* into two groups is built on the content and genre of the individual hymns. Theological differences between the two categories have also been detected.

Scholars have continuously returned to this issue in search of better arguments to support the initial claims. Questions remain, however, and more often than not, the studies have presumed their conclusions about authorship from the outset. In a recent study by Douglas, he identifies linguistic connections between the hymns in columns 10–17.[13] He argues on this basis that they were composed by a single author, who he identifies as the Teacher of Righteousness. His study, however, only proves that the hymns are linguistically related, not that they stem from the same author, let alone the Teacher of Righteousness.[14] One can identify similar linguistic links in the canonical Psalms, but this does not prove authorship. At best, linguistic connections can only suggest authorship, but there must be more substantive evidence, such as the text itself claiming to be written by a specific person. Likewise, Schuller's reconstruction of the cave 4 material only demonstrates that the hymns of the *Hodayot* were transmitted separately for some time. The different collections do not prove authorship nor can they. The analysis by Wise, in which he focuses on terms found in the "Teacher Hymns" and other literature about the Teacher, appears fruitful and provides a way forward in this discussion.[15] Again, however, this cannot prove that the Teacher was the actual author. His students may have composed these hymns in remembrance, just as the pesharim were composed after the Teacher's death but (partly) in light of his life.[16]

---

[10] Holm-Nielsen is typically credited with dismantling the claim that the Teacher of Righteousness composed all of the hymns. He argued that the *Hodayot* consists of different genres, so it cannot stem solely from the Teacher of Righteousness (*Hodayot*, 320; cf. pp.316–31).For a history of the debate and literature, see Douglas, "Teacher Hymn Hypothesis Revisited."

[11] See the initial study by Jeremias, *Der Lehrer der Gerechtigkeit,* 168–77.

[12] Schuller thinks that 4QH^c and possibly 4QH^f contained only the "Teacher Hymns," while 4QH^a contained only the "Community Hymns" ("Cave 4 Hodayot Manuscripts," 144, 145, 148–49).

[13] Douglas, "Teacher Hymn Hypothesis Revisited." The numbering system for the columns and lines of 1QH^a used in this study is taken from Stegemann/Schuller, *1QHodayot^a*.

[14] Douglas' reconstruction of the historical background in col. 10 and 12 exploits the metaphorical language ("Teacher Hymn Hypothesis Revisited," 159–66; also Garnet, *Salvation and Atonement,* 13–31).

[15] Wise, "Concept of a New Covenant."

[16] Cf. Thyen, *Studien zur Sündenvergebung,* 81–85.

For this study, however, the question of authorship need not be resolved. This study does not oppose the possibility that individual hymns may stem from the Teacher, but neither does it assume that any do. Regardless of whether the Teacher of Righteousness wrote every hymn, a few, or none does not alter how one understands the theological and anthropological statements.

Another issue raised by study of the *Hodayot* concerns the unity of the theological claims. Some scholars drive a wedge between the various hymns, usually in terms of authorship, but also based on genre and word usage, thereby arguing that one should not attempt to understand the text as presenting a unified perspective on various subjects. For example, when discussing the genre of the *Hodayot*, Hopkins argues that there is "a constant shifting of emotions and themes" which "creates a thematic and emotional tension" that should not be dismissed since this tension "must be recognized as the most important element in *1QH*."[17] She faults Merrill for using three passages to form a basic understanding of predestination from which to understand the rest of 1QH^a. She claims that this process "robs the collection of its rich diversity."[18] Diversity in form and wording, however, does not necessarily mean diversity in thought.

Two other points should be noted. First, the repetition of key thoughts and expressions with the same basic meaning suggests that a coherent thought pattern underlies and joins the individual hymns together. As Licht notes, "The same things are said over and over again."[19] The repetition certainly creates a sense of monotony, but it also helps the interpreter to understand better the author's points. There can be little doubt that a pessimistic anthropology runs throughout the material and that the focus is on God's deliverance. The repetition makes these points clear. Second, while it is correct that one should not force unanimity when none exists, neither should one create contradictions where they are not evident. Some scholars juxtapose statements about some subject, such as predestination and free will or judgment and mercy, to demonstrate that the author(s) advocated contradictory positions.[20] They are able, then, to favour one perspective over the other, choosing whichever best fits their argument. The result is that scholars reveal more about their own views than they do the views of the ancient text. The *Hodayot* may not (indeed do not) fit everything together in a manner that satisfies current philosophical and theological arguments, but it does presume the teaching of the community that authored it. As Licht points out, the text was written for those familiar with the "underlying doctrine," and "coming to the text from the outside, we are

---

[17] Hopkins, "Qumran Community," 329–30.
[18] Hopkins, "Qumran Community," 329–30n.22; referring to Merrill, *Qumran and Predestination*.
[19] Licht, "Doctrine," 3.
[20] VanLandingham *Judgment and Justification*, 114–15, 119 (on predestination and free will); 122–23 (on judgment and mercy).

compelled to reconstruct the doctrine which underlies it, if we honestly try to understand the scroll."[21] The goal of this chapter is to explain how the hymnists understood the relationship between God and humanity, and on this issue there is a unified perspective that runs throughout the *Hodayot*.

Finally, the issue of genre needs to be addressed. Some scholars think that the prayer, poetic genre biases one to contrasting God's character and actions with the sinfulness of humans.[22] The genre, VanLandingham argues, does not give an accurate picture of what people believed because it is predisposed towards one perspective.[23] This generalised claim about the content of this genre, however, is not consistent with the surviving material. It is correct that hymns and poems often describe God as transcendent and praise him for his mercy, but this is not a distinctive feature of this genre. Moreover, the hymnic, poetic genre does not consistently contain a pessimistic anthropology. Of the 200 or so hymns and prayers found in the Dead Sea Scrolls, only a few actually present a pessimistic anthropology (cf. 1QS 10–11; 4Q392; 4Q393; 4Q400 2 7; 4Q507; 4Q509+505; 4Q511 [4Q*Songs of the Sage*[b]] 28; 29; 30).[24] With the exception of the *Words of the Luminaries* (4Q504–506), the pessimistic anthropology is certainly not a dominate theme in these writings. In other poetic material, human inability is simply ignored (e.g. 1QM 13–14; *Songs of the Sabbath* [4Q403–407]; 4Q502; 4Q503). This suggests that while hymns are more suited than legal texts for contrasting God's righteousness with human sinfulness the hymn or prayer genre is not bound to this contrast. The pessimistic anthropology presented in the *Hodayot* cannot be discounted simply because of the genre.[25]

B. Divine Saving Acts and Human Obedience

The primary interest of the *Hodayot* is to praise God. The individual hymns usually open, so far as can be told, with either "I give you thanks Lord" (אודכה אדוני) or "Blessed are you Lord" (ברוך אתה אדוני). This is often followed by a description of what God has done to redeem the elect from their sinfulness or enemies. These opening phrases set the focus on God's character and actions.

---

[21] Licht "Doctrine," 3.
[22] Cf. Sanders, *Paul and Palestinian Judaism*, 167; Condra, *Salvation for the Righteous Revealed*, 169–170.
[23] VanLandingham, *Judgment and Justification*, 122, 135.
[24] For a survey of the hymns and prayers, see Chazon, "Hymns and Prayers;" idem, "Prayers from Qumran." One should also note the approximately forty copies of the canonical psalms found in the Dead Sea Scrolls (see Flint, "The Book of Psalms," 454).
[25] "[H]ymns must not be divorced from doctrine, because they are often the most innocent expression of it" (Carson, *Divine Sovereignty*, 82).

Whereas Ben Sira insisted that each agent act at the appropriate time, one following the other and neither at the same time, the *Hodayot* presents a view of divine and human agency that, while prioritising God's actions, coordinates human action within the sphere of divine action. Ben Sira's emphasis on the human agent is reversed by claiming that God acts first to restore the broken relationship. After God has taken the initial steps, the human is enabled to obey God's will because God remains at work through his spirit. Assigning the first act to God is necessary not because the hymnists think grace is better than law observance, but because the human is a frail, sinful creature incapable of obeying the commandments. In a variety of ways, the hymnists explain how God overcomes the human dilemma. The uniting factor in all of these means of redemption is the divine spirit. It is these divine saving acts that lead the hymnists to write. The *Hodayot*, as a whole, are reflections on how God redeems sinners from themselves and restores to them the glory once held by Adam.

The following sections will analyse three divine acts: predestination, the giving of knowledge, and purification. The role assigned to the spirit will be specifically highlighted. It will also be noted how these divine acts relate to human action. Finally, the understanding of the divine-human relationship set forth here will be compared with Sanders' description of covenantal nomism. First, however, one must understand the hymnists' portrayal of the incapacity of the human agent, for it is this factor, itself gained through divine revelation, that makes clear precisely why the hymnists prioritise divine action.

1. The Creaturely Limitations of Humanity

From the initial studies of the *Hodayot*, scholars have recognised the pessimistic anthropology that dominates the hymns.[26] Humans are described as worthless creatures predisposed to wickedness and destined for death. These ideas, Ringgren notes, "are presented [in the Qumran texts] with such emphasis that they almost become the leading motif in the Qumran concept of man. In any case they are repeated so often in the psalms that there is an overwhelming impression of man's nothingness and depravity."[27] Even if Ringgren overstates the importance of this idea for the sect's anthropology, he is correct in his observation about the *Hodayot*. While this repetition can make the hymns monotonous, it contributes to the overall focus on divine action by reminding the reader how pathetic humans are. The use of repetition also gives the *Hodayot* a sense of simplicity, and many studies have merely reproduced the overt claims that humans are worthless and sinful without any attempt to grasp the interconnectedness of these two themes or the underlying logic.[28] The anthropology is

---

[26] For summaries of the anthropology of the *Hodayot*, see Hyatt, "View of Man;" Licht, "Doctrine," 10–11. For the Dead Sea Scrolls generally, see Lichtenberger, *Menschenbild*.

[27] Ringgren, *Faith of Qumran*, 95.

[28] E.g. VanLandingham, *Judgment and Justification*, 119–35.

deceptively complex. What makes the anthropology of the *Hodayot* stand out is not its pessimism, which is similar to other texts, but the exact form that the pessimism takes: humans are necessarily morally incompetent because they are formed from material that wastes away.

Here it is necessary to state clearly what "salvation" means for the hymnists since this has significant implications for how they construct the human problem. An eschatological tension runs right through the *Hodayot*. In the current age, salvation consists (at least) of joining the human community of the redeemed, possessing knowledge, and being in a state of purity despite one's sinfulness. These present salvific measures are not the fullness of salvation, however, for the hymnists look toward another period when they will dwell both with the human community and with the holy ones (11.20–24) and possess "all the glory of Adam" (4.27). To be certain, the community perceives of itself as already participating in worship with the angels and possessing Adam's glory, but the fullness of these realities has not yet dawned.[29] In this future state, a "transformation" will take place as the human's dusty, fleshly origin and sinful disposition are left behind. The human does not become "angelic" or "divine," but those portions of the creaturely condition, such as the dusty origins and the resulting disposition toward disobedience, that hinder him or her will be removed.[30] This future expectation for transformation provides the context over against which the hymnists develop their anthropology.[31] The hymnists do not confine the anthropological problem that prevents the human from entering into this eternal bliss solely to disobedience. Rather, the problem extends to the very core of the human, the material from which he or she was created.

At the risk of creating distinctions that the hymnists may not have consciously made, it is useful to divide the phrases and words used to develop the anthropology into two categories: descriptions drawn from the realm of creation (material), and expressions about righteousness and wickedness (moral). The distinction between the two will allow us to highlight the distinctive point of each semantic field and to identify any potential scriptural backgrounds. First, phrases and words referring to the material composition of the human will be noted. This language is used to emphasise the human's creaturely limitations. Second, statements about humans as morally weak will be noted briefly. This distinction between the two categories, while heuristically helpful, is not maintained in the hymns. The two categories are brought together and mutually in-

---

[29] Fletcher-Louis overemphasises the present time aspects (*All the Glory of Adam*, 96; cf. Lichtenberger, *Menschenbild*, 224–27).

[30] For the idea of "transformation," see Fletcher-Louis, *All the Glory of Adam*, 104–12 ("Transformation in the Hodayot"). He claims that the transformation is to an "angelomorphic existence" or a "'divine' humanity" (105, 112). This seems to overstate the evidence.

[31] It is not possible to determine which came first, the pessimistic anthropology or the conception of the salvific state, but the two ideas do overlap and reinforce one another.

terpret one another so that phrases that originally referred only to the human's frailty and insignificance now testify to the reason one transgresses. The hymnists trace the anthropological problems of frailty and sinfulness back to the material from which humans were formed. This perspective is arrived at, it appears, by interpreting Genesis 2.7 through Genesis 3.19.

a. The Material Weakness of Humanity

In 18.3–9 the hymnist contemplates why God would reveal his mysteries and wisdom to a human being. He asks, "What, then, is man—he is earth, pinched off [clay] and to the dust he will return (ומה אפהו אדם ואדמה הוא ח[מר] קורץ ולעפר תשובתו)—that (כי) you have given him insight into wonders like these . . . ?" (lines 5–6).[32] Three things should be noted about the interjected comment. First, it is fundamental to the concept of humanity that the person is formed from the earth. The hymnist is playing on the lexical connections between the terms אדם and אדמה. The human is by definition a product of the earth. Second, death appears to be the inevitable outcome of human existence. This appears, on the one hand, to contradict the hymnist's expectation that he and others will attain to eternal glory. On the other hand, it underscores the need not only for divine intervention, but also for God to transform the hymnist's current condition. The creaturely condition that leads to one's demise must be overcome. Finally, this statement draws on scriptural ideas and language. The phrase "pinched off clay" likely comes from Job 33.6, where it is one of several comments about humans coming from clay or dust (4.19; 10.9; 30.19). The dust and clay language, which always has a negative connotation in Job, signals frailty and limitation. More significant for the hymnist's view are Genesis 2–3. The idea that humans are formed from the earth originates in Genesis 2.7 where the author records that "YHWH God formed the man from the dust from the ground" (וַיִּיצֶר יְהוָה אֱלֹהִים אֶת־הָאָדָם עָפָר מִן־הָאֲדָמָה). The claim that humans will return to the dust, which is widespread throughout the OT (see below), is first stated in Genesis 3.19: "and you will return to the dust" (וְאֶל־עָפָר תָּשׁוּב). The combination of Genesis 2.7 and 3.19 in 1QH ͣ 18.5–6 indicates that the hymnist thinks the two belong together. The hymnist's dislike for the material from which the human is formed can be accounted for if Genesis 3.19, with its negative perspective on humanity's origins, functions as the lens through which the hymnist reads the neutral statement in 2.7 about the material God used to create Adam. The hymnist's understanding of humanity and its future is ultimately rooted, then, in a particular understanding of the

---

[32] The grammar of these lines is not entirely clear. This translation follows Stegemann/Schuller, *1QHodayot ͣ*, 238. García Martínez/Tigchelaar think the question is "What, then, is man?" and the answer begins with "he is nothing but earth" (*Dead Sea Scrolls Study Edition*, 187 [hereafter *DSSSE*]). They begin a new sentence at כי. Either way is consistent with the points drawn here.

sacred texts. These three points provide the basic problem that the hymnist has with the human being as a creature: he is formed from material that wastes away. This depiction of the human problem is conveyed in several ways. Here we will focus on a few of the key expressions used to remind the reader that he or she is a frail, weak creature destined to die. These expressions do not point in and of themselves to the sinfulness of the human.

"Son(s) of man/Adam" (e.g. 7.19 [4QH^a 8 i 11]; 9.29, 36; 12.31; 19.6) and "born of a woman" (5.31; 21.2, 9; 23.13) point to the birth of each human and may hint at the first man and woman. The phrase "son(s) of Adam" (בני אדם) is common in the OT, although it is often difficult to determine if an author is referring to humanity in general or specifically to the first human, Adam. The same ambiguity appears in the *Hodayot*. At the least the phrase, along with "son(s) of man" (בני איש), recalls the fact that humans are created beings. The phrase "born of a woman" comes from Job, where it indicates the frailty and mortality of humanity (14.1; 15.14; 25.4).

The expression "kneaded from water" (5.21; 9.21; 11.24; 20.25) may draw on a tradition about the water rising to cover the earth before God created the first man.[33] It recalls the origins of humanity from dust and highlights the frailty and worthlessness of the human being. The phrases סוד ערוה ("foundation of shame") and מקור נדה ("source of impurity") also occur several times (5.32; 9.24; 20.28). The terms ערוה and נדה have sexual overtones (e.g., Lev 12.5; 18.6–19) and can refer metaphorically to shame, filth, and impurity due to one's sinfulness (Lam 1.17; Ezek 23.19). The terms in the *Hodayot*, according to Licht, "transfer a deep sexual disgust to the contemplation of human nature in general."[34]

Another term to note is בשר (flesh), which appears 29x in Stegemann's and Schuller's reconstruction of the *Hodayot*. It is used in several ways. It stands for all humans as creatures (5.33; 7.34) or a particular part of the human body (16.34). In 7.25 "hand of flesh" parallels אדם and אנוש. Most often, it indicates the weakness and mortality of humanity. Those made of flesh are unable to understand God's mysteries (5.30–31; 7.34) and are insignificant within creation (12.30; 26.35). The "flesh" cannot be relied on for protection (18.25) and fails under the pressures of life (16.34). In 18.25, "flesh" may mean either one's personal abilities or other humans. Either way, the context contrasts God's care and protection with the securities created by humans. As a "spirit of flesh," the hymnist cannot follow God's will nor can he protect himself from evil spirits (4.37).[35] The hymnists' use of בשר to describe the human condition as weak and insignificant follows the typical use of the term in the OT. "Flesh" is like

---

[33] Lichtenberger, *Menschenbild*, 81–84; cf. Greenfield, "Root 'GBL'." The difficulty with this interpretation, though, is the date at which the tradition is first clearly presented.

[34] Licht, "Doctrine," 10.

[35] Cf. Holm-Nielsen, *Hodayot*, 249n.26.

B. Divine Saving Acts and Human Obedience 85

the grass of the field, and although it possess a form of glory, it withers and dies (Isa 40.3; cf. Ps 78.39). If God removes his spirit, all flesh would perish (Job 34.15). One should not put confidence in the powers of flesh for they are fleeting (Jer 17.5) and cannot stand against God (2 Chron 32.8). Weakness characterises flesh (Job 6.12). God does not see like flesh does (Job 10.4) because he is the opposite of flesh (Isa 31.3; cf. Dan 2.11). As Bratsiotis accurately summarises, "The characteristics, then, of *basar* are its creatureliness, its absolute dependence on God, its earthly nature, and its weakness, inadequacy, and transitoriness."[36]

"Flesh" itself is not inherently flawed, and the view taken by the hymnists is not identical to some later "Gnostic" perspectives on the flesh as intrinsically evil. Yet, there is in the *Hodayot* a consistent negative description of the flesh. Even in general statements such as 5.33 and 7.34, there is a negative overtone. The flesh is something that impedes the human from participating in worship with the angels. The idea that one must be delivered from the "flesh" appears in 7.27–30. The passage describes the creation of the righteous person who adheres to God's demands and is given salvation. The description concludes, "You have raised his glory מבשר." בשר can refer to humanity, and the preposition מן would be translated "above." This would mean that God established the righteous person with honour over humanity in general or more specifically the wicked.[37] Alternatively, the word could mean "from flesh," indicating that God has removed the righteous person from the realm of flesh and all its limitations.[38] The latter option appears to be correct. The term "flesh" in the *Hodayot* rarely means simply "humanity" without any hint at the weakness and insignificance of humans. Twice in the immediate context, "flesh" represents inability. Humans are unable to direct their own futures (line 25), and they lack the ability to understand God's ways (line 34). Line 30 contributes to the idea that in salvation God restores to humanity "all the glory of Adam" (4.27). By giving the righteous a glory apart from flesh, the hymnist does not deny the creaturely state of the human being. Instead, he looks toward the restoration of the human's true creaturely characteristics.[39]

A final set of expressions that highlight the human's creaturely limitations are those that use the words "clay" and "dust." The ideas expressed with these terms have already been noted in the discussion of 1QH^a 18.3–9 above. The

---

[36] Bratsiotis, "בשר," *TDOT*, rev. ed., 2:328.

[37] Holm-Nielsen, *Hodayot*, 228, 231n.19.

[38] Fletcher-Louis, *All the Glory of Adam*, 134. Fletcher-Louis' claim that this removal "from flesh" refers in part to "a fully sexual life" based on some OT texts in which "flesh" refers to the genitals (e.g. Lev 6.3; 12.3) is unconvincing. "Flesh" never has sexual connotations in the *Hodayot*.

[39] Holm-Nielsen's contention that this interpretation results in a rejection of the flesh comparable to "Gnostic" views is mistaken (*Hodayot*, 231n.19).

phrases "creature of clay" (יצר [ה]חמר) and "creature of dust" (יצר [ה]עפר) appear several times.[40] As a creature of clay, the hymnist is amazed that God would bring one of such humble origins into eternal life and give him the opportunity to praise God with the sons of heaven (11.22–25). The terms conveniently highlight the idea that humans are creatures formed from perishable material. The dusty origins of humanity distinguish it from God (12.30; 18.5–14), for he is the Creator and eternal. He is omnipotent and omniscient, while humans, because they are from clay and dust, are unable to understand God's ways (20.29) or even determine their own (18.7). These various statements highlight the weakness of humans. They are frail creatures formed from the ground and are wasting away. The statements also draw attention to the insignificance of the human being. Being a creature made from dust denotes mortality and weakness and underscores the fact that humans were created and are, thus, infinitely distinct from their Creator.

At the end of their earthly existence, humans will return to the dust, which reminds them that they are creatures and not eternal beings (18.5–7; 20.28–29; 23.24). The idea of humans returning to the dust at death is widespread throughout the OT (see Job 17.16; 20.11; 21.26; 34.15; Ps 7.6 [Eng 5]; 22.15 [16], 30 [29]; 104.29; Qoh 3.20; 12.7).[41] These passages are based on the tradition recorded in Genesis 3.19. As a result of his transgression, God tells Adam that at the end of his life he will return to the ground. Adam's existence will end the same way it began because he is a creature formed from the dust of the earth. The simple statement "for you are dust" reminds Adam that he is a part of the created world. His quest to become like God (cf. v.5) brings the humbling reminder that he is nothing like God. The idea that humans return to the dust at death marks the end of their existence, thus signifying the frailty of their frames. Apart from divine intervention, humans will perish.

Through these phrases and others, the hymnists set forth clearly the frailty and weakness of the human creature. By using language from creation, the hymnists indicate that the problem of frailty and weakness is innate to the human being because he or she is a creature. The scriptural roots of some of the expressions and terms give a sense of authority to this description. The problem inherent to the human, though, goes further. Alongside these statements about humanity as frail, weak, and mortal creatures are statements that emphasise the sinfulness of the human nature.

---

[40] E.g. column 21. See Lichtenberger, *Menschenbild*, 77–81.
[41] Isa 26.19 and Dan 12.2 describe the hope of resurrection by remarking that those lying in the dust will rise again (also contrast Ps 30.10 [9] with Isa 26.19).

b. The Moral Weakness of Humanity

The contrast between God as righteous and humans as sinners is evident throughout the hymns. Because this idea is widely recognised, it is not necessary to go into much detail. Left to his own devices, the human dwells in impurity, which results in him rejecting God's ways (1QH^a 4.31). In moments of doubt, the hymnist recalls his transgressions and those of his ancestors, and he worries that he may have forsaken God's covenant (12.34–36). He writes, "I said, 'Because of my transgression, I have forsaken your covenant'" (ואני אמרתי בפשעי נעזבתי מבריתכה) (line 36).[42] As he notes earlier, "righteousness does not belong to humans" (לוא לאנוש צדקה) (line 31). By contrast, God is holy (5.18), full of truth (12.41), and knowledge (17.17). The hymnists exclaim repeatedly that righteousness belongs to God (4.32; 6.26; 7.37; 8.27, 29; 9.28; 12.32; 20.22, 34). His judgment is always in accordance with justice and impartial (7.37–38).

Each human remains a sinner from birth until death (12.30–31). Even the righteous do not escape this sinful status when they enter the community of the redeemed.[43] VanLandingham argues, though, that statements about humans as sinners only apply to those outside the community because statements about human depravity are followed by statements about those in the community.[44] His examples, however, do not support his claim that those in the community are freed entirely from their sinful dispositions. The constant use of the first person pronoun shows that the hymnists never thought they escaped their sinful state even after God redeemed them.[45] Even after experiencing redemption, the hymnists still describes themselves as "a man of offense" (22.8) and sharing "the lot of the scoundrels (חלבאים)" (11.26).[46] While one may be more righteous than his neighbour, his righteousness will not suffice when he stands before God's judgment seat (17.14–17; cf. 9.27–28; 15.31–32; 22.29). Even the members of the community of the elect would be declared guilty if it were

---

[42] For this translation, cf. García Martínez/Tigchelaar, *DSSSE*, 171; Stegemann/Schuller, *1QHodayot^a*, 166. Abegg translates as "I said in my transgression, I am abandoned by Your covenant" ("Thanksgiving Psalms," 97; cf. Holm-Nielsen, *Hodayot*, 78, 86n.92; Mansoor, *Thanksgiving Hymns*, 130). בפשעי, however, probably goes with the verb נעזבתי not אמרתי, and it describes the reason why the hymnist thinks he has rejected the covenant. The ב preposition is causative. His sin prevents him from partaking in the realm of salvation. This seems to fit the context better, since the hymnist is contemplating the possibility that he might be banned from salvation due to his sin.

[43] See also Merrill, *Qumran and Predestination*, 38–39; Sanders, *Paul and Palestinian Judaism*, 274–82; Condra *Salvation for the Righteous Revealed*, 179–80.

[44] VanLandingham, *Judgment and Justification*, 121.

[45] Kuhn, "New Light," 102–03; cf. Frey, "Flesh and Spirit," 382.

[46] The translation of 11.26 is García Martínez/Tigchelaar, *DSSSE*, 167. Cf. Holm-Nielsen, *Hodayot*, 69n.22.

not for God's grace since their own obedience does not count as righteousness before God's judgment (cf. 9.25). Those destined for salvation still possess the same sinful nature as the rest of humanity.

c. The Problem of Being a Creature

The heuristically useful distinction between the descriptions of humans as materially weak and as morally weak is not maintained in the *Hodayot*. The hymnists consistently bring the two semantic fields together to present a composite picture of humans as physically frail and morally deficient individuals. The language seems to indicate that humans are sinners precisely because of their dusty origins. By combining the two language types, they both are redefined and inherit the meanings of the other one. Weakness in terms of mortality is transformed to mean weakness in terms of morality.[47]

Several times the hymnists simply lists descriptions of humans. For example, in the midst of a hymn about creation, one writes,

I am a creature of clay and kneaded with water, a foundation of shame and spring of impurity, a furnace of iniquity and a building of sin, a spirit of error and perversion, without knowledge and terrified about (your) righteous judgment. (9.23–25; cf. 5.32)

The two semantic categories are placed next to one another in order to develop a holistic picture of the human being as a frail and sinful being. There is no attempt here to explain any potential relationship between the terms. Within the context, though, one senses a critique of the human situation. In comparison with the rest of creation, the human is nothing because of his origins and disposition toward sin.

Elsewhere the two semantic categories become mutually interpreting as the connotations of one are transferred to the other. This mixture of thought between humans as weak and sinful creatures can be seen in the use of ערוה and נדה. The metaphorical meanings of these terms refer to the character of the individual based on his or her sinful deeds. A person incurs "shame" or is identified as "filthy" because he or she has disobeyed the commandments. The original application of these terms in a sexual way, though, remains in the background, and it is the combination of this original meaning with the metaphorical one that the hymnists exploit. They use these terms precisely because they bring the ideas of creation and unrighteousness together.[48]

In column 12, the hymnist recounts how God has established him as a leader within the community. Through God's assistance, he has worked wonders

---

[47] Cf. Braun, "Römer 7, 7–25," 4–11; Smith, *What Must I Do*, 55–58.

[48] Smith suggests that the phrase "shameful nakedness" may allude to Adam's and Eve's realization that they were naked (עֵירֹם) and the resulting "shame" (Gen 3.7) following Adam's sin (*What Must I Do*, 56). עֵירֹם is not used, however, with the same negative connotations that ערוה has in either the OT or the Dead Sea Scrolls.

among the people (lines 29–30). He proceeds to contrast this divinely given situation with his natural abilities: "What is flesh compared with this? What creature of clay can magnify wonders?" (line 30). Based on the use of "flesh" and "creature of clay," one would expect the hymnist to claim that humans are incapable of such wondrous deeds because they are frail creatures and insignificant within the spectrum of creation, but he does not. Instead, he describes how humans are sinful: "He is in iniquity from the womb and until old age in the guilt of unfaithfulness" (line 31). The reason humans are incapable of doing such wonders is because they are predisposed from birth to sin. The human's problem with sin is traced to his origins as a creature formed from clay and flesh. The hymn continues by contrasting the individual's inability to establish his own path with God's determination of every person's way (lines 31–33).

The same idea appears also in 11.20–26. The hymnist praises God for redeeming him from condemnation and placing him within the angelic community (lines 10–24). The connection between the human as a frail creature and as a sinner appears first in two parallel sentences:

I know that there is hope
   for someone you formed from dust
      for an everlasting council.
You have purified
   the depraved spirit from great transgression
      so that he can stand in service with the host of the holy ones
      and can enter into communion with the congregation of the sons of heaven.
   (lines 21–23)

"Formed from dust" is parallel to "depraved spirit," and "everlasting council" parallels "the host of the holy ones" and "the congregation of the sons of heaven." What prevents the human from participating in these groups is both one's material weakness and one's moral weakness. The hymnist then asks, "But I, a creature of clay, what am I? Kneaded from water, and for whom am I to be reckoned? What is my strength?" (lines 24–25). As in 12.30, one would expect the hymnist to describe how humans are weak because of the material from which they were formed. Instead, just as in 12.31, he explains that humans are prone to wickedness: "For I stand at the border of wickedness and share the lot of the scoundrels" (lines 25–26). Being formed from the earth's clay, the hymnist possesses no strength and the result is his sharing of the same lot as the scoundrels. The underlying logic seems to be this: because he is a weak creature, he is prone to evil. As he writes in 9.29, "to the sons of Adam belongs the service of iniquity and deeds of deceit."

In column 5, the hymnist ponders his place within the vast realm of creation. He asks, "[But what is] the spirit of flesh to understand all these things and to have insight into the great [wonder] of [your] counsel? And what is someone born of a woman among all your awesome works?" (5.30–31). The implication of the questions is that because the human is a creature, he has no great place within creation. As in 12.30–31, though, the hymnist continues by noting the human's sinfulness: "He is a structure of dust, kneaded with water, his counsel is [the iniquity of sin], shame of dishonour, and a sp[ring of] impurity; and a corrupt spirit (ורוח נעוה) rules over him" (lines 32–33). The reason a human cannot understand God's ways or is insignificant within the spectrum of creation is because he is both a creature and a sinner. The human is insignificant within creation because, unlike the rest of creation, he breaks God's commands.

The significance of the reply given to these questions about the place of the individual can be seen by comparing the hymnists' answers with the answer given the question "what is man?" in Psalm 8. In Psalm 8, the psalmist expresses wonder over why God takes any interest in humanity. Compared with the majesty of the heavens, humanity deserves no accolades. He queries, "What is man that you are mindful of him, the son of man that you care for him? (v.4). God decided to elevate the status of humanity by placing humans just below the angels (v.5) and making them rulers over the rest of creation (vv.7–8). The psalmist takes an optimistic perspective of humanity.

Already in the OT, one finds other answers being given to the question "what is man?" The answer in Psalm 144.3–4 is that humans are like breath and a fleeting shadow. This negative answer focuses on the frailty of humanity. Job queries also about God's interest in humanity: "What is man that he could be pure, or one born of a woman that he could be righteous?" (15.14). As the question indicates, Job's interest is in the moral capacity of humanity. The authors of the *Hodayot* likewise do not recall the marvellous role assigned to humanity. They rather describe humans as sinful beings (1QH[a] 5.32; 12.31). The answer provided to the questions by the authors of 1QH[a] 5 and 12, Job, and Psalm 144 is the precise opposite of that given by the psalmist of Psalm 8. Psalm 144 does not make explicit any connection between humans as creatures and as sinners. Job hints at a connection with the phrase "born of a woman," but he does not draw out the implications of this connection. The negative answer to the question "what is man?" given in the *Hodayot*, though, brings the problem associated with humanity's creaturely condition closer to humanity's problem with sin. Noticing that Job 15.14 and Psalm 144.3–4 use the same language may have provided the necessary key for the hymnists to combine the two answers into one: humans are unworthy because they are sinful creatures. The reason that humans are not ascribed the same glorious role in the *Hodayot* as they are in Psalm 8 is because the hymnists view the creaturely condition as a fundamental problem because of its connections with sin.

In each of these sections, the hymnists juxtapose the human's creaturely state, which signifies frailty and insignificance, with his or her sinful state. These questions address the place of the human within the vastness of creation by defining what it means to be human. The answers provided to them, however, indicate that the human's problem is more than simply insignificance and

B. Divine Saving Acts and Human Obedience

frailty. The concept of being human has been defined as being a sinner through the combination of the language about the human as a creature and as a sinner. The human is frail and weak not only because he or she is a creature, but also because he or she is a sinner.

In 20.27–38 the hymnist contrasts himself as a sinner and creature with God who is just and Creator. The one taken from the dust is nothing (line 34b), incapable of understanding God's glory (line 33), and will return to the dust at death (lines 29–30, 34). The hymnist exclaims, "And I, from dust [I] have been taken [and from clay] I have been [pi]nched as a source (למקור) of impurity, and disgraceful shamelessness, a pile of dust, and mixed with [water . . .], and a dwelling of darkness" (lines 27–28).[49] Assuming the reconstruction is correct,[50] the opening statement "from dust [I] have been taken [and from the clay] I have been [pi]nched" is scriptural language. The first part comes from Genesis 2.7 and the tradition to which it belongs. The second part is from Job 33.6, which is the only place where the two words חמר and קרץ appear together. In Elihu's speech, the statement affirms his solidarity with Job as a human. He stands before God just as Job does, that is, as a created being drawn from the clay of the Earth. In the *Hodayot*, these expressions are clarified by the following list of descriptors. The ל preposition on למקור indicates that the human has been created in a certain manner; in this case, "as a source of impurity," that is, as a sinful being. In the opening statement, then, the hymnist is not interested solely in defining humans as created beings, as the language in its scriptural context indicates. Rather, the fact that humans are creatures testifies to their state as sinners. By connecting the human's sinful condition with its origins, the issue of sin becomes inherent to the very essence of the human being.

Some scholars find the notion of sinfulness particularly in the term "flesh" (בשר). It is depicted as frail and is associated with the evil ways of humanity (5.30–33). In 12.30–31 the hymnist connects the two even closer. He queries about the place of "flesh" within the spectrum of creation and whether a "creature of clay" can do wonders like God. He remarks that those defined as flesh and creatures of clay are "in iniquity" from birth until death. Commenting on this text, which, he maintains, provides the closest connection between "flesh" and sin, Frey writes, "בשר does not only express human weakness and frailty, but also a state of being characterized by inescapable sinfulness and basic opposition with the creator."[51] The one formed from flesh and clay is incapable of doing anything but sin. Like the other terms and expressions derived from

---

[49] Compare García Martínez/Tigchelaar, *DSSSE*, 193; Abegg, "Thanksgiving Psalms," 109; Lohse, *Texte*, 159; Maier/Schubert, *Qumran-Essener*, 229. Mansoor (*Thanksgiving Hymns*, 175) translates lines 29–30 as a continuation of lines 27–28 (quoted above). Holm-Nielsen (*Hodayot*, 198) separates them with a semi-colon. The verb ותשובת in line 29 likely starts a new sentence.

[50] See Stegemann/Schuller, *1QHodayot^a*, 257.

[51] Frey, "Flesh and Spirit," 382; cf. Mansoor, *Thanksgiving Hymns*, 61–62.

the realm of creation, בשר is juxtaposed with language depicting humans as morally corrupt and through this proximity, it comes to represent human sinfulness. Through the negative connotations attributed to the "flesh," the hymnists convey the moral and material weakness of humans.

The connection between "flesh" and sin should not be overemphasised, however. This is done, for example, when one attempts to categorise the hymns as either "Teacher Hymns" or "Community Hymns" based on whether this word refers to frailty or is connected with sin. The term appears three times in the so-called "Teacher Hymns" where it indicates particularly the frail state of humans (15.20; 16.32, 34).[52] The lack of any explicit connection with sin, though, is not uncommon for the *Hodayot*, and this cautions against using this word as a criterion for authorship.[53] Flesh is undoubtedly portrayed as weak and insignificant and on several occasions assumes connotations of sinfulness and wickedness.

Scholars have sought for the origins of the *Hodayot*'s pessimistic outlook. Rejecting any notions of "original sin," Licht contends that the description of humans as sinful is a reflex of the claim that God alone is righteous.[54] This formulation, however, probably establishes a logical framework that the hymnists did not perceive. Moreover, both ideas are clearly set forth in the scriptures, and because the hymns are so dependent on these texts, it is unlikely that the hymnists only arrived at the view that humans are sinful after they realised that God alone is just. VanLandingham points to the canonical Psalms as the source for the hymnists' view. He catalogues several texts from the Psalms that portray humans as sinful, frail, and worthless. The *Hodayot*, he claims, emphasises and develops the same themes but does not change any of them.[55] Certainly parallels can be detected, but VanLandingham downplays the radicalness of the *Hodayot*.[56] Furthermore, he has not adequately noted the impact of Genesis 2–3 on the hymnist. Indeed, the closest parallels to the *Hodayot* in the Psalms (e.g. Pss 8; 103) are those that have lexical and thematic connections with Genesis 2–3.

Fletcher-Louis rightly notes that "much of the *Hodayot* is a sustained and extended meditation on the anthropology of Genesis 2:7."[57] Yet, he fails to notice (partly because he downplays the pessimistic anthropology) that the hymnists' interpretation of Genesis 2.7 is mediated through their reading of the

---

[52] 12.30 was originally considered part of the "Teacher Hymn" in 12.6–13.6, but others have argued that 12.30b–13.6 was added later to the "Teacher Hymn" (now identified as 12.6–30a) by the community (Becker, *Das Heil Gottes*, 54–55; Frey, "Flesh and Spirit, 382n.86). The distinction here, as Sanders points out, is driven by the particular view of "flesh" and sin taken by Becker and Frey (*Paul and Palestinian Judaism*, 323).

[53] See 7.25, 34; 17.16; 21.7, 9.

[54] Licht, "Doctrine," 11–12.

[55] VanLandingham, *Judgment and Justification*, 132–33.

[56] Cf. Gen 6.5; 8.21; Pss 51.5; 144.3–4; Isa 40.6; Jer 17.9.

[57] Fletcher-Louis, *All the Glory of Adam*, 107.

B. Divine Saving Acts and Human Obedience

punishment given to Adam in 3.19.[58] There Adam is told that he will return "to the ground," "to the dust," because he comes from the dust. This latter verse functions as the lens through which the hymnists interpret the description of the creation of the first man. Reading the creation of Adam in 2.7 in light of his subsequent failure and punishment (3.1–19), the hymnists maintain that the very material used to create Adam is the ultimate cause of his failure. For the hymnists, then, the creation of humanity from dust becomes a negative reality that represents both frailty and moral weakness. Whatever the neutral statement about Adam's formation from dust might have meant, in light of the form of punishment given by God, namely, the return to the dust, Adam's dusty origins are interpreted as a significant problem. Because Adam functions as the representative of all humanity, his situation is then transposed to all humans, which means that his descendents assume his dusty origins and all that it implies (mortality, sinfulness, etc.). While the hymnists nowhere blame Adam for the current predicament of the human race, they nevertheless view Adam's sin and assigned punishment as the reason that the human being is given to sin, frailty, and insignificance.[59]

The hymnists' view is not itself particularly new or novel, for parallels can be found elsewhere. Several statements in the OT join creation language with notions of sinfulness. In fact, the connection between frailty and sinfulness that the hymnist makes between Genesis 2.7 and 3.19 may have been spurred by Psalm 103. The psalmist is confident that God will remove his sins because God "knows our frame, remembering that we are dust" (vv.10–14). The *Hodayot*, however, offers a sustained reflection on this relationship and pushes the relationship further until the anthropology becomes "an almost pathological abhorrence of human nature."[60] This extreme criticism of the human being as a creature must not be downplayed by drawing endless comparisons. In the hymnists' view, the ultimate cause of the human's sinful condition is the material that forms his or her frame. "[H]is sins are not the result of error, carelessness, or human malice which may be overcome through the power of human will, nor are the consequence of having been misled. Rather, they are rooted in a

---

[58] Yates remarks, "It is obvious even from a quick reading of the sectarian scrolls found near Qumran that Genesis 2:7a, as interpreted by Gen. 3:19, plays a central role in the anthropology of the community" (*Spirit and Creation in Paul*, 64). He does not develop this insight, however.

[59] The closest one comes to a notion of "original sin" is 17.13: "In my troubles you comfort me. I delight in forgiveness and regret פשע ראשון." Dupont-Sommer translates the phrase as "original sin" (*Essene Writings*, 231; cf. Brownlee, "Anthropology and Soteriology," 227–28), but the context focuses on the hymnist's personal failure, not something he inherited. It is unlikely that he is attributing his moral failings to Adam's transgression (cf. Licht, "Doctrine," 11; Mansoor, *Thanksgiving Hymns*, 159; Holm-Nielsen, *Hodayot*, 276–77; Hyatt, "View of Man," 283).

[60] Licht, "Doctrine," 10.

basic human weakness as a created being, against which man is powerless to act alone."[61] This flesh, dust formed, water kneaded, shameful, filthy, depraved spirit must be disposed of before the human can participate in the fullness of salvation.

d. Summary

The picture of humanity pervading the *Hodayot* highlights weakness, insignificance, and ultimately sinfulness. The hymnists distinguish sharply between God and humanity. The former is Creator of all things and always acts in accordance with justice, while the latter is one part of creation (although an important part) and when left to its own ways, always acts unjustly. Using language associated with creation, the hymnists describe humanity as frail and insignificant, formed from perishable material like dust, clay, and flesh. Terms associated with righteousness and sin depict the human as morally deficient. One cannot obey God's demands and will be found guilty at the Final Judgment. The hymnists combine these two conceptions of the human so that each type of description helps explain the other. Humans are morally corrupt, incapable of acting righteously or understanding God's ways because they are formed from the dust and are made of flesh. Although parallels can be found in other texts, the *Hodayot* stands out because of the connection made between the material and moral weaknesses of the human being. The human is necessarily immoral because he or she is created from feeble material. The combination of the two semantic fields results in a comprehensive critique of the human being.

This picture of the human predicament differs remarkably from Ben Sira's optimistic portrayal of humanity. For Ben Sira humans only sin because they choose to. Disobedience is not the inevitable result of human nature because humans have a neutral disposition. They can obey or disobey, and the choice is solely up to the individual (Sir 15.14–17). The ability to choose, in fact, is given to humans at creation. The contrast could not be more drastic. The ability that Ben Sira claims God gave at creation is denied by the hymnists who attribute the human's moral failures to the material from which he or she is formed. Just as Ben Sira's optimism is fundamental to his conception of the divine-human relationship, the hymnists' pessimism is crucial.

2. Divine Action as the Basis for Human Action

The depravity of humanity, and the resulting incapacity to accomplish anything righteous, creates a significant problem for the human because this condition will keep one from attaining salvation. The solution to this problem is not a renewed effort on the human's part, but instead divine intervention. The interaction of the divine and human agents in the *Hodayot* consistently gives priority

---

[61] Nitzan, *Qumran Prayer*, 337.

B. Divine Saving Acts and Human Obedience

to God. God determines from before creation who will be righteous or wicked, and through his spirit, he enacts his eternal decree, gives knowledge, and purifies from sin. Through these divine acts, the human is empowered to obey God's will because the spirit of God is working through the human.

A clear example of this perspective is 8.26–33, which brings together several important themes: divine action in the forms of predestination, giving knowledge, and purification, which are all enacted through the spirit; and human response through spirit-enabled obedience. In this paragraph, two parallel statements describe the priority of divine action, which then serves as the basis for human action. In the first (lines 28–29), the hymnist resolves to purify his hands and oppose all evil because he "knows" that God has "recorded (רשמתה) the spirit of the righteous one." Throughout the hymns, knowledge belongs to God alone who imparts it to those he elects. In this passage, the divinely given knowledge is the understanding that God establishes the human as righteous by giving his spirit to the human, which is itself an act of predestination. With the verb רשם, the hymnist portrays God as writing down the person's status prior to creation rather than God keeping an account of what the righteous person does.[62] The only scriptural occurrence refers to what was written in the book of truth, which probably refers to a heavenly book that contains what will come in the future (Dan 10.21). What is inscribed is the "spirit of the righteous one" (1QH^a 8.28). This could mean either that God has given a certain type of spirit (e.g. the spirit of holiness) to a person, which because of this spirit the person becomes righteous. Alternatively, the "spirit" could be the human's disposition – in this case, towards righteousness – and God by inscribing it confirms that a person's disposition will become reality.[63] The former option is a stronger form of predestination and coheres better with the context. The relevant part of line 29 reads אל יצדק איש מבלעדיך, "no one is righteous besides you." Righteousness belongs to God alone. Because of this claim, line 28 cannot mean that the human is righteous according to his own inclination. The person described as righteous only has this characteristic because God has allowed him to be made this way. Line 28, then, means that God actively assigns a certain characteristic, which describes a certain lifestyle of obedience to the Torah, and this is accomplished by giving the spirit. The description of God's work focuses on past actions that occurred apart from the hymnist's present existence.

The hymnist's response that is described in line 28b arises from God's gift of knowledge. He chooses to purify himself, which is further defined as avoiding evil. His response to God's grace is obedience to the divine will. His desire to

---

[62] Contra Gaster, *Dead Sea Scriptures*, 202: "Thou dost keep a record of every righteous spirit."

[63] Sekki suggests that it is "nothing more than a reference to any righteous member of the sect," and "*ruaḥ* could be dropped completely" without affecting the meaning (*The Meaning of Ruaḥ at Qumran*, 106).

purify himself is confirmation that he is one worthy of the accolade "righteous" (צדיק) that God assigned to him through predestination. God's past act of determining the future of the righteous person provides the basis from which the person makes God's decision a reality in the present. The hymnist's response, therefore, is not a secondary step independent of God's redemption. As the next lines make clear, his response is grounded in God giving him a certain type of spirit that moves him to perform certain tasks.

The second statement (lines 29b–32a) describes how the hymnist "appeases" (ואחלה פניך) God because God has given him a particular spirit (ברוח אשר נתתה [בי]) to accomplish for him a series of items. The spirit was given by God "to lavish" (להשלים) his mercy on the hymnist, "to purify" (לטהרני) him, and "to draw [him] near" (להגישני). Damage at this point in the scroll makes it impossible to know how lines 30–31 related to these clauses.[64] Nevertheless, the sequence of actions depicts God's work as the basis for and reason that the hymnist acts. The ל preposition on each of the infinitives indicates the purpose or reason that God gave his spirit to the hymnist. The hymnist claims that the act of appeasing God is something done by himself, while ascribing it to God who placed his spirit in the hymnist. There is no tension between divine and human action, as if placing an emphasis on God's actions somehow lessens the significance and necessity of human action or vice versa. The two are interrelated but priority is also given to God.

Lines 32–33 conclude this paragraph with an appeal for divine protection. The hymnist beseeches God to prevent something (perhaps an evil spirit or evil doers) from joining with him. He also asks God to keep him from abandoning the "statutes of the covenant" because of afflictions that he might encounter. Recognising his own inability and wayward nature, he seeks assistance from God. The expectation for obedience is underscored in this line, for the hymnist does not think that God's gracious deliverance described in the previous lines can be abstracted from the demand for obedience. While his obedience is not the reason God acts to redeem him, it is nonetheless a necessary part of the life of the redeemed.

Two points should be noted. First, the complementary relationship between divine and human action appears in the two statements about purification. On the one hand, the hymnist claims that he purifies himself (line 28), while on the other, he attributes his purification to God through his holy spirit (line 30).[65] The act of purification can be described as something accomplished by the hymnist or by God. The hymnist's actions, however, are never accomplished apart from something done by God. Because God gave him knowledge, the hymnist vows to purify his ways and to avoid committing evil. The significance

---

[64] The series of infinitives indicating what God has accomplished for the hymnist continues through line 32 and possibly line 33 according to Stegemann/Schuller, *1QHodayot*ª, 109, 114–115.

[65] The two terms ברר and תהר are synonyms.

of the hymnist's action is not lessened because it is rooted in God's action, for it is precisely because God acted on behalf of the hymnist that he decides to act. In addition, God's action is not somehow dependent on the hymnist's willingness to reject wickedness. The underlying assumption seems to be that the human will act in accordance with God's decisions.

Second, one could argue on the basis of the phrases "for those who love you," "for those who keep your comm[and]ments," and "they who turn to you in truth and with a perfect heart" (lines 31, 35) that God's decision to act for the human is either based on his foreknowledge of or is a response to the obedience of a human. Either way, God's action is subsequent to and determined by human action. Such a conclusion, however, over-interprets the intent of the expressions. The expressions identify those who are recipients of God's gracious actions by indicating how they are best known, namely, as those who obey God's commandments. They do not mean, however, that these people acted in such a manner as to earn God's grace. The phrases indicate the importance of obedience, indeed the expectation for it, but they do not reverse the pattern of divine and human action.

The pattern observed in this analysis of 8.26–33 appears throughout the *Hodayot*. God acts in a certain manner to overcome the ill effects of the human's creaturely, sinful nature, and with this basic problem corrected, the human is enabled to understand, worship, and obey God, all the while relying on God for assistance. The following three sections investigate how the divine-human relationship works in relation to three key concepts: predestination, knowledge, and purification. In each section, attention will be drawn to the role assigned to the spirit.

a. Predestination

The idea of predestination assumes divine providence and foreknowledge. Before creating each being and part of creation, God knew what they would do (9.9–10, 26–27; 15.16). His knowledge extends from before creation until its ending, and he has assigned each creature, whether in the heavens or on earth, its task (9.11–17). Specifically about humans, one hymnist writes, "In the wisdom of your knowledge you det[er]mine their course before they came, and according to [your] wi[ll] everything [happ]ens and apart from you nothing is done" (9.21–22; cf. 7.26–27). The preceding lines describe how God distributed the tasks of humanity throughout its generations (9.17–21). The hymnists accept many of the dualistic notions found in other Qumran texts.[66] They affirm that the world is divided between good and evil, and humanity is split into the righteous and wicked. This division occurred when God created humanity (7.26–31; 12.39: "For you created the just and the wicked") and, at least, im-

---

[66] On dualism in the Dead Sea Scrolls, see Frey, "Different Patterns," 280–85.

plies double predestination.[67] Although the *Hodayot* rarely mentions double predestination, some passages make good sense when interpreted with this idea as a background.[68] God created the righteous for "eternal salvation and endless peace" and the wicked "for the day of slaughter" (7.29–30). The hymnists maintain that God is ultimately responsible for the final outcome of each human because he assigned to each a particular spirit (6.22–23).

The concept of predestination has been thoroughly explored by others, and it is not necessary to cover the same ground again.[69] Attention is drawn here to two motifs used to explain how God establishes his will in one's life. The question of the purpose of this teaching will then be addressed, followed by a short explanation of how the hymnists relate predestination and "free will."

Motifs of Predestination. Among the many ways to explain God's pre-temporal decisions, two in particular stand out in the *Hodayot*: God establishes each human's path, and God assigns a particular spirit to each person.

The hymnist asserts, "From [God] comes the path of every living being" (7.35). This statement follows the hymnist's reflections on the creation of the righteous and wicked. God created the just one in order for him "to walk on all (your paths)" (lines 27–28). The wicked, who were created "for the day of slaughter," walk on an evil path (lines 30–31). God determined the destinies of these two persons when he created them. Ultimately, a human's destiny depends on the spirit that God created for him or her: "The path of man is not established (תכון) except by the spirit which God formed for him to perfect the path of the sons of Adam" (12.32–33). Unlike Ben Sira, who envisions God placing the human before two paths and instructing the human to choose his or her own destiny, the hymnist maintains that God determines the human's destiny when he places the human on the path of righteousness or wickedness.

As a descendent of Adam and formed from clay, the human cannot establish his own path (7.25–26, 34; 12.31), and apart from divine intervention, the human remains captive to this inability. Thus, the hymnist appeals to God, "How can I make straight (my) path unless you establish [my] ste[ps? How] can [my] steps stand [unless you] strengthen (me) with strength?" (20.37–38). He places his hope in God because, as a human, he is unable to follow the path of righteousness. The hymnists' view is adopted from the scriptures. While humans are instructed to follow the righteous path (Deut 11.28; 28.9; Prov 4.26–27), it is recognised that they cannot fully establish their paths (Prov 20.24; Jer 10.23)

---

[67] 12.39 cannot mean simply that God created all human beings, as Wernberg-Moeller suggests ("Reconsideration of the Two Spirits," 415n.5), not least because it is a condensed form of 7.26–31.

[68] Merrill, *Qumran and Predestination*, 41–42.

[69] On the *Hodayot* see Merrill, *Qumran and Predestination*. For the Dead Sea Scrolls generally, see Lange, *Weisheit und Prädestination*; idem, "Wisdom and Predestination in the Dead Sea Scrolls."

B. Divine Saving Acts and Human Obedience

and are dependent on God, who firmly plants each person (2 Sam 22.33; Ps 37.23; Prov 3.6; 16.9).[70] Only by divine assistance will the hymnist be able to walk before God on the path that leads to life (1QH^a 15.17).[71]

Along with indicating predestination, this image also reveals the connection between predestination and obedience. The language of walking according to God's ways appears in Deuteronomy alongside "commandments," "statute," and "judgments" (26.17) and indicates that walking according to God's way means keeping the Torah.[72] In later traditions, the kings are evaluated according to whether they follow God's way like David and Asa[73] or the evil ways of Jeroboam and the Israelite kings.[74] The image, therefore, has an ethical orientation. Within the *Hodayot*, this connection is made when the hymnists contrast those who have not followed God's path with those who do follow God's will (1QH^a 12.18–28). The just are those who "keep your covenant" and "walk on all (your paths)," while the wicked are those who "walk on a path that is not good" and "reject your covenant" (7.28, 31). Adherence to God's way means obeying the demands of the covenant.

Predestination, therefore, is not an abstract doctrine that stands by itself. It is rather a practical concept that emphasises God's sovereignty, while also establishing human ability. The connection between predestination and obedience also shows that the divine and human are not competing agents. Predestination does not dismiss or devalue human action. It enables the human to obey the divine demand because when God chooses the person for righteousness he establishes the person on the path of life. While it is correct that one is elected to be obedient, one should not deduce from this that salvation (or election) is based on obedience.[75] Obedience is the outcome and purpose of the divine decision.

This connection between predestination and obedience may help to explain those instances in which the hymnists describe the wicked as refusing to walk in God's ways. In 12.18 the wicked are described as those who "have not chosen the p[ath of] your [heart]." Their rejection of God is not attributed to a pre-temporal decision, but to their own wayward actions. Similarly, in 14.22–24 the hymnist complains about those who once followed his teaching but, having been enticed by deception, have rejected him and God. They have disobeyed God, who "commanded them to seek fortune far from the paths" of the deceivers. The point in both texts is not to teach free will, but to indicate

---

[70] See Koch, דֶּרֶךְ, *TDOT* 3:282–93; Merrill, דרך, *NIDOTTE* 1:989–93.

[71] 4.33 likely conveys the same idea: "But I know that [. . .] the path of your chosen one." García Martínez/Tigchelaar (*DSSSE*, 148) reconstruct [תישר] ("you smoothen"), while Stegemann/Schuller (*1QHodayot^a*, 71) suggests ה[כינותה] ("you determine;" cf. Holm-Nielsen, *Hodayot*, 249n.18).

[72] Cf. Exod 18.20; Deut 10.12; 11.22; 19.9; 28.9; 30.16; Jos 22.5; 1 Kings 2.3, 4.

[73] E.g. 1 Kings 3.14; 8.25; 22.43.

[74] E.g. 1 Kings 15.26, 34; 16.2, 19, 26; 2 Kings 8.18.

[75] Contra VanLandingham, *Judgment and Justification*, 106.

that the righteous are those who observe the Torah. In 7.30–31 predestination and human freedom are set side by side: "But the wicked you have created for the [pur]pose of your anger and from the womb you set them apart for the day of destruction, for (כי) they do not walk on a path that is good but they reject your covenant."[76] The author seems to present two contradictory ideas in these lines since he says that God predestined the wicked for destruction but their end is determined by which path they have chosen.[77] Rather than accusing the hymnist of contradiction in the space of one sentence, the statement, along with the others just noted, can be interpreted as describing human responsibility not necessarily free will. God is just in punishing the wicked because they have actually disobeyed, but, at the same time, they were predisposed to disobedience because God determined that they would walk on evil paths. While this solution may not be philosophically acceptable to many today, it is coherent with the hymnists' view of predestination and responsibility.

Another way of speaking about God's determination of a person's destiny is through the motif of God allocating to a person a particular type of "spirit" (רוח). The divine will is manifest in the present by the spirit that God assigns to each person. While the term רוח has a variety of referents in the Dead Sea Scrolls, in the *Hodayot* two connotations are important for the teaching about predestination.[78] It stands for spiritual beings that influence humans either positively by assisting them to be obedient or negatively by attempting to cause the righteous to sin. In the former case, the spirit can be connected directly with God, for it is "the spirit of your holiness" (6.24). The other important use connects directly with the human being and indicates the person's disposition toward a certain type of lifestyle, either righteousness or wickedness. God ultimately determines the person's disposition when he creates a person and assigns a certain spirit to him or her. The two connotations are brought together when the hymnists describe God giving his holy spirit to some humans.

In the creation hymn in column 9, the term רוח functions as a convenient term to summarise all the aspects of creation. God is credited with creating every spirit: "You formed every spirit and [their] work [you determine]ed and the judgment of all their deeds" (9.10–11).[79] In lines 12–13, the term refers to angels. In the following lines, it refers to heavenly beings such as the sun and stars (lines 13–14) and to meteorological events (lines 14–15). Finally, humans

---

[76] For this reconstruction see Stegemann/Schuller, *1QHodayot*ᵃ, 104.

[77] Licht, "Doctrine," 7; VanLandingham, *Judgment and Justification*, 114.

[78] For the Dead Sea Scrolls generally, see Sekki, *Meaning of Ruaḥ*. His treatment addresses the syntactical use of רוח, which does have its limitations since it assumes more consistency than may have existed.

[79] אתה יצרתה כול רוח ופ̇ע̇ול̇ת̇ם̇ הכינות̇ה̇ ומשנט לכול מעשיהם. Stegemann/Schuller's reconstruction and Newsom's translation (*1QHodayot*ᵃ, 118, 130). See the notes on p.123 for explanation.

possess a "spirit" (line 17). God assigns to each type of spirit certain tasks according to his own pleasure. The sun, moon, and stars travel their paths, while the storms accomplish their purposes (lines 13–15). "The spirit of humanity" was created to live eternally and to each generation certain tasks have been assigned (lines 17–18). God has determined the course of each generation (lines 21–22) and rewards or punishes each generation for the actions of the previous one (lines 19–20).

Holm-Nielsen and Hübner claim that in lines 10–11 the author is referring to two governing beings that rule over humanity and fight against one another.[80] The doctrine is most fully explained in the Two-Spirits sermon of 1QS 3.13–4.26, which describes how God created two governing spirits, the Spirits of Truth and Deceit, and assigned to them a portion of humanity. This pre-temporal decision determines one's final destiny. Although one can be influenced by either Spirit (3.19), a person's lot is determined prior to creation (4.16, 25). The sins of the sons of light are traced to the Angel of Darkness and his cohorts, but God assists his chosen ones (3.24). He purifies them by the spirit of holiness and provides knowledge and wisdom (4.20–23). This text does not only describe a psychological battle raging in the mind of one desiring to join the community, although it does depict the conflict between choosing good or evil.[81] A clear cosmic dualism and predestination underlies this text, since humanity is divided into two groups based on God's decision and ruled over by one of the two spirits.

In spite of sharing the focus on divine sovereignty, predestination, and using the word רוח, the two texts have no other similarities. The hymn in 1QHª 9 nowhere mentions the two spirits or even implies that cosmic spirits rule over part of humanity or wage war against one another. Humanity is not divided into "lots" but viewed instead as a whole. The cosmic dualism that lies at the heart of the Two-Spirits sermon is missing from this creation hymn. The idea could have been inserted easily and would have cohered with the general teaching of the hymn, but to find the two-spirits doctrine here is to read the concept into the text not to derive it from the sentence.

The creation hymn emphasises God's role in determining how each being or aspect of creation remains under his control and does as he intends. It uses the

---

[80] Holm-Nielsen, *Hodayot*, 20n.10; Hübner, "Anthropologischer Dualismus," 269–70. Sekki thinks the statement refers to "demons" because of the syntactical construction רוח כול and because the hymnist is contrasting the creation of the spiritual and material worlds with humanity (*Meaning of Ruaḥ*, 168–69). The syntactical construction, however, is not as uniform as Sekki maintains since כול as a modifier of רוח is not used exclusively as a reference to spiritual beings (cf. 7.23). He also has misunderstood the context, for the contrast is not between, on the one hand, the spiritual and material worlds and, on the other, humanity but between the heavens (9.11b–15a) and the earth (lines 15b–22) (cf. Lange, *Weisheit und Prädestination*, 211).

[81] Contra Wernberg-Moeller, "Reconsideration of the Two Spirits." See Charlesworth, "Critical Comparison," for a response.

term "spirit" as a summarizing word to indicate the similarities between the various aspects of creation. While differences between the beings can be identified, each is united in that they are all spiritual beings under the direction of God.

The same statement, with slight modifications, found in 9.10–11 occurs also in 7.35. Because of human weakness, God "created the spirit (אתה יצרתה רוח) and established its tasks [before eternity], and from you is the way of all living beings (כול חי)." Again, the characteristic features of the Two-Spirits sermon are missing.[82] There is no mention of a Good or Evil Spirit nor are humans divided into lots under the control of a governing spirit.[83] The second part of the line, "from you is the way of all living beings," parallels the first. רוח and כול חי are either synonymous, referring to the human being, or רוח may be more specific in that it might refer to the human's disposition. The use of רוח earlier in this hymn (line 26) suggests the latter interpretation. God gives to each person a certain spirit, and he also determines what each person will do. In contrast to the inability of the human to direct his or her own ways (line 34), God secures the person's future. The statements in lines 34–35 parallel those in lines 25–27, which also develop the contrast between human weakness due to its creaturely condition and God's sovereignty as the one who possess control over "the impulse of every spirit" (יצר כול רוח) (line 26) and determines its tasks before even creating it.

The phrase אתה יצרתה רוח found in 7.35 and 9.10–11 also appears in 18.24: "for you have formed the sp[irit of your servant and according to] your [wi]ll you have established me."[84] Rather than describing God as the Creator of all humanity, the statement focuses on God's role in the life of the elect. The statement is more specific than the others since it indicates the creation of the elect, which brings the concept of predestination to the foreground.

The connection between "spirit" language and predestination also appears in 1QHᵃ 6.22–23. Stegemann and Schuller reconstruct the text as follows: ותשכל עֿבדך] ב   גור]לֿוֹת אנוש כי לפי רוחות תפֿילם בין טוב לרשע [וֿתכן]תם פעולתם°°[   ] The translation provided is: "And you have caused your servant to have insight [lo]ts of humankind. For according to (their) spirits you cast (the lot) for them between good and evil, [and] you have determined [   ] *tm* their recompense."[85] The lacunae make the text very ambiguous, and several alternative reconstructions and a variety of interpretations have

---

[82] Contra Hübner, "Anthropologischer Dualismus," 269; cf. Frey, "Flesh and Spirit," 380.

[83] Sekki connects this line and line 26 with the two-spirits doctrine because he understands "spirit" in 1QS 3 as a spiritual disposition (*Meaning of Ruaḥ*, 134). His reading of 1QS 3.13–15 is incorrect at this point.

[84] The reconstruction is generally accepted.

[85] Stegemann/Schuller, *1QHodayotᵃ*, 88, 96. See also p.92 for the notes on the text and plate IV.

B. Divine Saving Acts and Human Obedience

been offered.[86] The first two words are arrived at by the placement of fragments 44.3 (ות), the third line of SHR 4284 frg (שכל), and 22.7 (upper part of *lamed* and עבדך). The reconstruction גור[ל]וֹת by Stegemann and Schuller is rare.[87] Others opt for a form of רוח[88] or leave the space blank.[89] The letters prior to לם on תּפִֿילם have been reconstructed in several ways. Most agree that a *waw* or *yod* preceded the letters. Mansoor restores [ע]וֹלם ("[ete]rnal"),[90] but this does not fill the space, which seems to have room for 2–4 letters.[91] Others propose a form of the verb בדל ("to divide, separate").[92] This seems to be what lies behind the translation by Abegg: "For by their spirits You distinguish between the good and the wicked."[93] If one accepts this reconstruction, then second person masculine singular (תבד[י]לם) is more likely than third masculine singular (Lohse) because of the context. The *mem* on תבד[י]לם would be the third masculine plural suffix,[94] and it most likely refers to humanity as a whole.[95] Stegemann and Schuller think the gap is not large enough for this word.[96] Their proposal of תפילם requires only space for two letters, and they think it is more probable because גורלות often occurs with נפל (cf. 11.23; 15.37). Their argument is circular, however, since they reconstruct גור[ל]וֹת on the basis of their reconstruction of תפילם, and then use the reconstruction of גור[ל]וֹת to justify reconstructing תפילם. The space prior to תםֿֿ is also filled in various ways. Many read [לה]תם (from תמם), translating it as either "to destroy"[97] or with the idea of perfection,[98] but this does not adequately fill the gap.

---

[86] García Martínez/Tigchelaar reconstruct the sentence as ותשלכ עבדך [. . .רוח]ת אנוש כי לפי רוחות . . . ולם בין טוב לרשע [ות]כן [. . .להוד]עתם פעולתם and translate it: "And you teach to your servant [. . . the spirit]s of man, for corresponding to the spirits . . . them between good and evil and set over them [to sho]w them their actions" (*DSSSE*, 152–53).

[87] Cf. Maier/Schubert, *Qumran-Essener*, 232: "[. . .] des Menschen, denn gemäß den Geistern ihres [Lo]ses (?) im Guten oder im Fevel [. . .] ihr Werk."

[88] García Martínez/Tigchelaar, *DSSSE*, 152.

[89] Sukenik, *Dead Sea Scrolls*, plate 48; Lohse, *Texte*, 162.

[90] Mansoor, *Thanksgiving Hymns*, 181n.4; also Dupont-Sommer, *Essene Writings*, 244.

[91] Cf. Holm-Nielsen, *Hodayot*, 220n.5.

[92] See Lohse, *Texte*, 162: יַבְדִּ[י]לֵם, which is Hiphil imperfect 3ms with 3mp suffix: "denn entsprechend den Geistern [scheidet] er sie zwischen dem Guten und dem Frevelhaften" (p.163). Holm-Nielsen suggests hiphil infinitive (*Hodayot*, 220n.5).

[93] Abegg, "Thanksgiving Psalms," 88. Cf. Vermes, *Complete Dead Sea Scrolls*, 248: "[For Thou hast divided men] into good and evil in accordance with the spirits of their lot;" Gaster, *Dead Sea Scriptures*, 196: "[and stray not in the waywar]dness of men, but, through the spirit of [discern]ment which is theirs, [distinguish] the good from the wicked [and keep] their deeds undefiled."

[94] Cf. the translation of García Martínez/Tigchelaar and Lohse.

[95] Cf. Holm-Nielsen, *Hodayot*, 220n.5.

[96] They claim that one must presume that the material "has crumpled laterally about 2 mm" which it had done in the previous two lines. The damage in lines 19–21, however, is not obvious in line 22 (Stegemann/Schuller, *1QHodayot^a*, 93).

[97] Mansoor, *Thanksgiving Hymns*, 181.

[98] Gaster, *Dead Sea Scriptures*, 196: "keep undefiled."

Although the textual issues make any interpretation uncertain, one can still judge some more plausible than others. Many commentators find in this text the notion of the two-spirits doctrine.[99] This suggestion has more to commend it than attempts to find the concept in 7.35 and 9.11. Not only is the term רוח used, but also the contrast between good and evil coheres with the description in 1QS 3–4. The statement seems to develop a notion of predestination or determinism. Nevertheless, it is doubtful that the hymnist is drawing on this concept, at least explicitly. The context does not develop the idea, and the lack of cosmic dualism in the rest of the *Hodayot* makes it somewhat suspect to find it here and only here.[100] One can make good sense of the statement without importing a concept that is not explicitly mentioned or required. While the "two spirit" idea may reside in the background,[101] at the very least, one cannot agree with Merrill that "the two spirits are clearly mentioned."[102]

Reconstructing בדל as a hiphil infinitive, Holm-Nielsen proposes that the lines describe the righteous person's capability to differentiate between good and evil.[103] He bases his interpretation on the analogous statement in 15.15, which uses similar terms. The hymnist describes his role in God's judgment of each human: "For all those who strive against me, you condemn guilty at the judgment, dividing (להבדיל) by me between the righteous and the wicked (בין צדיק לרשע)." Two problems arise, however. First, 15.15 is not an accurate parallel, since it describes the role of the righteous hymnist in God's judgment of wicked and righteous persons. It does not refer to "spirits," nor does it describe the moral choice that the righteous person makes. Second, the *Hodayot* does not depict humans as choosing between either a spirit of good or evil. The righteous person remains a sinner and a depraved spirit until death, but the *Hodayot* never depicts a psychological battle within one's will.

---

[99] Ringgren, *Faith of Qumran*, 75; Merrill, *Qumran and Predestination*, 28; Dupont-Sommer, *Essene Writings*, 244n.2; VanLandingham, *Judgment and Justification*, 114; cf. Licht "Doctrine," 91n.83.

[100] The idea of personal, evil spirits is not foreign to the *Hodayot*. According to the common reconstruction of 4.35, the hymnist seeks divine protection from "evil spirits" that would try to prevent him from obeying God's commandments. "Belial" also is mentioned several times although no details about him are provided. The term בליעל appears eleven times (10.18, 24; 11.29, 30, 33; 12.11, 14; 13.28, 41; 14.4; 15.6), but often it is not clear if it should be understood as a personal name or as a noun meaning "worthless, destructive, or wicked." The primary interest throughout the *Hodayot* is not this figure's rule over humans but in the similarities between his actions and the wicked. In 12.13–15, for example, the hymnist writes that God hates "all the thoughts (מחשבת) of Belial," but the hypocrites "plan (יחשובו) the devices of Belial" when they do not seek God properly (cf. 10.18).

[101] Cf. Hyatt, "View of Man," 280; Licht, "Doctrine," 6.

[102] Merrill, *Qumran and Predestination*, 28.

[103] Holm-Nielsen, *Hodayot*, 220n.5. Cf. Ringgren, *Faith of Qumran*, 76.

B. Divine Saving Acts and Human Obedience

Sekki disputes the widely accepted claim that this statement (6.22–23) develops the notion that God predestines a person's spiritual disposition. He notes that the following lines portray the hymnist's religious attitude as changing as he progresses within the community. The statements imply spiritual growth and human activity, which Sekki takes to mean that a person's spiritual disposition could not have been "determined unchangeably from birth."[104] His conclusion, however, fails to account for statements throughout the *Hodayot* (and even in 1QS 3–4) that those predestined for salvation will still sin. The disposition is unchangeable in that God determines that it will be manifest during the person's life and culminate in the person's final salvation, but this does not mean that the person always and only lives in accordance with it. Moreover, Sekki's contention that human activity renders the notion of predestination inappropriate is inaccurate because throughout the *Hodayot* human action is seen as the outworking of a prior divine action. There is, then, no opposition to understanding 6.22–23 as describing God assigning to individual humans a disposition toward good or evil.

The sentence in 6.22–23 most likely describes God assigning one type of spirit to each human rather than God giving each human over to a certain Spirit. The dualistic idea is found not in the cosmic realm but on the individual level as God distinguishes between the righteous and the wicked according to the spirit he has assigned them. Whereas the cosmic dualism evident in the Two-Spirits sermon focuses on groups of individual persons, the Hymns focus on the individual person. 6.22–23 utilise an ethical dualism to demonstrate God's sovereign control over the destinies of each human being.

The texts analysed thus far indicate a close relationship between the concept of divine sovereignty and the term "spirit" (רוח). God rules over all the "spirits," whether spiritual or material beings, because he is the Creator. He determines the tasks that each will do. He separates humanity according to the type of spirit he assigns them, whether good or evil, which suggests a notion of double predestination. 6.22–23 evidences the use of "spirit" to refer to a spiritual disposition, which in this case is assigned by God. Licht aptly summarises, "The term spirit . . . is thus best defined as the vehicle of determination, or as the carrier of divinely ordained characteristic, or that part of the human being which receives these characteristic traits – i.e. man's personality."[105]

Apart from divine intervention, humans are "a spirit of flesh" (5.30). The combination of רוח and בשר indicates that the human has a disposition associated with the status of being a creature. "Flesh" stands in this context for weakness, inability, and ultimately sinfulness. A "corrupt spirit" also rules the human (lines 32–33). Although the verb "rules" (משלה) could suggest that the

---

[104] Sekki, *Meaning of Ruaḥ*, 131 (emphasis added). He is contrasting this text with 1QS 3–4, 1QH^a 7, and 4Q186.

[105] Licht, "Doctrine," 91; cf. Frey, "Flesh and Spirit," 380, 382n.83.

hymnist is thinking about an external force that asserts its own will and desires onto the human,[106] it probably indicates the control that the sinful condition of the human spirit has over the human. The expression is the last in a string of phrases intended to demonstrate the complete worthlessness and sinfulness of the human. Each of these phrases describes how the hymnists view the human agent. They are not concerned with external, personal beings that influence humanity, but rather with the control exerted over the human by his or her own depraved nature.[107] This is consistent with the other uses of the phrase רוח נעוה (8.18; 9.24; 11.22; 19.15). This "depraved spirit" is something from which God redeems the elect.

Unlike the wicked, who are left to their depraved spirits, the righteous are given another spirit. God himself intervenes by putting his spirit into the righteous, thereby both electing some unto salvation while also overcoming the negative impact and effects of their depraved spirits. Since humans are unable to direct their paths because they are "flesh" and "creatures of clay," God "creates" for some a spirit that "establishes" their path (12.32).[108] The statement highlights divine action in the specific form of predestination, for God gives to some a spirit that overcomes their creaturely weaknesses. The term "spirit," Sekki rightly concludes, refers to the type of disposition that God gives to the human.[109] Sekki, however, downplays the act of predestination, choosing instead to emphasise human action. He argues that the statement, in dependence on Ezekiel 36, means "that God himself must create the kind of disposition in man which enables him to lead a godly life."[110] The context indicates precisely the opposite conclusion. Predestination is clearly evident in 1QH^a 12.39 ("for you created the just and wicked"), and this portion of the hymn is devoted to God's redemptive acts. It is not by human action that one overcomes the effects of one's creaturely, sinful condition and secures one's own path. Rather, it is by God's mercy, and to this one clings despite affliction (line 37).

The expression "by the spirit which you put in me" (ברוח אשר נתתה בי) functions as a technical phrase to denote God's salvific actions (5.36; 8.29; 20.14–15; 21.34). God intervenes in the human's life and not only alters one's being, but also actually imparts a new spirit, his own spirit, that leads the human into knowledge and teaches him how to obey God. The language is reminiscent of Ezekiel 11 and 36–37.[111] The Lord declares to Ezekiel his intention to give a new spirit to the people and to replace their heart of stone with a heart of flesh (11.19; 36.26). This new spirit is identified with God's own spirit

---

[106] Mansoor, *Thanksgiving Hymns*, 179n.7; Brownlee, "Anthropology and Soteriology," 229.
[107] Sekki, *Meaning of Ruaḥ*, 138–39.
[108] Cf. Frey, "Flesh and Spirit," 380.
[109] Sekki, *Meaning of Ruaḥ*, 124–28.
[110] Sekki, *Meaning of Ruaḥ*, 128.
[111] See Yates, *Spirit and Creation in Paul*, 78–82.

B. Divine Saving Acts and Human Obedience

(36.27; 37.14). God also will purify the people from their uncleanliness and idol worship (11.18; 36.25). Because God has cleansed them and given a new spirit, the people will obey his commandments (11.20; 36.27). Although key points from these chapters are missing, the hymnists likely derive the phrase ברוח אשר נתתה בי from these sections.[112] They find here a clear statement of God's intent to redeem his people. The hymnists transpose the language from its original application to the people as a whole to reflect their individualistic theology. God's spirit is placed in the individual, not just the community of the redeemed. From this perspective, God's decision to give his spirit represents predestination since not all receive the spirit. The hymnists never ponder why they are chosen, but they likely view their acceptance as an act of grace. They learn from Ezekiel 36.31 that God gives his spirit and restores the people despite their sin.

The spirit is assigned several titles that relate to the various functions that it has. It is the "spirit of knowledge" (1QH^a 6.36), who unveils God's mysteries, exposes human sinfulness, and reveals the way of righteousness. The spirit is associated with God's holiness and in this role purifies sinners (8.30).[113] The two titles and the roles they represent are not carefully distinguished, for the "spirit of your holiness" often reveals knowledge. The hymnist can also speak of God placing "spirits" in him (מרוחות אשר נתתה בי) (4.29), which likely stands for the various roles that the single spirit of God has.[114] Within these roles, the spirit, as an external being, assists the human to be obedient to God's commandments. He works against the "fleshly spirit" of the human. The spirit is not a reward for obedience, but rather the cause of one's obedience.[115] The

---

[112] There is no mention of idolatry (11.18, 21; 36.25) or returning to the land (11.16–17; 36.24, 28–30, 33–38; 37.14), and the phrase "heart of flesh" (11.19; 36.26) would probably not have appealed to the hymnist because of the negative connotations they assign to "flesh." The phrase ברוח אשר נתתה בי has also been adopted slightly, but this is to be expected since the Lord is speaking in Ezekiel.

[113] Cf. Licht, "Doctrine," 92.

[114] Sekki suggests that רוחות refers to the human spirit, but this is less likely than the interpretation offered here (*Meaning of Ruaḥ*, 136). The hymnist never says that humans have multiple spirits, dispositions, or anything else. Although the preposition on רוח is typically ב not מן, the clause otherwise matches the standard formula drawn from Ezekiel. The context does not mention "spiritual qualities such as righteousness and insight" (136) that could be acquired within the community (nor is the community even hinted at). The attempt by Sekki to contrast this hymn with 1QH^a 7 (and 1QS 3–4) on the basis that 1QH^a 4 gives evidence that one's spiritual disposition has not been established from birth as 1QH^a 7 (and 1QS 3–4) implies completely misunderstands the function of predestination in the *Hodayot*. The hymnist does not describe two groups of people that are completely separated and, at least for the righteous, uninfluenced by the other. The hymnist maintains throughout that he had an evil spirit from birth, although God had determined to give him a spirit of righteousness. He was predetermined to have God's Spirit at birth, although until the moment of revelation he would be controlled by the evil spirit.

[115] Cf. Mansoor, *Thanksgiving Hymns*, 76.

108   *Chapter 2: God's Gracious Acts of Deliverance in the Hodayot*

idea that God gives his spirit apart from human obedience reinforces the doctrine of predestination as well as underscores the gracious nature of God's actions.

These motifs discussed above indicate God's involvement in the lives of all humans right from the outset. He determines who will be among the righteous or the wicked prior to birth. The righteous he creates to be obedient and to enjoy eternal life, but the wicked he creates for destruction. He establishes the path of the righteous and gives to them his spirit of holiness. The concepts analysed develop a doctrine of predestination that informs much of the hymnists' thoughts about the divine-human relationship.

Purpose of Predestination. The scholarly discussion about the Qumran doctrine of predestination (1) has focused primarily on the relationship between predestination and free will and (2) usually combines various statements from diverse documents without first understanding the function of predestination within a certain text. While an explanation of the concept may appear to handle the texts as a whole, one often finds that the explanation fails to address adequately the particulars of a single text. In terms of the *Hodayot*, Merrill's *Qumran and Predestination* focuses on this document. He traces the connection of predestination with various other teachings and demonstrates its importance for the hymnists, even concluding that it is the fundamental doctrine of the *Hodayot*.[116] Nevertheless, he provides no rationale for why predestination is so important to the hymnists.[117] While possible reasons are hinted at occasionally, a full explanation is never provided.

A reason for the focus on predestination and election does present itself: this teaching serves to counter the pessimistic anthropology. Because the human's moral failings extend back to his origin, God's actions must extend back that far also. Predestination sets God's actions prior to any human action, thereby overcoming the negative effects of human nature and making the human completely dependent on God's unconditional grace. One hymnist explains how God knew him prior to his birth and watched over him even as a child (17.29–30). Concerning the just one, another writes, "From the womb you established him for the period of approval," and his obedience was determined by God at the outset (7.27–30). He will be redeemed from the inabilities that plague him as a creature (cf. lines 25–27). In other instances, the hymnists explain how God reverses the problem of the sinful nature by overcoming their creaturely status. As a creature of clay, a human cannot understand God's ways without him opening one's ears and eyes, thus making it possible for one to grasp the truth.[118] The doctrine of predestination provides the solution to humanity's problem with sin since ac-

---

[116] Merrill, *Qumran and Predestination*, 57.

[117] In a section entitled "The Importance of Predestination in 1QH," he discusses possible sources for the concept but never states why it is important (Merrill, *Qumran and Predestination*, 12–15).

[118] 6.15; 9.23; 20.36–37; 21.6; 22.26, 31; 25.12. Cf. Schnabel, *Law and Wisdom*, 174.

B. Divine Saving Acts and Human Obedience

cording to this teaching God acts for his own pleasure to redeem those whom he chooses. He reverses the effects of their depraved natures.

The contrast between the human spirit that is "fleshy" and "corrupt" and the divine spirit that purifies and gives knowledge further enhances the suggestion that the concept of predestination counters the problem of human sin by overcoming it from its beginning point. The human spirit is characterised by inability, weakness, and sinfulness, and because of the human's natural spirit, no human can comprehend God's mysteries or obey the covenant's demands. The intervention of God, however, marks a drastic change, for the human's wretched spirit is replaced by God's spirit of holiness and knowledge, which then enables the human to understand and obey. God overcomes the human's creaturely condition by giving his own spirit which is not limited by the sinfulness of the creature. This gracious divine act represents predestination since God gives his spirit only to those he desires. The inherent problem faced by the human due to one's creaturely sinfulness is addressed prior to one's birth, although it takes a lifetime for the solution to manifest itself fully.

This link with creation is supported also by Yates' recent argument that one finds a contrast between the original creation and the new creation in the statements that describe a spirit as "formed" in humankind and as "given" to humans by God. The former draw on Genesis 2.7 and the latter on Ezekiel 37.6, 14.[119] With constant hints to the original creation, Ezekiel 36–37 refers to an eschatological event in which creation is renewed through God's spirit.[120] This is what one finds in the *Hodayot* when the hymnists draw upon Ezekiel 36–37 and place their references within creation contexts.[121] Because this divine act of imparting his spirit is understood as an eschatological act of recreation, one can draw the conclusion that election is intended to overcome the problems that the hymnists identify with the original creation.

It is incorrect, therefore, to claim, as some do, that predestination functions as the basis of the hymnists' thought and spurs their reflections on human depravity.[122] These two vital teachings seem to be interlocking blocks that support and develop one another. One cannot determine simply from the hymns which idea the hymnists developed first. Both ideas are found in the scriptures, and it is more likely that the hymnists radicalised the scriptural teachings than that they conceived of one idea prior to the other.

---

[119] Yates, *Spirit and Creation in Paul*, 81–82.
[120] Yates, *Spirit and Creation in Paul*, 76–82.
[121] Yates, *Spirit and Creation in Paul*, 31–34, 38–41.
[122] Merrill, *Qumran and Predestination*, 12–13, 57; Condra, *Salvation for the Righteous Revealed*, 172–73.

The concept of predestination emphasises divine action and is ultimately an expression of God's grace.[123] The decision to elect someone occurs apart from and without any regard for what a human being does. The concept cannot be reduced to foreknowledge in the Hodayot because predestination is viewed as an eternal decision made by God prior to creation. The concept, however, should not be considered abstractly and apart from its intended goal. The notion is not devoid of human action since the goal of God's decision to elect someone is that the depraved, creaturely condition will be altered in order that the human may be obedient. The reason God assigns his spirit to certain individuals is his sovereign will, and by the spirit, the human is able to obey God's commands. The language of walking according to God's way refers to obedience to the Torah. When God establishes the righteous person's path, he determines that he or she will obey the Mosaic Torah (as interpreted by the community). Obedience is the intended goal and outcome of God's decision to act. Predestination is not a speculative doctrine concerned only with the mysterious, hidden will of God. It is, instead, a practical doctrine focused on addressing a particular problem, human sinfulness, in order to accomplish a particular result, human obedience.

Predestination and "Free Will." While the doctrine of predestination establishes divine action at the forefront of the divine-human relationship, this idea does not absolve the human agent of responsibility for one's actions. The hymnists maintain throughout that humans are ultimately responsible for their action. The seeming incoherence of the relationship between statements about human agency and those about predestination (divine agency) reflects, according to many scholars, a profound difficulty that runs throughout the *Hodayot* and the other Qumran literature.[124] In terms of the *Hodayot* specifically, several solutions have been offered, none of which are satisfactory.[125]

VanLandingham thinks the hymns are unclear, due of course to their genre, and that Qumran theology must have included human freedom. He bases this claim on the various commands, vows, and prayers for repentance found in the *Hodayot*, which "make no sense unless humans can choose their own path."[126]

---

[123] Contra VanLandingham, *Judgment and Justification*, 115. His further claim that "in the *Hodayot*ᵃ God predestines the righteous and the wicked, but not directly the damned and those not" contradicts the text, since the hymnist maintains that God created the righteous, who will be given eternal life, and created the wicked, who will be punished (see 7.27–32). If God assigns a person to one group or the other, then the outcome is assured.

[124] On Qumran thought generally, see Sanders, *Paul and Palestinian Judaism*, 264–68; Bockmuehl, "1QS and Salvation at Qumran," 396–97.

[125] Several scholars suggest that the hymnists were not systematic thinkers and never perceived the tension between predestination and free will (e.g. Licht, "Doctrine," 7). Holm-Nielsen argues that predestination was a theoretical perspective used to explain the current situation while experience showed free will (*Hodayot*, 281–82). This is similar to Sanders' view of the Dead Sea Scrolls as a whole ("Dead Sea Sect," 29–32).

[126] VanLandingham, *Judgment and Justification*, 113–15 (quote from 113).

B. Divine Saving Acts and Human Obedience

Two points should be noted, however. First, this argument fails to account for the hymnists' pessimistic anthropology. The human agent cannot obey God's commands by virtue of his or her nature. The hymnists' understanding of sin and the human nature rule out an absolute freedom. Second, the commands are only given to the elect not the general population, and the prayers for assistance and forgiveness can only be offered by those in the community. The hymnists do not describe a situation in which one is free to do as one pleases. Each is under the constraint of one's spirit or inclination, a disposition assigned by God prior to creation.

Merrill advocates another position. God has put spirits into the world to influence human beings, and he knows who will respond to which spiritual influence. Those who will respond to his grace, Merrill argues, God draws to himself through the community. Those who choose to act wickedly, he rejects.[127] In this perspective, predestination is a response to human decisions. This solution, however, reduces predestination to foreknowledge, thus emptying it of any meaning for the hymnists. Nowhere in the *Hodayot* is obedience made the basis for God's decision to elect someone to salvation.

Rejecting these types of solutions, Hopkins proposes that God gives to certain persons the ability to respond to his revelation, which they may accept or reject according to their own decision, while assigning others to wickedness, thereby making it impossible for them to respond to his revelation even if they so desired.[128] As with the other attempts noted above, this explanation should be rejected. Not only is Hopkins forced to turn to 1QS and CD as a basis for this view, a methodology that she repeatedly chastises other scholars for adopting,[129] but it is the exact opposite of what one might deduce from some statements in the *Hodayot*. According to the common interpretation of 7.27–32, which provides the clearest explanation for double predestination in the *Hodayot*, the hymnist gives a reason for why the wicked are predestined for the day

---

[127] Merrill, *Qumran and Predestination*, 42–43; 46–51.

[128] "This cosmological dualism can be combined with the idea of predestination by saying that only those whom God has preordained for righteousness may receive his revelation, although they do not have to. Those predestined to wickedness, however, have been blinded to God's enlightening revelation, so that even if they wanted to they could not receive it. Thus those who are predestined with the ability to respond to God's revelation may influence their own destinies by the attitude which they adopt toward such revelation" (Hopkins, "Qumran Community," 350). For a similar assessment, she notes Holm-Nielsen, *Hodayot*, 281–82, especially n.16; and Brownlee, "Anthropology and Soteriology," 214.

[129] For the references to 1QS and CD, see Hopkins, "Qumran Community," 351. For her critique of how many scholars subject 1QH^a to 1QS, see 349 and elsewhere. The only evidence she adduces from 1QH^a is 6.30, which indicates different levels of righteousness within the community (351). This hardly supports her point that those predestined for righteousness can reject God's call.

of slaughter, but the righteous are not said to accept God's revelation.[130] It is the wicked who have rejected God, not the righteous who have chosen God.[131]

These three proposals also impose a particular definition of "free will" onto the *Hodayot*. For these actions to be genuine human actions, it is implied, humans must be morally free and thus capable of determining their own direction. The hymnists, however, do not conceive of human action in this manner. The only genuine human actions are those accomplished with divine assistance. The human agent is not human because he can act independently of God; rather, one is truly human because he or she depends on God for empowerment. The contradiction between predestination and free will that some commentators find in the *Hodayot* judges it solely based on their own conceptions of what true freedom is. For the hymnists, however, these ideas of freedom fail to grasp both the radical inability of humanity and the all-encompassing power of God.

This difficulty in relating predestination with certain understandings of free will ignores or downplays the hymnists' understanding of the relationship between human and divine action. According to the hymnists, underlying every action taken by a human is a corresponding action made by God. To walk according to God's heart means God must have established this as the path for one to walk. One acquires knowledge only because God has revealed it. The wicked perform deeds of unrighteousness because God gave them a spirit of wickedness. A person's actions reveal the category to which one belongs, and one's actions are the outworking of a decision made by God. There are no random coincidences; rather, there is always a cause and effect, which has God as the ultimate cause.

The hymnists can exhort one to obedience or describe themselves as avoiding sin because they know, by virtue of God's revelation, that God has already empowered them to obey and avoid sin. Likewise, they can claim that one is damned based on disobedience, while claiming that God's eternal decision underlies this person's actions. Thus, the "blatant contradiction" in 7.30–31, as Licht calls it, arises more from the interpreter's failure to perceive the underlying logic than the author's inability to think clearly.[132] God's pre-temporal decision to create some people righteous and others wicked is repeatedly stated in the context (see lines 27–28, 30, 35, 37). When the wicked actually reject God's covenant and do evil, they manifest the decision made by God.[133]

---

[130] Mansoor, *Thanksgiving Hymns*, 56–57.

[131] Contra Merrill, *Qumran and Predestination*, 41, nothing is said here about election unto salvation being based on God's knowledge of who would choose him.

[132] Licht, "Doctrine," 7; cf. VanLandingham, *Judgment and Justification*, 114: "obvious contradiction."

[133] This interpretation of 7.30–31 is the opposite of Brownlee. He argues that God foreknew that the wicked would disobey him, but he proceeded to create them anyways, which cements their destiny. He writes, "If God foresees that certain people will turn out wicked and yet he proceeds to create them, he is thereby foreordaining their wicked lives" ("Anthropology and Soteriology," 236). Nothing is stated in the context about divine foreknowledge and God's act being determined by what humans do.

With this emphasis on divine providence, the hymnists differ considerably from Ben Sira. According to Ben Sira, God created humans with free will and the moral capacity to obey. Human freedom is absolutely necessary in order to protect God from the charge of being responsible for evil (Sir 15.14–17). The hymnists, however, do not give thought to this tension because they do not think humans are capable of living morally apart from divine assistance. They come close to attributing the origin of evil to God with their idea that humans are morally depraved due to the material from which they are created and the claim that God created the wicked. Nevertheless, they maintain that the wicked are ultimately responsible for their disobedience. The pessimistic anthropology in the *Hodayot* necessitates, for the hymnists, divine intervention, and the possibility of a human obeying of his or her own will is simply ludicrous.

To summarise: Predestination functions to counteract the anthropological problem by setting divine action temporally before the human comes into existence. God determines what path each person will travel and assigns to each a particular spirit. For those destined to righteousness, he imparts his own spirit as the means of predestination. The hymnists' focus on predestination highlights the basic pattern of the divine-human relationship. God initiates the salvation process and sustains those he elects. The emphasis on divine action, however, does not eliminate the human. Those elected for salvation by God reveal the divine decision when they obey the Torah. Predestination is not an abstract teaching. It rather leads to the human becoming a real agent, one empowered by God to obey his will.

b. The Gift of Knowledge

In his account of creation, Ben Sira explained that God gave knowledge of good and evil to humans (Sir 17.6–7). God did this to enable humans to determine their own destiny. With knowledge comes responsibility and power. Ben Sira's interest is the human. The statements about knowledge in the *Hodayot*, though, focus on God's gracious act, not the human's capacity to choose. Knowledge is imparted only to the elect. Whereas Ben Sira prioritised the human over God, the hymnists do the opposite. As will be noted below, the emphasis placed on God is necessary because of the hymnists' pessimistic anthropology, but it does not eliminate the human. The divine act of imparting knowledge becomes a means through which one obeys. Again, the spirit plays a crucial role.

The gift aspect of knowledge is evident in the claim that only the elect possess God's knowledge. "To the sons of truth you have given intelligence" (18.29). The hymnist thanks God because "you have made known to me (הודעתני) the foundation of truth" (19.19), and the servant of God is the one who has "the insight of knowledge to understand your wonders" (lines 30–31). Knowledge cannot be acquired apart from God revealing it to an individual. Sanders has correctly argued that "knowledge is the means and sign of election. One is brought into the covenant by being given knowledge and knowledge of God's secrets characterizes the elect."[134] Possessing knowledge serves to distinguish the elect from the non-elect, and it is on this basis that the community will allow a person to join.[135] In one of the few references to the community and particularly entrance into the community, the hymnist explains that a person is brought near (אגישנו) "according to his intelligence" (6.29–30).[136] This indicates that a person possesses some insight before entering the community. The fact that a person has some intelligence likely indicated to the community authorities that the person was elected by God. In this respect, knowledge has a very real function as a "sign of election."

The knowledge of God's dealings with humanity is beyond the grasp of the human because of one's creaturely, sinful state. One remains ignorant of God and his ways unless God intervenes. As the rhetorical questions at the end of column 20 show, God alone can enlighten and instruct. The focus throughout this hymn is on God's position over creation.[137] Creation works like a clock (lines 4–14), never faltering from its predetermined tasks "because the God of knowledge has established it" (lines 13–14). Despite God revealing the order of creation to him, the instructor admits that he does not fully understand God's mysteries (lines 22–23). His inability to understand results from his sinful state, for he is formed from clay and he will return to the dust. Even at the judgment, he will not be able to provide an account of his actions (lines 27–34). His only hope is for God to give him knowledge. Thus, he appeals to God:

> What can I say unless you open my mouth? How can I understand unless you instruct me? What can I [say] without you opening my heart? How can I make straight (my) path unless you establish [my] ste[ps? How] can [my] steps stand [unless you] strengthen (me) with strength? How can I arise [. . .]? (lines 36–38)

The hymnist declares his inability and places himself completely at the mercy of God. He turns to the God of knowledge for he recognises, only because God has revealed it to him, that he stands in need of enlightening (cf. 6.26; 12.6; 21.5–6). He acknowledges that God alone can instruct him and give him knowledge.

---

[134] Sanders, *Paul and Palestinian Judaism*, 259.

[135] According to the *Community Rule*, the novice enters the community by taking an oath to obey the Torah (1QS 5.7–11). His intelligence and adherence to the Torah are evaluated by the members of the community (5.20–22; cf. 6.18).

[136] Abegg translates the verb אגישנו in line 30 as "I will advance him" ("Thanksgiving Hymns," 88). This suggests movement within the hierarchical leadership of the community. Stegemann and Schuller suggest that from לפי in line 29 until the end of line 33 "could be a citation of the text of the entrance ceremony, perhaps the words spoken concerning those being received, a 'liturgy' in which the one responsible for the new candidate stated his obligations" (*1QHodayot*ᵃ, 93).

[137] Several damaged spots, especially at the beginning and end of lines, create some ambiguity, but the general sense of the hymn is clear.

B. Divine Saving Acts and Human Obedience

In a hymn about creation, the author remarks, "These things I know through your knowledge because you opened my ears to wondrous mysteries" (9.23). These "wondrous mysteries" are the order and regulation of creation (lines 9–22), which God established by his wisdom and knowledge (lines 9, 16, 21). The human cannot comprehend how God created the world because he himself is a product of the world, a creature who remains in sin and "depraved without knowledge" (lines 23–25). The "God of knowledge" (line 28) must reveal himself and his ways to the human. The pattern of divine and human action is clear from this sentence, for the hymnist claims knowledge of God's actions because God has revealed it to him.

The expressions "you open my ears/eyes/heart" appear throughout the hymns as a statement about what God has done in order to reveal himself and his ways to humanity. The expressions denote how the human was previously closed off to God and the path to salvation, but now how God, by mercy and grace, has imparted his knowledge to the human and revealed the means to salvation. The hymnist is limited in his abilities, so he asks of God: "[Ho]w can I see without you opening my eyes and hear [without you opening my ears]?" (21.5–6). God opens one's ears and heart to hear his truth (9.23; 14.7; 22.31), thereby empowering his elect to obey his commandments (21.10) and to proclaim his knowledge (20.33–34). God's action perplexes the hymnist for God has not revealed the truth to the righteous but to one who has "uncircumcised ears" (21.6). These expressions contrast with the pessimistic anthropology, which attribute human inability to one's creatureliness. A human cannot understand God because his or her ears are unable to hear and his or her eyes incapable of seeing. The hymnist knows about the order of creation only because God has "opened my ears," and God has done this "although I am a creature of clay" (9.23). By opening one's ears, eyes, or heart, God intervenes directly at the source of the problem.

Elsewhere the hymnist thanks God for giving him a "spirit of knowledge."[138] Lying behind this simple statement is an elaborate theology, part of which has already been discussed. The connection between predestination and the divine spirit was observed above. In this context, one should note how the divinely appointed means for giving knowledge is though the spirit. On several occasions, the hymnists write, "I know because of the spirit which you have given me" (5.35–36; 20.14–15; 21.34). The spirit is the imparter of knowledge.

By giving the spirit, who reveals God and his ways to the human, God takes the initiative in the salvation process. Because of this divine action, the human agent acts. The progression is clear in 6.23–25: "I know because of your knowledge that in your kindness toward m[a]n [you] have enlar[ged his share with] your holy spirit. Therefore, you cause me to draw near to your knowledge (תגישני לבינתך), and as I approach, I oppose all doers of evil and men of

---

[138] 6.26: "I, your servant, you have gifted me (חנותני) with a spirit of knowledge."

guile." The relationship is initiated by God who reveals himself to the hymnist through his holy spirit, the bearer of divine knowledge. The hiphil verb תגישני suggests that God remains the underlying cause of the hymnist's actions. Although the hymnist can describe himself as approaching God, he acknowledges that his opposition to wickedness is the result of God drawing him. He would not oppose evil if God had not revealed the truth to him and given him the spirit to assist him. The action, though, is not attributed to God in such a manner as to eliminate the reality of the hymnist's action. He can claim to approach God and to oppose evil as his own doings even while acknowledging God's underlying work. Divine and human are not set in opposition here, and although divine action is given priority, this does not make the human action insignificant or negotiable. The expected result of God's action is human obedience.

The crucial role of the spirit in the imparting of knowledge appears in 20.14–16, which also juxtaposes divine and human action. The instructor knows God "because of the spirit which you put in me" (ברוח אשר נתתה בי) (lines 14–15). Although God has revealed himself to Moses and the prophets, this knowledge can only be accessed if God has given the spirit. The giving of the spirit and understanding motivates the hymnist to "listen faithfully" to God's "wonderful counsel" (line 15). The hymnist has prioritised divine action and made it the basis from which he acts. The phrase "through your spirit of holiness" (ברוח קודשכה) modifies "listen."[139] In 1QH^a ברוח always modifies the preceding verb, and often it explains how the hymnist accomplishes something. The hymnist's ability to listen to God comes by means of the spirit. This modifying phrase places the emphasis on divine action, but it does not negate the hymnist's part.

Because of his insight into God's actions, the hymnist worships God, seeks forgiveness for his transgressions, and desires to serve God more faithfully (8.24–25). Knowledge of God's dealings spurs him to greater obedience (6.19–21; 8.28). His vow to not sin is rooted in the prior revelation given by God. He asserts "I know" (ואני ידעתי), which summarises in the simplest manner possible all that God has revealed to and accomplished for him (6.28–29).[140] Similarly, in lines 19–21, the hymnist thanks God for "putting instruction in the heart of your servant," which results in him restraining himself from sin. The knowledge of God's dealings with humans provides a basis from which one can act righteously. With knowledge comes the power to avoid wickedness and to live righteously.

---

[139] So García Martínez/Tigchelaar, *DSSSE*, 193; Lohse, *Texte*, 159; Abegg, "Thanksgiving Psalms," 108; Maier/Schubert, *Qumran-Essener*, 228. Stegemann and Schuller put it with the following sentence (*1QHodayot^a*, 260)

[140] In the other occurrences of the phrase ואני ידעתי (or just the verb), it is followed by a clause, usually introduced by כי, that contains the content of what the hymnist knows. See e.g. with כי: 6.23–24; 7.25, 35; 12.31; 19.10; 24.29–30; with אשר: 14.10; without any particle: 17.9; 20.14.

B. Divine Saving Acts and Human Obedience

These texts reveal a close connection between obedience and knowledge. In order for one to actually obey, God must have revealed his knowledge to the person. Without this revelation a person will be misled by the "hypocrites" who exchange God's law with "flattering teachings" (12.11). VanLandingham misses this connection between knowledge and obedience. His preoccupation with "works" has led him to downplay the importance given to knowledge in the *Hodayot*. In his attempt to dismiss the idea of predestination in the *Hodayot* and the Dead Sea Scrolls generally, he remarks, "Ultimately, responsibility lies in what one does, not in what one knows."[141] He fails to realise that obedience is possible only because God has revealed to a person the correct manner in which to obey. The dividing line between the elect and non-elect is not simply knowledge, but neither is it solely obedience. Knowledge of God's ways indicates how one should obey. Torah observance is not straightforward until a person knows how a particular command should be interpreted.[142] Those outside the community cannot obey until God gives insight and understanding. When a person is removed from the community because of his disobedience, this is proof that he never possessed knowledge and was never among the elect. If he had possessed knowledge, then he would not have disobeyed. The community does not set works and knowledge in opposition, for the means to correct obedience is through understanding.

c. Purification from Sin

A final divine act to note is the claim that God himself purifies one from sin. The community was painfully aware of their sinful deeds and the need for purification. This acute understanding of human sinfulness pervades the *Hodayot*, and the hymnists mention often the need for purification. They maintain that only God can accomplish purification. Relying on God's own testimony to Moses about his character, the hymnist recounts that God forgives transgression and sin and atones for unfaithfulness. Although God judges with fire, he protects his servants and establishes them by forgiving their sin and giving to them "all the glory of Adam" and eternal life (4.23–27; cf. Exod 34.5–8). God himself "will purify" his people "in order to cleanse (them) from guilt" (1QH^a 14.11). As is written elsewhere, "All the sons of your truth you bring to forgiveness before you in order to [cl]eanse them from their transgressions by your great goodness and by the abundance of your me[r]cy, in order to make them stand before you forever" (15.32–34; cf. 5.3–35). In the lines prior to this statement, God's justice is contrasted with the sinfulness of creation. No human can withstand God's anger. Because of his grace (חסד) and mercy (רחם), however, he

---

[141] VanLandingham, *Judgment and Justification*, 113.

[142] The purpose of 4QMMT is to provide further instruction since the recipients only have partial understanding, which results in incomplete obedience (see C 27–30=4Q398 14–17 ii).

has revealed his ways to the hymnist (15.30). Because he has forgiven one's sins, he has reversed the impending result of judgment.[143] The result of God purifying a person is that he is able to stand "with the hosts of the holy ones and enter into communion with the sons of heaven" (11.22–23). The act of purification, therefore, is directed not only at the problem of sin and guilt, but it also is a "cleansing of impurity associated with being human" (cf. lines 11–15).[144] The very one who falters before God and deserves punishment now stands in God's presence because God forgave and cleansed him.

As with so many other themes, the spirit of God has a crucial role in the purification of God's elect. It is by the holy spirit that one is purified (8.30) and guilt is removed (23.33). The contrast between the God-given holy spirit that purifies and the depraved human spirit further heightens the notion of human sinfulness. The human cannot free himself from bondage to his own creaturely, sinful state without divine assistance. God gives to those he elects a spirit that works to overcome the fleshly, sinful nature of the human. The spirit functions as the bearer of predestination as well as the cleansing agent. One might even say that it is the enactor and maintainer of election.

Purification from sin does not become a foundation for licentiousness, but rather the motivation for the human to pursue righteousness.[145] The hymnist's knowledge that God has established him as righteous motivates him to purify himself and avoid all evil (8.28). The hymnist attributes his desire to be holy to God's previous cleansing action: "For the sake of your glory, you cleanse (טהרתה) man from his transgression in order that he might make himself holy (להתקדש) for you from all abominations of impurity and from guilt of unfaithfulness" (19.13–14). להתקדש is the first of five infinitives that describe the results of God's cleansing work.[146] These infinitives summarise the totality of salvation as one is united with the community of the redeemed and transferred from death to life, which results in one being a part of the new creation (lines 14–17). Divine and human action are not in opposition; rather, divine action enables human action. The symmetry of divine and human action stands out in the clauses indicating from what God has cleansed humans, namely "transgression," and the human decision to pursue holiness by avoiding "all abominations of impurity and guilt of unfaithfulness." Holm-Nielsen correctly notes "that it is God's cleansing which forms the background; as a mortal being, man is quite

---

[143] Nitzan points out that the *Hodayot* reflects on how God has made repentance possible but is not actually a request for forgiveness (*Qumran Prayer*, 337–40).

[144] Falk, "Psalms and Prayers," 31.

[145] Cf. 9.34–35: On the basis of his lovingkindness and mercy, God has "strengthened the spirit of man against afflictions" and "cleansed" him from sin "in order that he can recount the wonders" of God to the rest of creation.

[146] The others are: להוחד ("to join;" line 14); להרים ("to be raised up;" line 15); הציתהלו ("and to stand;" line 16); להתחדש ("to be renewed;" line 16).

unable to sanctify himself."¹⁴⁷ Because God has acted on behalf of the human, though, the human can pursue what God set out to accomplish. Without God undertaking this task, the human remains incapable of living righteously, but because God cleanses his chosen people, one can live in accordance with God's commands.

Along with purifying the elect from sin, God strengthens them so that they will not continue to commit sins or fall prey to spirits of wickedness (4.35; 9.34; 15.9–12). The hymnist recognises that the human spirit is weak and given to transgress God's will. With God's assistance and protection, though, the human can obey God's will:

> [Prevent] your servant from sinning against you and from stumbling over all the words of your will. Strengthen [. . .] against spirits of [wickedness in order that he might] walk (וֹלה]תהלך]) in all that you love and to despise all that [you] hate [and in order to do] good in your eyes. [. . .] in my bowels, for your servant (is) a spirit of fle[sh]. (4.35–37)¹⁴⁸

Two types of human action are available. Apart from divine action, the hymnist can only follow the will of his fleshly spirit. When God intervenes, the hymnist can then imitate God. In order to obey God's will, the human is dependent on God, who alone can overcome the effects of the human's depraved spirit.¹⁴⁹

d. The Hodayot as Covenantal Nomism?

This study has shown that the divine-human relationship revolves around God's gracious acts of deliverance for the individual. Obedience does not merit salvation. It is instead the outworking of God's mercy. In concluding this study of the *Hodayot*, it is worth briefly commenting on the similarities between this study's explanation of the divine-human relationship and covenantal nomism. In Sanders' definition of covenantal nomism not only is grace prioritised over works, but also the interaction between God and humans is set firmly within a covenantal framework. He writes, "[C]ovenantal nomism is the view that one's place in God's plan is established on the basis of the covenant and that the covenant requires as the proper response of man his obedience to its commandments, while providing means of atonement for transgression."¹⁵⁰ At one

---

¹⁴⁷ Holm-Nielsen, *Hodayot*, 292n.

¹⁴⁸ See Holm-Nielsen, *Hodayot*, 249nn.21–26, for a discussion of the textual problems. Also, Stegemann/Schuller, *1QHodayotᵃ*, 71–72.

¹⁴⁹ Hopkins is certainly wrong when she states, "Repentance, or the proper disposition becomes a prerequisite for election, forgiveness, and cleansing" ("Qumran Community," 346; cf. VanLandingham, *Judgment and Justification*, 125: "Even in the *Hodayotᵃ*, a text that emphasises the role of God's grace in the process of eternal salvation more than any other text in Second Temple Judaism, salvation and eternal life result from human effort."). Whatever the accuracy of this statement for 1QS or other Dead Sea Scrolls, it completely distorts the *Hodayot*.

¹⁵⁰ Sanders, *Paul and Palestinian Judaism*, 75.

level, covenantal nomism may be a succinct summary of the salvific pattern found in the *Hodayot*. The emphasis, as this study has shown, clearly falls on God's gracious acts of deliverance. He predestines based on unmerited grace, gives knowledge to whom he wishes, purifies the sinners, and all this is done despite the human's sinfulness. Nothing the human does has merit before God. Along with initiating the relationship, God sustains it. His spirit is the source of obedience, and the human cannot act in a manner pleasing to God apart from his assistance. The central focus of the hymns is God's grace and mercy.

At this level, covenantal nomism accurately captures the salvific pattern depicted in the *Hodayot*: God acts first in grace, and the human responds with obedience. This similarity, however, requires one to work with a reduced definition of covenantal nomism.[151] In this definition, covenantal nomism stands for any soteriological pattern that prioritises grace over works. The specifics of covenantal nomism are lost entirely, despite the fact that it is these specific aspects that make covenantal nomism a viable concept. One way to assess more accurately the appropriateness of defining the soteriological pattern in the *Hodayot* as covenantal nomism is to ask how the hymnists understood the interaction between God and the individual in relation to "getting in" and "staying in."

"Getting in" according to Sanders is by grace not works. He pointed to God's election of Israel as a sign of this gracious aspect. The *Hodayot* likewise emphasises God's role in establishing the relationship. "Getting in" is only possible through divine intervention because the human is a sinner. The individual can do nothing to merit God's mercy. On this point, the *Hodayot* and covenantal nomism agree.

According to Sanders, "staying in" the covenant is through obedience. Obedience is the "proper response" of the elect and, he claims, it "maintains one's position in the covenant, but it does not earn God's grace as such."[152] Several lines in the *Hodayot* imply that obedience is both the response of the elect and necessary to maintain the relationship. For example, the hymnist purifies himself in light of what he knows God has done for him (8.28). Those who have abandoned the hymnist's teachings for the path of Belial have forfeited their place among the redeemed (14.22–24; cf. 22.27). This loss of salvation suggests that obedience has the role of maintaining one's place within the community of the redeemed.

Concerning the issue of "getting in" and "staying in," one finds in the *Hodayot* ideas that cohere well with Sanders' definition of covenantal nomism. Gathercole has challenged the accuracy of covenantal nomism because it lacks an eschatological perspective.[153] He suggests that the issue at stake is not only

---

[151] Cf. Carson, "Summaries and Conclusions," 543–45.
[152] Sanders, *Paul and Palestinian Judaism*, 75, 420 (emphasis removed).
[153] Gathercole, *Where is Boasting?*

getting in and staying in, but also, and perhaps more importantly, getting into the next age. He demonstrates that according to many Second Temple texts entrance into the next age was based on both election and obedience. According to the *Hodayot*, though, entrance into the next stage is dependent solely on election. Without obedience in this life, one will not enter into the next age, but entrance into the next age is solely according to God's grace. Those few instances that do mention judgment reflect on how no one will endure it without God's grace (e.g. 15.32). Human obedience will not stand at the judgment.

Although Gathercole's critique of covenantal nomism exposes a serious flaw in Sanders' description of Judaism, it does not render the idea of covenantal nomism inappropriate for the *Hodayot*. A problem with summarizing the *Hodayot* under the heading covenantal nomism does appear, though, in the role assigned to the spirit. Sanders did maintain that the salvation process was undergirded throughout by God's grace, but nowhere does he make sufficient room for the spirit as an enabling agent.[154] Sanders' formulation of getting in through grace (divine activity) and staying in through obedience (human activity) distinguishes too sharply between divine and human action. The *Hodayot* portrays obedience as something done by the human through the spirit. The human can claim to act because he is convinced that God is working in him. Obedience is not simply the "proper response" of the elect, but rather it follows necessarily from God's gift of the spirit. The separation between divine and human activity created by Sanders' formulation does not cohere with the combination found in the *Hodayot*.

While covenantal nomism accurately captures much of the thought in the *Hodayot*, its inability to account fully for the role assigned to the spirit cautions against claiming that the interaction between God and humanity in the *Hodayot* is formulated on the pattern of covenantal nomism. This conclusion does not invalidate covenantal nomism as an accurate description of other texts nor even of the sectarian Dead Sea Scrolls themselves. The validity of covenantal nomism must be tested text by text since wholesale acceptance or rejection will result in distortions or generalisations.

e. Summary

It would be an understatement to claim that the hymnists think salvation is accomplished by God. In the hymns, they repeatedly praise God for his bestowal of grace and mercy onto a frail, sinful creature. This section has highlighted three crucial expressions of divine salvific acts: predestination, the giving of knowledge, and purification from sin. God initiates the salvation process as the teaching on predestination demonstrates. God's role is not confined only to the

---

[154] Sanders, *Paul and Palestinian Judaism*, 422. According to the *Index of Subjects*, Sanders does not even mention the Spirit in his account of Judaism.

initial stage. Rather, he continues working in the individual through his spirit. The stress placed on divine agency does not eliminate human agency. On the contrary, each of the ideas discussed here contained not only clear statements about what God does, each also connects to how the human lives. Predestination was to a particular way of life, while knowledge reveals itself in obedience to the Torah. Purification leads to obedience not more sinning. The divine acts produce a human agent who through the spirit obeys the Torah. Ultimately, God's decisive acts of mercy overcome the creaturely problems of frailty and sinfulness. It is in reliance on God that the human being becomes truly human.

C. Conclusion

Running throughout the *Hodayot* are two interlocking themes. On the one hand, humans are described as frail, sinful creatures. Their creation from the dust means that they are morally deficient, and the only outcome is death since none can stand before God. On the other hand, every opportunity is taken to describe how God delivers from this predicament. God intervenes into the human dilemma when he decides before creation who will be saved and who will not. God purifies the elect and gives knowledge to them. These divine saving acts of mercy are accomplished through God's spirit, which, functioning as the agent of predestination, sustains and enables the human being. The emphasis on divine action does not turn the human agent into a purely passive recipient. These divine acts ultimately culminate in the individual following the Torah as interpreted by the community. Human obedience is made possible because God himself has intervened.

The *Hodayot* provides an example of Josephus' claim that the Essenes attributed everything to God, and it is the exact opposite of Ben Sira. At the most fundamental level, the two texts differ in which character takes centre stage. Ben Sira focuses his attention on the human, while the hymnist emphasises how God has acted. This crucial difference results in conceptions of the divine-human relationship that are fundamentally opposed to one another. Here are four key differences:

1) Ben Sira views the human as fully capable of determining his or her own destiny. The hymnists describe the human as a creature of dust bent to sin and without the ability to obey God.

2) Both authors maintain that God is sovereign, but the hymnists highlight predestination. God determines the way of each human. Ben Sira argues that each human determines his or her own way by choosing to obey or disobey the Torah.

3) In the *Hodayot*, divine action is the basis for human action, while in Ben Sira the relationship is reversed. God responds to the human by rewarding with "life" or punishing with "death."

C. Conclusion

4) In accomplishing the task of obedience, the hymnists insist that the human remains fully dependent on God, who gives his spirit to assist the elect. Ben Sira views divine assistance through Wisdom as the reward for perseverance. Divine assistance is not an important idea for Ben Sira because the human possesses within himself or herself the ability to obey the divine will.

These points highlight the fundamental differences between Ben Sira and the hymnist. While their conceptions of the divine-human relationship have the same goal, namely salvation (although they view this differently), they present contrasting and conflicting ways of attaining the goal. According to Ben Sira, the divine-human relationship is initiated and sustained by humans, while the hymnists think it is initiated and sustained by God. Where one speaks of God, the other speaks of humans.

The divergences between the two texts indicate the variety of views held among Jews of this time period. Judaism was not monolithic. While each works with the same concepts, images, and language and even in dependence on the same scriptures, they arrive at different understandings. Neither is less Jewish for taking a different perspective, but neither does their Jewish heritage bind them to certain conclusions. These diverging views between two thoroughly Jewish authors provide a context within which to explore Paul's description of what God did through Jesus the Messiah and its impact on the divine-human relationship.

Chapter 3

Sin, the Spirit, and Human Obedience in Romans 7–8

When considering what Paul expected of the human agent in salvation, the most natural starting point, since at least the Reformation, has been the Pauline antithesis between justification by faith (in Christ) versus works (of the law) (Gal 2.16; Rom 3.20–26; cf. Phil 3.9). The antithesis has served as a hermeneutical framework for interpreting all of Paul's soteriological statements. A common interpretation runs along these lines.[1] In the antithesis, both aspects refer to actions taken by humans, but they are qualitatively different. Faith in Christ is not a deed, but an acknowledgement of what God has done apart from human obedience and in spite of the human's sinfulness.[2] Salvation, according to this part of the antithesis, is given entirely apart from any human doing. It is an act of pure unconditional grace. Works of the law stands for legalism. That was the problem of the Jews who sought through their law observance to earn salvation and to put God in their debt. "Works of the law" is a subcategory of "works," which means that Paul is rejecting any deeds not just obedience to the Torah. The antithesis, in this reading, is used to oppose any possibility of human action in the salvation process.

This reading of the antithesis has been questioned at almost every point. First, Sanders' description of Judaism as covenantal nomism leads to a re-evaluation of the opposition between faith and works that the traditional reading has found in the antithesis. If all Jews agreed that salvation was by grace not works, then the opposition between divine and human action has no historical basis. The antithesis simply cannot be between faith and "doing." Thus, for Sanders, the key contrast of the antithesis is Christ and the law.[3] Sanders' account of Judaism provides the context for the interpretation of the antithesis as a conflict over whether Gentiles had to become Jews in order to be full members of the people of God.[4] Because all agreed that salvation was based entirely on God's grace, the polemic that the traditional reading finds in the antithesis between faith and works is removed. "Works of the law" indicates obedience to the Torah, and, according to Dunn, represents the "nomism" aspect of "covenantal nomism."[5]

---

[1] Although with differences, see Westerholm, *Perspectives*; Bell, *No One Seeks for God*, 239–75; Kim, *Paul and the New Perspective*, 57–70.

[2] Human inability and sinfulness is a key element for this interpretation. See Schreiner, *The Law and Its Fulfillment*, 41–71; Smith, *What Must I Do*, 73–160.

[3] Sanders, *Paul and Palestinian Judaism*, 482. Cf. Räisänen, *Paul and the Law*, 164–77.

[4] Sanders, *Law*, 17–64; Dunn, "New Perspective on Paul: whence," 23–33.

[5] Dunn, "New Perspective on Paul: whence," 23. See also Wright, *Saint Paul*, 132.

In the antithesis, then, Paul is arguing that Gentiles do not need to adopt the particular practices of the Jewish people in order to enjoy the covenantal blessings. This reading, while not necessarily opposed to the Reformation reading, does at least soften the harsh polemic against "works" and Judaism that others have found in the antithesis.[6] The issue in the antithesis is not "how is one saved – by faith or by works?" but "how do Gentiles become full members of God's people – by faith in Christ or by works of the law?"[7] For our purposes, this criticism of the traditional reading questions the opposition between divine and human action that the traditional interpretation identified.

A second challenge to the traditional reading arises from those who interpret the phrase πίστις Χριστοῦ as referring to Christ's faithfulness (Gal 2.16 [2x], 20; 3.22; Phil 3.9; Rom 3.22, 26).[8] The content of the antithesis according to this reading is more "Christological" than "anthropological" since the issue is not what the individual human does but what Christ has done.[9] Christ's fidelity is his obedience to God's call for him to die on the cross. Paul's antithesis, therefore, contrasts human action ("works of the law") with divine action, thus removing the particular issue that the traditional interpretation found in it. This second challenge, unlike the first, agrees with the traditional reading that the antithesis is about the divine-human relationship, but in focusing on Christ's faithfulness/obedience, it is a significant challenge to the traditional reading.

Alongside these two alternative interpretations of the antithesis, other issues have been raised against the traditional understanding of the antithesis as an opposition between the human acts of faith and works. For example, how does judgment by works fit into this scheme that rejects works as necessary for salvation?[10] Should "works of the law" be understood as a subcategory of "works" or is "works" shorthand for the longer phrase?[11] Is Paul only criticizing obedience to the Torah, but not rejecting "works" outright as necessary for salvation? What do "faith (in Christ)" and "works (of the law)" mean?[12]

---

[6] Rejection of the Augustinian and Lutheran interpretations is central to Wright's arguments (*Saint Paul*, 120).

[7] See Wright, *Saint Paul*, 119; Dunn, "Paul and Justification by Faith." See also the neglected article by Barth, "Jews and Gentiles: The Social Character of Justification in Paul."

[8] The literature on this issue is enormous. In favour of the "Christ's faithfulness" reading, see e.g. Hays, *Faith*[2], 141–62, 272–97; Johnson, "Rom 3:21–26 and the Faith of Jesus;" Stowers, *Rereading Romans*, 194–226. On the debate see now Bird and Sprinkle, eds., *Faith of Jesus Christ*.

[9] Hays, *Faith*[2], 277.

[10] VanLandingham argues vehemently in his *Judgment and Justification* that the antithesis has no implications for the Final Judgment, which is determined solely on the basis of obedience.

[11] See Moo, "'Law,'" 94–99; Rapa, *Meaning*, 53–70. On the scholarly debate over the phrase "works of the law" in Paul and Qumran, see de Roo, *'Works of the Law'*.

[12] E.g., Watson argues that "faith in Christ" refers to the way of living within the Christian community and "works of the law" is the way of life in the Jewish community (*Paul, Judaism, and the Gentiles*[2], 148, 212). Similarly, Jewett emphasises the communal dimensions of faith and explicitly rejects any hint of individual response to the Gospel in Paul's faith language (*Romans*, 146, 276–78).

Regardless of how one answers these questions and which position is taken on the antithesis, the controversy indicates that it is no longer profitable to begin a discussion of divine and human agency in Paul from the antithesis. Indeed, the antithesis is not only too controversial, it is incomplete in itself to address fully the issue of divine and human agency. The antithesis is a piece of rhetoric, a shorthand catch phrase of a much larger issue in Paul. As such, it must be placed within a broader context to make sense. It cannot be the controlling criterion for how one understands the relationship between faith and obedience and divine and human action in Paul, not least because it is intended to summarise (not dictate) Paul's view.

In place of the antithesis as the starting point, Romans 7.7–8.13 presents itself as a viable candidate. Here is an argument about contrasting patterns of human activity developed as an intra-Jewish debate. In 7.7–25 Paul explains what life under the Torah looks like. The Torah gave a commandment – "You shall not covet" (v.7; cf. Exod 20.17; Deut 5.21) – to its hearers, and they were to obey it.[13] Romans 7 focuses on human inability, as Paul describes the human's failure to obey the Torah. The result is nothing less than death. In Romans 8, the situation is the opposite. Now because of and on the basis of God's intervention, obedience becomes a possibility, and life is a reality because of the indwelling Spirit. Whereas the former path takes its direction from a word found on a stone tablet (cf. 2 Cor 3.7), this path takes its direction from the divine Spirit who now indwells those found in Christ. The goal of obedience in both patterns is "life," for this is what the law offered to the one who successfully kept the commandment (7.10) and what is attained by the Son's death and given to the one in whom the Spirit dwells (8.6, 11, 13). Paul's argument in 7.7–25 is about the human's (failed) attempt to please God (cf. 8.8) by keeping the commandment of the Torah, and in 8.1–13 it is about the human's (successful) act of pleasing God through the Spirit's guidance.

This chapter explores how Paul develops the two patterns for obedience. It will be argued that in 7.7–25 Paul portrays the ἐγώ as the human agent of the two-ways pattern. Paul seeks to show the powerlessness of the two-ways tradition to produce an adequate obedience to the Torah. By contrast, in 8.1–13, he adopts an alternative Jewish understanding of the divine-human relationship that focuses on God's act of deliverance and the imparting of his Spirit as the empowering agent. Obedience is possible because of the Spirit of God. Paul contends that under the law the human has no agency, but in Christ the human becomes an agent.

---

[13] Throughout this section, Paul constantly emphasises the idea of "doing" or "practising" the law. Note the various terms used: πράσσειν (vv.15, 19); ποιεῖν (vv.15, 16, 19, 20, 21); κατεργάζεσθαι (vv.15, 18).

A. Paul's Critique of the Two-Ways Theology (7.7–25)

Romans 7.7–8.13 is typically recognised as two parts of an argument, although there is little agreement over the precise connection.[14] The recounting of God's act in Christ in 8.1–4 is the response to the desperate cry for redemption that concluded chapter 7. Although recognising this connection, scholars still struggle to identify clearly the main point of the two sections and their place within the argument of Romans. Some regard 7.7–25 as an excursus in which Paul seeks to clarify his position on the law.[15] While others reject the idea that 7.7–25 is an excursus, they also hold that it is centrally about the Torah. Here Paul, it is claimed, gives his great "defence" of the law.[16] Having linked the Torah so closely with sin earlier in the letter (3.20; 4.15; 5.20; 6.14; 7.5), he now qualifies those statements. He emphatically declares the law as "good" (7.13), indeed as "holy" and "the commandment" as "holy, just, and good" (v.12). He argues that the law was the "unwilling" partner, usurped by Sin.[17] The law was intended for humanity's good, but in the hands of Sin, it could not fulfil its goal of giving life. Instead, it was used as an instrument of death.

A reading along these lines has almost universal support. Nevertheless, it is questionable on several grounds. There is, in fact, little reason to think that Paul is interested in defending the Torah itself. Actually, it is *Paul's* view of the law and especially its relationship to sin that needs defending. As Seifrid notes, "Paul here defends his Gospel against the potential Jewish objection that

---

[14] Most scholars make a paragraph break between 8.11–12. This seems incorrect, however, for two reasons. First, vv.12–13 continue the contrast between "Spirit" and "flesh" found in vv. 4–11, and the theme of "life" continues until v.13 (Moo, *Romans*, 473; Byrne, "Living Out," 580). Second, aside from Romans 8.12, the phrase ἄρα οὖν occurs 10x or 11x in the Pauline corpus, but in none of these instances does it start a new paragraph (Rom 5.18; 7.3, 25; 9.16, 18; 14.12 [disputed], 19; Gal 6.10; Eph 2.19; 1 Thess 5.6; 2 Thess 2.15). It functions the same in Romans 8.12 where Paul draws out the practical conclusion of his description of life according to the Spirit or according to the flesh. The paragraph should not be extended to v.17, for, although v.14a functions as a transition, the concept of adoption is introduced in v.14b and is the main point of vv.14–17. Verse 17 concludes with the idea of suffering that occupies Paul's thought throughout the rest of chapter 8. Verses 14–17 function as a hinge, reassuring believers of their status as God's children and introducing the idea of suffering as preparation for the discussion of hope (vv.31–39; cf. 5.1–11).

[15] Moo, *Romans*, 424.

[16] Kümmel, *Römer* 7, 9; Bultmann, "Romans 7," 153; Bornkamm, "Sin, Law and Death," 88–89; Beker, *Paul the Apostle*, 104–08; Stuhlmacher, *Romans*, 105; Dunn, *Romans*, 1:376–77; idem, *Theology of Paul*, 157–59; Fee, *God's Empowering Presence*, 509; Moo, *Romans*, 423; Garlington, *Faith, Obedience and Perseverance*, 118; Schreiner, *Romans*, 358–59; Tobin, *Paul's Rhetoric*, 219.

[17] Kruse, *Paul, the Law, and Justification*, 211.

it compromises the holiness of *Torah*."[18] Although this reading offered by Seifrid and others is better, it also does not represent accurately what Paul does in this section. Paul does not soften any of his previous comments about the relationship of the law to sin.[19] He remains on the offensive and has no intent to reverse his previous statements. He maintains an intimate connection between the law and sin, while clarifying that the law itself is not evil. If this is a defence of the law or even his own view of the law, then Paul fails miserably since he introduces ideas that his Jewish contemporaries would find objectionable. For example, he describes God's law as being taken hostage by Sin. What Jew would find in this a defence of the law? Paul also declares the law as incapable of dealing with the problem of Sin. Paul's fellow Jews, however, thought the law was God's solution to the evilness of humanity.[20] Far from separating the law from Sin, Paul maintains that the law is intimately connected with Sin, and this despite being holy.

Also questionable is the argument that Paul is primarily focused on the Torah in 7.7–25. Moo, for example, contends that throughout chapter 7 "[t]he main topic is the Mosaic law" while "anthropology – the identity and situation of the 'I' of vv.7–25—is a subordinate issue in Rom. 7."[21] Similarly, Schreiner writes, "The theme of verses 7–25, therefore, is not anthropology and existential human experience but the goodness of God's law."[22] Undoubtedly, Moo, Schreiner, and others are correct to oppose the view espoused by, for example, Käsemann, who claimed that with the exception of v.14a in vv.14–25 "the Torah recedes completely into the background and everything focuses on anthropology, which in turn is no less important than the question of the law in vv.7–13."[23] Certainly the unceasing interest in the identity of the ἐγώ gives the impression that anthropology is the main point of the passage.[24] Reducing anthropology to a "subordinate issue," however, is not the appropriate way to

---

[18] Seifrid, "Subject of Rom 7:14–25," 324; cf. Räisänen, *Paul and the Law*, 67; Kruse, *Paul, the Law*, 208; Byrne, *Romans*, 209; Kuula, *The Law, the Covenant*, 242; Esler, *Conflict and Identity*, 239.

[19] Cf. Romanello, "Impotence of the Law," 522–23.

[20] See Sir 21.11 ("whoever keeps the law masters his thoughts"); *4 Ezra* 7.116–131. Although much later, R. Raba (d. AD 352) remarks, "Though God created the evil inclination, he created the law as an antidote against it" (*b. B. Bat.* 16a; cf. *b. Qidd.* 30b; *Sifre Deut.* 45; '*Avod. Zar.* 5b; *b. Sukkah* 52b). See Porter, "The Yeçer Hara," 127–30; van der Horst, "Note on the Evil Inclination," 61.

[21] Moo, *Romans*, 409; cf. Stendahl, "Introspective Consequence," 212; Wilckens, *Brief an die Römer*, 100; Fee, *God's Empowering Presence*, 509n.110.

[22] Schreiner, *Romans*, 358; cf. Romanello, "Impotence of the Law," 512–13.

[23] Käsemann, *Romans*, 192. He acknowledges that the Torah is also referenced in vv.16b and 22 later in his commentary (ibid., 199). Cf. Bornkamm, "Sin, Law and Death," 95.

[24] The literature debating the identity of the ἐγώ is massive. For reviews see Lambrecht, *Wretched "I"*, 59–91; Lichtenberger, *Das Ich Adams*; Middendorf, *The "I" in the Storm*, 15–51, 133–225; Jewett, *Romans*, 441–45.

A. Paul's Critique of the Two-Ways Theology (7.7–25)

correct the imbalance. Maintaining that Paul is interested in only either anthropology or the Torah arises from a serious methodological error, namely, the false assumption that a passage has only one dominant concept.[25] In reality, though, Paul's arguments often involve a complex relationship between several issues, in this case, Sin and the law and their impact on the human agent. The argument of 7.7–25 cannot be reduced to either anthropology or Torah.[26] The former overlooks vv.7–12, while the latter misses crucial elements in vv.7–12 and cannot explain the anthropological focus in vv.14–21. When both issues are allowed equal weight, it emerges that the question of the relationship between the law and sin is answered by describing how the human relates to each. Throughout 7.7–25 the argument is advanced by Paul's characterization of the inability of a human to obey the divine will revealed in the Torah. He is not "develop[ing] an abstract doctrine of the law" but rather explaining how the relationship between the holy, just, and good law and Sin impacts the life of the human being.[27] He answers the question about the relationship between the law and Sin through anthropology.

When more factors are introduced into the mix, 7.7–25 not only becomes more coherent, it also begins to make sense in the unfolding argument of Romans. Byrne rightly identifies 6.1–8.13 as a single unit concerned with the issue of obedience.[28] Here Paul takes up various objections to his law-free gospel, objections that were first voiced in 3.8.[29] Paul has set πίστις Χριστοῦ against "works of the law" (3.20, 22), and whatever these phrases mean precisely, they indicate a fundamental contrast between Christ and the Torah. Paul's disparaging remark in 5.20–21 further distances the Christian from the Torah. The issue raised in the ethical argument of 6.1–8.13, then, is whether this Torah-less proclamation can actually produce an obedient people. That is, does the dismissal of the Torah have as its inevitable result wickedness (6.14–15)?[30] In the view of Paul's Jewish contemporaries, it certainly does. Paul seeks to demonstrate that it does not.

---

[25] Take, for example, Räisänen, *Paul and the Law*, 112–13: "[I]t should be remembered that the passage is not really meant to be an anthropological lecture. It is concerned with the law, and it is hardly safe to base any other Pauline 'doctrines' on it." Also Sanders, *Law*, 77.

[26] Cf. Weber, "Geschichte des Gesetzes."

[27] Quote from Jewett, *Romans*, 440. He continues, "but rather to clarify its bearing on the situation of the Roman church." My description asks what is Paul saying, while Jewett's asks what is Paul doing. The two need not be in conflict.

[28] Byrne, "Living out," 562–63. For the place of chapter 7 in the context of the letter, see Schnackenburg, "Römer 7 in Zusammenhang des Römerbriefes;" and Catchpole, "Who and Where." Both trace the influence of the Adam-Christ typology of 5.12–21 on 7.7–25.

[29] Dillon, "Spirit as Taskmaster." Cf. Campbell, "Romans III," 259–60.

[30] Theobald, "*Concupiscentia*," 262–63.

Paul argues in 6.1–23 that obedience is possible because Christians are identified with Christ through baptism. This act of initiation re-enacts Christ's death and resurrection, which indicates that believers are freed from Sin's control. They now become slaves to God rather than Sin, and Paul instructs them to produce in their lives the righteousness that God has given by faith in Christ. Freedom from the law, then, does not result in wickedness because one now becomes enslaved to Christ. This point is reinforced through the marriage analogy in 7.1–6. Paul's point is simply that death brings freedom from the law and enables service to God.

Within this broader context, Paul argues in 7.7–25, contrary to other Jews, that obedience is not possible within the realm of the Torah. Paul turns the objection against the Gospel on its head: rather than his law-free message producing wickedness, the attempt to live by the Torah has as its inevitable outcome the doing of evil. Placing the Torah at the centre of one's existence means that one comes under Sin's rule. Sin deceives the human and causes his desire to obey the Torah to be manifest as evil. Indeed, this is the only outcome possible according to the speaker (v.21). Rather than making obedience possible, as Paul's objectors claimed, the Torah actually makes the problem worse.

Romans 7.7–25 must be read as the negative counterpart to 8.1–13.[31] In the latter, Paul explains how obedience will finally be possible. Verses 1–4 do not simply provide the solution to the speaker's plea for redemption. They are rather the key component in explaining what makes obedience possible. God's act in Christ and his Spirit destroys Sin's hold on the human. The ethical impossibility described in 7.7–25 becomes a possibility because God has acted.[32] 8.5–13 then elaborate on how obedience becomes a daily possibility. Those found in Christ and given the Spirit are empowered to fulfil the righteous requirement of the Torah (v.4). The life that the ἐγώ sought through the law is now given by the Spirit of life. Set in contrast to 7.7–25, Paul argues that obedience is possible not in the realm of the law but in the realm of the Spirit. Those who seek life through the law will fail because they have oriented their lives around the wrong nexus, but those found in Christ will have life and be obedient.

The argument of 7.7–25 is about far more than the Torah. It is a crucial part of Paul's argument for how the Gospel, on the one hand, "is the power of God unto salvation for all who believe, to the Jew first and to the Greek" (1.16) and on the other hand, produces among Gentiles (and Jews) an "obedience of faith" (1.5; cf. 16.26). 7.7–8.13 is fundamentally about the capacity of the human agent to produce an adequate obedience, an obedience that is ultimately "pleasing to God" (8.8).

---

[31] Byrne compares the two sections to "panels of a diptych" (*Romans*, 213) and suggests that Paul is employing "his favorite rhetorical technique of antithesis" (p.209).

[32] See Byrne's headings to Rom 7.14–25, "Life Under the Law – Ethical 'Impossibility'," and 8.1–13, "Life in the Spirit – Ethical 'Possibility'" (*Romans*, 224, 234).

A. Paul's Critique of the Two-Ways Theology (7.7–25)

In Romans 7.7–25 Paul describes the human encounter with the Torah. He models this encounter after the human agent of the two-ways tradition. At the conclusion of his sermon to the people of Israel, Moses exhorts the people "Choose life in order that you might live" (Deut 30.19). He has immediately prior to this call told the people that if they obey, God will give them the land and many days, but if they disobey and worship other gods, their days will be short (vv.16–18). This text provides the Scriptural foundations for the two-ways soteriological pattern that appears in other OT texts and early Jewish writings.[33] This pattern has already been observed in Ben Sira who provides the classic Jewish rendition of it:

> God created (the) man from the beginning, and he gave him into the hand of his inclination. If you choose, you may keep the commandment, and you will understand to do his will. . . . Before a man are life and death, and whichever he chooses will be given to him. (Sir 15.14–17)

This statement, as Ben Sira expounds in his work, emphasises human agency. There are two key aspects to the two-ways paradigm of the divine-human relationship: The means to life is through Torah observance. Moses sets this forth in his appeal to the people to obey, and some later Jewish interpreters rely upon this text as their scriptural basis for their own arguments about the necessity of law observance for covenant blessings.

The human possesses within himself the capacity to act morally. This is to be assumed by Moses' exhortation (Deut 30.15–20), but it is clearly stated by Ben Sira when he writes that God places the human "into the hand of his inclination" (Sir 15.14). He uses the verb "to choose" three times in vv.15–17 to indicate that humans can determine their own destiny. The individual can choose for himself or herself whether to obey the commandments or not (v.15). The withdrawal of the divine presence further undergirds the idea that humans are morally capable.

In Paul's narrative, the Torah appears on the scene, and the human, who had been experiencing life, is now confronted with the divine demand "do not covet." This commandment was given for the human's life, but in actuality it brought Sin to life and resulted in the human's death. Sin found in the Torah the means to assert its deadly rule over humanity, and through deception it twisted the human's right intent to obey the Torah into the production of evil. Sin took up residence in the human and made the human a prisoner of war, a slave to its own demands. Sin's rule over the human is manifest daily as the human attempts to do good but learns that all he or she produces is evil. Death is revealed in this frustrated attempt to keep the Torah, and death will be the final result of the human who attempts to live under and through the Torah. Paul is not just engaging with the Torah in itself but with the two-ways tradition as evidenced in Ben Sira. According to the two-ways tradition, law observance is straightfor-

---

[33] Cf. Josh 24.14–28; Jer 21.8; *1 En.* 94.1–5; *Pss. Sol.* 9.1–5; *4 Ezra* 7.3–24, 127–29.

ward once the commandments are known. According to Paul, knowing the law is exactly when the problems begin.³⁴

What Paul describes in this passage is a "narrative of disillusionment."³⁵ The ἐγώ represents anyone, most particularly a Jewish person (cf. 7.1), who lives under the Torah and strives to keep its commandments. As contemporary Jewish texts indicate, those who obeyed the Torah would be given life. Paul, however, challenges this depiction by arguing that experience and theology do not cohere. Whereas his contemporaries claimed that life was a possibility through the Torah, Paul argues that the one who exists under the law experiences only death. Whatever rational and theological arguments could be put forward are contradicted by the reality that the human, whose identity is found in and through the Torah, is experiencing death daily and only has eschatological death for a future.

When reading Romans 7.7–25 it is helpful to distinguish two levels of reading. The first is Paul's level. At this level one seeks to understand what Paul is doing with the words and argument of the passage. What is Paul's depiction of human agency? How does Paul understand the impact of Sin and the law on the human agent? This is the level at which most commentators are working since most are interested in how this section fits within Paul's broader argument and how Paul views the Torah and human (in)ability. Another level can be added to this one: the view of the ἐγώ. At this level one is interested in how the ἐγώ views his ability and responsibility. Does he think he can keep the law? How does he understand his existence before and after the law comes? These two levels are not exclusive, for the views of the ἐγώ are controlled by Paul.³⁶ Nev-

---

³⁴ Seifrid argues that Romans 7 is modelled on the penitential prayers found in the OT and Second Temple texts ("Subject of Rom 7:14–25," 322–23). The prayers, especially in the *Hodayot*, focus on the individual. All the passages describe the person "from a limited perspective determined by group or personal guilt," but they set this within a larger context "which is dependent upon divine mercies" (322). In these texts, the human is portrayed "from the limited perspective of his or her intrinsic soteriological resources" (323). It is unclear, though, how a penitential prayer would function within the context of Romans 6–8.

³⁵ I owe this phrase to Prof. Francis Watson.

³⁶ This reading strategy is employed simply to help bring out the particularities of the narrative and does not imply that Paul would exclude himself from the situation of the speaker. Attempts to separate Paul from the situation described are numerous and flawed. Most recently Stowers' suggestion that Paul employs *prosopopoiia*, which "is a rhetorical and literary technique in which the speaker or writer produces speech that represents not himself or herself but another person or type of character" ("Romans 7.7–25," 180), has received wide support (e.g. Witherington, *Romans*, 179–80; Das, *Solving*, 227–31; Jewett, *Romans*, 443–44). Stowers supported his reading by appealing to Origen's interpretation of this passage as *prosopopoiia*, and he concluded that Paul could not be describing himself since the rhetorical device did not allow it ("Romans 7.7–25," 193–98; *Rereading Romans*, 264–69). His appeal to Origen, however, is uncritical since, as Thurén notes, Stowers does not account for Origen's own historical context and his desire to present Saint Paul without any defects ("Romans 7 Derhetorized," 423–24, 428–30). Additionally, Jewett has demonstrated how this rhetorical device can be combined

ertheless, the two levels can be distinguished, which may help clarify some of the exegetical problems in this section.

1. The Death of the ἐγώ

The two-ways paradigm consists of two aspects. First, life is contingent on law observance. Second, the human possesses the moral capacity to obey the Torah, and God does nothing to intervene or influence the human. Each of these can be seen in Paul's characterization of the ἐγώ.

a. The Law and Life

Although Paul focuses throughout the narrative on the law's relationship to death, he does explicitly state that the commandment was intended for life in v.10: "the commandment which is unto life" (εἰς ζωήν). Only three other times does Paul mention the law's relationship with life (Gal 3.12, 21; Rom 10.5). In two of these he cites Leviticus 18.5. Here in Romans 7 the scriptural background is not Leviticus 18.5 but Deuteronomy 30.15, the scriptural foundation for the two-ways tradition.[37] The four terms "life," "death," "good" and "evil" used throughout Romans 7 are drawn from this text. As in Ben Sira's interpretation of Deuteronomy 30.15, Paul views "life" and "death" as alternative outcomes available from law observance. "Good" and "evil" are not further descriptors of the outcomes of obedience or transgression, but "the modes of conduct" that the law defines as "good" or "evil."[38] Paul's interest in Deuter-

---

with the suggestion that Paul is writing autobiographically (*Romans*, 443–73; cf. Holland, "Self against Self," 268–71). Watson is probably correct that Paul, now in Christ, takes up the persona of one "under the law" (cf. 1 Cor 9.20), and his description of this way of life has validity because he had at one time been under the law (*Paul, Judaism, and the Gentiles*², 290). Philippians 3.4–6 does not contradict this reading since there Paul is describing his situation from within Judaism, while in Romans 7.7–25 he is reflecting back from his Christian position. The rhetorical differences between the texts are ignored by those who deny that Paul includes himself within the identity of the ἐγώ in Romans 7.

[37] Luck, "Das Gute und das Böse," 225–26. Cf. Ziesler, *Romans*, 188; Seifrid, "Romans," 632–33.

[38] Watson, *Paul and the Hermeneutics of Faith*, 506. Bultmann argued that in vv.14–25 "good" and "evil" are synonyms of "life" and "death" respectively. What one sought through keeping the law was life, and what one attained by disobedience was death. In vv.14–25, then, "the object of the 'willing' is not the fulfilling of the 'commandments,' but 'life' (ζωή). What is really willed in all our doing is 'life'; but what comes out of all our doing is 'death' (θάνατος)" ("Romans 7," 152; idem, *Theology of the New Testament*, 248. He is followed by Käsemann, *Romans*, 202–04; Bornkamm, "Sin, Law and Death," 96; Furnish, *Theology and Ethics*, 141–43; Meyer, "Worm at the Core," 74–75; Luck, "Das Gute und das Böse," 233–34). The verbs ποιέω and πράσσω do not support this reading. The ἐγώ does not simply desire good (life) and hate evil (death), but instead he desires to do good and hates that he does evil. The emphasis is on deeds.

onomy 30.15–20 connects him with the two-ways tradition. While life and law observance is not confined solely to the two-ways tradition, it is this interest in Deuteronomy 30.15–20 that suggests that the two-ways tradition is the appropriate background.[39]

Like the other texts that bring the law and life together, the relationship between law and life in Romans 7.10 is debated. Dunn accurately summarises the two current options when he asks: "Does Paul mean that the commandment was intended to *bring about life*, to lead to life (NEB, NJB), that is, a life not yet possessed, or to *promote* life, to regulate and prosper life already possessed?"[40] The traditional reading has followed the former option – that law observance leads to life. Representatives associated with the New Perspective, following Sanders' description of the role of the law in Palestinian Judaism, have argued for the latter position. The law does not give life (cf. Gal 3.21) but explains how the covenant member should act within the covenantal relationship.[41]

The narrative description of the speaker's encounter with the law is complex, but the evidence points to the idea that the law was intended to lead to life. Prior to the giving of the law, the speaker claims to possess life (v.9). Following Sanders' description of covenantal nomism, this life could be equated with existence in the covenant. Life, therefore, would be a gracious gift from God, and the giving of the law, also a gift, would be intended to regulate the speaker's life. His obedience would be the natural response of one given such a wonderful gift from God.

Despite the coherence of this reading and admittedly its potential to account for the speaker's claim to possess life prior to the law, the picture of the human agent is far more complicated than this explanation allows. Two points should be noted, both of which suggest that the purpose of the law is to bring about life. First, the parallel clause εἰς θάνατον must mean that the law leads to death (v.10),[42] and this clause cannot be dismissed as easily as Dunn implies.[43] Death throughout this passage is condemnation. This suggests that the life connected with the law is also eschatological. Just as the law can lead to final death, it also can lead to eternal life. Second, the ἐγώ dies because of his disobedience. His repeated failure (vv.15–20) results in the sombre conclusion "I died" (v.10a) and causes him to cry out in desperation "Who will redeem me from the body

---

[39] On Lev 18.5 in Second Temple Judaism and Paul, see Sprinkle, *Law and Life*.

[40] Dunn, *Romans*, 1:384 (emphasis original).

[41] Jervis argues that the commandment in view is "the commandment inherent to life in Christ" ("Sin's Use," 196; emphasis removed). Part of her justification for this view is that Paul would not write that the Torah was "unto life" (cf. Gal 3.21) (204–205). She ignores the OT and Jewish background that Paul draws upon in this statement and his citation of Lev 18.5 in Rom 10.5 and Gal 3.12. He denies that the law does actually give life in Rom 7.7–25; 10.5; and Gal 3.12, but he can repeat the view of Leviticus and his contemporaries.

[42] Moo, *Romans*, 439n.58.

[43] Dunn, *Romans*, 1:384.

A. Paul's Critique of the Two-Ways Theology (7.7–25) 135

of this death?" (v.24). Apparently, the "life" he possessed prior to the arrival of the law was insufficient to guarantee his future destiny. His ultimate destiny, therefore, is determined not by his state prior to his encounter with the law, but by how well he succeeds in keeping the commandment. Accordingly, life is contingent on the speaker's law observance not God's grace. These points indicate that law observance does not merely regulate one's existence. It is the means to life if the commandment is kept.[44]

The perspective on obedience described in Romans 7.7–25 does not cohere with Sanders' interpretation of obedience in Judaism. Against the description of Judaism as crass legalism, Sanders argued that law observance did not earn salvation. Election, which in Sanders' model equals salvation, is based entirely on God's mercy.[45] While humans should obey the law, their obedience did not ultimately affect whether they were in or out of the covenant. Their place in the covenant depends solely on God. Sanders claimed that the intent to keep the Torah was sufficient. He writes, "God *made the condition for remaining in the covenant* the free intent to obey the commandments, not their successful fulfilment."[46] Only those who deliberately rejected the covenant would be condemned.[47] Deliberate rejection is indicated by the refusal to keep the covenant stipulations. Within this scheme salvation is based entirely on God's grace, while condemnation is ascribed to the human who refuses to obey. Actual obedience, while desired, is not necessary for the intent to obey is sufficient to indicate one's desire to please God.

Sanders' interpretation of obedience within Judaism does not match the experience and thought of the ἐγώ. The ἐγώ sought to obey the law. He desired to do the good, but constantly produced evil (vv.18–19). He did not deliberately reject the law, and even at the end claims that in his mind he serves God's law (v.25). He intended to keep the law. His intent, however, was insufficient to secure his life. He unwillingly disobeyed, and the result was death. The intent to obey, which according to Sanders is all that is required of the human to enjoy covenantal blessings, is not enough for the ἐγώ. It is on account of the actual act of obedience that the covenantal blessings are given, not mere intent.

Throughout Romans 7.7–25 Paul establishes a symmetrical relationship between life and law observance. The one who obeys lives, and the one who disobeys dies. His description of the function of law observance coheres with the position taken in the two-ways paradigm. Like Ben Sira's description of the human agent (Sir 15.14–17), the ἐγώ stands at a junction between life and

---

[44] Cf. Thurén, *Derhetorizing Paul*, 113–14.
[45] Cf. Enns, "Expansions of Scripture," 98; Westerholm, *Perspectives*, 344–46.
[46] Sanders, *Paul and Palestinian Judaism*, 93 (emphasis original); cf. 107–10.
[47] Sanders, *Paul and Palestinian Judaism*, 94.

death. God has set before him "the commandment which is unto life,"[48] and his decision whether to accept or reject it will determine whether he has life or death. If he obeys then life is given; if he disobeys then death. As with Ben Sira's view, the law contains within it the instructions necessary for life, and the one who obeys will receive life from God.

The ἐγώ strives to keep the commandment since he knows that his very life depends on it. Contrary to advocates of the two-ways pattern and the ἐγώ, Paul denies in Romans 7 that the law is successful in accomplishing its goal. Rather than giving life, the law empowers Sin, and death comes to the ἐγώ. As will be seen, Paul's view about the introduction of Sin through the law critiques the widely-held Jewish view that life could be found through obedience to the Torah.

b. Moral Optimism

The fact that the options between life and death are set before humans indicates, for the two-ways tradition, that humans possess within themselves the capacity to obey the Torah. In Romans 7.7–25 the ἐγώ is portrayed as thinking that he possesses the capacity to obey the law. In vv.7, 9 the speaker describes himself as ignorant of sin and he assumes that he possesses life, and in vv.15–20 his attempts to obey the law imply that he thinks he has the ability to keep it.

Ignorant of Sin and disobedience (v.7c), the human considers himself to be alive (v.9a). The two statements, "I would not have known Sin" and "I was alive once apart from the law," have caused significant problems for interpreters. Most interpreters are concerned at this point with the identity of the ἐγώ, but this issue is less important than the claims made by the speaker. He perceives of himself as possessing some form of innocence since he has no knowledge, whether experientially or purely noetic, of Sin. Reminiscent of 3.20, one task of the law is to define what sin is. The idea likely extends beyond simple knowledge of sin to include the actual experience of sin.[49] Jewett captures the sense well: "The verb γινώσκω refers to knowledge gained through experience, thus implying that without the presence of a law, he would have been unaware of sin."[50] There may be in this statement the added notion of Sin as power: only through the law can one experience this

---

[48] Compare Ben Sira's description of the law as "the law of life" (Sir 17.11; 45.5). Also *Pss. Sol.* 14.2; *4 Ezra* 14.29–30.

[49] So Moo, *Romans*, 433–34; Schreiner, *Romans*, 366–68. Contrast Cranfield, who suggests that it is a change in understanding not experience (*Romans*, 1:348), while Dunn emphasises the experiential aspect at the expense of the noetic (*Romans*, 1:378).

[50] Jewett, *Romans*, 446. Paul is speaking exclusively about the Torah, however. Wasserman misses the force of this statement when she compares the speaker's encounter with the Torah to the view that giving a wicked person laws only entices him or her to transgress more ("Paul

A. Paul's Critique of the Two-Ways Theology (7.7–25) 137

ruling power. Regardless of when and how the ἐγώ has come to understand Sin, it must be noted that for a time period he thinks of himself as innocent. While from Paul's perspective the ἐγώ was still a sinner even without the law (cf. 1.18–32; 2.12; 3.9–18; 5.13–14), from his own view the speaker considers himself as sinless.

The second clause, "I was alive once apart from the law" in v.9a, has been at the centre of the debate concerning the identity of the ἐγώ since it does not fit well any of the standard descriptions, expect perhaps Adam.[51] What is important for our purposes is not the identity of the ἐγώ, but the claim that he makes. While some commentators think otherwise,[52] it seems highly likely that the speaker thinks he possesses eschatological life. Being alive means "the fullness of human existence – the life ultimately to be enjoyed as 'eternal life'."[53] This interpretation of ζάω matches ἀποθνῄσκω and is consistent with other uses of the verb and noun (ζωή) throughout this part of Romans (cf. 8.1, 13).[54] This understanding of "life" coheres well with the claim of ignorance in v.7c.[55] The speaker does not share Paul's assertion that "all are under Sin" (Rom 3.9) or the pessimistic anthropology of the *Hodayot*, *4 Ezra*, or *2 Baruch*. The confusion over the meaning of ζάω arises, in part, because the perspective of the ἐγώ is not distinguished from Paul's. Reducing "life" to simply existence is only necessary when one interjects Paul's claims about the human agent as a sinner. The ἐγώ, however, does not (yet) share Paul's view.

---

among the Philosophers," 407–09; citing Plato, *Rep.* 8.563d-e; Josephus, *Ant.* 1.60; Polybius, *Hist.* 1.81; Seneca, *De clem.* 1.23). Paul's speaker is not like the wicked person in these accounts, who attempted to use laws to curve his evilness. He already knows right from wrong. The speaker of Romans 7, however, only learns good from evil after the law tells him not to covet. Before the law's arrival, he did not even know something called "good" or "evil" existed.

[51] For the identification of the speaker as Adam, see e.g. Käsemann, *Romans*, 261; Dunn, *Romans*, 1: 381–83; Hofius, "Schatten Adams;" Lichtenberger, *Das Ich Adams*; Watson, *Paul, Judaism, and the Gentiles*[2], 282–83. (Busch argues that Paul is referring to Eve not Adam ["Figure of Eve"].) A recent interpretation that is gaining popularity identifies the ἐγώ as a Gentile "God-fearer" (cf. Stowers, *Rereading Romans*, 273–78; Tobin, *Paul's Rhetoric*, 239–40; Das, *Solving*, 221). While Gentiles are included in the discussion, an exclusive reference to Gentiles seems mistaken. The primary focus in fact, as 7.1 indicates, is on those who "know the law," which is most naturally taken as a reference to Jews. If Paul is recounting the giving of the law at Sinai, then this description of the speaker as alive prior to the law matches well Israel's condition prior to the giving of the law. As Watson has shown, the post-Sinai accounts in the Pentateuch, in Paul's mind, highlight Israel's failure to obey and her death (*Paul and the Hermeneutics of Faith*, 354–80).

[52] Cranfield, *Romans*, 1:351–52; Moo, "Israel," 125, 132n.29; Middendorf, *The "I" in the Storm*, 80.

[53] Byrne, *Romans*, 222.

[54] See particularly Wilckens, *Brief an der Römer*, 82.

[55] Davies describes this period when Sin is dead (v.8) and Paul is alive as "the age of innocence" (*Paul and Rabbinic Judaism*, 24). The claim that this is the period before the bar mitzvah (so Davies, *Paul and Rabbinic Judaism*, 24–25; Gundry, "Moral Frustration," 232–33; Burnett, *Salvation of the Individual*, 192–95) is unnecessary.

138 Chapter 3: Sin, the Spirit, and Human Obedience in Romans 7–8

Verses 15–20 are marked by extreme pessimism. The ἐγώ repeatedly notes that what he desires to accomplish he fails to do, and what he desires to avoid he actually does. Often lost in the overwhelming negative impression of the passage, though, is the speaker's underlying assumption that he can be obedient. His repeated attempts to keep the commandments indicate that he thinks he possesses the ability to obey. He assumes that what he wishes to do he can accomplish. His optimism is made in direct contrast to his acknowledgement that he is "fleshly, enslaved to Sin" (v.14). Sin's rule is not considered comprehensive. It can be resisted and overcome.

The description of the ἐγώ mirrors the portrait of the human in Sirach 15.11–20. According to Ben Sira, the options of life and death are set before each human, and the human possesses within himself or herself the ability to determine one's own destiny. Like Ben Sira's description of the human agent, the speaker of Romans 7.7–25 thinks he can obey the Torah and thereby acquire the life that it offers. The reality of his death is not cemented in his mind, for he thinks that life is still available and therefore that death is also an option.[56] In these verses, he actively pursues the life offered by the Torah by choosing to obey its commandments. He recognises at the outset that his life is marked with repeated failure, but he nevertheless remains confident that if he tries he can succeed.[57]

As the description of his condition progresses throughout the section (vv.15–20), the speaker becomes more and more aware of his inability. Verse 15b states the contradiction that exists between the speaker's willing and doing, and it is this disjunction between thought and action that he wants to understand. He acknowledges in v.17 that Sin dwells within him and causes him to act contrary to his will. This leads to the confession that "good does not dwell within me, that is in my flesh" (v.18a).[58] His acceptance that Sin dwells within him (v.17) contrasts with his acknowledgement that good does not dwell within him (v.18).[59] Where Sin is, good cannot be. Yet, despite realising that good does not reside within his being, he continues to pursue "the good" (vv.18b-19). He holds out hope that he can overcome the power of Sin that has affected his flesh. Again, though, the reality of Sin's rule turns the speaker's good desires into evil, and

---

[56] Middendorf argues that the ἐγώ does not pursue "righteousness" through the law because "he has no doubt about the futility of pursuing 'a Law of righteousness' (9:31)" since acquiring righteousness "by works" (v.32) "is an impossibility" (*The "I" in the Storm*, 194). Such a conclusion conflicts with the speaker's attempts to attain life through his obedience. Only after the desperate attempts to obey does the evgw, conclude that he needs God's help. Prior to this plea, however, he pursues life through his obedience.

[57] If he has adopted Ben Sira's depiction of the path to life, he would assume that the struggles to obey are the tests of Wisdom so that as long as he continued striving to obey, Lady Wisdom would eventually reward him with her presence and gifts (cf. Sir 4.11–20; 6.18–37; 14.20–15.10). His failure and frustration are only temporary.

[58] On the translation of v.18, see Keck, "Absent Good."

[59] The verb οἰκέω is used in both instances.

rather than obeying the Torah, he breaks it and does evil. Repeating the sombre conclusion of v.17, the speaker declares in v.20 that Sin dwells within him. He has learned the full extent of his death, realising now that he is incapable of putting his intentions into action. Verse 21 encapsulates the speaker's problem as a rule of life: "when I will to do the good, evil is present with me" (v.21). Confidence has given way to disillusionment as the reality of death has settled in.

The moral optimism of the human agent is also highlighted through the absence of the divine agent. Throughout the narrative of Romans 7.7–25, the ἐγώ acts on his own. God is not mentioned as the ἐγώ struggles to transform his willing into doing. While the divine hand can be seen at various points, for example in giving the law and presumably in creating the ἐγώ, he offers no assistance to the human agent. Despite the contention to the contrary by some prominent commentators, the divine Spirit is not mentioned as assisting the ἐγώ to fight against Sin.[60] The ἐγώ stands in a similar place as the human described by Ben Sira in Sirach 15.11–20. Having been created with the ability to choose life or death, the human agent stands alone at the junction. It is his decision which path to take, and God will not interfere since "he [God] gave him into the hand of his inclination" (v.14b). Likewise, the ἐγώ stands alone, and when faced with the choice of life or death, he chooses life. As he pursues this path, he finds that he must walk it alone, just as Ben Sira said.

Ben Sira claimed, though, that Wisdom would eventually assist those who endured her trials (Sir 4.11–19; 6.18–37; 14.20–15.10). The discipline was only temporary, and afterwards the human would enjoy all Wisdom's benefits. Paul, however, denies this aspect. No divine Spirit, no Wisdom, not even the Torah assists the ἐγώ as he attempts with all his will and might to keep the divine law that promises to reward him with life. Having been placed in the service of Sin, the law cannot help the ἐγώ escape Sin's enslavement nor can it assist him to obey the commandments. The ἐγώ is truly alone.

---

[60] Cranfield, *Romans*, 1:359–60; Dunn, "Rom. 7,14–25," 262; Packer, "'Wretched Man' Revisited," 80; Garlington, *Faith, Obedience, and Perseverance*, 126–29. Laato asserts that Paul's silence means nothing (*Paul and Judaism*, 123–24), but while one cannot always read between the lines, in this instance his silence speaks volumes especially since he has contrasted life in the flesh with life in the Spirit (7.5–6) and will do so again (8.5–13). Moreover, Laato's suggestion that "the positive attitude of the 'I' towards the spiritual law (7:14) without doubt" (ibid., 124; cf. Cranfield, "Sanctification as Freedom," 37) arises from the Spirit is inaccurate. Paul indicates that his contemporaries had a "positive attitude" toward the law (Rom 9.30–10.4; Phil 3.2–6), but he would not claim that they had the Spirit of Christ residing within them (see Ridderbos, *Paul*, 128–29). Also, the struggle described in Rom 7.14–20 does not indicate that the speaker is a Christian (contra Dunn, "Rom. 7.14–25," 271–73; Garlington, *Faith, Obedience, and Perseverance*, 120–21) for the same or similar tension is described in Jewish (cf. Pr. Man.) and Greco-Roman texts (Euripides, *Medea* 1077b-1080). Similarly Campbell's remark that none deny that Romans 6 is about Christian existence although the Spirit is not mentioned there fails to take account of the context ("Identity," 59).

To summarise: In Romans 7.7–25 Paul engages with the two-ways tradition. He models the human agent, identified as ἐγώ, after the human described in, among other places, Sirach 15.14–17. Here Ben Sira develops ideas found in Moses' exhortation to the people in Deuteronomy 30.15–20. Life and death are set before the human in the form of the Torah, and all that is required is for one to obey its commandments. The human possesses the capacity to obey for God has given him free will. God himself assures that the human can determine his or her own destiny by leaving the human to himself or herself. Like this description of the human agent, the speaker of Romans 7 is offered the law that leads to life. He thinks that he can obey it as his repeated attempts to obey reveal (vv.15–20). God himself, just as Ben Sira said (Sir 15.15), leaves the human alone to determine for himself what path to take.

Having adopted this understanding of the human agent, however, Paul proceeds to expose its fallacies. The ἐγώ does not possess the ability to obey because Sin has taken it from him. The result of all his efforts to obey is nothing less than death, for under Sin's control he has chosen the path of death. The law that was supposed to give him life, in reality, becomes the instrument of death.

2. Sin's Takeover of Human Capacity

In Romans 7.7–25 Paul depicts life under the law and in the process critiques the view of the law held by some of his Jewish contemporaries. Specifically, he targets the two-ways theology advocated by Ben Sira and others and based in a particular reading of Deuteronomy 30.15–20.[61] It was already noted how Paul's description of the ἐγώ is similar to the human of Sirach 15.11–20. Both are created with "free will" and the capacity to obey; both are confronted with the "law of life;" and both are left by God to determine their own destinies. Obedience to the law is the means to life, which while defined differently is the goal for both. Paul and Ben Sira are both dependent on Deuteronomy 30.15–20. These parallels suggest that Paul has something similar to Ben Sira's view in mind as he writes Romans 7.7–25. Against this optimistic analysis of human capacity, Paul argues that it fails to account for the radical nature of Sin (ἁμαρτία). In this context Sin stands not simply for wrongdoing or inappropriate, base desires. Rather, Sin is a demonic-like being that invades the human realm, asserts its rule over the human, infects his flesh, and leads to his demise. With the introduction of this third agent, Paul charges that the two-ways scheme as

---

[61] I am not saying that the two-ways soteriological model was Paul's only target. I am only suggesting that it makes a viable candidate, and one that has not been seriously considered. Nickelsburg is the only scholar, to my knowledge, that has seen in Romans 7 the two-ways scheme ("The Incarnation," 593–96). He argues that the whole of Rom 5–8 is structured on the two-ways, two-spirits motif. This seems, however, to equate any mention of "two ways" as being *the* two-ways tradition. For other potential backgrounds, see Borgen, "Contrite Wrongdoer," and the discussion of the *akrasia* tradition below.

exemplified by Ben Sira is too simplistic. Although the ἐγώ thinks he possesses freedom and has the ability to obey, Paul denies that he can act because he is ruled by Sin. The introduction of this third actor leads to a re-evaluation of the human's moral capacity.

a. The Concept of Sin

There is virtual agreement among scholars that Paul personifies ἁμαρτία in most of its occurrences in Romans 5–7. In the view of many commentators, Paul's description of ἁμαρτία is linked with an "apocalyptic" background and understood as more than the act of disobedience or wrongdoing. "Sin" (with a capital S) is a cosmic power, even a personal being, with its own agency that invades the human realm and works against God. Comparing "sin" with Satan's deceptive tactics (cf. 2 Cor 11.14), Käsemann writes about "sin" in Romans 7.7–13, "Here sin is a power.... It has a demonic character."[62] ἁμαρτία is not the act of wrongdoing, but a personal being that deceives, enslaves, and ultimately kills.

This widely adopted view has been challenged in recent years. Kaye notes that the instances in which ἁμαρτία is described in personal terms in Romans 5.12–21 and 7.7–25 are consistent with the literary style of the passages and do not require the conclusion that ἁμαρτία is a power.[63] Additionally, he maintains that throughout Romans ἁμαρτία refers to human's actively doing wrong. Wasserman has recently claimed "that proponents of this theory have done little to defend it in historical terms and that they deny Paul the use of metaphor and personification."[64] Yet, the literary arguments made by Kaye are not conclusive and obvious parallels appear across a range of Jewish literature in which a demonic being is described as ruling over and through human agents.[65]

The description of Sin as a personal being has significant parallels with the account of personal, cosmic beings in the Dead Sea Scrolls. The Two-Spirits Treatise describes the rule of two cosmic beings, the Prince of Lights and the Angel of Darkness, that wage war against each other and its assigned lot of humanity (1QS 3.13–4.26). Although cosmic beings, they are also described

---

[62] Käsemann, *Romans*, 198; cf. Grundmann, "ἁμαρτάνω," *TDNT* 1:311.

[63] Kaye, *Argument of Romans*, 34–57. His study remains the most carefully argued challenge to the "power" reading.

[64] Wasserman, "Paul among the Philosophers," 402. Cf. Forbes, "Paul's Principalities and Powers." Many who have rejected the "power" interpretation have opted, on the basis of philosophical traditions, for interpreting ἁμαρτία as the irrational, base passions that reside within each individual (see below).

[65] Wasserman has dismissed these parallels with the comment: "one finds little basis for such conceptions of sin in Jewish texts that describe the work of nonhuman or demonic beings. With the possible exception of col. 3 of the *Rule of the Community* from Qumran (1QS 3), there are virtually no extant texts that depict external powers entering the body and controlling the person in the way that the [apocalyptic] theory envisions" ("Death of the Soul," 798).

as dwelling within each individual. While some have used this statement to eliminate any cosmic notions, the claim likely attempts to explain why humans act wickedly. They are not only under the lordship of a wicked cosmic being, this same being also invades and dwells within each individual, including the righteous, causing all to act wickedly. In attributing the evil deeds to the spirit dwelling within and ruling over each individual, the authors do not absolve the individual of his or her deeds. The human is still guilty, even though the Angel of Darkness causes one to disobey.

Paul's description of "Sin" as a personal being compares with the description of "Mastema" (משטמה) and "Belial" (בליעל) as personal beings in many Jewish texts. The words משטמה and בליעל mean "enmity" and "worthlessness" respectively, but in the literature they are also names for real beings that rule over "demonic" armies and assert their rule in the human realm by causing humans to act wickedly (cf. *Jub.* 11.5; 1QS 2.5–9; 1QM 1.1; 13.2–4; 4Q286 7 ii). Whether the author is referring to the actions of enmity or worthlessness or the Beings designated by these names is unclear at times (e.g. 1QS 10.21; 1QH[a] 10.24). Nevertheless, in some texts personal beings are identified by these names. Like the authors of these texts, Paul could portray "sin" in a general way as disobedience, and he can also use the same word to describe a personal being that rules over humanity apart from Christ.

Another analogous concept is the Rabbinic teaching on the "Evil Inclination" (יצר הרע).[66] The rabbis generally described sin as rebellion against God and in a concrete form as disobedience to the Torah.[67] They surmised that the cause of sin was the human's impulse to evil.[68] The Evil Inclination was part of the human nature because it was created by God.[69] Alongside this anthropological understanding of the Evil Impulse, the Rabbis personified it.[70] At times the

---

[66] Statements about the יצר and its tendency toward evil are found in the OT (Gen 6.5; 8.21; Deut 31.21), and these may be the basis for later ideas. While Ben Sira can describe the human "inclination" as morally neutral (Sir 15.14), the author of *4 Ezra* repeatedly uses the expression "evil heart" (3.20–22; cf. "evil thought" in 7.92; see Stone, *4 Ezra*, 63–67). Some Dead Sea Scrolls also describe the human as possessing an "evil inclination" (cf. CD 2.14–16). A formal contrast between a Good and an Evil Inclination appears in later texts, such as *T. Jud.* 20.1, *T. Ash.* 1.3, and the Rabbinic literature, but it is not clear when exactly the contrast was first developed. For discussion of these texts and others, see Porter, "Yeçer Hara," 136–56; Marcus, "Evil Inclination in the Epistle of James." The date of the Rabbinic tradition makes a formal comparison with Paul difficult, but this only affects arguments attempting to trace dependence.

[67] Schechter, *Some Aspects of Rabbinic Theology*, 219–41.

[68] *b. Sabb.* 105b; *Sifre Deut.* 33.

[69] The Rabbis argued that the two *yods* in the word וייצר in Gen 2.7 indicates that God himself created humanity with two "inclinations," both a good one and an evil one (*b. Ber.* 61a; *Sifre Deut.* 45). They also based this idea on the occasional spelling of לבב with two *beths* instead of one (לב) (e.g. Deut 6.5; 11.13; *m. Ber.* 9:5) or the plural use of "hearts" (Ps 7.10; *m. Mishle* 12) (see Porter, "Yeçer Hara," 101–02; 110–11; Moore, *Judaism*, 1:479–80, 484–85).

[70] *b. Sukkah* 52b. See Moore, *Judaism*, 1:492.

A. Paul's Critique of the Two-Ways Theology (7.7–25)

Rabbis went beyond mere personification to equate the Evil Inclination with Satan and the Angel of Death: "Resh Lakish said: Satan, the evil prompter, and the Angel of Death are all one" (*b. B. Bat.* 16a [Soncino]). The Evil Impulse from this perspective is more than the human inclination toward evil or even a personification of the passions. The Evil Inclination has become a personal being with its own agency. In the interpretation of Genesis 4.7 in *Gen. Rab.* 22.6, the Evil Inclination is identified as the Tempter who lies behind Cain's murder of Abel. The movement from inclination to personal being is available already in the biblical text which describes sin as crouching at the door. To be sure, the Rabbis typically describe the Evil Inclination in impersonal terms, but they can also speak of it as a personal being. This provides a clear historical parallel to Paul's use of ἁμαρτία as a description of human wrongdoing and as a power that reigns over and in each human.[71] A background for interpreting Paul's language of "sin" as referring to a personal being is there despite Wasserman's hasty dismissal of it.

Kaye's arguments against the "power" reading are more serious than Wasserman's since his actually deal with Paul's statements. He claims that "sin" always refers to the act of wrongdoing in Romans and that the depiction of "sin" as a personal being is the result of the personal tone of 5.12–21 and 7.7–25. Neither argument, however, is conclusive. First, Kaye is correct that "sin" refers to acts of evil at times in Romans (cf. 5.20). Those who seek to distance "Sin" as a power from the act of sinning, as if Paul had no interest in disobedience, are mistaken.[72] Nevertheless, the focus on the act of sinning does not rule out the possibility that Paul conceived of a power known as "Sin" being the cause of disobedience. The either/or mentality is not helpful. Second, Kaye rightly notes the personal tone of 5.12–21 and 7.7–25, but his argument assumes that the literary form caused Paul to describe "sin" in a personal manner. Yet, could Paul not have used the personalised literary form because he needed it to express the personal nature of Sin? Which came first, the form or the concept? There is no reason to assume that Paul only portrayed Sin so personally because of the literary form. Indeed, with an apocalyptic background in mind, it is likely that Paul could portray Sin in such personal terms because it had become something that had its own agency.[73] It is a being with its own history and actions.[74]

---

[71] Several scholars have argued that Paul is working with the two impulses teaching in Romans 7 (Davies, *Paul and Rabbinic Judaism*, 23–27; Marcus, "Evil Inclination in the Letters of Paul," 15–16; Shogren, "*Reduction ad absurdum*"). Cf. the critique by Porter, "Pauline Concept," 9–13.

[72] This is a problem found in the, otherwise outstanding, work of Martyn. See e.g. his *Galatians*, 95–97.

[73] See Southall's critique of Kaye's position in *Rediscovering Righteousness in Romans*, 104–05.

[74] For the language of Sin having its own history, see Gathercole, "Sin in God's Economy."

These objections to the interpretation of "Sin" as a cosmic power in Romans 7.7–25 are unfounded. It is most likely that Paul did perceive of "Sin" here as a quasi-personal being with its own agency.[75] Sin is a foreigner to the human realm, and it invaded this realm because of Adam's transgression (5.12). True to its name, Sin acts in the human realm to cause humans to do evil deeds that are contrary to the Torah. Sin's stranglehold over the individual must not be divorced from the actual act of sinning, for it is when humans sin that they reveal themselves to be under Sin's control.

b. Sin's Destructive Reign

Paul's statements about Sin in 7.7–25 assume the prior depiction of Sin as a ruling power associated with the old era found in 5.12–6.23. It always opposes God and his will and manifests its rule over humanity when individuals act wickedly. Sin, Paul claims, entered the world through Adam's transgression, and it brought death in its wake (5.12). Paul establishes from the beginning of human history the connection between Sin and death (cf. v.21). He describes in chapter 6 how Sin enslaves humans. It acts like a master dictating to its slaves how they should use their bodies to obey "its desires" (6.12) and to act in lawlessness (v.19). With Sin as their master, humans were free from righteousness. Sin works contrary to God's will and opposes grace, obedience, and righteousness.

In 7.7–25 the picture darkens. Whereas in chapters 5–6 Sin appears as an outside force working with humans, in 7.7–25 it enters into the human.[76] Paul envisions the power designated by the name Sin taking up residence within the individual human. From its internalised position, it frustrates one's will and determines his or her actions. The description of Sin's rule also intensifies in 7.7–25. In chapter 6, Paul uses master-slave language to describe Sin's relationship to humanity. Throughout chapter 7, he describes the human's relationship to Sin through military terminology. The human is sold into slavery to Sin (πεπραμένος ὑπὸ τὴν ἁμαρτίαν) (v.14). The law of Sin "wages war" (ἀντιστρατεύω) against the law in the speaker's mind and takes him as a prisoner of war (αἰχμαλωτίζω) (v.23). The human loses the battle that he attempted to wage against Sin (vv.15–20) and becomes a slave and a prisoner.

In vv.9–10 Paul writes that Sin was dead at one point but became alive after the entrance of the law into history. The arrival of the law is, for Paul, a historical event with drastic consequences for the life of Israel. While Sin entered the world after Adam's transgression and brought death along with it (5.12), it is

---

[75] Southall questions the "power" and/or "personal" reading on the methodological grounds that it fails to adequately account for the literary motif of personification (*Rediscovering Righteousness in Romans*, 105–11). In the end, however, he still argues that Paul is doing something with "sin" beyond just wrongdoing.

[76] Dodson, "The 'Powers' of Personification," 109–23.

A. Paul's Critique of the Two-Ways Theology (7.7–25)

not reckoned apart from the law (v.13). However the parenthetical comment in vv.13–14 be interpreted, Paul establishes the law as a separate event in human history and prepares for the statements in 7.7–11. The statement that Sin is not counted compares with the statement that Sin is dead apart from the law. Describing Sin as dead does not mean non-existent, but rather powerless.[77] With the arrival of the law, Sin gains a new lease on life, just as it had when Adam transgressed the commandment. With the arrival of the law, Sin acquires its own agency.

Sin uses its newfound power to wreak havoc in the life of the individual who seeks life through the law. It finds in the law a "bridgehead" (vv.8, 11) from which to wage its deadly attacks. The law becomes "the power of Sin" (1 Cor 15.56), and it provides no assistance to the human to free oneself from Sin's enslavement.[78] It is powerless against Sin (cf. 8.3). In the speaker's current situation, the Torah is outside him, imposing its demands but offering nothing to assist him to satisfy them, while Sin dwells within him, issuing its own commands and bringing them to fruition.[79]

Sin's reign over the speaker is oppressive and destructive. Paul's description of the human encounter with Sin emphasises how the human has no control. Under Sin the human lacks the ability to do as one pleases. Hofius notes that the liberation documents given to a slave stated that the slave was now able to do as he or she pleased (ἐποιῶν ὃ κα θέλῃ). Paul's statements in vv.15–19 parallel this expression, and in the negative form, they "indicate for the slave that he is not lord of himself or his doings."[80] Based on this connection, Paul's description of the speaker's inability further highlights his bondage to Sin and emphasises that he is "not the free subject of his activity."[81]

The human's inability is highlighted through the speaker's claim that the evil he does was not done by himself but by "Sin dwelling in me" (7.17, 20). Along with the military terminology employed in vv.14, 23, this admission indicates that, contrary to Garlington, Sin's attack on the human cannot be reduced to mere oppression.[82] The ἐγώ is entirely incapable of bringing his will to do good to its desired end because Sin dwells within him. This statement in

---

[77] Hofius, "Schatten Adams," 130–31.

[78] Cf. Ziesler, "Tenth Commandment," 49.

[79] In v.18 the speaker remarks, "I know that good (ἀγαθόν) does not dwell (οὐκ οἰκει) within me." Prior to this he has acknowledged that the law is "good" (καλός [v.16]; ἀγαθός [vv.12, 13]). ἀγαθός in v.18 is not a general notion of what is right but specifically the Torah. Theissen, *Psychological Aspects*, 220; Hofius, "Schatten Adams," 139; contra Wasserman, *Death of the Soul*, 107

[80] Hofius, "Schatten Adams," 139: ",,Tun, was man nicht will" und ,,nicht tun, was man will" ist mithin kennzeichnend für den Sklaven, der nicht Herr seiner selbst und seines Tuns ist."

[81] Hofius, "Schatten Adams," 139.

[82] Garlington writes, "While Paul is no longer *willingly* a bond slave of 'sin' (6:15–18, 22), 'sin,' nevertheless, continues to oppress him" (*Faith, Obedience, and Perseverance*, 123; emphasis original).

vv.17, 20 is often viewed as Paul's admission that the ἐγώ is not guilty of his sins. However, Paul does not absolve the ἐγώ of his responsibility. Instead, the claim serves to enhance the picture of Sin's all-encompassing control. The human under Sin's rule is incapable of bringing his will to its intended goal, and he merely serves as a pawn in Sin's destructive game.[83] The human will indeed be judged for his transgressions, as the cry for help indicates (v.24), but he also realises that he remains helpless in the situation. Sin's rule is comprehensive and deadly.

Sin's indwelling rule does not mean that the ἐγώ ceases to act. The human still acts on his will to do good, but through Sin's deception (v.11), he is tricked into doing evil.[84] The ethical categories of "good" and "evil" have been reversed due to Sin's deception.[85] This has the practical result that when the speaker thinks he is doing the law he actually is acting contrary to the commandment.[86] Perhaps the closest analogy is Paul's persecution of the church (Gal 1.13; 1 Cor 15.9; Phil 3.6).[87] In seeking to annihilate the church, Paul was actually working against God and his Messiah. He was sinning against God while seeking to keep the Torah. This confusion over the meaning of "good" and "evil" is in direct conflict with the two-ways tradition. This tradition holds that God himself made known to humans the difference between "good" and "evil." Moses said, "See I have put before you today life and death, good and evil" (Deut 30.15 LXX). Similarly, when describing the creation of humanity, Ben Sira thinks that God himself gave humans knowledge and "showed to them good and evil" (Sir 17.7). God's first commandment is "beware of all evil" (v.14). Against this tradition, though, Paul claims that although God revealed good and evil in the Torah, Sin has deceived the human. The content of each category has been switched so that what God defines as evil, the human now calls good and what God says is good, the human identifies as evil. The two-ways tradition collapses when the human cannot tell the difference between good and evil as God defines them.

---

[83] Cf. Bergmeier, "Röm 7,7–25a (8,2)," 109–10: "Die Rede vom „Gesetz der Sünde" signalisiert somit die Unfreiheit des Willens. „Recht bzw. Unrecht zu tun *mit unserer Hände Werk*", geschieht nicht nach unserer eigenen Wahl und Freiheit."

[84] For a perceptive analysis of how Sin deceives, see Chester, *Conversion*, 185–94. Cf. Gathercole, "Sin in God's Economy," 166–69, who follows Chester.

[85] "Given that it is the commandment . . . that provides sin with the opportunity to deceive the pre-conversion self, it is difficult to see how the deception can involve anything other than a failure to recognise certain actions as transgressions of that commandment" (Chester, *Conversion*, 186).

[86] Bultmann's idea that Paul is critiquing the attitude of self-righteousness that is manifest through the attempt to do the law must be rejected ("Romans 7;" idem, *Theology of the New Testament*, 247–48; cf. Bornkamm, "Sin, Law and Death;" Käsemann, *Romans*, 184–204; Hübner, *Law in Paul's Thought*, 70–78). The problem Paul addresses is precisely the opposite: the failure to actually do the law. For a critique of the Bultmannian reading, see Räisänen, "Use of ἐπιθυμία and ἐπιθυμεῖν;" Beker, *Paul the Apostle*, 239–40.

[87] See Chester, *Conversion*, 183–86; Jewett, *Romans*, 444; idem, "Basic Human Dilemma."

A. Paul's Critique of the Two-Ways Theology (7.7–25)   147

Sin's deception appears in the speaker's confusion over why his attempt to do good manifests evil (Rom 7.15–20). Having been enslaved to Sin (v.14b), the speaker unwillingly produces evil.[88] Haacker's contention that "sin" means "weakness," that is the failure to act on one's good intentions, confuses the definition of sin with the problem created by one's enslavement to sin, namely, the inability to manifest one's good intentions as one pleases.[89] The problem described in vv.15–20, as Meyer argues, "is not simple frustration of good intent, but good intention carried out and then surprised and dumbfounded by the evil it has produced."[90] The production of evil, despite the intent and attempt to do good, is positive proof that the human's agency has been lost to Sin, so that his actions are now ascribed to "Sin dwelling in me" (vv.17, 20). Meyer's statement indicates an important point that is often overlooked. The speaker did not actively choose evil. He intended to do good and actually put his intention into action. It is only when that intention is manifest that he realises he has done evil. Sin's deceptive work is revealed not by causing the human to consciously do evil but by manifesting his intention to do good as evil. The speaker can, therefore, summarise his condition as: "So then I find the 'law' that, when I will to do the good, evil is present with me" (v.21).[91] Evil manifests itself in the very act of trying to do good because the ethical categories have been reversed. It is not just the case that evil is simply present when the speaker desires to do

---

[88] Achtemeier rightly argues, "This passage does not describe the problems we have in trying to do the good." It rather discusses "the problem of those who can do nothing but evil, since the power of sin over them remains unbroken" (*Romans*, 125).

[89] Haacker, *Römer*, 145–46: Paul "deutet die Sünde ... vielmehr als Schwachheit, nämlich, wie die Fortsetzung lehrt, als ein Zurückbleiben hinter guten Absichten und ein Mißlingen gerade auch des Gutgemeinten."

[90] Meyer, "Worm at the Core," 76.

[91] Some argue that νόμος is here a reference to the Torah so that the speaker is saying, "I find with reference to the Torah that when I will to do good, evil is always near" (Meyer, "Worm at the Core," 79; Keck, *Romans*, 190; Schreiner, *Romans*, 376–77; Das, *Paul, the Law*, 231 [see for others]; Jewett, *Romans*, 469). More likely, though, Paul is summarizing what he has previously described in vv.15–20 as a "rule" or general principle (Winger, *By What Law?*, 183–85; Moo, *Romans*, 460; Haacker, *Römer*, 147; Starnitzke, *Struktur*, 260–61; Watson, *Paul, Judaism, and the Gentiles*², 293). The meaning "principle" or "rule" for νόμος was established by Räisänen ("Paul's Word-Play," although translating it as either [so Witherington, *Romans*, 201; Tobin, *Paul's Rhetoric*, 243; NASB] loses the rhetorical effect). Moreover, the parallel between v.10 and v.21 created by some is inaccurate (contra Dunn, *Romans*, 1:392; Wright, *Climax*, 198; Das, *Paul, the Law*, 231). εἰς ζωήν and εἰς θάνατον (v.10) are not the opposites of τὸ καλόν and τὸ κακόν (v.21) respectively. The former indicate the goal of obedience to the Torah, that is what the Torah intended to give but actually gave. This cannot be said for the latter since the Torah did not give either καλός or κακός. The parallel between v.10 and v.21 can only be maintained if one accepts Bultmann's argument that καλός and κακός refer not to obedience or disobedience to the Torah, but the end result sought by every religious person, life, and its opposite, death. Verse 21 can be paraphrased as: "I have discovered the 'law': because my good desires produce evil when I seek to obey the Torah (that is, 'the good'), this means that evil is inevitable when I try to obey."

good. Rather, "evil is close at hand precisely as I seek the good."[92] As Watson argues:

> [T]he relationship between willing the good and doing the evil is not a merely contingent one. Rather, Paul's law is that willing the good has doing the evil as its necessary consequence. The attempt to make one's conduct conform to God's law, in full recognition that what the law prescribes is holy and just and good, generates only evil: that is the desperate situation of the person who is under the law of Moses and who delights in it and acknowledges its goodness.[93]

Despite the speaker's belief, evil and good are not two possible outcomes of his decision to keep the commandment. Evil will always be the outcome of his decision and attempt to observe the law. The ἐγώ cannot escape evil for it manifests itself each time that he attempts to obey the Torah.

With the point that the speaker did not consciously choose to disobey, we are at some distance from the *akrasia* (weakness of the will) tradition that many have identified as the background to vv.15–20.[94] In Greek literature, Euripides has Medea say,

> Yet I am conquered by evils. And I understand the deeds I am about to do are evil, But anger is greater than my resolves. Anger, the cause for mortals of the greatest evils. (Medea 1077b–1080)[95]

The idea is even clearer in Ovid's retelling of the Medea story:

> But some strange power draws me against my will, and desire persuades me one way, and my mind another. I see the better and approve, but I follow the worse. (Met. 7.20–21 [Miller, LCL])

The conflict between knowing what is right but doing what is evil expressed in these statements reappears in a variety of philosophical contexts as the phi-

---

[92] Watson, *Paul, Judaism, and the Gentiles*[2], 293.

[93] Watson, *Paul, Judaism, and the Gentiles*[2], 294. Cf. Epsy, "Paul's 'Robust Conscience'," 172.

[94] See especially Theissen, *Psychological Aspects*, 212–19; van den Beld, "Romans 7:14–25 and the Problem of *Akrasia*;" Stowers, *Rereading Romans*, 260–64, 279–81; Tobin, *Paul's Rhetoric*, 232–36, 242. (I am dependent on these scholars for the texts listed below.) Also, Thielman, *From Plight to Solution*, 104–07; Engberg-Pedersen, "Reception," 47, 54–56; Carter, *Power of Sin*, 190–91; Lichtenberger, *Das Ich Adams*, 176–86; Das, *Solving*, 223–26. Wasserman contends that Paul is not speaking about the problem of *akrasia*, but of ἀκολαστία, which is the case of extreme immorality (*Death of the Soul*, 98–103). The criticisms of Cranfield (*Romans*, 1:359) and Dunn (*Romans*, 1:389–40) miss the mark since they rely on identifying the ἐγώ as a Christian. There is no mention of the Spirit in these verses (Cranfield) nor is the anguish increased because of an eschatological tension (Dunn; cf. Chang's critic of Dunn ["Christian Life in a Dialectical Tension?"]).

[95] ἀλλὰ νικῶμαι κακοῖς. καὶ μανθάνω μὲν οἷα δρᾶν μέλλω κακά, θυμὸς δὲ κρείσσων τῶν ἐμῶν βουλευμάτων, ὅσπερ μεγίστων αἴτιος κακῶν βροτοῖς. Translation from Tobin, *Romans*, 233; Greek from Way, LCL. On the translation of this text, see Gill, "Did Chrysippus Understand Medea?" On the debate about whether this text is original and applies to the *akrasia* debate, see Rickert, "Akrasia and Euripides' Medea."

A. Paul's Critique of the Two-Ways Theology (7.7–25)

losophers debate the reason for this conflict. The Stoic tradition claimed that the person does evil because he or she lacks knowledge of what is right.[96] The Platonic tradition maintained that the problem results from a conflict between the rational and irrational parts of a human.[97] The account in Romans 7.15–20 is thought to describe an inner conflict between the speaker's mind and his base desires.[98] His mind wills to follow God's law, but his base desires, which are located in his flesh, overwhelm him and cause him to do evil. He does not take responsibility for his actions but attributes the evil to the "passions [ἁμαρτία] dwelling in me" (vv.17, 20). Stowers concludes, then, that the speaker suffers from a "moral schizophrenia."[99]

It seems clear that Paul is at least familiar with this perception on human ability, but recent attempts to align Paul with either philosophical interpretation or with the tradition as a whole underestimate the differences between Paul and the tradition. Paul's view does not square with either of the standard positions, which indicates that other issues have influenced his view.[100] The reference to deception (v.11) and the speaker's confusion over what is happening (v.15) could indicate that the issue is one of knowledge.[101] These two themes might connect Paul with the Stoic position. The speaker's problem, however, is not one of knowledge since he knows the law and what is expected of him.[102] He even recognises after further reflection that the outcome of his willing, despite his intention, is evil. Verse 15 describes the speaker's failure to grasp the full extent to which he is enslaved to Sin. Indeed, contrary to the Stoic position, it is precisely because good and evil are made known to the speaker in the Torah that he begins to sin (vv.7–11).

Paul's statements are closer to the Platonic position, but it is not clear that ἁμαρτία should be understood as "passion" or "desire." While Paul does write about "sinful passions" (τὰ παθήματα τῶν ἁμαρτιῶν) (v.5) and the fundamental error committed by the ἐγώ is ἐπιθυμία (v.7; cf. 6.12), his use

---

[96] E.g. Epictetus, *Discources*, 2.17.18–19, 21; 2.26.1–7.

[97] E.g. Galen, *Hippoc. et Plat.* 4.2.27; 4.6.19–22. Book 4 addresses the problem of the relationship between the mind and the passions.

[98] The scholars proposing this background have their differences, some minor, some major, but the basic outline of the interpretation is fairly consistent. Huggins ("Alleged Classical Parallels," 156–57) proposes that the portrayals of Medea be classified as "fatal fault" not *akrasia* (cf. Aristole, *Poet.* 13.5 [1453a 6–10]). Fatal fault points to a momentary mistake of judgment but not a lifetime of weakness. Ovid, however, places his description of Medea's struggle at the beginning of her life, and, by returning to it later in his story (*Met.* 7.92–93), he suggests that her life was marked by failure.

[99] Stowers, *Rereading Romans*, 280. Cf. Engberg-Pedersen, "Reception," 51.

[100] Tobin recognises the difficulty of placing Paul within either tradition (Paul's Rhetoric, 235). Stowers (*Rereading Romans*, 279) and Wasserman ("Paul among the Philosophers") place Paul within the Platonic tradition, while Engberg-Pedersen (*Paul and the Stoics*, 239–46; "Reception," 55–56) and Huttunen (*Paul and Epictetus*, 101–25) situate him in the Stoic tradition.

[101] For "deception" in the Stoic pattern, see Euripides, *Discources*, 1.28.6–8.

[102] Keck, *Romans*, 188.

of ἁμαρτία is distinct. ἁμαρτία causes one to have ἐπιθυμία: "But Sin (ἡ ἁμαρτία), receiving an opportunity through the commandment, worked in me all kinds of desire (πᾶσαν ἐπιθυμίαν)" (7.8). Similarly, in 6.12 Paul instructs the readers not to submit to Sin's lordship by allowing their "mortal bodies" to obey "its desires" (ταῖς ἐπιθυμίαις αὐτοῦ).[103] Sin expresses its reign by causing people to have inappropriate desires, but Sin is not identical to the desires. The speaker's problem is not desire, but the rule of Sin that causes him to desire.[104] While Paul is overtly interested in how "sin" expresses itself as "desire," his understanding of "sin" cannot be reduced to the irrational, appetitive desires. The attempt to situate Paul within the Platonic perspective confuses the result of Sin's impact on the ἐγώ with the actual problem from which the ἐγώ suffers.

Regardless of whether Paul's statements mirror either perspective of the *akrasia* tradition, his overall presentation of the ἐγώ differs at one crucial point, namely, the ἐγώ does not actively choose to sin. According to the *akrasia* tradition, while the person desires to do good he or she *actively* chooses the evil. This is clear in Medea's statement: "I see the better and approve, but I follow the worse" (Ovid, *Met.* 7.20–21 [Miller, LCL]). Despite knowing what is correct, she, of her own volition, chooses to do evil. The *akrasia* tradition requires that one interpret the speaker of Romans 7 as consciously willing the good and consciously choosing the evil. In Paul's description of the ἐγώ, however, this person desires the good but had his desire to do good twisted into evil by Sin. He has a single desire: to obey God's will as revealed in the Torah.[105] This alone occupies his mind and is what he attempts to do. The ἐγώ does not consciously engage in evil. It is instead the consequence of Sin's deceptive use of the law (v.11). There is no division in his desire.[106] The speaker's failure to actualise his desire to obey the Torah is the consequence of Sin dwelling within him (vv.17, 20, 23). Sin prevents him from doing the good that he sought by twisting his otherwise right desire to obey the Torah into transgressing the Torah. The conflict between "willing" and "doing" refers to the conflict between the ἐγώ and Sin, with the latter always turning the former's thoughts into the practice of evil.[107]

---

[103] Cf. Gen 4.7.

[104] Keck, *Romans*, 183.

[105] Nygren, *Romans*, 291; Packer, "The 'Wretched Man' Revisited," 77; Chester, *Conversion*, 190–93.

[106] Contra Stowers, *Rereading Romans*, 279–80. Meyer rightly states, "Paul is not talking about the conflict between the rational and the irrational in the human self, nor about two selves at different levels, as though one were under the power of sin and the other not. Both 'inmost self' (v.22) and 'members' (v.23) are but two aspects of the same self that is 'sold under sin'" ("Worm at the Core," 76).

[107] Contra Packer ("The 'Wretched Man' Revisited," 77) and Engberg-Pedersen (*Paul and the Stoics*, 244), there is no hint that the ἐγώ occasionally does the good that he desires. He is a complete failure. The suggestion that Paul is describing a Christian in Romans 7.13–25 cannot account for the complete failure and hopelessness of the speaker's situation.

A. Paul's Critique of the Two-Ways Theology (7.7–25)

The similarity between Paul's statements and the *akrasia* tradition shows that he was aware of this perspective on the relationship between willing and doing.[108] The attempt to place Paul within this tradition as it developed in the philosophical debates, however, leads to distortions in Paul's argument in Romans 7.7–25.[109] Fundamental differences exist, which should not be minimised, and these differences are significant enough to indicate that Paul rejects the standard Greco-Roman philosophical solutions to the problem of human inability. He stands as a critic of this conception of human agency.

With the introduction of this third actor, Paul attacks the foundations of the two-ways paradigm. No longer is it just God and the individual. Now other agents are involved in the relationship, agents for which the two-ways scheme cannot account. Paul's criticism is not just of the worldview held by the two-ways tradition. His criticism has a practical effect on the daily lives of those who attempt to live by the two-ways perspective. Fundamental to the two-ways tradition is the claim that the human can of his or her own volition decide to follow the law and having made that decision put his or her will into action. In his debate with other positions, Ben Sira makes human freedom and the capacity to obey central to his argument. God has left the human to determine his own destiny (Sir 15.14). He has the ability to keep the commandment (v.15). When the human sins, this is the result of his own will. God has certainly not caused the human to sin (vv.11–12), and since God is the only other agent in Ben Sira's two-agent drama, the human alone is to blame.

In contrast to Ben Sira, for whom the human agent must choose to sin, Paul asserts that the human agent will sin because he is a servant of Sin. Sin's reign over the human results in a different understanding of human capacity than that set forth by Ben Sira.[110] The human has no "free will" that allows him to choose between obedience or disobedience, life or death. Whereas in Ben Sira's view "ought" implies "can," in Paul's view "can" does not follow from "ought." As Martyn argues,

---

[108] Aletti argues that Paul is drawing on both Jewish traditions and the *akrasia* tradition with the result that both Jews and non-Jews can identify with the ἐγώ ("Rm 7.7–25 encore une fois").

[109] Comparison should be made with 4 Maccabees. The author explicitly addresses from a philosophical argument the issue of whether reason can control passion or desires (1.1, 12–13). He lists various examples of persons who controlled desire with reason, and he even cites the Tenth commandment as the reason one should avoid desire (2.5). While Paul's argument in Romans 7 is often paralleled with 4 Maccabees (Tobin, *Paul's Rhetoric*, 230–31), differences are rarely noted. Especially crucial is the explicit interest in philosophy in 4 Maccabees. This is lacking in Paul, and at the least suggests more caution when comparing Paul with the philosophical schools. Also, the author of 4 Maccabees thinks the law instructs the mind in what to avoid, but Paul holds that the law actually empowers Sin to bring about desire (Huggins, "Alleged Classical Parallels, 159). Cf. also the use of the Tenth commandment by Philo in *Decal.* 142–153, 173–174, and *Spec.* 4.79–131.

[110] Cf. Bergmeier, "Gesetz im Römerbrief," 72–73.

[W]ith a third actor in the drama, it is an understatement to say that the assumption of human moral competence cannot be maintained in its old and simple form. That is to say, with a third actor having power to set up its own "rule" – under God's ultimate sovereignty, to be sure – we obviously have a moral drama in which God's commandeering "ought" is far indeed from implying a simple "can" on the part of the human agent. Indeed in the Apocalyptic Moral Drama generally there is no human autonomy, for the human agent and his activity can be separated neither from the activity of God nor from the activity of the third actor."[111]

Life under the law, for Paul, is an existence without agency, for the human loses to Sin his or her ability. Under the law, human agency is illusionary. From Paul's perspective, those who adopt the two-ways pattern have failed to comprehend the depth of the human condition. They do not apprehend the true heinousness of Sin and the disastrous consequences it has for the human being.

3. Conclusion

In Romans 7.7–25, Paul critiques the widely-held view that one can attain life through obedience to the Torah. The ἐγώ represents anyone who attempts to live by the law and to acquire eschatological blessings through it. Particularly, he corresponds to Ben Sira's description of the human agent (Sir 15.11–20). Both look to the Torah as the means to life and both attempt to obey it. For Ben Sira the human is fully capable. Paul, however, portrays the human as incapable and continuously committing the evil he sought to avoid. His life is marked by failure and frustration and ultimately results in death. Sin reigns in his body, and while he resists with his mind, he finds that Sin ultimately determines his actions. He is a prisoner caught in Sin's web of death. Paul's conclusion is diametrically opposed to Ben Sira's: attempting to acquire life through the Torah only results in death.

Whereas Ben Sira sought to defend human freedom and responsibility with his argument that the human can respond to the divine demand, Paul argues that human freedom and ability are illusionary when one lives under the law. There is no correspondence between ought and ability for the person under the law according to Paul. The human agent who desires to order his or her life according to the commandments of the Torah will always fail. The law, then, cannot be the means to redemption from Sin's hold. Life cannot come through the Torah since the path of the Torah is a dead end – literally.

---

[111] Martyn, "New Created Agent," 10 (underline original). He is commenting on 1QS 3–4, but the statement is applicable to Paul.

B. Obedience Accomplished through the Spirit (8.1–13)

In Romans 6.1–8.13 Paul addresses the issue of whether his law-free gospel can manifest itself in obedient people. In 7.7–25 he argued that a prominent Jewish view on human agency, the two-ways tradition, cannot produce an adequate obedience. The human agent only disobeys. In 8.1–13 he adopts another Jewish pattern of human agency, which he modifies in light of his Christological conceptions. In this other perspective, obedience is made possible when God resolves the human problem and gives his Spirit as a source of empowerment. This results in the creation of human moral capacity and ultimately in the human being obedient.

Paul has often been portrayed as a maverick Jew, whose ideas find no home in the Jewish world. This is the case particularly when scholars describe Paul's soteriology. All other Jews, it has been claimed, held that salvation came through obedience, but Paul realised that salvation came through faith. In his rebuttal of this reading of Judaism, Sanders, according to some, failed to integrate Paul, and the picture of Paul as an anomaly within a grace-oriented Judaism sparked the New Perspective. The attempt by Dunn and other New Perspective proponents to integrate Paul into Sanders' Judaism, however, has come at a great price. We have already seen how in Romans 7.7–25 Paul critiques a common view of the divine-human relationship held by some Jews. The New Perspective, at this point, has sacrificed both Ben Sira's claims and Paul's criticisms in the attempt to make Paul fit a certain perspective on Judaism. Against Ben Sira only, Paul's perspective does make him a maverick who has radicalised divine action and eliminated human agency. Yet, the perspective offered by Ben Sira, while a (the?) dominant Jewish view of divine and human agency, was not the only Jewish explanation of the divine-human relationship available. The pattern of divine and human action developed in Romans 8.1–13 bears a remarkable similarity to that of the *Hodayot*: both present divine action as the solution to the human dilemma, and both emphasise the indwelling and empowering presence of the divine Spirit.

In the *Hodayot*, the hymnists develop an extremely pessimistic anthropology. They describe humans as sinful creatures bound by their very nature to disobedience. As "creatures of clay," they are ruled by their perverse spirits, and they only and always displease God. The solution to this problem is divine intervention. Among the various divine actions undertaken to alter the human's evil disposition, the constant thread uniting them all is the divine spirit. Temporally speaking, the first divine action is election. God decides prior to creation who will receive his grace and mercy. These God assigns to walk righteous paths, and he gives them his spirit. God's pre-temporal decision is manifest in history by the imparting of his spirit, who liberates the human from one's perverse spirits. The spirit gives knowledge to the elect, which enables the human to obey the Torah. The spirit empowers the human to obey.

Paul shows a familiarity with this tradition in two or three ways. First, the *Hodayot* explicitly connect the spirit with predestination. As the argument of Romans 8 progresses, Paul moves from the Spirit (v.27) to predestination (v.29; cf. 9.1–29). Paul does not connect directly the Spirit with predestination, but the movement from one to the other may indicate that Paul had some familiarity with this Jewish tradition. Second, Paul and the *Hodayot* share an emphasis on the divine Spirit as the means to obedience. The Spirit empowers one to fulfil God's will. Moreover, both authors have derived their understanding of the Spirit from Ezekiel. A third possible connection could be the pessimistic anthropology. Both texts highlight human incapacity, but the *Hodayot* expresses a much more negative evaluation of the creatureliness of humanity.

While it is impossible to know if Paul had read the *Hodayot* or encountered a *Hodayot*-like theology prior to or after his conversion, the similarities in thought, especially regarding the Spirit, indicate that Paul was not a maverick Jew, who had no knowledge of Palestinian traditions. Indeed, the similarities suggest the exact opposite: in Romans 7.7–8.13 Paul participates in an intra-Jewish debate over the divine-human relationship and specifically the human capacity to obey. In contrast to the two-ways paradigm advocated by Ben Sira, Paul follows a tradition described in the *Hodayot* that highlights divine action at every point and views this as the source for human action. The Spirit is imparted to humans as the enabling agent, and his presence establishes human agency.

1. The Christological Modification

The centre of Paul's thought emerges in the alterations he makes to this pattern of divine intervention. Christ's death on the cross is the decisive point when God broke into the age of the flesh (7.5) to resolve the human dilemma created by Sin and exacerbated by the law.[112] Paul modifies the pattern of the divine-human relationship to account for this event (1) by making it, rather than the pre-temporal decision of God, the point at which God intervenes and (2) by redefining the divine identity around Christ.

Whereas the Torah was incapable of dealing with Sin, "God condemned Sin in the flesh" of his Son, who was sent in "the likeness of sinful flesh and for sin" (v.3). Three points should be noted about this verse. First, God has acted with the specific purpose of destroying Sin's hold over humanity. With a sense of irony, Paul writes that "God condemned Sin." The expression is striking, for the very act (sin) and Being (Sin) that lead to the ἐγώ deserving condemnation (v.1; cf. 1.18) is now charged by God and bears the full weight of his wrath.

---

[112] Martyn writes, "There, in the thoroughly real event of Christ's crucifixion, God's war of liberation was commenced and decisively settled, making the cross the foundation of Paul's apocalyptic theology" (*Galatians*, 101).

B. Obedience Accomplished through the Spirit 155

κατακρίνω is always used in a forensic sense in the NT and LXX to denote the reality that punishment will come on those guilty of sinning.[113] In some occurrences, the term has the added notion of not only passing sentence, but also bringing about that sentence.[114] This double sense appears here.[115] In condemning Sin itself, God at the same time breaks its strangle-hold over the human agent.[116]

The irony continues: whereas Sin brought death to the ἐγώ (7.11; cf. 1.32; 5.17), it is by another's death that Sin is condemned.[117] "In the flesh" (8.3) refers to Jesus' physical body as the place where the condemnation takes place. It is in the very place that Sin had exercised its deadly rule (7.14, 18) that it itself is finally killed.[118] There is also a reversal of roles here. The death that the ἐγώ experienced in his body is transferred to the Son who, having embodied Sin in his flesh, assumes the speaker's death for him. The condemnation that all individuals deserve (cf. 5.18) is removed from them. As the act of baptism symbolises (6.3–7), believers are identified with Christ in his death and resurrection with the result that they no longer live to Sin. The transition from being "fleshly" and under the law happens not in the absence of death, but through death (cf. 7.4). What is avoided is the death (that is, the condemnation) due because of one's sinfulness since this is taken up by the Son who, being "in the likeness of sinful flesh," had Sin condemned in his flesh.[119]

Second, the Son participates in the human dilemma when he comes "in the likeness of sinful flesh" (ἐν ὁμοιώματι σαρκὸς ἁμαρτίας). The phrase "sinful flesh" recalls the claim, "I am fleshly, sold into slavery under Sin" (Rom 7.14). The combination of the two terms "flesh" and "sin" as descriptive of both the ἐγώ and the Son signifies the Son's full identity with the situation of the ἐγώ.[120] The difficulty of this phrase is the noun ὁμοίωμα, which can express complete identity (Phil 2.7) or similarity (Rom 1.23; 5.14; 6.5). Many reject the idea of complete identification in 8.3 because this would indicate that

---

[113] Cf. Sus 1.53; Mk 10.33; Rom 2.1.

[114] Cf. 1 Cor 11.32; 2 Pet 2.6.

[115] Schreiner, *Romans*, 402. Moo limits it to the judicial sense (*Romans*, 480–81).

[116] God's act of condemning Sin, however, is not dependent on the believer's fulfillment of the law as Elliott contends (*Rhetoric of Romans*, 248). Similarly, Lowe argues that there is no condemnation for those in Christ (8.1) because of (γάρ) the Spirit's transforming work (v.2) ("'There is No Condemnation'"). This interpretation misreads v.2 as referring to sanctification and ignores the description of God's act in Christ in v.3. See the response by McFadden, "Fulfillment of the Law's *Dikaiōma*."

[117] Dunn, *Romans*, 1:422.

[118] Bell, "Sacrifice," 8.

[119] One should not press the point too hard that God condemns Sin not Jesus (such as Wright, *Climax*, 213, does), for it is in Jesus' flesh that God's act of condemnation is executed (Gathercole, "Justified by Faith," 177). Jesus bears God's wrath when he embodies Sin within his flesh.

[120] Contrast Witherington: "'The likeness of sinful flesh' means Christ had real flesh, but it was not fallen and sinful flesh" (*Romans*, 213).

Christ himself sinned and would be deserving of punishment.[121] Yet, as Bell correctly points out, Paul is not referring to "Jesus committing sins; rather he is saying that Jesus fully participated in the sphere of humanity where a sinful existence is inevitable."[122] The Son took the same identity as other humans, a flesh ruled by Sin and subject to death, but unlike other humans he did not succumb to Sin's rule.[123] He conquered Sin by being obedient to the point of death, the divine will for his life (Phil 2.7; cf. Heb 5.8–9). As Fitzmyer writes,

> He came in a form like us in that he became a member of the sin-oriented human race; he experienced the effects of sin and suffered death, the result of sin, as one "cursed" by the law (Gal 3:13). Thus in his own self he coped with the power of sin. Paul's use of the phrase *sarx hamartias* denotes not the guilty human condition, but the proneness of humanity made of flesh that is oriented to sin.[124]

God's solution to the human problem is for his own Son to become human, and this action, rather than protecting the divine from the human problem caused by Sin, identifies the divine as truly participating in it.[125]

Third, God's ability to solve the human problem is set in direct contrast with the Torah. The Torah is incapable of dealing with Sin not because of some inherent fault, but rather because it is weakened by the more powerful flesh. God, working through his Son and his Spirit (v.2), however, destroys Sin's hold on the human when the Son appears in flesh. The seemingly powerful flesh that weakened the law turns out to be weak itself. This contrast between the Torah and God serves to heighten the significance of divine action in Paul's thought. Whereas the Torah left the human to confront the power of Sin on his or her own, God invades the human realm to destroy Sin's power.[126]

---

[121] E.g. Moo, *Romans*, 479–80. The sinlessness of Christ was a common early Christian viewpoint (John 7.18; 8.46; 2 Cor 5.21; Heb 4.15; 7.26; 1 Pet 2.22). Barnick argues that ὁμοίωμα always indicates complete identity ("Sinful Flesh,"), but Gillman, despite agreeing with Barnick's conclusion about the meaning of Rom 8.3, rightly criticises his lexical study ("Another Look").

[122] Bell, "Sacrifice," 6–7 (emphasis original). Jewett sidesteps the debate over ὁμοίωμα by interpreting σὰρξ ἁμαρτίας "as the perverse quest for honor that poisons every human endeavor" so that there is no problem with "Christ enter[ing] fully and without reservation into that social arena with all its evil consequences, at the cost of his own life" (*Romans*, 484). This concept of sin, however, is too limited to the social realm and fails to account for the problem created for the divine-human relationship (cf. also Carter's work, *Power of Sin*, which suffers from the same problem). See Barclay, "Is it Good News," 103–06.

[123] Barrett, Romans, 156; Käsemann, *Romans*, 217; Schmithals, *Römerbrief*, 262; Byrne, *Romans*, 236; Fee, *Pauline Christology*, 247; Wright, "Romans," 578.

[124] Fitzmyer, *Romans*, 485.

[125] Byrne, *Romans*, 236; cf. Dunn, *Theology of Paul*, 202–03.

[126] Verse 3a also clarifies the referent of νόμος in v.2. While some scholars think "the law of the Spirit of life" is the Torah under the influence of the Spirit (e.g. Dunn, *Romans*, 1:416;

B. Obedience Accomplished through the Spirit

The Christological modification extends also to the concept of God.[127] First, what God did in Christ defines who he is. He is "the one who raised Christ from the dead" (v.11b; cf. 4.24). God is now to be understood as God the Father and his Son is the one who he raised from the dead (1.4). God is also to be understood as the one who invaded the world by sending his Son to condemn Sin (8.3). In each of these statements, Paul's understanding of God and his activity is connected with the Christ-event. The events of Jesus' life, especially his death and resurrection, define who God is.

Second, this redefinition of the divine identity manifests itself in Paul's understanding of the Spirit. While in the OT and Second Temple Judaism the Spirit is associated with God alone, Paul claims that the Spirit must also be associated with the person and activities of Jesus. The Spirit is not simply the "Spirit of God." He is now known as "the Spirit of him who raised Jesus from the dead" (v.11a) and the "Spirit of Christ," the one resurrected and exalted by God.[128] Although often overlooked Paul only rarely speaks of the Spirit as being "of Christ" (Rom 8.9; Gal 4.6; Phil 1.19; cf. 2 Cor 3.17).[129] Dunn misunderstands the phrase "Spirit of Christ" (Rom 8.9) to mean an identification of the risen and exalted Christ with the Spirit. He writes, "As is generally recognized, Χριστός [in v.10] is used here synonymously with πνεῦμα θεοῦ = πνεῦμα Χριστοῦ"[130] While Paul undoubtedly links the Spirit and Christ together, it is not clear that he intends the two to be identified as one.[131] First, in other passages Paul clearly maintains a distinction between the Spirit and Jesus (e.g. 1 Cor 12.4–6; 2 Cor 13.14; Eph 4.4–6).[132] These passages should be borne in mind when discussing the three passages that link the Spirit and Christ with a genitive. Second, Christ's relationship to the Spirit is analogous to God's relationship to his Spirit. The Spirit is the presence and experience of God, but not the full embodiment of the person of God. That the Spirit is distinct from God the Father is clear because it is through the Spirit that one addresses God as Fa-

---

idem, *Theology of Paul*, 647; Schreiner, *Romans*, 400; Das, *Paul, the Law*, 228–32; Martyn, "Nomos;" Jewett, *Romans*, 481), the opening clause of v.3 indicates that the Torah cannot liberate from Sin (see Cranfield, *Romans*, 1:376; Keck, "'Law of Sin and Death,'" 49; Fee, *God's Empowering Presence*, 522–23; Moo, *Romans*, 474–75; Thielman, *Paul and the Law*, 201–02).

[127] See especially Watson, "Triune Divine Identity." Also, Fee, "Christology and Pneumatology."

[128] Cf. Meyer, "Holy Spirit," 8–9.

[129] This connection is made explicit in only three out of 145 occurrences of πνεῦμα in the Pauline corpus (Fee, *God's Empowering Presence*, 14–15).

[130] Dunn, *Romans*, 430; cf. Sanday and Headlam, *Romans*, 197 (but note the qualifications on pp.199–201); Leenhardt, *Romans*, 207; Starnitzke, *Struktur*, 178; Jewett, "Question of the 'Apportioned Spirit'," 197.

[131] Cf. Calvin, *Romans*, 165; Barrett, *Romans*, 159; Moo, *Romans*, 491; Schreiner, *Romans*, 413–14.

[132] See Gabriel, "Pauline Pneumatology."

ther (8.15).¹³³ Just as the "Spirit of God" is not God (the Father) himself, neither is the "Spirit of Christ" the risen Christ. He is the presence and experience of Christ, which is why Paul can write "Christ in you" (v.10a), but not Christ himself. Paul is not identifying the Spirit as the risen Christ, but he is attempting to express his understanding of God in light of his understanding of God's action in Christ. In so doing, he views the "Spirit of God" as the "Spirit of Christ," for he has already related God and Jesus as Father and Son (1.3–4; 8.3). Identifying the Spirit with both the Father and Son is simply a further extension of Paul's attempt to redefine the Jewish concept of God around Jesus.

Third, the linking of the Spirit with Christ not only signals a drastic redefinition of God, but also distinguishes Paul's conception of divine empowerment from his contemporaries. While other Jews pointed to the Spirit as the means to obedience, Paul insists that the Spirit must be connected with Christ. It is not enough to claim that the Spirit of God helps one. Rather, the Spirit that assists must be the Spirit of Christ.

This Christological modification to the pattern of the divine-human relationship already found in the *Hodayot* is significant. Whereas in the *Hodayot*, God's acts of deliverance were attributed to the outworking in time of his mysterious will to elect some unto salvation, Paul claims that God has invaded time in his Son (cf. Gal 1.4; 4.4–6). The theoretical consequences are that Paul both orients God's engagement with humanity around the Christ-event, and he redefines the concept of God around Jesus Christ. The practical result is that human agents, now free from Sin's grasp, are able to lead, through the Spirit of Christ, obedient lives that emulate God's act in Christ.

2. The Establishment of Human Ability

Much like the *Hodayot*, Paul sets forth the Spirit as the divine agent who empowers the human to obey God's will. The Spirit is God's and Christ's presence in the intermediate time between Christ's ascension and his return. As the embodiment of the divine presence, the Spirit's task, according to 8.4–13, is to enable those "in Christ" to please God by fulfilling the righteous requirement of the Torah. In this capacity, the Spirit creates human agency where Sin had prevented it.

Developing the antithesis of 7.5–6, Paul contrasts the Spirit with the flesh in 8.4–13. πνεῦμα is the divine Spirit imparted to believers, and σάρξ can be understood as a personal power or, more likely, a sphere of influence.¹³⁴ Paul's

---

¹³³ Fay, "Was Paul A Trinitarian?" 342.

¹³⁴ There is general agreement that in Romans 8.4–13 πνεῦμα and σάρξ are not anthropological terms for the constituent parts of the human being. Recently, though, van Kooten has argued for the anthropological reading (*Paul's Anthropology*, 383–88). He suggests that to live by the "flesh," as the lower plain of human existence, means acting immorally and following base desires, but to live by the "spirit," as the higher plane of existence, is to act morally and in

use of the term σάρξ is deliberately ambiguous. Here it likely summarises the argument of 7.7–25. Being enslaved to Sin and attempting to acquire life through law observance is to live according to the "mindset of the flesh," which results in death (8.5–6). The Spirit-flesh dualism is used in 8.1–13 primarily to highlight the change in aeons that has occurred because of God's act in Christ. The movement from one aeon to the next signals a change in lordship.[135] The human who is "in Christ" no longer exists in the flesh or under Sin's control. Now he or she lives in the age of Christ and under the "lordship" of the Spirit.

Paul's description of the Spirit is deliberately set up to contrast with the power of Sin. Both Sin and the Spirit are external agents that invade the human realm and take up residence within the human. From this internal position, Sin enslaves the human as a captive of war and rules over one's actions (7.14b, 23). The human loses the ability to enact his or her will. Every action done is attributed to "Sin dwelling in me" (vv.17, 20). While Sin destroys and prevents human agency, the Spirit creates it. Like Sin the Spirit establishes itself in the human. The indwelling of the Spirit is repeatedly emphasised in 8.9–11. Those who are "in the Spirit" are those in whom the Spirit resides (οἰκέω). Resurrection is accomplished by God through his Spirit which dwells within believers. The possession language is found also in the expression "Christ in you" (v.10). Paul's typical pattern is to speak of the believer being "in Christ." Here he reverses the formula in order to highlight the indwelling power of God as the characteristic of the believer and as the source of the believer's ability to obey. While Paul can describe both Sin and the Spirit as dwelling in a human, he does not think about them ruling in the same manner. Where Sin usurps the human's ability, the Spirit gives ability. Sin prevents the human from acting upon his or her desire to obey, but the Spirit enables obedience. Paul views the Spirit as the enabler who establishes human agency, so that the believer is neither a puppet moved at God's whim nor an independent agent capable of acting apart from the Spirit.

---

conformity to God's Spirit. Thus, throughout Romans 8.4–13 Paul is not speaking of the divine Spirit which guides the human agent in the fulfilment of the just requirement of the law, but of the human, who, having been assimilated to Christ through baptism, sets his mind on the things of the "spirit" and acts accordingly. Four points, however, demonstrate that Paul is not thinking about the constituent parts of the human. First, the term πνεῦμα occurs 34x in Romans, and the overwhelming majority refer to God's Spirit not the human's spirit. Second, the σάρξ-πνεῦμα dualism appears 3x in Romans prior to 8.4–13, and in each πνεῦμα is the divine Spirit (1.3–4; 2.28–29; 7.5–6). While σάρξ is anthropological in 1.3 and 2.28, 7.5–6 develops the γράμμα-πνεῦμα contrast, which is also found in 2.29. In this contrast, as the parallel in 2 Cor 3.3–6 shows, πνεῦμα is the Spirit. σάρξ in 7.5 indicates a realm within which humans dwell. Third, σάρξ and πνεῦμα in 8.1–13 derive their meaning from 7.5–6. To introduce an anthropological meaning would cause great confusion. Fourth, in 8.1–13 Paul relies on Ezekiel's portrait of divine intervention. In Ezekiel 11.19–20, 36.26–27, and 37.1–14, the divine Spirit is imparted to the human and enables obedience. The OT background is unmentioned by van Kooten. These four points indicate that Paul is not using σάρξ and πνεῦμα in an anthropological sense.

[135] Sanders, *Paul and Palestinian Judaism*, 497–98.

One should take note here of the scriptural background for Paul's understanding of the Spirit's agency. Like the *Hodayot*, Paul's view of the Spirit is informed by Ezekiel's statements about God giving his Spirit to enable his people to obey.[136] The Lord tells Israel that he will give to them a new spirit (Ezek 11.19; 36.26), which is identified as his own Spirit (36.27; 37.14). This new Spirit gives the people life (37.14) and leads them in obedience to the commandments (11.20; 36.27). Although Paul does not use the phrase "I will put my spirit in you" from Ezekiel as the *Hodayot* had done, the background should be clear enough. The Spirit and life are connected together throughout Romans 8.1–13. The Spirit is called the "Spirit of life" in v.2, and those who have "the mind of the Spirit" have "life and peace" (v.6) because "the Spirit is life" (v.10).[137] Paul attributes the future resurrection of believers to the Spirit's presence in their lives (v.11).[138] Paul also emphasises that the Spirit dwells within the believer, as just noted. Finally, he argues that the human is able to be obedient because of the Spirit's empowerment (vv.4, 13). The believer fulfils the "righteous requirement of the law" (τὸ δικαίωμα τοῦ νόμου) because the Spirit resides within and gives the ability to obey. This is precisely what Ezekiel was told would happen to the people: "I will put my Spirit in you and cause you to walk in my statutes [τοῖς δικαιώμασίν] and to keep and to do my judgments" (36.27; cf. 11.20).

This background in Ezekiel seems rather clear, but it is sometimes conflated with Jeremiah's promise of a "new covenant" (31[38].31–34).[139] The two are not identical however. Jeremiah relates that God "will put my law in their

---

[136] See particularly Yates, *Spirit and Creation*, 143–56.

[137] The referent of πνεῦμα in v.10 is disputed. Based on the contrast with "body," some suggest that it is the human spirit that is "alive" (Wright, *Climax*, 202 [he has since changed his view; see "Romans," 584n.269]; Fitzmyer, *Romans*, 491; NIV). The broader context, however, indicates that πνεῦμα is the divine Spirit: (1) life is connected with the Spirit throughout this section (vv.2, 6, 11, 13); and (2) according to v.11, which is expounding on v.10b, the human is given life because of the divine Spirit dwelling within (see Barrett, *Romans*, 159; Dunn, *Romans*, 1:427; Fee, *God's Empowering Presence*, 550–51; Schreiner, *Romans*, 414–15).

[138] NA[27] accepts διὰ τοῦ ἐνοικοῦντος αὐτοῦ πνεύματος ἐν ὑμῖν at the end of v.11, which means "through his Spirit who is indwelling in you." An alternative textual tradition has διὰ τὸ ἐνοικοῦν αὐτοῦ πνεύματος ἐν ὑμῖν: "because of his Spirit who is indwelling in you." The first reading means that the Spirit is the agent who gives resurrection life, while the second indicates that possession of the Spirit is the reason God makes alive. Both variants are strongly supported, thereby making external evidence inconclusive (Cranfield, *Romans*, 1:391–92). Schreiner (*Romans*, 417) rightly notes, against Fee (*God's Empowering Presence*, 543, 553), that the Spirit is the active agent who brings to life in Ezekiel 37. Those who accept the genitive reading typically view the Spirit as an intermediary agent in the act of resurrection (cf. Moo, *Romans*, 493; Wright, "Romans," 585). The two readings are not that different then, and whichever variant is original, the basic point remains the same: only those who have the Spirit will experience life.

[139] So Bruce, *Romans*, 161–62; Lyonnet, "Rom 8,2–4 à la lumière de Jérémie 31 et d'Ézéchiel 38–40;" Zeller, *Brief an die Römer*, 153.

B. Obedience Accomplished through the Spirit

minds and write it on their hearts," which leads to obedience because each person knows the law (vv.33–34). Ezekiel writes that God implants his Spirit and through the Spirit one obeys the law. Paul's statements are based on Ezekiel's because he claims that the Spirit is imparted to believers not the law. As in Romans 7, the law remains outside the human as a demand that must be met. Paul claims in 8.1–13 that it is met not because it is placed within each person but because the Spirit directs the lives of those "in Christ." This subtle difference between what God puts in each person is important for Paul's argument. He is able to distance himself and his gospel from the law, while also maintaining that the law is fulfilled by those who believe his gospel.[140]

The Spirit establishes human agency when it creates the possibility for obedience by freeing the human from Sin's enslaving rule. "The law of the Spirit of life in Christ Jesus has set you free from the law of Sin and death" (8.2). Paul's claims about freedom in chapter 6 and 7.1–6 culminate in this statement.[141] It is here that the readers learn that their freedom has been accomplished for them by the Spirit. Paul uses the same slavery language (although not the military terminology) to depict the human's service to both Sin and God, but, in a striking paradox, while slavery to Sin is bondage, slavery to the Spirit is freedom. "But having been freed from Sin, you became slaves to righteousness" (6.18). Again: "But now having been freed from Sin, but enslaved to God" (v.22).[142] The freedom from Sin accomplished by the Spirit, rather than resulting in licentiousness, creates the possibility for the believer to obey God's will. The Pauline conception of freedom is not one of an absolute freedom wherein the believer becomes an autonomous being. In Paul's worldview, the human is always connected with one ruling power or another, either God or the agents of evil (Sin and the Flesh).[143] Freedom from Sin, for Paul, is freedom to God, and it is when a person is united to Christ and walking by the Spirit that he or she is truly free.

The Spirit not only frees the human and thereby creates the possibility for obedience. He also functions as the empowering agent through whom believers "please God" (8.8). Positively, the Spirit assists believers to do precisely what Sin had prevented, namely, fulfil the Torah's righteous requirement (τὸ δικαίωμα τοῦ νόμου) (v.4). A significant number of scholars contend that in v.4 Paul continues to describe what God has done in Christ for believers.[144]

---

[140] In a different context (2 Cor 3.1–6), however, Paul is able to conflate Jeremiah 31[38].31–34 and Ezekiel 36–37. The differences likely arise from the social contexts of the two letters and Paul's argumentative strategy.

[141] Because he identifies the speaker of Romans 7 as a Christian, Cranfield is forced to take the claim of freedom in 8.2 in a weakened sense as indicating only partial freedom from Sin's tyranny ("Sanctification as Freedom," 38–40).

[142] Cf. Gal 5.1, 13.

[143] Käsemann, "Primitive Christian Apocalyptic," 136.

[144] E.g. Melanchthon, *Romans*, 166–67; Ziesler, *Romans*, 208; Wright, *Climax*, 212; Keck, *Romans*, 200; Pate, *Reverse of the Curse*, 266–67; Lichtenberger, *Das Ich Adams*, 196–97.

Because of the judicial language in vv.1, 3, τὸ δικαίωμα τοῦ νόμου is "the righteousness required by the law" (Byrne) or "the just requirement of the law" (Moo), which Moo explains as "the demand for perfect obedience, or for righteousness."[145] Calvin and Moo argue that the law's demand cannot be satisfied by the human agent. Christ, however, because of his perfectly obedient life or death (or both) has satisfied this requirement, which is transferred to the human when one believes in him.[146] The Christian does not actively fulfill the law, as the passive πληρωθῇ, which must be given its full weight as a divine passive, indicates.[147] Unlike the ἐγώ who sought to keep the Torah by his own volition, those in Christ, here described as those "who walk according to the Spirit," have τὸ δικαίωμα τοῦ νόμου fulfilled on their behalf. The passive indicates that God is the one who actually satisfies the δικαίωμα of the law. Käsemann pointedly writes, "God alone fulfills what he demands. He does it paradoxically on the cross with the sending of his Son as a sin-offering, and therefore apart from and even in opposition to our cooperation."[148] This is implied also by the participial clause that characterises those who benefit from Christ's death. The participial is not conditional ("if we walk") nor modal ("by our walking") but descriptive of those in whom the law's righteousness is fulfilled.[149] Likewise, ἐν ἡμῖν, translated as "in us," suggests that this requirement is not accomplished by believers.[150] Moo summarises the thought: "[T]he law's just demand is fulfilled in Christians not through their own acts of obedience but through their incorporation into Christ."[151]

Despite the theological attractiveness of this interpretation, it should be rejected. The passive voice does not automatically indicate divine action and preclude all human action.[152] Rather, the passive prevents one from assuming that the human agent acts alone after God has freed him or her from Sin's enslavement. Without the passive, one could parallel Paul's statement to Ben Sira's conception of Wisdom assisting the obedient. In Ben Sira's view, the human remains the primary actor, and it is precisely this conception that Paul avoids by

---

[145] Byrne, "Living Out," 569; idem, *Romans*, 237 (cf. Fitzmyer, *Romans*, 487); Moo, *Romans*, 482, 484.

[146] Calvin, *Romans*, 160; Moo, *Romans*, 483.

[147] Keck, "Law of Sin and Death," 52; Byrne, "Living out," 569; Moo, *Romans*, 482–84; Fitzmyer, *Romans*, 487.

[148] Käsemann, *Romans*, 218–19.

[149] Conditional: Fitzmyer, *Romans*, 488. Modal: Cranfield, *Romans*, 385; VanLandingham, *Judgment and Justification*, 238 (although the ultimate conclusion drawn by these two is radically different). Descriptive: Moo, *Romans*, 484.

[150] So Keck, *Romans*, 200; cf. Fee, *God's Empowering Presence*, 536n.191.

[151] Moo, *Romans*, 484.

[152] Schreiner notes that the use of the passive of πληροῦν in 2 Cor 10.6, Phil 1.11, Col 1.9, and Eph 5.18 do not exclude human activity (*Romans*, 405). His examples, however, are not particularly strong, for the point in the verses is often that God has done something for the human or it is an activity that the human can accomplish alone.

using the passive. The human, in Paul's view, never acts without the constant reminder that it is God himself who is acting through the human to fulfil the just requirement.[153] The Spirit is not merely an aide who comes alongside, as Wisdom was for Ben Sira. Instead, the Spirit indwells the human and actually brings about the fulfilment of the "just requirement." Paul's use of the passive compares with the use of the hiphil in the *Hodayot* to express the notion that God is the underlying cause of the human's obedience (see 1QH[a] 6.24). The passive is absolutely necessary and should not be downplayed or ignored, but neither does it rule out human agency.[154] The point of the passive is to make human agency actually possible by grounding it in divine action.

The broader context further supports interpreting 8.4 as being about human action. The argument throughout 7.7–8.13 concerns the ability of the human to fulfil the Torah, and the issue in 6.1–8.13 is whether Paul's law-free gospel results in sinful behaviour or obedience. His interlocutor holds that obedience is only possible when the human orders his or her life around the Torah. Paul has argued that a Torah-centred existence actually results in disobedience (7.7–25), and he now completes the argument by claiming that only those in possession of (and possessed by) Christ's Spirit fulfil the Torah. His gospel about Christ does result in obedience. The ἵνα at the beginning of 8.4 indicates that the purpose for God's liberating act was to secure for himself an obedient people. Far from resulting in sinful behaviour (cf. 3.8), Paul's proclamation of the gospel was intended to result in obedience (cf. 1.5; 15.18). The human under the law could not obey the divine demand placed before him and instead he "bore fruit unto death" (7.5). The believer, however, no longer lives under the law or in the flesh, and he or she instead bears fruit unto God (v.4). As 7.6 indicates the human's transition from being in the flesh and under the Torah's rule is so that one might serve God according to the Spirit. This is exactly what Paul expresses in 8.1–4. God has freed humans from Sin's grasp, and this results in obedience.

In 8.3–4 Paul argues that his gospel has the specific purpose of creating an obedient people who, with the Spirit's enablement, fulfil the Torah's just requirement. The issue remains of what τὸ δικαίωμα τοῦ νόμου means. The term δικαίωμα is used by Paul only in Romans. In 1.32 and 2.26 it has the meaning "ordinance." Significantly, in 2.26 circumcision is excluded from "the requirements of the law" (τὰ δικαιώματα τοῦ νόμου). In 5.16, 18 it is used

---

[153] Compare the logic of Phil 2.12–13. Paul exhorts the Philippians to "work out your salvation with fear and trembling" and grounds this command in the divine act: "for (γάρ) God is the one working in you both to will and to work concerning his good pleasure."

[154] Cf. Zeller, *Brief an die Römer*, 153: "Das ist zunächst passiv als Intention des Werkes Gottes beschrieben, geschieht aber durch unseren aktiven „Wandel" gemäß der Wirklichkeit, in der wir uns nun befinden, nämlich dem Geist." Contrast Engberg-Pedersen (*Paul and the Stoics*, 371n), who thinks the passive is irrelevant and to give any emphasis to it is to fall under "the long shadow of traditional Protestantism."

rhetorically in contrast with κατάκριμα and παράπτωμα, and means "righteousness" or "righteous act." Since Paul writes about human action in 8.4, δικαίωμα cannot mean the righteousness required by the law or the life that the law intended to give. To accept either of these would make attaining righteousness and life dependent on the human agent. Paul maintains in Romans (cf. 3.20–24; 11.6) and his other letters (cf. Gal 2.15–16; Phil 3.9) that the human cannot attain righteousness or life through obedience to the law or any other human endeavour.

The singular δικαίωμα is striking since it does not match Romans 2.26 nor conform to the Septuagintial use. It is rarely used in the LXX with reference to a single commandment, and when so used the specific commandment is always identified in the immediate context (cf. Exod 21.9; Num 31.21; Ruth 4.7).[155] In Romans 8.4, though, no specific commandment is clearly identified. Watson, therefore, thinks Paul "construes the law not as a multiplicity of demands but as a singular, comprehensive demand" that is different from the γράμμα (cf. 7.6), and Schreiner indentifies specifically the "moral norms."[156] Yet this reading also attributes to δικαίωμα a meaning that is unparalleled in the LXX. Although δικαίωμα can be used in the singular to classify multiple commandments as a whole, these are always identified.[157] The evidence of the LXX, therefore, is not helpful for establishing Paul's usage.

The identification with the "moral norms" suggested by Schreiner is unlikely. Not only is the category "moral norms" anachronistic, but Paul only rarely appeals to the Torah's commandments themselves for ethical instruction.[158] Moreover, at points where Paul could have used the Torah to direct his congregations, he does not. For example, the situation of the man having sexual relations with his stepmother in the Corinthian church (1 Cor 5.1–13) could

---

[155] So Ziesler, *Romans*, 207; Watson, *Paul, Judaism, and the Gentiles²*, 299. The phrase τὸ δικαίωμα τοῦ νόμου appears in the LXX only at Num 31.21.

[156] Watson, *Paul, Judaism, and the Gentiles²*, 299; Schreiner, *Romans*, 407; idem, "Abolition and Fulfillment," 59–65. Cf. Dunn, *Romans*, 1:423; Bayes, *Weakness*, 88–92.

[157] E.g. Num 35.29 which concludes the laws about avenging and the cities of refuge.

[158] In the undisputed epistles, Paul appeals to Deut 25.4 in 1 Cor 9.8–10, but he denies the literal sense and interprets it allegorically. Also, 1 Cor 14.34 (if authentic) is often understood as a reference to the Torah. Here, however, Paul does not appear to have a specific command in view, but he makes a deduction from the narrative of the Torah. This verse parallels then 1 Cor 10.1–14 in which Paul appeals to events recounted in the Torah as instruction for the church. Note here that Paul does not utilise specific commandments but narrative events. The Sinai legislation is not drawn on.

B. Obedience Accomplished through the Spirit

have been resolved by appealing to the Torah (cf. Deut 23.1 [22.30]; 27.20).[159] The avoidance of the Torah is significant indeed. When Paul does appeal to the commandments as ethical injunctions, he reduces the Ten Commandments to a single commandment: love your neighbour (Rom 13.8–10). Paul does not revitalise the "moral norms" of the Torah in his churches, and while his ethics are virtually identical to the Torah, he does not claim the Torah's commandments as support for his position.[160]

Elsewhere in the Pauline corpus, the verb πληροῦν or the noun πλήρωμα occur with the noun νόμος five times. Except Galatians 4.4, which is irrelevant to this discussion, and Romans 8.4, the law to be fulfilled is identified explicitly as the love commandment (Gal 5.14; Rom 13.8, 10). In Galatians 5.13, Paul exhorts the readers to not misuse their freedom to satisfy the flesh, but "to serve one another in love." He continues, "For the whole law is fulfilled in one word, in this: love your neighbour as yourself" (v.14).[161] The parallels with Romans 8.1–13 are clear. The Roman Christians, as with the Galatians, have been set free from Sin and the flesh and now they live according to the Spirit. The primary expression of the Spirit's guidance in one's life is love.[162] Romans 13.8–10 is even more explicit. Paul writes, "For the one who loves another fulfils the law" (v.8). After listing several of the ten commandments, including the commandment not to covet (v.9), he concludes, "Love for a neighbour does not produce evil. Therefore, love is the fulfilment of the law" (v.10). The entire law, including the "moral norms," is reduced to the single

---

[159] Paul's conclusion, "Purge the evil from among you" (1 Cor 5.13), is likely drawn from Deuteronomy (17.7; 19.19; 21.21; 22.21; 24.7; cf. 13.5). Yet this command lacks any specificity and functions as a refrain indicating that evil is not to be found among the people of God. In his study on scripture and ethics in 1 Cor 5–7, Rosner is only able to identify general motifs from the Torah that have influenced Paul's argument in 5.1–13 (*Paul, Scripture and Ethics*, 61–93). Where he is able to locate specific commands that may have influenced Paul, the ideas are too widespread to claim that Paul is actually expecting his readers to obey the Torah's commandments. Rosner finds no specific commandments that Paul tells his readers to follow. There seems to be a serious methodological flaw in Rosner's and others' works, namely if there is similarity, then Paul is dependent on the Torah and he expects his readers to obey it. Paul's ethics are undoubtedly similar, but his lack of specific reference to the Torah indicates that he does not view the Torah as something to be done or obeyed by his congregations.

[160] See Moo, "Law of Christ;" Westerholm, *Perspectives*, 408–39 (esp. 431–39).

[161] The connection between 5.14 and 6.2 is disputed. The latter reads: "Bear one another's burdens and thus you will fulfil the law of Christ" (ἀναπληρώσετε τὸν νόμον τοῦ Χριστοῦ). See Barclay, *Obeying the Truth*, 126–35, for the options.

[162] This is probably why "love" (ἀγάπη) appears first in the list of the "fruit of the Spirit" (Gal 5.22).

commandment "love your neighbour as yourself."[163] The love commandment functions as Paul's summary of the entire ethical instruction in the Torah.[164]

Although in 8.4 Paul does not explicitly mention the love commandment, the repetition of the fulfilment language in 13.8–10 makes the connection likely. It is not necessary for the readers to understand on the first reading of 8.4 that loving one another is the fulfilment of the commandments. As the letter progresses, they would make the connection (Paul hopes) and realise that in expressing love to one another, especially across the divide created between the weak and strong (14.1–15.13), they are fulfilling the law's requirement. In 8.4 Paul is describing the outcome of God's act in Christ and is not detailing how the community will enact the fulfilment of the law.[165] The outcome of God's act is that believers, in contrast to the ἐγώ, will be obedient (cf. 8.8). The righteous requirement of the law is fulfilled as the Spirit of Christ produces in us the love that Christ showed in his death for us (cf. 5.5–8).

This enactment of love is possible only because the Spirit of life dwells within believers and serves as a source of power. Likewise the ability to avoid committing evil deeds is possible only by the Spirit: "For if you live according to the flesh, you will certainly die. But if by the Spirit [πνεύματι] you put to death the practices of the body, you will live" (8.13). "The practices of the body" refers to the acts and thoughts of the flesh that are manifest in the body. To live "according to the flesh" is to perform "the practices of the body." The expression connects back to the description of Sin as dwelling within the body

---

[163] Ziesler argues that the "just requirement" is the tenth commandment, which the ἐγώ was unable to keep but believers do (*Romans*, 207). The connection with the love commandment is more likely, however, since Paul uses the tenth commandment to summarise what the law demands of those under its rule and the love commandment to summarise how one lives according to the Spirit. The tenth commandment, as a prohibition – "You shall not" – stands negatively for what the law demands, while the love commandment presents positively what believers do. Cranfield argues that the righteous requirement of the law is fulfilled by those who walk according to the Spirit when they have faith in God, which is revealed in their obedient lives (*Romans*, 1:384–85). Yet this reading conflicts with Paul's argument that the law does not rest on faith but doing, "the one who does these things will live by them" (Lev 18.5 quoted in Rom 10.4; Gal 3.12), as Gal 3.11–12 makes clear (cf. Moo, *Romans*, 482).

[164] For the identification of the "just requirement of the law" as the love command, see also Bruce, *Romans*, 161; Fee, *God's Empowering Presence*, 537; Kruse, "Paul, the Law, and the Spirit," 126–27; Wells, "Grace, Obedience," 223–25.

[165] Romans 8.1–13 is, in form, a description of the benefits of being in Christ and how those in Christ act (Moo, *Romans*, 486; Fee, *God's Empowering Presence*, 539). Underlying this description is an "implied exhortation" for the Roman Christians to see themselves as those in Christ and therefore to act accordingly (Lambrecht, "Implied Exhortation;" Engberg-Pedersen, *Paul and the Stoics*, 250–52). This implied exhortation should not be dismissed, but neither should it be made the central point. The failure to hold the two together appears in each of the studies just noted. It is the tension between these two that allows Paul to leave undefined the "righteous requirement of the law."

(6.6) and causing the body to die (7.24; 8.10). Through the Spirit's enabling guidance, one is able to kill these evil deeds. Paul likely placed πνεύματι at the beginning of the clause for emphasis. He wants the readers to understand that they cannot overcome the flesh and Sin alone. Only with the Spirit's help can this be accomplished. Moo rightly concludes:

> Holiness of life, then, is achieved neither by our own unaided effort – the error of "moralism" or "legalism" – nor by the Spirit apart from our participation – as some who insist that the key to holy living is "surrender" or "let go and let God" would have it – but by our constant living out the "life" placed within us by the Spirit who has taken up residence within.[166]

As with the passive voice and the reference to the Spirit in v.4, the emphatic placement of πνεύματι reminds the readers that the obedience required for life arises from a unification between the divine and human agents. The presence of the divine Spirit does not negate human action. Rather, it enhances the importance of the human act. Paul's warning is addressed to an agent who, because of Christ's death and his indwelling Spirit, now possesses the ability to please God. Paul's account of the moral capacity of those in Christ is radically opposed to the description of human moral capacity in 7.7–25. The human's essence has been completely reformed, and now under the lordship of Christ and led by the Spirit, one is able to be addressed with moral demands and to fulfil them.

The warning in v.13 should not be passed over too quickly, for it provides a crucial key to understanding Paul's view of agency.[167] He threatens eschatological death to any who, despite being united to Christ ("brothers"), continue to live according to the flesh. His warning also indicates that, in some manner, eternal life is dependent on obedience. VanLandingham argues vehemently that this verse indicates that eternal life is contingent solely on what the human does. He writes, "This conditional sentence indicates that life or death depends on what the believer does, not the Spirit."[168] While Christ's death rectified the past transgressions of the believer and enables the possibility, with the Spirit's inspiration, for him or her to act righteously, the outcome at the judgment is ultimately determined by his or her obedience.[169] Whether one lives or dies is determined by his or her obedience or disobedience, and God's actions in Christ and his Spirit play no part in determining one's eternal destiny.

---

[166] Moo, *Romans*, 495–96.

[167] Warnings of this sort are fairly common in Paul's letters, e.g. Gal 6.7–9; 1 Cor 10.1–13; 2 Cor 13.5. See Schreiner, *New Testament Theology*, 573–85.

[168] VanLandingham, *Judgment and Justification*, 239.

[169] VanLandingham, *Judgment and Justification*, 335. VanLandingham's entire project is deeply concerned with demonstrating that humans have "libertarian" free will and that the Spirit does not affect this. Because of this particular understanding of free will, he consistently sets the action of humans against God's, and he insists that the Spirit does little more than "inspire" (meaning: encourage) obedience (cf. p.187, 238)

VanLandingham's interpretation is questionable at numerous points. He ignores the connections between the Spirit and life earlier in the section (vv.2, 6, 10). These statements culminate in the emphatic claim of v.11: those in whom the Spirit dwells will be raised, just as Jesus was. Literally, "your mortal bodies will be made alive."[170] If the genitive is the correct reading, then the connection between the Spirit and life is even greater, for it is "by his Spirit which is dwelling in you" that God makes alive. The future life of the believer is attributed to the presence of the "Spirit of life" within the believer.[171] This reference to the "mortal body" prepares one for the phrase "practices of the body" in v.13 and suggests some continuity between the promise of bodily resurrection because of the Spirit's presence and the act of obedience on the part of the human with the Spirit's enablement. When the warning of v.13 is read within this context of the Spirit's connection with life, the conclusion emerges that the believer's act to destroy the practices of the body that results in life is the outworking of the Spirit's life-giving presence within the believer.

This conclusion (that obedience is the outworking of the Spirit's act to make alive) does not negate the human act of obedience, not least because Paul, unlike VanLandingham, finds no conflict between the divine and human agents. On the contrary, this conclusion actually enhances the significance of obedience. The warning, on the one hand, prevents one from drawing the conclusion that Paul eliminates human agency with his emphasis on God's invading action in Christ and the Spirit. The warning is addressed to the human agent, and even with the Spirit's empowerment, the human must act in obedience. Believers are not mere robots controlled by the Spirit, as the non-Christian is under the control of Sin (7.7–25). Without the daily re-enactment of Christ's death, the believer declares himself or herself to be separated from the Spirit that gives life. On the other hand, Paul does not reverse his claims about what God has done and is doing. As seen already, even the warning, with the emphatic placement of πνεύματι, underscores the importance of divine action for human action. The warning, with its mixture of divine and human action, indicates that Paul's conception of the divine-human relationship cannot be reduced to an oppositional framework. The divine and human do not stand opposed to one another. The warning rather reveals the joining of the divine and human agents.

---

[170] Engberg-Pedersen argues that the phrase "the body is dead" in v.10 must be taken seriously as a claim that the Roman Christians' bodies have truly died and become "a hollow shell ... as compared with the *pneuma* inside the shell" ("Material Spirit," 192). His emphasis on the problem found in the body, however, does not explain Paul's statement in v.11 that the body will be made alive. Paul speaks here neither of the body "literally die[ing] (*completely*, we might say)," which must mean something like the body ceasing to exist, nor of it being "transformed *completely* by the *pneuma*" (p.193; emphasis original).

[171] Cf. Blackwell, "Christosis," 120–22; Bertone, "Function of the Spirit," 93–96.

B. Obedience Accomplished through the Spirit

God now participates in human obedience, and his engagement with the human makes human action all the more important.[172]

Paul's view, therefore, is at some distance from the two-ways paradigm. While Paul lays both "death" and "life" before the human, he does not Christianise the two-ways pattern.[173] In the two-ways scheme, the human stands *alone* before life and death, and he or she makes the decision to follow one path or the other independent of divine action. In Paul's view, however, the human agent does not stand before life and death alone. The Spirit of Christ dwells within him or her. The presence of the divine agent from the beginning is a significant difference between Paul and the two-ways scheme.[174] Additionally, it would be inaccurate to describe the believer's obedience as a "response" to God's act in Christ, as some have done who describe Paul in terms of covenantal nomism.[175] Conceiving of obedience in this manner makes it a secondary step following from God's act. For Paul, though, obedience is a continuation of God's act. There is no separation between God's deliverance of the human in Christ and God's Spirit conforming believers into the image of Christ. Indeed, Christian obedience is the re-enactment of the Christ-event in the daily lives of the individual and the community, and this is done when the Spirit empowers believers to "put to death the practices of the body" (8.13) or, stated positively, to "fulfil the righteous requirement of the Torah" (v.4).[176] Obedience is not simply the human's independent response to God's gracious deliverance from Sin. Rather, it is a continuation of God's gracious work in the believer's life.

Like the *Hodayot*, Paul holds the divine and human agents together. For the hymnist, God's gift of the Spirit of knowledge is the enactment of the pre-temporal decision by God to elect him into the community of the redeemed. This Spirit imparts knowledge to the human and empowers him to resist his own creaturely failings. His obedience to the knowledge given by the Spirit is the expression of God's mercy working, through the Spirit, in him. God's hand is

---

[172] "[F]or Paul, God's saving agency includes human agency within its scope, establishing it on a wholly new foundation rather than excluding or eliminating it" (Watson, *Paul, Judaism, and the Gentiles*², 213).

[173] Contra Dunn (*Romans*, 449) and Fee (*God's Empowering Presence*, 558), who suggest that Paul is following Deuteronomy 30.15–20. In one sense, everyone works with the two-ways scheme, for "life" and "death" are the only two options. The issue then is how one formulates the actions of the divine and human agents in relation to the two ways.

[174] This difference is completely missed by VanLandingham (*Judgment and Justification*, 239), who seriously underestimates the significance of the Spirit's involvement.

[175] Hooker, "Paul and 'Covenantal Nomism'," 52; Garlington, 'Obedience of Faith', 264–65; Yinger, *Judgment*, 288–90; Dunn, *Theology of Paul*, 632. Each of these acknowledges that the term "covenantal nomism" is inaccurate, but they contend that the basic structure of covenantal nomism is identical to Paul's framework. For a reply, see O'Brien, "Was Paul a Covenantal Nomist?" (although he misses some key issues).

[176] Cf. Gorman, *Cruciformity*, 56–61. He describes Christian love as the Spirit's work to replicate Christ's love in the believer and the community.

seen at every stage, but this does not eliminate the need for the human to act upon the knowledge he receives. In fact, the failure to be obedient is a sign that one does not possess the Spirit and therefore is outside the bounds of God's grace.

The similarities with Paul, given the Christological modifications, are obvious. God's gift of the Spirit is the continuation of his work in his Son which has brought freedom for the human from Sin's control. Those freed by Christ's death are united both with Christ and with others so that they form a community known as those "in Christ." Those in Christ possess his Spirit, who in giving life also gives power to resist the flesh. Their obedience is the outworking of God's mercy in their lives and the evidence of the Spirit in their lives. Just as in the *Hodayot*, God's activity is clearly visible at each point. Also, as in the *Hodayot*, the failure for the human to be obedient is evidence that he or she does not possess the Spirit of Christ and remains under Sin's control.

The insistence by both the hymnist and Paul that those in their salvific communities lead lives pleasing to God does not collapse into "works-righteousness." Both do make eternal life contingent on the human agent's enactment of God's work in them. But neither author describes human activity as independent of divine action. This is a significant difference from what has traditionally been understood as "works-righteousness" or "legalism." Legalism refers to the human agent acting apart from divine assistance with the goal of attaining (eternal) life or righteousness. For both Paul and the hymnist, any attempt to be obedient apart from divine intervention is simply impossible. Both hold that human action is the expression of the divine impartation of life, so that far from trying to earn life, the human is revealing the life already possessed. The failure to obey reveals that one does not have life. The obedience of the believer, in either the Essene/Qumran community or the Christian community, is absolutely necessary so that without it salvation is impossible, but it is not the sole means to attaining salvation, even at the final judgment, for obedience is the outworking of the divine act.[177]

C. Conclusion

Romans 7.7–8.13 is a unified section in which Paul argues against the presumption that obedience is only possible when one's life is oriented around the law. This lifestyle does not please God and will not result in life and blessing, for it only brings death. God has acted in his own Son, Jesus Christ, to destroy Sin's hold over the human agent, and the result is freedom to live for God through

---

[177] "Preserving ourselves is not an independent thing that is added paradoxically to the divine preservation. God's preservation and our self-preservation do not stand in mere coordination, but in a marvellous way they *are* in correlation. One can formulate it best in this way: *our* preservation of ourselves is entirely oriented to *God's* preservation of us" (Berkouwer, *Faith and Perseverance*, 104; emphasis original).

his empowering Spirit. The Spirit leads the human in the act of fulfilling the righteous requirement of the law and in putting to death the evil practices associated with the flesh. Obedience is produced through the Spirit, and the charge of the interlocutor is found to be groundless.

On the issue of divine and human agency, this section of Romans indicates that Paul did not set the divine and human agents in opposition to one another. Paul rejects, on the one hand, the model set forth in the two-ways tradition in which the human agent must be emphasised at the expense of the divine agent. On the other hand, while Paul's pessimistic anthropology leads him to emphasise God's act in Christ, this is not done at the expense of the human agent. The freedom and redemption secured through Christ creates the possibility for human action so that the human becomes a real agent. The human and the divine Spirit work together to maintain the life given because of Christ's death. There is no opposition between the divine and human agent, as if when one works the other ceases. Rather, Paul holds both together arguing that only when both act together can the human obey in a manner pleasing to God.

The conclusions drawn from this study of Romans 7.7–8.13 can be related to two recent debates about Paul. First, scholarship has tended to read Paul's letters in light of a monolithic understanding of Judaism. More recently, however, scholars have begun to take the diversity of Judaism seriously,[178] and in this section of Romans, Paul witnesses to this diversity. Here he engages in an inter-Jewish debate carried out on two fronts. In 7.7–25 he challenges the two-ways tradition on anthropological grounds. The human cannot keep the law in a manner sufficient to bring about life. A divine action is required to resolve the human problem (v.24). Sanders dismissed the anthropological element of the argument by claiming that it produced excessive contradictions because the human plight is a deduction from Paul's claim that God acted in Christ to redeem all.[179] Paul's real reason for rejecting the law, Sanders argued, is because he believed that God acted in Christ, not because he thought humans were incapable of keeping the law. Sanders is correct that Paul's rejection of the law as God's means of salvation arises from his conviction that God acted in Christ, and this

---

[178] See Elliott, *Survivors of Israel*.

[179] Sanders, *Law*, 79–80. On the movement of Paul's thought from solution to plight, see Sanders, *Paul and Palestinian Judaism*, 442–47, 474–502. Thielman claims that Paul's thought moved from plight to solution because he, like other Jews, thought they were still in exile because of their disobedience (*From Plight to Solution*; cf. Wright, *New Testament*, 268–72; note also Scott, ed., *Exile*; idem, *Restoration*). The Christ-event resolved the problem of the exile, which came about because of the people's unfaithfulness to the covenant. This argument is questionable on two grounds. First, it is not clear that all or even a majority of Jews thought they were still in exile (Seifrid, "Blind Alleys," 86–92). Second, Sanders did not deny that in Jewish thought there was a plight from which humans needed redemption. Rather, he claimed that Paul perceived of the plight in much deeper terms. The solution necessitated a more profound understanding of the plight so Paul configured the human plight as enslavement to Sin.

point has not been adequately appreciated.[180] Nevertheless, it does not follow that Paul did not develop a coherent anthropological explanation for why the law is not God's means to salvation. Paul's pessimistic anthropology may be a secondary deduction drawn from his belief that God acted in Christ to save, but it becomes an important point in his claim against Torah observance as the means to divine blessing. In 7.7–25 he engages a Jewish view of law observance solely on Jewish premises (that is, he does not mention Christ except in a parenthetical comment [v.25]), and he disputes the claim that one can actually fulfil the law on anthropological grounds: because the human is a servant of Sin, he or she always does evil and will never attain to the life promised by the law. The argument is not nearly as convoluted as Sanders claimed when read against the backdrop of the two-ways tradition.

In 8.1–13 Paul challenges another Jewish perspective, although without the straightforward polemical engagement. This other perspective is basically that of the *Hodayot*. Paul actually has several points of agreement with this view. Both have a pessimistic anthropology, prioritise divine action, and claim that obedience is possible only through the empowering of the divine Spirit. Yet, Paul finds this option flawed because it lacks any reference to Jesus as the Messiah. Here Sanders' insistence that Paul rejected Judaism because it lacks Jesus as the Christ is entirely accurate. Divine action for Paul must be understood as the Christ-event, and while Paul has a doctrine of election, this too must be brought into conformity with God's action in Christ.

This study of Romans 7.7–8.13 shows that Paul's critique of his contemporary Jews cannot be limited to a single line of thought, whether that be the claim that all Jews were legalists, Judaism was not Christianity, or Judaism restricted God's grace to Jews alone. This latter interpretation, associated with the (so-called) New Perspective, finds, in fact, little basis in Paul's critique at this point of Romans.[181] The New Perspective has rightly emphasised the social context in which early Christianity and especially Paul's mission and theology developed. Nevertheless, Paul's opposition to the law cannot be restricted to Jewish exclusiveness without neglecting major portions of his thought. The argument of Romans 7.7–8.13 makes little sense against the backdrop of ethnic pride. Paul's problem with his fellow Jews is not simply that they claim that a person must obey the law nor that they confined salvation to only those who bore the marks of the Jewish nation. He certainly had problems with these issues, but more than that, he objected to any view that denied to Jesus the central place.

---

[180] This is due partly to confusion over the meaning of Sanders' claim that *"this is what Paul finds wrong in Judaism: it is not Christianity"* (*Paul and Palestinian Judaism*, 552; emphasis original).

[181] Cf. Moo, "Israel and the Law," 207–08. Contra Longenecker, *4 Ezra and Romans 1–11*, 233.

C. Conclusion

A second point at which this interpretation of Romans 7.7–8.13 can help clarify recent debates is Paul's conception of salvation and the role assigned to Paul's antithesis between faith in Christ and works of the law. It was noted at the beginning of this chapter how Paul's antithesis has been interpreted in recent scholarship and how these various options have controlled how one interprets other aspects of Paul's soteriological thought. This complex history of interpretation and the fundamental character assigned to this antithesis in some circles makes discussion of it difficult. Here the purpose is simply to offer some comments on what the antithesis and Pauline soteriology broadly might mean in light of the interpretation of Romans 7.7–8.13 offered previously.

One argument typically advanced in favour of interpreting πίστις Χριστοῦ as Christ's faithfulness is that the traditional reading ("faith in Christ") accords too significant of a role to human faith.[182] Regardless of whether the other arguments for the faith of Christ are persuasive, this one fails to convince. As explained above, Romans 8.13 ascribes a major role to the human agent in the ultimate possession of eternal life. Justification, as with salvation broadly conceived, is grounded for Paul in divine initiative and sustained by divine actions, but this does not make the human agent passive. The divine act in Christ (the gospel) brings forth faith and obedience as the human acknowledgment of what God has done. Priority always belongs to God, as those who argue for Christ's faithfulness correctly note, but this does not negate the human act. The elimination of the human agent in justification by πίστις Χριστοῦ is unnecessary. While this point does not abolish the possibility that the faith of Christ interpretation is correct, it at least shows that the theological argument does not work.[183]

If justification by faith alone in Christ alone is viewed as the totality of Paul's soteriology, then the correct interpretation must encompass Paul's exhortation to obedience and those statements where he indicates that obedience is part of the means to life. Bell's claim that for Paul "salvation is not dependent on sanctification" cannot account for Paul's expectation that believers' lives be marked by obedience.[184] Additionally, Paul's warnings that disobedient believers will be punished and may even lose their salvation cannot fit within Bell's scheme. It will not suffice to claim that Paul's warnings and judgment by works

---

[182] Cf. Hays, *Faith*², 150–53; idem, "Paul's Hermeneutics," 129–30. The theological argument is usually supported by interpreting Paul's use of Habakkuk 2.4 in Romans 1.17 (cf. Gal 3.11) as referring to Christ (see Campbell, "Romans 1:17," 281–84; idem, *Deliverance of God*, 610–16; Hays, *Faith*², 279–81).

[183] For more comprehensive arguments against interpreting πίστις Χριστοῦ as Christ's faithfulness and in favour of interpreting the phrase as a reference to the human act of faith in Christ, see Dunn, "Once More;" Matlock, "Detheologizing;" idem, "Rhetoric of pistis;" Cranfield, "On the Πίστις Χριστοῦ Question;" Silva, "Faith versus Works of the Law," 227–34; Watson, *Paul, Judaism, and the Gentiles*², 238–45.

[184] Bell, *No One Seeks for God*, 274.

language only refers to rewards, since, as Romans 8.13 makes clear, eschatological death will come even to the believer who does not "through the Spirit put to death the practices of the body."

In Paul's broader conception of salvation, the contrast between faith and works that is fundamental to the justification passages cannot be read so as to exclude the human agent from acting within the salvation process. Faith cannot be disconnected from obedience since for Paul faith entails obedience. He tells the Galatians that neither circumcision nor un-circumcision matter. What has value is "faith working through love" (Gal 5.6). The goal of Paul's missionary work is to produce among the Gentiles "the obedience of faith" (Rom 1.5; 16.26). However the genitival relationship be understood, there is a link between faith and obedience, and this connection is fundamental to Paul's soteriology.[185] Faith, in Paul's thought, functions as the source, from the human perspective, for good deeds. Genuine faith must reveal itself in obedience to Christ's law.

Romans 8.4–13, along with other passages, indicates that the human must be obedient in order to enter into eternal life. Paul's view, however, cannot be described as "legalism" or "works-righteousness" since he holds that the obedient life necessary in order to enter into eternal life is produced through the Spirit's power. Schreiner aptly writes, "[P]erseverance is the fruit of faith and grounded in God's sustaining and electing grace. Yes, works are necessary to be saved. No, this is not works righteousness, for the works are hardly meritorious. The grace of God is so powerful that it not only grants us salvation apart from our merits, but also transforms us."[186] The transformation brought about by the Spirit reveals itself in the human when the human acts in a manner pleasing to God. And this act of obedience done by the human through the Spirit is absolutely necessary. Salvation cannot be reduced solely to justification. It must also encompass sanctification and culminate in glorification. Without obedience in this life, one will not enter into the next life, but entrance into the next life is solely according to God's grace.

Paul is not opposed to human "doing," even within the salvation process, but he is opposed to a human "doing" that seeks to fulfil the law as the means to divine blessing. God's blessings have already been poured forth in Jesus' death and resurrection, which means that human activity is not oriented toward attaining what God himself has already given. Rather, human activity is the outworking of God's transformative grace as the human is brought into fellowship with Christ and his body through the Spirit for the purpose of being conformed to the image of Christ and in the end being glorified.

---

[185] On the grammatical construction, see Garlington, *Faith, Obedience and Perseverance*, 10–31.

[186] Schreiner, "Perseverance and Assurance," 53. Cf. Watson, *Paul, Judaism, and the Gentiles*[2], 213–14.

Conclusion

Throughout the Second Temple Period, Judaism was constantly redefining itself in light of various challenges that arose. Whether those issues be the return from exile, the Maccabbean revolt, or the Roman invasion, Jews attempted to correlate their understanding of God and the sacred scriptures with the immediate problem. This study has been principally concerned with how ancient Judaism viewed divine and human agency. In the introduction the question was raised about the legitimacy of this topic. It was argued on the basis of Josephus's portrayal of the Jewish schools (*J.W.* 2.119–166; *Ant.* 13.171–173; 18.11–25) that the topic was discussed by ancient Jews and that different perspectives were put forth by the three schools. Plotting the schools along a single line, Josephus places the Essenes and Sadducees at the extremes and sits the Pharisees in the middle. Josephus' model is neat and certainly masks the complexity of these groups, but his portrayal of the schools indicates that the topic of divine and human agency is not only a modern one. Josephus' statements open the way for a study of ancient Jewish views on this issue. This study has not attempted to defend Josephus' representation of the schools, but it has taken seriously Josephus' claim that a diversity of views were put forth by Jewish thinkers.

This study has used Sirach and the *Hodayot* to represent the ends of Josephus' spectrum. Ben Sira opposes those who overemphasise God's mercy or deny their responsibility for their sins (chapter 1). He employs the two-ways pattern to argue that the primary actor in the divine-human relationship is the individual human (Sir 15.14–17). The human possesses the moral capacity to obey and Torah observance leads to life and blessing. Rather than placing obedience within a covenantal context of pure grace, Ben Sira models the divine-human relationship after the Creator-creation relationship. In this relationship God is viewed as the giver of commandments and creation obeys those commandments. The giving and obeying of the commandments is foundational to the divine-human relationship not because it signifies pure electing grace, but because this is the way that God interacts with all of creation. In his portrayal of the divine agent, Ben Sira's primary focus is God as judge. Even here, though, his real interest lies with the human agent since the act of judgment is the re-action of God to what the human has done. Ben Sira's view of divine and human agency prioritises human action throughout.

At the other end of the spectrum sits the *Hodayot* (chapter 2). This text could hardly emphasise God's gracious saving acts more. Humans are described as mere creatures, frail and sinful beings destined for death. God overcomes the human's creaturely limitations by electing some and giving his Spirit. Predestination is stressed throughout the *Hodayot* because it brings the focus onto God and it gets behind the problem of the human race. Through the Spirit the human is given knowledge and purified from transgression. The outcome of all these divine acts is that the human can obey the Torah. Transformation from a creature of dust comes solely through God's grace, and even when making the claim that humans obey, the hymnist's focus remains on God. The view put forth in the *Hodayot* opposes the view taken by Ben Sira.

This argument for the diversity among Judaism fits squarely with neither the old perspective claim that in general Judaism was legalistic nor Sanders' claim that with the exception of *4 Ezra* Judaism was a religion of grace. The perspectives on divine and human agency put forth by Ben Sira and the *Hodayot* indicate that Judaism was not monolithic. Attempts to discover in these texts a single pattern, such as covenantal nomism, will inevitably flatten out the distinctions that are visible on the surface of the texts. Covenantal nomism runs counter to Sirach's insistence that life comes through Torah observance, and it misses out on the *Hodayot*'s stress on the continuing role of the Spirit. This study, therefore, has questioned the applicability of covenantal nomism as the basic soteriological structure of Second Temple Judaism. It would be too much to conclude from this study that covenantal nomism is nowhere found in Second Temple Judaism. It may capture well the ideas of some texts, but it was not the only view taken by Jewish thinkers.

A return to the older claim that all of Judaism was "legalistic" is inaccurate also. On the one hand, the term prejudices the analysis since it has negative connotations in contemporary usage where it typically refers to an attempt to earn one's salvation through works which results in boasting about one's works. Ben Sira rejects boasting and egotism, but he does argue that "life" is attained through obedience. In order for the discussion about the relationship between grace and works to move forward, scholars must realise that prioritising human agency is not the same as "legalistic works-righteousness." On the other hand, the charge that Judaism was legalistic cannot account for texts like the *Hodayot*. Here one finds a form of Judaism that prioritises divine agency and speaks primarily, almost exclusively, about grace and mercy. Election by grace is foundational to the *Hodayot*. The charge of legalism is nothing less than distortion.

With this spectrum of views, it becomes possible to situate Paul firmly within his Jewish context without dismissing or downplaying his emphasis on divine grace, which has often been judged as distinctive. This study used Romans 7.7–8.13 as a way into Paul's thought (chapter 3). In this passage Paul engages in an intra-Jewish debate about human ability and divine intervention. Romans 7.7–25 was paralleled to Ben Sira and the two-ways tradition that he used. Paul's ἐγώ is the human agent of the two-ways tradition, who is standing before the options of life and death and has the law of life available to him. Paul opposed this view through his portrayal of Sin as a malevolent power. In Romans 8.1–13 Paul adopted a perspective similar to the *Hodayot*. Paul traces all divine action back to the Christ event. Here God has intervened into the human dilemma by sending his Son to destroy Sin's hold over humanity. In contrast to the incapable human of Romans 7, the human in Romans 8 is empowered by the Spirit to obey. Paul argues that human obedience is necessary for salvation, but this obedience is generated by the divine Spirit that indwells and empowers each human who believes in Christ.

Taking the diversity of Judaism seriously allows one to place Paul within the Jewish spectrum. His claims about divine action do not need to be softened, nor is it necessary to dismiss his criticisms of obedience to the law as the means to life. The complexity of Paul's view, in that it prioritises divine action while also encompassing human action, fits squarely within the spectrum of Jewish views during the Second Temple Period. Paul's claims about Jesus as the Messiah certainly led to his Jewish contemporaries considering him beyond the pale, even ascribing to him the derogatory charge of "apostate."[1] The way he formulates the relationship between divine and human agency, however, is not itself outside the spectrum of possibilities. What ultimately puts Paul beyond the tolerable limits of Judaism, in the minds of many of his contemporaries, is not his claims about grace, faith, and the relegation of works, but his placement of Christ at the centre of his worldview rather than the Torah.[2]

In the analysis of Romans 7.7–8.13, this study has challenged attempts to limit Paul's critique of Judaism solely to Christological claims, the place of Gentiles within the people of God, or anthropological differences. Paul argues against a Ben Sira-style theology that attributes salvation primarily to law observance. Paul's critique is anthropologically oriented and concerns the human act of "doing." This should not be understood as a blanket rejection of human obedience, but Paul does take issue with forms of human obedience that are motivated by the attempt to attain life. Paul's disagreement with other Jews, however, is not confined solely to anthropological ideas. Had the apostle Paul read the *Hodayot*, he probably would have found much of it favourable, but his fundamental problem with it would have been its lack of Christological reference. Here his disagreement with other Jews is Christological. We have seen also that the claim by Dunn, Wright, and others that Paul's principal problem with other Jews concerned the acceptance of Gentiles into the people of God has no basis in Romans 7.7–8.13. This may be the case elsewhere, but it does not explain the totality of Paul's debate with other Jews. Paul's ability to argue

---

[1] See Barclay, "Paul among Diaspora Jews." It should be noted that how Paul was viewed by his contemporaries is not his own view of himself. Although rejecting certain aspects of his past (Phil 3.4–11), he continues to think in very Jewish terms. His ethics are Jewish even if he does not tie them to the Torah, he shares the same scriptures and is deeply influenced by them, and he is genuinely concerned about the salvation of his fellow Israelites according to the flesh (Rom 9–11). Whatever aspect of Judaism Paul rejects, it is not the whole structure of Judaism. See Hagner, "Paul as a Jewish Believer."

[2] Identifying Paul as an apostate and outside the limits of Judaism does not make him unique. The sectarian scrolls identify certain other Jews ("seekers after smooth things") as apostates.

on multiple levels should be considered more seriously in the attempt to relate him to his Jewish contemporaries.

All three texts maintain that obedience is a necessary component in salvation. Ben Sira argued that obedience was the means to life, while the *Hodayot* and Paul according to Romans 8 describe obedience as the outworking of God's Spirit in the person's life. No one can conceive of a "saved" person who does not live in obedience. Even in the case of the *Hodayot* and Paul, both of which stress the priority of divine action, the human agent is not portrayed as merely a passive recipient of grace. The human's life is transformed, and this transformation leads to obedience. Indeed, without obedience one simply cannot enter into eternal life. In arguing for the necessity of obedience, Paul and the *Hodayot* do not adopt a Ben Sira-like view that ultimately attributes salvation to human deeds. They seek rather a unification of the divine and human agents through their stress on the divine Spirit as God's empowering agent. Through the Spirit the human obeys. Any claim that prioritises the human must be rejected and any view that eliminates the human must also be dismissed.

This latter point is significant for how one construes Pauline soteriology. It cannot be reduced to the claim that salvation is accomplished solely by God apart from the human. Paul's view of divine action takes up within itself the human agent. The whole of salvation can be attributed to neither at the expense of the other. Paul, to be certain, prioritises divine action, and he seeks throughout his letters to highlight God's work and not his own. Yet, he never eliminates himself as an active agent. He is rather the agent through whom God works and simultaneously the agent at work.

One should also note that much of the discussion about divine and human agency in these three texts revolved around particular scriptural passages. Ben Sira derived the two-ways pattern (Sir 15.14–17) from his interpretation of Deuteronomy 30.15–20, and he showed a keen interest in the creation accounts (Sir 17.1–14). In the Praise to the Fathers (Sir 44–50), which is a rehearsal of scriptural traditions and is an exercise in interpretation, Ben Sira draws attention to the obedient lives of Israel's heroes. The *Hodayot* relied heavily on the scriptures in its anthropological claims. Particularly of interest were the accounts of Adam's creation from dust (Gen 2.7), his punishment for his transgression (3.19), and the traditions that reflect on these two (e.g., Pss 8; 103). Its idea of the Spirit as given by God was derived from Ezekiel 11 and 36–37. In his critique of the two-ways pattern in Romans 7.7–25, Paul engages with Deuteronomy 30.15–20 and the way that it was interpreted by others. Also, Paul's understanding of the Spirit's empowerment was based on Ezekiel 11 and 36–37. All three sources consciously used the scriptures to formulate their views of divine and human agency. This study has not pursued the hermeneutical issues raised by this engagement with scripture, and profitable research could be carried out on this issue.[3]

---

[3] See already Watson, *Paul and the Hermeneutics of Faith*.

Another matter that would benefit from more research concerns the place of other Jewish texts within the spectrum of views available in the Second Temple Period. This study employed Ben Sira and the *Hodayot* to represent the end views, but it might be the case that a text pushes beyond these two in its prioritising of the divine or the human agent. One might take, for example, the Two-Spirits Treatise found in 1QS 3–4. Running through this text is a rigid determinism that seems to extend even beyond the statements about predestination in the *Hodayot*. The views held by Jews of this period might even be further apart than this study has demonstrated. A study of how the two-ways tradition was developed in, for example, *1 Enoch* 94–104, *Psalms of Solomon* 9.1–5 and *4 Ezra* 7.3–24, 127–29 would also be worthwhile. Here the issue of scriptural engagement would come to the forefront, and one could track both how this tradition developed and changed and how it functioned within the broader claims about divine and human agency made by each author.

Additionally, this study has focused on Palestinian Jewish views of divine and human agency. A wider referent that includes both Diaspora Jewish and Greco-Roman sources would be extremely helpful.[4] The philosophical schools debated vigorously the relationship between fate and free will. A study of these texts that attempts to correlate them with Paul would help clarify Paul's place within the Greco-Roman intellectual world.

Some questions about Pauline soteriology still remain unanswered. Particularly, the function of the antithesis between faith in Christ and works of the law is not fully resolved. Some implications for how one understands the antithesis were drawn at the end of chapter 3, and the point was made that the importance of the antithesis may have been overstated by some scholars. Further study needs to address the rhetorical function of the antithesis as well as its overall function within Paul's thought. Moreover, this study confined itself almost exclusively to Romans 7.7–8.13. The results drawn from this study, therefore, need to be placed into a much broader context. This broader context needs to discuss statements like Galatians 2.20 and Philippians 2.12–13 as well as concepts like grace and judgment by deeds.[5] This study is a starting point for a broader statement of how Paul viewed divine and human agency but more work is needed.

This study has been an initial and a limited attempt at dealing with the issue of divine and human agency in Second Temple Judaism. As scholarship advances beyond Sanders' description of Judaism as covenantal nomism, old questions are now being reopened. The old answers to some of these questions may prove to be accurate, but in other instances new answers must be put forth. This study hopes to have brought some clarity to the variety of options available to Jews in the Second Temple Period and to have provided a way to understand Paul within that context.

---

[4] See the studies by Barclay on Paul and Philo ("'By the Grace of God I am what I am'") and Engberg-Pedersen on Epictetus and Paul ("Self-sufficiency and Power").

[5] See Barclay, "Grace and the Transformation of Agency in Christ."

Bibliography

Primary Literature and Translations

Abegg, Martin. "Thanksgiving Psalms (The Thanksgiving Scroll) (1QH, 1Q35, 4Q427–432)." Pages 84–114 in Wise, Michael, Martin Abegg, Jr., and Edward Cook. *The Dead Sea Scrolls: A New Translation.*

Baba Bathra: Translated into English with Notes, Glossary and Indices. Translated by Maurice Simon and Israel W. Slotki. *The Babylonian Talmud, vol. 3.* London: Soncino Press, 1935.

Beentjes, Pancratius C. *The Book of Ben Sira in Hebrew.* VTSup 68. Leiden: Brill, 1997.

Danby, Herbert, trans. *The Mishnah.* London: Oxford University Press, 1950.

Dupont-Sommer, A. *The Essene Writings from Qumran.* Translated by Geza Vermes. Oxford: Basil Blackwell, 1961.

García Martínez, Florentino, and Eibert J.C. Tigchelaar. *The Dead Sea Scrolls Study Edition.* 2 volumes. Leiden: Brill, 1998.

Gaster, Theodor H. *Dead Sea Scriptures.* 3d ed. Garden City: Anchor Press/Doubleday, 1976.

Euripides. Translated by A.S. Way. 4 vols. Loeb Classical Library. Cambridge: Harvard University Press, 1912–1935.

Josephus. Translated by H. St. J. Thackeray et al. 10 vols. Loeb Classical Library. Cambridge: Harvard University Press, 1926–1965.

Lohse, Eduard. *Die Texte aus Qumran: Hebräisch und Deutsch.* Munich: Kösel-Verlag, 1971.

Maier, Johann and Kurt Schubert. *Die Qumran-Essener: Texte der Schriftrollen und Lebensbild der Gemeinde*, vol. 2. Munich: Ernst Reinhardt, 1973.

Ovid. Translated by Frank Justus Miller et al. 6 vols. 2d ed. Loeb Classical Library. Cambridge: Harvard University Press, 1977–1989.

Rahlfs, Alfred, ed. *Septuaginta.* Stuttgart: Deutsche Bibelgesellschaft, 1935, 1979.

Schechter, Solomon and Charles Taylor. *Wisdom of Ben Sira: Portions of the Book Ecclesiasticus.* Cambridge: University Press, 1899. Repr., Amsterdam: APA-Philo Press, 1979.

Schuller, Eileen M. "*Hodayot.*" Pages 69–254 in *Qumran Cave 4.XX: Poetical and Liturgical Texts: Part 2* by Esther Chazon et al. DJD XXIX. Oxford: Clarendon, 1999.

Stegemann, Hartmut with Eileen Schuller and translation by Carol Newsom. *Qumran Cave 1.III: 1QHodayot^a with Incorporation of 1QHodayotb and 4QHodayot^{a-f}.* DJD XL. Oxford: Clarendon, 2009.

Sukenik, E.L. *The Dead Sea Scrolls of the Hebrew University.* Jerusalem: Magnes, 1955.

Vermes, Geza. *The Complete Dead Sea Scrolls in English.* London: Penguin, 1997.

Ziegler, Joseph, ed. *Sapientia Iesu filii Sirach.* 2d ed. Septuaginta 12/2. Göttingen: Vandenhoeck & Ruprecht, 1980.

Secondary Literature

Achtemeier, Paul J. *Romans*. Interpretation. Atlanta: John Knox, 1985.
Aitken, J.K. "Biblical Interpretation as Political Manifesto: Ben Sira in His Seleucid Setting." *JJS* 51 (2000): 191–208.
–. "Divine Will and Providence." Pages 282–301 in *Ben Sira's God*. Edited by Renate Egger-Wenzel.
Alexander, Philip S. "Torah and Salvation in Tannaitic Literature." Pages 261–301 in *Justification and Variegated Nomism: Volume 1 – The Complexities of Second Temple Judaism*. Edited by D.A. Carson, Peter T. O'Brien, and Mark A. Seifrid.
Aletti, Jean-Noël. "Rm 7,7–25 encore une fois: enjeux et propositions." *NTS* 48 (2002): 358–76.
Argall, R.A. *1 Enoch and Sirach: A Comparative Literary and Conceptual Analysis of the Themes of Revelation, Creation, and Judgment*. SBLEJL 8. Atlanta: Scholars, 1995.
Barclay, John M.G. "'By the Grace of God I am what I am': Grace and Agency in Philo and Paul." Pages 140–57 in *Divine and Human Agency in Paul and His Cultural Environment*. Edited by John M.G. Barclay and Simon J. Gathercole.
–. "Grace and the Transformation of Agency in Christ." Pages 372–89 in *Redefining First-Century Jewish and Christian Identities: Essays in Honor of Ed Parish Sanders*. Edited by Fabian E. Udoh. Notre Dame: University of Notre Dame Press, 2008.
–. "Introduction." Pages 1–8 in *Divine and Human Agency in Paul and His Cultural Environment*. Edited by John M.G. Barclay and Simon J. Gathercole.
–. "Is It Good News that God is Impartial? A Response to Robert Jewett, Romans: A Commentary." *JSNT* 31 (2008): 89–111.
–. *Obeying the Truth: Paul's Ethics in Galatians*. Edinburgh: T&T Clark, 1988
–. "Paul among Diaspora Jews: Anomaly or Apostate?" *JSNT* 60 (1995): 89–120.
Barclay, John M.G., and Simon J. Gathercole, eds. *Divine and Human Agency in Paul and His Cultural Environment*. LNTS 335. New York: T&T Clark, 2006.
Barker, Paul A. *The Triumph of Grace in Deuteronomy*. Carlisle: Paternoster, 2004.
Barnick, Vincent P. "The Sinful Flesh of the Son of God (Rom 8:3): A Key Image of Pauline Theology." *CBQ* 47 (1985): 246–62.
Barrett, C. K. *A Commentary on the Epistle to the Romans*. BNTC. London: Adam & Charles Black, 1971.
Barth, Markus. "Jews and Gentiles: The Social Character of Justification in Paul." *JES* 5 (1968): 241–61.
Baumbach, Günther. "The Sadducees in Josephus." Pages 173–95 in *Josephus, the Bible, and History*. Edited by Louis H. Feldman and Gohei Hata. Leiden: Brill, 1989.
Baumgarten, Joseph, and Menahem Mansoor. "Studies in the New *Hodayot* (Thanksgiving Hymns)—I." *JBL* 74 (1955): 115–24.
–. "Studies in the New *Hodayot* (Thanksgiving Hymns)—II." *JBL* 74 (1955): 188–95.
–. "Studies in the New *Hodayot* (Thanksgiving Hymns)—III." *JBL* 75 (1956): 107–13.
Bayes, Jonathan F. *The Weakness of the Law: God's Law and the Christian in New Testament Perspective*. Carlisle: Paternoster, 2000.
Beall, Todd S. *Josephus' Descriptions of the Essenes Illustrated by the Dead Sea Scrolls*. SNTSMS 58; Cambridge: Cambridge University Press, 1988.
Becker, Jürgen. *Das Heil Gottes: Heils- und Sündenbegriffe in den Qumrantexten und im Neuen Testament*. Göttingen: Vandenhoeck & Ruprecht, 1964.
Beentjes, Pancratius C. "God's Mercy: 'Racham' (pi.), 'Rachum', and 'Rachamim' in the Book of Ben Sira." Pages 100–17 in *Ben Sira's God*. Edited by Renate Egger-Wenzel.

Beentjes, Pancratius C., ed. *The Book of Ben Sira in Modern Research: Proceedings of the First International Ben Sira Conference 28–31 July 1996 Soesterberg, Netherlands.* BZAW 255. Berlin: de Gruyter, 1997.
Beker, J. Christiaan. *Paul the Apostle: The Triumph of God in Life and Thought.* Philadelphia: Fortress, 1984.
Beld, A. van den. "Romans 7:14–25 and the Problem of *Akrasia*." *RelS* 21 (1985): 495–515.
Bell, Richard H. *No One Seeks for God: An Exegetical and Theological Study of Romans 1.18–3.20.* WUNT 1/106. Tübingen: Mohr Siebeck, 1998.
–. "Sacrifice and Christology in Paul." *JTS* 53 (2002): 1–27.
Bergmeier, Roland. "Das Gesetz im Römerbrief." Pages 31–102 in idem, *Das Gesetz im Römerbrief und andere Studien zum Neuen Testament.* WUNT 1/121. Tübingen: Mohr Siebeck, 2000.
–. "Röm 7,7–25a (8,2): Der Mensch – das Gesetz – Gott – Paulus – die Exegese im Widerspruch?" Pages 103–12 in idem, *Das Gesetz im Römerbrief und andere Studien zum Neuen Testament.* WUNT 1/121. Tübingen: Mohr Siebeck, 2000.
Berkouwer, G.C. *Faith and Perseverance.* Translated by Robert D. Knudsen. Grand Rapids: Eerdmans, 1958.
Bertone, John A. "The Function of the Spirit between God's Soteriological Plan Enacted But Not Yet Culminated: Romans 8.1–27," *JPT* 15 (1999): 75–97.
Bird, Michael F., and Preston M. Sprinkle, eds. *The Faith of Jesus Christ: Exegetical, Biblical, and Theological Studies.* Peabody: Hendrickson, 2009.
Blackwell, Ben C. "Christosis: Pauline Soteriology in Light of Deification in Irenaeus and Cyril of Alexandria." PhD Thesis, Durham University, 2010.
Blenkinsopp, Joseph. *Wisdom and Law in the Old Testament: The Ordering of Life in Israel and Early Judaism.* Rev ed. Oxford: Oxford University Press, 1995.
Block, Daniel I. "The Grace of Torah: The Mosaic Prescription for Life (Deut 4:1–8; 6:20–25)." *BSac* 162 (2005): 3–22.
Boccaccini, Gabriele. *Beyond the Essene Hypothesis: The Parting of the Ways between Qumran and Enochic Judaism.* Grand Rapids: Eerdmans, 1998.
–. "History of Judaism: Its Periods in Antiquity." Pages 285–308 in *Judaism in Late Antiquity: Part Two, Historical Syntheses.* Edited by Jacob Neusner. Leiden: Brill, 1995.
–. "Inner-Jewish Debate on the Tension between Divine and Human Agency in Second Temple Period." Pages 9–26 in *Divine and Human Agency in Paul and His Cultural Environment.* Edited by John M.G. Barclay and Simon J. Gathercole.
–. *Middle Judaism: Jewish Thought 300 B.C.E. to 200 C.E.* Minneapolis: Fortress Press, 1991.
Boccaccini, Gabriele, ed. *Enoch and Qumran Origins: New Light on a Forgotten Connection.* Grand Rapids: Eerdmans, 2005.
Bockmuehl, Markus. "1QS and Salvation at Qumran." Pages 381–414 in *Justification and Variegated Nomism: A Fresh Appraisal of Paul and Second Temple Judaism: Volume 1 – The Complexities of Second Temple Judaism.* Edited by D.A. Carson, Peter T. O'Brien, and Mark A. Seifrid.
Borgen, Peder. "The Contrite Wrongdoer – Condemned or Set Free by the Spirit? Romans 7:7–8:4." Pages 181–92 in *The Holy Spirit and Christian Origins.* Edited by Graham N. Stanton, Bruce W. Longenecker and Stephen C. Barton.
Bornkamm, Günther. "Sin, Law and Death: An Exegetical Study of Romans 7." Pages 87–104 in idem, *Early Christian Experience.* New York: Harper & Row, Publishers, 1969.
Botterweck, G.J., H. Ringgren, and Heinz-Josef Fabry, eds. *Theological Dictionary of the Old Testament.* Translated by J.T. Willis, G.W. Bromiley, and D.E. Green. 15 vols. 1974–2006.

Box, G.H., and W.O.E. Oesterley. "The Book of Sirach." In Charles, R.H., ed. *The Apocrypha and Pseudepigrapha of the Old Testament. Volume 1: Apocrypha*, 268–517. Oxford: Clarendon, 1913.
Braun, Herbert. "Römer 7, 7–25 und das Selbstverständnis des Qumran-Frommen." *ZTK* 56 (1959): 1–18.
Brown, Teresa R. "God and Men in Israel's History: God and Idol Worship in Praise of the Fathers (Sir 44–50)." Pages 214–220 in *Ben Sira's God*. Edited by Renate Egger-Wenzel.
Brownlee, William H. "Anthropology and Soteriology in the Dead Sea Scrolls and in the New Testament." Pages 210–40 in *Use of the Old Testament in the New and Other Essays: Studies in Honor of William Franklin Stinespring*. Edited by James M. Efird. Durham: Duke University Press, 1972.
Bruce, F.F. *The Epistle of Paul to the Romans: An Introduction and Commentary*. TNTC. London: Tyndale, 1963.
Büchler, A. "Ben Sira's Conception of Sin and Atonement." *JQR* n.s. 13 (1922–23): 303–14; 461–502; 14 (1923–24): 53–83.
Bultmann, Rudolf. "Romans 7 and the Anthropology of Paul." Pages 147–57 in *Existence and Faith: Shorter Writings of Rudolf Bultmann*. Translated by Schubert M. Ogden. London: Hodder and Stoughton, 1961.
–. *Theology of the New Testament*. 2 Volumes. Translated by Kendrick Grobel. New York: Charles Scribner's Sons, 1954.
Burkes, Shannon. *God, Self, and Death: The Shape of Religious Transformation in the Second Temple Period*. JSJSup 79. Leiden: Brill, 2003.
–. "Wisdom and Law: Choosing Life in Ben Sira and Baruch." *JSJ* 30 (1999): 253–76.
Burnett, Gary W. *Paul and the Salvation of the Individual*. BIS 57. Leiden: Brill, 2001.
Busch, Austin. "The Figure of Eve in Romans 7.7–25." *BibInt* 12 (2004): 1–36.
Byrne, Brendan. "Interpreting Romans Theologically in a Post-'New Perspective' Perspective." *HTR* 94 (2001): 227–41.
–. "Living Out the Righteousness of God: The Contribution of Rom 6:1–8:13 to an Understanding of Paul's Ethical Presuppositions." *CBQ* 43 (1981): 557–81.
–. *Romans*. SP. Collegeville: The Liturgical Press, 1996.
Calduch-Benages, Núria. "The Trial Motif in the Book of Ben Sira with Special Reference to Sir 2,16." Pages 13–51 in *The Book of Ben Sira in Modern Research*. Edited by Pancratius C. Beentjes.
Calduch-Benages, Núria, and J. Vermeylen, eds. *Treasures of Wisdom: Studies in Ben Sira and the Book of Wisdom: Festschrift M. Gilbert*. BETL 143. Leuven: University Press, 1999.
Calvin, John. *The Epistles of Paul the Apostle to the Romans and to the Thessalonians*. Edited by David W. Torrance and Thomas F. Torrance. Translated by Ross MacKenzie. Edinburgh: The Saint Andrew Press, 1960.
Campbell, David H. "The Identity of ἐγώ in Romans 7.7–25." Pages 57–64 in *Studia Biblica 1978: III. Papers on Paul and Other New Testament Authors*. Edited by E.A. Livingstone. Sheffield: JSOT Press, 1980.
Campbell, Douglas A. "Romans 1:17 – A Crux Interpretum for the πίστις Χριστοῦ Debate." *JBL* 113 (1994): 265–285.
–. *The Deliverance of God: An Apocalyptic Rereading of Justification in Paul*. Grand Rapids: Eerdmans, 2009.
Campbell, W.S. "Romans III as a Key to the Structure and Thought of the Letter." Pages 251–64 in *The Romans Debate*. Rev and Exp. Edited by Karl P. Donfried. Peabody: Hendrickson Publishers, 1991.
Carson, D.A. *Divine Sovereignty and Human Responsibility*. Atlanta: John Knox, 1981.

Bibliography

–. "Summaries and Conclusions." Pages 505–48 in *Justification and Variegated Nomism: Volume 1 – The Complexities of Second Temple Judaism*. Edited by D.A. Carson, Peter T. O'Brien, and Mark A. Seifrid.
Carson, D.A., Peter T. O'Brien, and Mark A. Seifrid, eds. *Justification and Variegated Nomism: Volume 1 – The Complexities of Second Temple Judaism*. Grand Rapids: Baker Academic, 2001.
–. *Justification and Variegated Nomism: A Fresh Appraisal of Paul and Second Temple Judaism: Volume 2 – The Paradoxes of Paul*. Grand Rapids: Baker Academic, 2004.
Carter, T. L. *Paul and the Power of Sin: Redefining 'Beyond the Pale'*. SNTSMS 115. Cambridge: Cambridge University Press, 2002.
Catchpole, David. "Who and Where is the 'Wretched Man' of Romans 7, and Why is 'She' Wretched?" Pages 168–80 in *The Holy Spirit and Christian Origins*. Edited by Graham N. Stanton, Bruce W. Longenecker, and Stephen C. Barton.
Chang, Hae-Kyung. "The Christian Life in a Dialectical Tension? Romans 7:7–25 Reconsidered." *NovT* 49 (2007): 257–80.
Charlesworth, James H. "A Critical Comparison of the Dualism in 1QS 3:13–4:26 and the 'Dualism' contained in the Gospel of John." Pages 76–106 in *John and Qumran*. Edited by James H. Charlesworth. London: Geoffrey Chapman, 1972.
–. *The Pesharim and Qumran History: Chaos or Consensus?* Grand Rapids: Eerdmans, 2002.
Chazon, Esther Glickler. "Hymns and Prayers in the Dead Sea Scrolls." Pages 244–70 in *The Dead Sea Scrolls After Fifty Years: A Comprehensive Assessment*. Volume 1. Edited by Peter W. Flint and James C. VanderKam. Leiden: Brill, 1998.
–. "Prayers from Qumran and Their Historical Implications." *DSD* 1 (1994): 265–84.
Chester, Stephen J. *Conversion at Corinth: Perspectives on Conversion in Paul's Theology and the Corinthian Church*. SNTW. Edinburgh: T&T Clark, 2003.
Collins, John J. *Jewish Wisdom in the Hellenistic Age*. Edinburgh: T&T Clark, 1997.
–. "The Origin of the Qumran Community: A Review of the Evidence." Pages 159–78 in *To Touch the Text: Biblical and Related Studies in Honor of Joseph A. Fitzmyer, S.J.* Edited by Maurya P. Horgan and Paul J. Kobelski. New York: Crossroad, 1989.
–. "The Root of Immortality: Death in the Context of Jewish Wisdom." *HTR* (1978): 177–92.
Condra, Ed. *Salvation for the Righteous Revealed: Jesus Amid Covenantal and Messianic Expectations in Second Temple Judaism*. AGJU 51. Leiden: Brill, 2002.
Cranfield, C. E. B. *A Critical and Exegetical Commentary on the Epistle to the Romans*. 2 volumes. ICC. Edinburgh: T&T Clark Limited, 1975, 1979.
–. "On the πίστις Χριστοῦ Question." Pages 81–97 in idem, *On Romans and Other New Testament Essays*. Edinburgh: T&T Clark, 1998.
–. "Sanctification as Freedom: Paul's Teaching on Sanctification with Special Reference to the Epistle to the Romans." Pages 33–49 in idem, *On Romans and Other New Testament Essays*. Edinburgh: T&T Clark, 1998.
Crenshaw, James L. "The Book of Sirach." In Leander K. Keck, ed. *The New Interpreter's Bible*. Vol. 5, *Wisdom Literature*, 601–867. Nashville: Abingdon Press, 2002.
–. "The Problem of Theodicy in Sirach: On Human Bondage." *JBL* 94 (1975): 47–64.
–. "The Restraint of Reason, the Humility of Prayer." Pages 206–21 in *Urgent Advice and Probing Questions: Collected Writings on Old Testament Wisdom*. Macon: Mercer, 1995.
–. "Theodicy." Pages 444–47 in vol. 6 of *ABD*. Edited by David Noel Freedman. 6 vols. New York: Doubleday, 1992.
Das, A. Andrew. *Paul, the Law, and the Covenant*. Peabody: Hendrickson Publishers, 2001.
–. *Solving the Romans Debate*. Minneapolis: Fortress, 2007.
Davies, William D. *Paul and Rabbinic Judaism: Some Rabbinic Elements in Pauline Theology*. London: SPCK, 1948.

de Roo, Jacqueline C.R. "God's Covenant with the Fathers." Pages 191–202 in *The Concept of the Covenant in the Second Temple Period*. Edited by Stanley E. Porter and Jacqueline C.R. de Roo.
–. *'Works of the Law' at Qumran and in Paul*. NTM 13. Sheffield: Sheffield Phoenix Press, 2007.
deSilva, D.A. "The Wisdom of Ben Sira: Honor, Shame, and the Maintenance of the Values of a Minority Culture." *CBQ* 58 (1996): 433–55.
Di Lella, Alexander A. "Conservative and Progressive Theology: Sirach and Wisdom." *CBQ* 28 (1966): 139–54.
–. "Fear of the Lord as Wisdom: Ben Sira 1,11–30." Pages 113–33 in *The Book of Ben Sira in Modern Research*. Edited by P.C. Beentjes.
–. "The Meaning of Wisdom in Ben Sira." Pages 133–48 in In *Search of Wisdom: Essays in Memory of John G. Gammie*. Edited by Leo G. Perdue, Bernard Brandon Scott, and William Johnston Wiseman. Louisville: Westminster/John Knox, 1993.
–. "Ben Sira's Doctrine on the Discipline of the Tongue." Pages 233–252 in *The Wisdom of Ben Sira: Studies on Tradition, Redaction, and Theology*. Edited by Angelo Passaro and Giuseppe Bellia.
Dillon, Richard J. "The Spirit as Taskmaster and Troublemaker in Romans 8." *CBQ* 60 (1998): 682–702.
Dodson, J.R. "The 'Powers' of Personification: Rhetorical Purpose in the *Book of Wisdom* and the Letter to the Romans." Ph.D. Thesis. University of Aberdeen, 2007.
Douglas, Michael C. "The Teacher Hymn Hypothesis Revisited: New Data for an Old Crux." *DSD* 6 (1999): 239–66.
Dunn, James D. G. *The Epistle to the Galatians*. BNTC. Peabody: Hendrickson, 1993.
–. "The Justice of God: A Renewed Perspective on Justification by Faith." Pages 187–205 in *The New Perspective on Paul*.
–. "New Perspective on Paul." Pages 89–110 in *The New Perspective on Paul*.
–. *The New Perspective on Paul: Collected Essays*. WUNT 1/185. Tübingen: Mohr Siebeck, 2005.
–. "The New Perspective on Paul: Whence, What, Whither?" Pages 1–88 in *The New Perspective on Paul*.
–. "Noch Einmal 'Works of the Law': The Dialogue Continues." Pages 407–22 in *The New Perspective on Paul*.
–. "Once More, πίστις Χριστοῦ." Pages 249–71 in Hays, Richard B. *The Faith of Jesus Christ: The Narrative Substructure of Galatians 3:1–4:11*. 2d ed. Grand Rapids: Eerdmans, 2002.
–. *The Partings of the Ways: Between Christianity and Judaism and their Significance for the Character of Christianity*. London: SCM, 1991.
–. "Paul and Justification by Faith." Pages 361–74 in *The New Perspective on Paul*.
–. "Rom. 7.14–25 in the Theology of Paul." *TZ* 31 (1975): 257–73.
–. *Romans*. 2 volumes. WBC. Dallas: Word Books, 1988.
–. "The Theology of Galatians: The Issue of Covenantal Nomism." Pages 167–86 in *The New Perspective on Paul*.
–. *The Theology of Paul the Apostle*. Grand Rapids: Eerdmans, 1998.
–. "Works of the Law and the Curse of the Law (Galatians 3.10–14)." Pages 111–30 in *The New Perspective on Paul*.
Egger-Wenzel, Renate, ed. *Ben Sira's God: Proceedings of the International Ben Sira Conference: Durham – Ushaw College 2001*. BZAW 321. Berlin: Walter de Gruyter, 2002.
Elliott, Mark Adam. *The Survivors of Israel: A Reconsideration of the Theology of Pre-Christian Judaism*. Grand Rapids: Eerdmans, 2000.

Elliott, Neil. *The Rhetoric of Romans: Argumentative Constraint and Strategy and Paul's Dialogue with Judaism.* JSNTSup 45. Sheffield: Sheffield Academic Press, 1990.
Engberg-Pedersen, Troels. "The Material Spirit: Cosmology and Ethics in Paul." *NTS* 55 (2009): 179–97.
–. "Once more a Lutheran Paul? (review of Francis Watson, *Paul and the Hermeneutics of Faith*)." *SJT* 59 (2006): 439–60.
–. *Paul and the Stoics.* Edinburgh: T&T Clark, 2000.
–. "The Reception of Graeco-roman Culture in the New Testament: The Case of Romans 7.7–25." Pages 32–57 in *The New Testament Studies as Reception.* Edited by Mogens Müller and Henrik Tronier. London: Sheffield Academic Press, 2002.
–. "Response to Martyn." *JSNT* 86 (2002): 103–14.
–. "Self-sufficiency and Power: Divine and Human Agency in Epictetus and Paul." Pages 117–39 in *Divine and Human Agency in Paul and His Cultural Environment.* Edited by John M.G. Barclay and Simon J. Gathercole.
Enns, Peter. "Expansions of Scripture." Pages 73–98 in *Justification and Variegated Nomism: A Fresh Appraisal of Paul and Second Temple Judaism: Volume 1 – The Complexities of Second Temple Judaism.* Edited by D.A. Carson, Peter T. O'Brien, and Mark A. Seifrid.
Eshel, Hanan. *The Dead Sea Scrolls and the Hasmonean State.* Grand Rapids: Eerdmans, 2008.
Esler, Philip F. *Conflict and Identity in Romans: The Social Setting of Paul's Letter.* Minneapolis: Fortress Press, 2003.
Epsy, John M. "Paul's 'Robust Conscience' Re-examined." *NTS* 31 (1985): 161–88.
Evans, Craig A. "Abraham in the Dead Sea Scrolls: A Man of Faith and Failure." Pages 149–58 in *The Bible at Qumran: Test, Shape and Interpretation.* Edited by P.W. Flint. Grand Rapids: Eerdmans, 2001.
Falk, Daniel. "Psalms and Prayers." Pages 7–56 in *Justification and Variegated Nomism: A Fresh Appraisal of Paul and Second Temple Judaism: Volume 1 – The Complexities of Second Temple Judaism.* Edited by D.A. Carson, Peter T. O'Brien, and Mark A. Seifrid.
Fay, Ron C. "Was Paul a Trinitarian? A Look at Romans 8." Pages 327–45 in *Paul and His Theology.* Edited by Stanley E. Porter.
Fee, Gordon D. "Christology and Pneumatology in Romans 8.9–11 and Elsewhere: Some Reflections on Paul as a Trinitarian." Pages 312–331 in *Jesus of Nazareth: Essays on the Historical Jesus and New Testament Christology.* Edited by Joel B. Green and Max Turner. Grand Rapids: Eerdmans, 1994.
–. *God's Empowering Presence: The Holy Spirit in the Letters of Paul.* Peabody: Hendrickson Publishers, 1994.
–. *Pauline Christology: An Exegetical-Theological Study.* Peabody: Hendrickson Publishers, 2007.
Fitzmyer, Joseph A. *Romans: A New Translation with Introduction and Commentary.* AB. New York: Doubleday, 1993.
–. *Tobit.* CEJL. Berlin: Walter de Gruyter, 2003.
Fletcher-Louis, Crispin H.T. *All the Glory of Adam: Liturgical Anthropology in the Dead Sea Scrolls.* STDJ 42. Leiden: Brill, 2002.
Flint, Peter W. "The Book of Psalms in the Light of the Dead Sea Scrolls." *VT* 48 (1998): 453–72.
Forbes, Chris. "Paul's Principalities and Powers: Demythologising Apocalyptic?" *JSNT* 82 (2001): 61–88.
Freedman, David N. and David Miano. "People of the New Covenant." Pages 7–26 in *The Concept of the Covenant in the Second Temple Period.* Edited by Stanley E. Porter and Jacqueline C.R. Roo.
Frey, Jörg. "Different Patterns of Dualistic Thought in the Qumran Library: Reflections on their

Background and History." Pages 275–335 in *Legal Texts and Legal Issues: Proceedings of the Second Meeting of the International Organisation for Qumran Studies Cambridge 1995: FS J.M. Baumgarten.* Edited by M. Bernstein, F. García Martínez, and J.I. Kampen. STDJ 23. Leiden: Brill, 1997.

—. "Flesh and Spirit in the Palestinian Jewish Sapiential Tradition and in the Qumran Texts: An Inquiry into the Background of Pauline Usage." Pages 367–404 in *The Wisdom Texts From Qumran and the Development of Sapiential Thought.* Edited by Charlotte Hempel, Armin Lange, and Hermann Lichtenberger. BETL 159. Leuven: University Press, 2002.

Furnish, Victor Paul. *Theology and Ethics in Paul.* Nashville: Abingdon Press, 1968.

Gabriel, Andrew K. "Pauline Pneumatology and the Question of Trinitarian Presuppositions." Pages 347–62 in *Paul and His Theology.* Edited by Stanley E. Porter.

Gammie, John G. "The Sage in Sirach." Pages 355–72 in *The Sage in Israel and the Ancient Near East.* Edited by John G. Gammie and Leo G. Perdue. Winona Lake: Eisenbrauns, 1990.

Gammie, John G., Walter A. Brueggemann, W. Lee Humphreys, and James M. Ward, eds. *Israelite Wisdom: Theological and Literary Essays in Honor of Samuel Terrien.* Missoula: Scholars Press, 1978.

García Martínez, Florentino, and Adam S. van der Woude. "A 'Groningen' Hypothesis of Qumran Origins and Early History." *RQ* 14 (1990): 521–41.

Garlington, Don B. *Faith, Obedience, and Perseverance: Aspects of Paul's Letter to the Romans.* WUNT 1/79. Tübingen: Mohr (Siebeck), 1994.

—. *'The Obedience of Faith': A Pauline Phrase in Historical Context.* WUNT 2/38. Tübingen: Mohr (Siebeck), 1991.

Garnet, Paul. *Salvation and Atonement in the Qumran Scrolls.* WUNT 2/3. Tübingen: Mohr (Siebeck), 1977.

Gathercole, Simon J. "Justified by Faith, Justified by his Blood: The Evidence of Romans 3:21–4:25." Pages 149–84 in *Justification and Variegated Nomism: Volume 2 – The Paradoxes of Paul.* Edited by D.A. Carson, Peter T. O'Brien, and Mark A. Seifrid.

—. "Sin in God's Economy: Agencies in Romans 1 and 7." Pages 158–172 in *Divine and Human Agency in Paul and His Cultural Environment.* Edited by John M.G. Barclay and Simon J. Gathercole.

—. *Where is Boasting? Early Jewish Soteriology and Paul's Response in Romans 1–5.* Grand Rapids: Eerdmans, 2002.

Gilbert, Maurice. "God, Sin and Mercy: Sirach 15:1–18:14," Pages 118–35 in *Ben Sira's God.* Edited by Renate Egger-Wenzel.

Gill, Christopher. "Did Chrysippus Understand Medea?" *Phronesis* 28.2 (1983): 136–49.

Gillman, Florence Morgan. "Another Look at Romans 8:3: 'In the Likeness of Sinful Flesh'." *CBQ* 49 (1987): 597–604.

Goldstein, J. "Jewish Acceptance and Rejection of Hellenism." Pages 66–87 in *Jewish and Christian Self-Definition: Volume 2: Aspects of Judaism in the Graeco-Roman Period.* Edited by E.P. Sanders with A.I. Baumgarten and Alan Mendelson. Philadelphia: Fortress, 1981.

Gorman, Michael J. *Cruciformity: Paul's Narrative Spirituality of the Cross.* Grand Rapids: Eerdmans, 2001.

Gowan, Donald E. "Wisdom." Pages 215–39 in *Justification and Variegated Nomism: Volume 1 – The Complexities of Second Temple Judaism.* Edited by D.A. Carson, Peter T. O'Brien, and Mark A. Seifrid.

Greenfield, Jonas C. "The Root GBL in Mishnaic Hebrew and in the Hymnic Literature from Qumran." *RQ* 2 (1960): 155–162.

Gundry, Robert H. "The Moral Frustration of Paul before His Conversion: Sexual Lust in Romans 7.7–25." Pages 228–45 in *Pauline Studies: Essays Presented to F.F. Bruce.* Edited by Donald A. Hagner and Murray J. Harris. Grand Rapids: Eerdmans, 1980.

Haacker, Klaus. *Der Brief des Paulus an die Römer*. THKNT. Leipzig: Evangelische Verlagsanstalt, 1999.
Hagner, Donald A. "Paul and Judaism: Testing the New Perspective." Pages 75–105 in Stuhlmacher, Peter. *Revisiting Paul's Doctrine of Justification: A Challenge to the New Perspective*. Downers Grove: IVP, 2001.
–. "Paul as a Jewish Believer – According to His Letters." Pages 96–120 in *Jewish Believers in Jesus: The Early Centuries*. Edited by Oskar Skarsaune and Reidar Hvalvik. Peabody: Hendrickson Publishers, 2007.
Harrington, Daniel J. "Wisdom at Qumran." Pages 137–52 in *The Community of the Renewed Covenant: The Notre Dame Symposium on the Dead Sea Scrolls*. Edited by Eugene Ulrich and James Vanderkam. Notre Dame: University of Notre Dame Press, 1994.
Hays, Richard B. *The Faith of Jesus Christ: The Narrative Substructure of Galatians 3:1–4:11*. 2d ed. Grand Rapids: Eerdmans, 2002.
–. "Paul's Hermeneutics and the Question of Truth (review of Francis Watson, *Paul and the Hermeneutics of Faith*)." *ProEccl* 26 (2007): 126–33.
Hengel, Martin. *Judaism and Hellenism: Studies in their Encounter in Palestine during the Early Hellenistic Period*. 2 volumes. Translated by John Bowden. London: SCM Press, 1974.
Hermisson, Hans-Jürgen. "Observations on the Creation Theology in Wisdom." Pages 43–57 in *Israelite Wisdom*. Edited by John G. Gammie, Walter A. Brueggemann, W. Lee Humphreys, and James M. Ward.
Hofius, Otfried. "Der Mensch im Schatten Adams." Pages 104–54 in *Paulusstudien II*. WUNT 1/143. Tübingen: Mohr Siebeck, 2002.
Holland, Glenn S. "The Self against the Self in Romans 7:7–25." Pages 260–71 in *The Rhetorical Interpretation of Scripture: Essays from the 1996 Malibu Conference*. Edited by Stanley E. Porter and D.L. Stamps. JSNTSup 180. Sheffield: Sheffield Academic Press, 1999.
Holm-Nielsen, Svend. *Hodayot: Psalms from Qumran*. ATDan. Aarhus: Universitetsforlaget, 1960.
Hooker, Morna D. "Paul and 'Covenantal Nomism'." Pages 155–64 in idem, *From Adam to Christ: Essays on Paul*. Cambridge: Cambridge University Press, 1990.
Hopkins, Denise Dombkowski. "The Qumran Community and 1QHodayot: A Reassessment." *RQ* 10 (1979–81): 323–64.
van der Horst, Pieter W. "A Note on the Evil Inclination and Sexual Desire in Talmudic Literature." Pages 59–65 in *Jews and Christians in Their Graeco-Roman Context: Selected Essays on Early Judaism, Samaritanism, Hellenism, and Christianity*. WUNT 1/196. Tübingen: Mohr Siebeck, 2006.
Hübner, Hans. "Anthropologischer Dualismus in den Hodayoth?" *NTS* 18 (1972): 268–284.
–. *Law in Paul's Thought. Studies in the New Testament and Its World*. Translated by James C.G. Greig. Edinburgh: T&T Clark, 1983.
Huggins, Ronald V. "Alleged Classical Parallels to Paul's 'What I Want to Do I Do Not Do, But What I Hate, That I Do' (Rom 7:15)." *WTJ* 54 (1992): 153–61.
Huttunen, Niko. *Paul and Epictetus on Law: A Comparison*. LNTS 40. London: T&T Clark, 2009.
Hyatt, James Philip. "View of Man in the Qumran 'Hodayot'." *NTS* 2 (1956): 276–284.
Jacob, Edmond. "Wisdom and Religion in Sirach." Pages 247–60 in *Israelite Wisdom*. Edited by John G. Gammie, Walter A. Brueggemann, W. Lee Humphreys, and James M. Ward.
Jeremias, Gert. *Der Lehrer der Gerechtigkeit*. SUNT 2. Göttingen: Vandenhoeck & Ruprecht, 1963.
Jervis, L. Ann. "'The Commandment which is for Life' (Romans 7.10): Sin's Use of the Obedience of Faith." *JSNT* 27 (2004): 193–216.
Jewett, Robert. "The Basic Human Dilemma: Weakness or Zealous Violence? Romans 7:7–25 and 10:1–18." *ExAud* 13 (1997): 97–109.

–. "The Question of the 'Apportioned Spirit' in Paul's Letters: Romans as a Case Study." Pages 193–206 in *The Holy Spirit and Christian Origins*. Edited by Graham N. Stanton, Bruce W. Longenecker and Stephen C. Barton.
–. *Romans: A Commentary*. Hermeneia. Minneapolis: Fortress, 2007.
Johnson, Luke Timothy. "Rom 3:21–26 and the Faith of Jesus." *CBQ* 44 (1982): 77–90.
Kaiser, Otto. "Der Mensch als Geschöpf Gottes: Aspekte der Anthropologie Ben Siras." Pages 1–22 in *Der Einzelne und seine Gemeinschaft bei Ben Sira*. Edited by Renate Egger-Wenzel and Ingrid Krammer. BZAW 270. Berlin: de Gruyter, 1998.
Kamell, Mariam J. 'The Soteriology of James in Light of Earlier Jewish Wisdom Literature and the Gospel of Matthew'. PhD Thesis, University of St. Andrews, 2010.
Käsemann, Ernst. *Commentary on Romans*. Translated by Geoffrey W. Bromiley. Grand Rapids: William B. Eerdmans Publishing Company, 1980.
–. "On the Subject of Primitive Christian Apocalyptic." Pages 108–37 in idem, *New Testament Questions of Today*. London: SCM Press, 1969.
Kaye, Bruce Norman. *The Argument of Romans with Special Reference to Chapter 6*. Austin: Schola Press, 1979.
Keck, Leander E. "The Absent Good: The Significance of Rom. 7.18a." Pages 66–75 in *Text und Geschichte: Facetten theologischen Arbeitens aus dem Freundes- und Schülerkreis Dieter Lührmann zum 60. Geburtstag*. Edited by S. Maser and E. Schlarb. Marburger theologische Studien 50. Marburg: N.G. Elwert, 1999.
–. "The Law and 'The Law of Sin and Death'." Pages 41–57 in *The Divine Helmsman: Studies on God's Control of Human Events Presented to Lou H. Silberman*. Edited by J.L. Crenshaw and S. Sandmel. New York: KTAV, 1980.
–. *Romans*. ANTC. Nashville: Abingdon Press, 2005.
Kim, Seyoon. *Paul and the New Perspective: Second Thoughts on the Origin of Paul's Gospel*. Grand Rapids: Eerdmans, 2002.
Kittel, G., and G. Friedrich, eds. *Theological Dictionary of the New Testament*. Translated by G.W. Bromiley. 10 vols. Grand Rapids, 1964–1976.
Knibb, Michael A. "Teacher of Righteousness." Pages 918-21 in vol. 2 of *Encyclopaedia of the Dead Sea Scrolls*. Edited by Lawrence H. Schiffman and James C. VanderKam. 2 vols. Oxford: Oxford University Press, 2000.
Kooten, George H. van. *Paul's Anthropology in Context: The Image of God, Assimilation to God and Tripartite Man in Ancient Judaism, Ancient Philosophy and Early Christianity*. WUNT 1/232. Tübingen: Mohr Siebeck, 2008.
Kraft, Robert A. "Early Developments of the 'Two-Ways Tradition(s),' in Retrospect." Pages 136–43 in *For a Later Generation: The Transformation of Tradition in Israel, Early Judaism, and Early Christianity*. Edited by Randal A. Argall, Beverly A. Bow, and Rodney A. Werline. Harrisburg: Trinity Press International, 2000.
Kruse, Colin G. *Paul, the Law, and Justification*. Peabody: Hendrickson Publishers, 1997.
–. "Paul, the Law, and the Spirit." Pages 108–30 in *Paul and His Theology*. Edited by Stanley E. Porter.
Kuhn, Karl Georg. "New Light on Temptation, Sin, and Flesh in the New Testament." Pages 94–113 in *The Scrolls and the New Testament*. Edited by Krister Stendahl. London: SCM, 1958.
Kuula, Kari. *The Law, the Covenant, and God's Plan: Volume 2: Paul's Treatment of the Law and Israel in Romans*. Göttingen: Vandenhoeck & Ruprecht, 2003.
Kümmel, W.G. *Römer 7 und das Bild des Menschen im Neuen Testament*. Munich: Chr. Kaiser, 1974.
Laato, Timo. *Paul and Judaism: An Anthropological Approach*. Translated by T. McElwain. South Florida Studies in the History of Judaism. Atlanta: Scholars Press, 1995.

Lambrecht, Jan. *The Wretched "I" and Its Liberation: Paul in Romans 7–8.* Louvain: Peeters, 1992.
–. "The Implied Exhortation in Romans 8,5–8." Pages 7–17 in *Collected Studies on Pauline Literature and on the Book of Revelation.* AnBib 147. Rome: Pontifical Biblical Institute, 2001.
Lange, Armin. "Wisdom and Predestination in the Dead Sea Scrolls." *DSD* 2 (1995): 340–54.
–. *Weisheit und Prädestination: Weisheitliche Urordnung und Prädestination in den Textfunden vom Qumran.* STDJ 18. Brill, Leiden, 1995.
Leenhardt, Franz J. *The Epistle to the Romans: A Commentary.* Translated by H. Knight. London: Lutterworth, 1961.
Levison, John R. *Portraits of Adam in Early Judaism: From Sirach to 2 Baruch.* Sheffield: Sheffield Academic Press, 1988.
Licht, Jacob. "The Doctrine of the Thanksgiving Scroll." *IEJ* 6.1 (1956): 1–13; 6.2 (1956) 89–101.
Lichtenberger, Hermann. *Das Ich Adams und das Ich der Menschheit: Studien zum Menschenbild in Römer 7.* WUNT 164. Tübingen: Mohr Siebeck, 2004.
–. *Studien zum Menschenbild in Texten der Qumrangemeinde.* SUNT 15. Göttingen: Vandenhoeck & Ruprecht, 1980.
Liesen, Jan. *Full of Praise: An Exegetical Study of Sir 39,12-15.* JSJSup 64. Leiden: Brill, 2000.
–. "A Common Background of Ben Sira and the Psalter: The Concept of תורה in Sir 32:14–33.3 and the Torah Psalms." Pages 197–208 in *The Wisdom of Ben Sira: Studies on Tradition, Redaction, and Theology.* Edited by Angelo Passaro and Giuseppe Bellia.
Longenecker, Bruce W. *Eschatology and the Covenant: A Comparison of 4 Ezra and Romans 1–11.* JSNTSup 57. Sheffield: JSOT Press, 1991.
Lowe, Chuck. "'There is No Condemnation' (Romans 8:1): But Why Not?" *JETS* 42 (1999): 231–50.
Luck, Ulrich. "Das Gute und das Böse in Römer 7." Pages 220–37 in *Neues Testament und Ethik für Rudolf Schnackenburg.* Edited by Helmut Merklein. Freiburg: Herder, 1989.
Lyonnet, Stanislas. "Rom 8,2–4 à la lumière de Jérémie 31 et d'Ézéchiel 35–39." Pages 231–41 in *Etudes sur l'Epître aux Romains.* AnBib 120. Rome: Pontifical Biblical Institute, 1990.
Mack, Burton L. *Wisdom and the Hebrew Epic: Ben Sira's Hymn in Praise of the Fathers.* CSJH. Chicago: University of Chicago Press, 1985.
Magness, Jodi. "Qumran Archaeology: Past Perspectives and Future Prospects." Pages 47–77 in *The Dead Sea Scrolls After Fifty Years: A Comprehensive Assessment.* Volume 1. Edited by Peter W. Flint and James C. VanderKam. Leiden: Brill, 1998.
–. *The Archaeology of Qumran and the Dead Sea Scrolls.* Grand Rapids: Eerdmans, 2002.
Maier, G. *Mensch und freier Wille: nach den jüdischen Religionsparteien zwischen Ben Sira und Paulus.* WUNT 1/12. Tübingen: Mohr (Siebeck), 1971.
Mansoor, Menahem. "Studies in the Hodayot—IV." *JBL* 76 (1957): 139–48.
–. *The Thanksgiving Hymns.* STDJ 3. Grand Rapids: Eerdmans, 1961.
Marcus, Joel. "The Evil Inclination in the Epistle of James." *CBQ* 44 (1982): 606–21.
–. "The Evil Inclination in the Letters of Paul." *IBS* 8 (1986): 8–21.
Marshall, I. Howard. "Salvation, Grace and Works in the Later Writings in the Pauline Corpus." *NTS* 42 (1996): 339–58.
Martin, James D. "Ben Sira – A Child of his Time." Pages 141–61 in *A Word in Season: Essays in Honor of William McKane.* Edited by James D. Martin and Philip R. Davies. JSOTSup 42. Sheffield: JSOT Press, 1986.
Martin, Luther H. "Josephus' Use of *Heimarmene* in the *Jewish Antiquites* XIII, 171–3." *Numen* 28 (1981): 127–37.

Martyn, J. Louis. "Epilogue: an Essay in Pauline Meta-Ethics." Pages 173–83 in *Divine and Human Agency in Paul and His Cultural Environment*. Edited by John M.G. Barclay and Simon J. Gathercole.

–. *Galatians: A New Translation with Introduction and Commentary*. AB. New York: Doubleday, 1997.

–. "The Newly Created Moral Agent in Paul's Letters." Paper presented at annual meeting of the Society of Biblical Literature. San Diego, Calif., November 2007.

–. "*Nomos* Plus Genitive Noun in Paul: The History of God's Law." Pages 575–87 in *Early Christianity and Classical Culture: Comparative Studies in Honor of Abraham J. Malherbe*. Edited by John T. Fitzgerald, Thomas H. Olbricht and L. Michael White. NovTSup 110. Leiden: Brill, 2003.

–. *Theological Issues in the Letters of Paul*. Nashville: Abingdon, 1997.

Mason, Steve. *Flavius Josephus on the Pharisees: A Composition-Critical Study*. StPB. Leiden: Brill, 1991.

–. "Josephus's Pharisees: The Philosophy." Pages 41–66, 433–37 in *In Quest of the Historical Pharisees*. Edited by Jacob Neusner and Bruce D. Chilton. Waco: Baylor University Press, 2007.

Matlock, R. Barry. "Almost Cultural Studies?: Reflections on the 'New Perspective' on Paul." Pages 433–59 in *Biblical Studies/Cultural Studies: The Third Sheffield Colloquium*. Edited by J. Cheryl Exum and Stephen D. Moore. JSOTSup 266. Sheffield: Sheffield Academic Press, 1998.

–. "Detheologizing the πίστις Χριστοῦ Debate: Cautionary Remarks from a Lexical Semantic Perspective." *NovT* 42 (2000): 1–23.

–.. "The Rhetoric of πίστις in Paul: Galatians 2.16, 3.22, Romans 3.22, and Philippians 3.9." *JSNT* 30 (2007): 173–203.

Mattila, Sharon Lea. "Ben Sira and the Stoics: A Reexamination of the Evidence." *JBL* 119 (2000): 473–501.

McFadden, Kevin W. "The Fulfillment of the Law's *Dikaiōma*: Another Look at Romans 8:1 4." *JETS* 52 (2009): 483–97.

Melanchthon, Philip. *Commentary on Romans*. Translated by Fred Kramer. St. Louis: Concordia Publishing House, 1992.

Merrill, Eugene H. *Qumran and Predestination: A Theological Study of the Thanksgiving Hymns*. STDJ 8. Leiden: Brill, 1975.

Meyer, Paul W. "Holy Spirit in the Pauline Letters: A Contextual Exploration." *Int.* 33 (1979): 3–18.

–. "The Worm at the Core of the Apple: Exegetical Reflections on Romans 7." Pages 62–84 in *The Conversation Continues: Studies in Paul and John. In Honor of J. Louis Martyn*. Edited by R.T. Fortna and B.R. Gaventa. Nashville: Abingdon, 1990.

Middendorf, Michael Paul. *The "I" in the Storm: A Study of Romans 7*. Saint Louis: Concordia Academic, 1997.

Moo, Douglas J. *The Epistle to the Romans*. NICNT. Grand Rapids: Eerdmans, 1996.

–. "Israel and Paul in Romans 7.7–12." *NTS* 32 (1986): 122–35.

–. "Israel and the Law in Romans 5–11: Interactions with the New Perspective." Pages 185–216 in *Justification and Variegated Nomism: Volume 2 – The Paradoxes of Paul*. Edited by D.A. Carson, Peter T. O'Brien, and Mark A. Seifrid.

–. "The Law of Christ as the Fulfillment of the Law of Moses: A Modified Lutheran View." Pages 319–76 In W. Strickland, W. VanGemeren, W. Kaiser, D.J. Moo, and G. Bahnsen. *The Law, the Gospel, and the Modern Christian: Five Views*. Grand Rapids: Zondervan, 1993.

–. "'Law,' 'Works of the Law,' and Legalism in Paul." *WTJ* 45 (1983): 73–100.

Moore, C.A. *Tobit*. AB. London: Doubleday, 1996.
Moore, George Foot. "Fate and Free Will in the Jewish Philosophies according to Josephus." *HTR* 22 (1929): 371-89.
–. *Judaism in the First Centuries of the Christian Era: The Age of the Tannaim*. 3 Vols. Cambridge: Harvard University Press, 1927.
Mowinckel, Sigmund. "Some Remarks on *Hodayot* 39.5-20." *JBL* 75 (1956): 265-76.
Murphy, Roland E. "Sin, Repentance, and Forgiveness in Sirach." Pages 260-70 in *Der Einzelne und seine Gemeinschaft bei Ben Sira*. Edited by Renate Egger-Wenzel and Ingrid Krammer. BZAW 270. Berlin: de Gruyter, 1998.
–. *The Tree of Life: An Exploration of Biblical Wisdom Literature*. 2d ed. Grand Rapids: Eerdmans, 1996.
–. "Yēṣer in Qumran Literature." *Bib* 39 (1958): 334-44.
Nickelsburg, George W.E. *Ancient Judaism and Christian Origins: Diversity, Continuity, and Transformation*. Minneapolis: Fortress Press, 2003.
–. "The Incarnation: Paul's Solution to the Universal Human Predicament." Pages 589-99 in *George W.E. Nickelsburg in Perspective: An Ongoing Dialogue of Learning*, volume 2. Edited by Jacob Neusner and Alan J. Avery-Peck. JSJSup 80. Leiden: Brill, 2003.
–. *Jewish Literature between the Bible and the Mishnah*. London: SCM, 1981.
–. *Resurrection, Immortality, and Eternal Life in Intertestamental Judaism*. HTS 26; Cambridge: Harvard University Press, 1972.
–. "Torah and the Deuteronomic Scheme in the Apocrypha and Pseudepigrapha: Variations on a Theme and Some Noteworthy Examples of its Absence." Pages 222-35 in *Das Gesetz im frühen Judentum und im Neuen Testament: FS Christoph Burchard*. Edited by Dieter Sänger and Matthias Konradt. NTOA/ SUNT 57. Göttingen: Vandenhoeck & Ruprecht, 2006.
Nickelsburg, George W.E., with Robert A. Kraft. "Introduction: The Modern Study of Early Judaism." Pages 1-30 in *Early Judaism and its Modern Interpreters*. Edited by Robert A. Kraft and George W.E. Nickelsburg. Philadelphia: Fortress Press, 1984.
Nitzan, Bilhah. *Qumran Prayer and Religious Poetry*. Translated by Jonathan Chipman. STDJ 12. Leiden: Brill, 1994.
Nygren, Anders. *Commentary on Romans*. Translated by Carl C. Rasmussen. London: SCM Press, 1952.
O'Brien, Peter T. "Was Paul a Covenantal Nomist?" Pages 249-96 in *Justification and Variegated Nomism: Volume 2 – The Paradoxes of Paul*. Edited by D.A. Carson, Peter T. O'Brien, and Mark A. Seifrid.
Oesterley, W.O.E. *Ecclesiasticus*. Cambridge: Cambridge University Press, 1912.
Packer, J.I. "The 'Wretched Man' Revisited: Another Look at Romans 7:14-25." Pages 70-81 in *Romans and the People of God: Essays in Honor of Gordon D. Fee on the Occasion of his 65th Birthday*. Edited by Sven K. Soderlund and N.T. Wright. Grand Rapids: Eerdmans, 1999.
Passaro, Angelo, and Giuseppe Bellia. *The Wisdom of Ben Sira: Studies on Tradition, Redaction, and Theology*. Deuterocanonical and Cognate Literature Series 1. Berlin: Walter de Gruyter, 2008.
Pate, Marvin C. *The Reverse of the Curse: Paul, Wisdom, and the Law*. WUNT 2/114. Tübingen: Mohr Siebeck, 2000.
Perdue, Leo G. *The Sword and the Stylus: An Introduction to Wisdom in the Age of Empires*. Grand Rapids: Eerdmans, 2008.
–. *Wisdom and Creation: The Theology of Wisdom Literature*. Nashville: Abingdon, 1994.
–. *Wisdom and Cult: A Critical Analysis of the Views of Cult in the Wisdom Literature of Israel and the Ancient Near East*. SBLDS 30. Missoula: Scholars Press, 1977.
Pinnock, Clark H., Richard Rice, John Sanders, William Hasker, and David Basinger. *The

Openness of God: A Biblical Challenge to the Traditional Understanding of God. Downers Grove: InterVarsity, 1994.
Porter, Frank Chamberlin, "The Yeçer Hara: A Study in the Jewish Doctrine of Sin." Pages 93–156 in *Biblical and Semitic Studies: Yale Historical and Critical Contributions to Biblical Science*. New York: Charles Scribner's Sons, 1901.
Porter, Stanley E. "The Pauline Concept of Original Sin in Light of Rabbinic Background." *TynBul* 41 (1990): 3–30.
Porter, Stanley E., ed. *Paul and His Theology*. Pauline Studies 3. Leiden: Brill, 2006.
Porter, Stanley E., and Jacqueline C.R. Roo, eds. *The Concept of the Covenant in the Second Temple Period*. JSJSup 71. Leiden: Brill, 2003.
Prockter, Lewis J. "Torah as a Fence against Apocalyptic Speculation: Ben Sira 3:17–24." Pages 245–52 in *Proceedings of the Tenth World Congress of Jewish Studies (Jerusalem, August 16–24, 1989): Division A: The Bible and Its World*. Edited by D. Assaf. Jerusalem: Magnes, 1990.
Räisänen, Heikki. *Paul and the Law*. WUNT 1/29. Tübingen: Mohr (Siebeck), 1983.
–. "Paul's Word-Play on νόμος: A Linguistic Study." Pages 69–94 idem, in *Jesus, Paul and Torah: Collected Essays*. Sheffield: Sheffield Academic Press, 1992.
–. "The Use of ἐπιθυμία and ἐπιθυμεῖν in Paul." Pages 95–111 idem, in *Jesus, Paul and Torah: Collected Essays*. Sheffield: Sheffield Academic Press, 1992.
Rapa, Robert Keith. *The Meaning of "Works of the Law" in Galatians and Romans*. Studies in Biblical Literature 31. New York: Peter Lang, 2001.
Reiterer, Friedrich Vinzenz. "Die immateriellen Ebenen der Schöpfung bei Ben Sira." Pages 91–127 in *Treasures of Wisdom*. Edited by Núria Calduch-Benages and J. Vermeylen.
–. "The Interpretation of the Wisdom Tradition of the Torah within Ben Sira." Pages 209–31 in *The Wisdom of Ben Sira: Studies on Tradition, Redaction, and Theology*. Edited by Angelo Passaro and Giuseppe Bellia.
Rickert, GailAnn. "Akrasia and Euripides' Medea." *Harvard Studies in Classical Philology* 91 (1987): 91–117.
Ridderbos, Herman N. *Paul: An Outline of His Theology*. Translated by John Richard De Witt. Grand Rapids: Eerdmans, 1975.
Ringgren, Helmer. *The Faith of Qumran: Theology of the Dead Sea Scrolls*. Translated by Emilie T. Sander. Philadelphia: Fortress, 1963.
Romanello, Stefano. "Rom 7,7–25 and the Impotence of the Law: A Fresh Look at a Much-Debated Topic Using Literary-Rhetorical Analysis." *Bib* 84 (2003): 510–30.
Rosner, Brian. *Paul, Scripture and Ethics: A Study of 1 Corinthians 5–7*. AGJU 22. Leiden: Brill, 1994.
Saldarini, Anthony J. *Pharisees, Scribes and Sadducees in Palestinian Society: A Sociological Approach*. Grand Rapids: Eerdmans, 2001.
Sanday, William, and Arthur C. Headlam. *A Critical and Exegetical Commentary on the Epistle to the Romans*, 5th ed. ICC. Edinburgh: T & T Clark.
Sanders, E.P. "The Covenant as a Soteriological Category and the Nature of Salvation in Palestinian and Hellenistic Judaism." Pages 11–44 in *Jews, Greeks and Christians: Religious Cultures in Late Antiquity: Essays in Honor of William David Davies*. Edited by Robert Hamerton-Kelly and Robin Scroggs. Leiden: Brill, 1976.
–. "The Dead Sea Sect and Other Jews: Commonalities, Overlaps and Differences." Pages 7–43 in *The Dead Sea Scrolls in their Historical Context*. Edited by Timothy H. Lim. Edinburgh: T&T Clark, 2000.
–. *Judaism: Practice and Belief 63 BCE – 66 CE*. Philadelphia: Trinity Press International, 1992.
–. *Paul and Palestinian Judaism*. Minneapolis: Fortress, 1977.

–. *Paul, the Law, and the Jewish People*. Philadelphia: Fortress, 1983.
Sanders, Jack T. "When Sacred Canopies Collide: The Reception of the Torah of Moses in the Wisdom Literature of the Second-Temple Period." *JSJ* 32 (2001): 121–36.
–. "Wisdom, Theodicy, Death, and the Evolution of Intellectual Traditions." *JSJ* 36 (2005): 263–77.
Sauer, Georg. *Jesus Sirach/Ben Sira*. ATD. Göttingen: Vandenhoeck & Ruprecht, 2000.
Schechter, S. *Some Aspects of Rabbinic Theology*. London: Adam & Charles Black, 1909.
Schmithals, Walter. *Der Römerbrief: Ein Kommentar*. Gütersloh: Gütersloher, 1988.
Schnabel, Eckhard J. *Law and Wisdom from Ben Sira to Paul*. WUNT 2/16. Tübingen: Mohr Siebeck, 1985.
Schnackenburg, Rudolf. "Römer 7 in Zusammenhang des Römerbriefes." Pages 283–300 in *Jesus und Paulus: Festschrift für Werner Georg Kümmel*. Edited by E. Earle Ellis and Erich Gräßer. Göttingen: Vandenhoeck & Ruprecht, 1975.
Schökel, Luis Alonso. "The Vision of Man in Sirach 16:24–17:14." Pages 235–45 in *Israelite Wisdom*. Edited by John G. Gammie, Walter A. Brueggemann, W. Lee Humphreys, and James M. Ward.
Schreiner, Thomas R. "The Abolition and Fulfillment of the Law in Paul." *JSNT* 35 (1989): 47–74.
–. *The Law and Its Fulfillment: A Pauline Theology of Law*. Grand Rapids: Baker Books, 1993.
–. *New Testament Theology: Magnify God in Christ*. Grand Rapids: Baker Academic, 2008.
–. "Perseverance and Assurance: A Survey and a Proposal." *SBJT* 2 (1998): 32–62.
–. *Romans*. BECNT. Grand Rapids: Baker Books, 1998.
Schuller, Eileen M. "The Cave 4 Hodayot Manuscripts: A Preliminary Description." *JQR* 85 n.s. (1994): 137–150.
–. "Some Contributions of the Cave Four Manuscripts (4Q427–432) to the Study of the Hodayot." *DSD* 8 (2001): 278–87.
Schwemer, Anna Maria. "Zum Verhältnis von Diatheke und Nomos in den Schriften der jüdischen Diaspora Ägyptens in hellenistisch-römischer Zeit." Pages 67–109 in *Bund und Tora: Zur theologischen Begriffsgeschichte in alttestamentlicher, frühjüdischer und urchristlicher Tradition*. Edited by Friedrich Avemarie and Hermann Lichtenberger. WUNT 1/92. Tübingen: Mohr Siebeck, 1996.
Scott, James M., ed. *Exile: Old Testament, Jewish, and Christian Conceptions*. JSJSup 56. Leiden: Brill, 1997.
–. *Restoration: Old Testament, Jewish, and Christian Perspective*. JSJSup 72. Leiden: Brill, 2001.
Seifrid, Mark A. "Blind Alleys in the Controversy over the Paul of History." *TynBul* 45.1 (1994): 73–95.
–. *Justification by Faith: The Origin and Development of a Central Pauline Theme*. NovTSup 68. Leiden: Brill, 1992.
–. "Romans." D.A. Carson and Greg K. Beale, eds. *Commentary on the New Testament Use of the Old Testament*, 607–94. Grand Rapids: Baker Academic, 2007.
–. "The Subject of Rom 7.14–25." *NovT* 34 (1992): 313–33.
Sekki, Arthur Everett. *The Meaning of Ruaḥ at Qumran*. SBLDS 110. Atlanta: Scholars Press, 1989.
Sheppard, Gerald T. *Wisdom as a Hermeneutical Construct: A Study in the Sapientializing of the Old Testament*. BZAW 151. Berlin: de Gruyter, 1980.
Shogren, Gary S. "The 'Wretched Man' of Romans 7:14–25 as Reductio ad absurdum." *EvQ* 72 (2000): 119–34.
Siebeneck, Robert T. "May Their Bones Return to Life: Sirach's 'Praise of the Father'." *CBQ* 21 (1959): 411–28.

Sievers, Joseph. "Josephus, First Maccabees, Sparta, The Three Haireseis—and Cicero." *JSJ* 32 (2001): 241–51.
Silberman, Lou H. "Language and Structure in the Hodayot (1QH 3)." *JBL* 75 (1956): 96–106.
Silva, Moisés. "Faith versus Works of Law in Galatians." Pages 217–48 in *Justification and Variegated Nomism: Volume 2 – The Paradoxes of Paul*. Edited by D.A. Carson, Peter T. O'Brien, and Mark A. Seifrid.
Skehan, Patrick W. and Alexander A. Di Lella. *The Wisdom of Ben Sira*. AB. New York: Doubleday, 1987.
Smith, Barry D. *What Must I Do to Be Saved? Paul Parts Company with his Jewish Heritage*. NTM 17. Sheffield: Sheffied Phoenix, 2007.
Snaith, John G. *Ecclesiasticus, or the Wisdom of Jesus Son of Sirach*. CBC. Cambridge: Cambridge University Press, 1974.
Southall, David J. *Rediscovering Righteousness in Romans: Personified dikaiosynē within Metaphoric and Narratorial Settings*. WUNT 2/240. Tübingen: Mohr Siebeck, 2008.
Sprinkle, Preston M. *Law and Life. The Interpretation of Leviticus 18:5 in Early Judaism and in Paul*. WUNT 2/241. Tübingen: Mohr Siebeck, 2008.
Stanton, Graham N., Bruce W. Longenecker, and Stephen C. Barton, eds. *The Holy Spirit and Christian Origins: Essays in Honor of James D.G. Dunn*. Grand Rapids: Eerdmans, 2004.
Starnitzke, Dierk. *Die Struktur paulinischen Denkens im Römerbrief: Eine linguistisch-logische Untersuchung*. BWANT. Stuttgart: W. Kohlhammer, 2004.
Stegemann, Hartmut. *The Library of Qumran: On the Essenes, Qumran, John the Baptist, and Jesus*. Grand Rapids: Eerdmans, 1998.
–. "The Qumran Essenes – Local Members of the Main Jewish Union in Late Second Temple Times." Pages 83–166 in *The Madrid Qumran Congress: Proceedings of the International Congress on the Dead Sea Scrolls, Madrid 18–21 March, 1991*. Edited by Julio Trebolle Barrera and Luis Vegas Montaner. STDJ 11.1. Leiden: Brill, 1992.
Stendahl, Krister. "The Apostle Paul and the Introspective Conscience of the West." *HTR* 56 (1963): 199–215.
Stone, Michael Edward. *4 Ezra*. Minneapolis: Fortress, 1990.
Stowers, Stanley K. *A Rereading of Romans: Justice, Jews, and Gentiles*. Hew Haven: Yale University Press, 1994.
–. "Romans 7.7–25 as Speech-in-Character (προσωποποιία)." Pages 180–202 in *Paul in His Hellenistic Context*. Edited by Troels Engberg-Pedersen. SNTW. Edinburgh: T&T Clark, 1994.
Stuhlmacher, Peter. *Paul's Letter to the Romans: A Commentary*. Translated by S. J. Hafemann. Louisville: Westerminster/John Knox Press, 1994.
Talmon, Shemaryahu. "Qumran Studies: Past, Present, and Future." *JQR* 85 n.s. (1995): 1–31.
Tcherikover, V. *Hellenistic Civilization and the Jews*. Translated by S. Applebaum. Philadelphia: The Jewish Publication Society of America, 1961.
Tennant, F.R. "The Teaching of Ecclesiasticus and Wisdom on the Introduction of Sin and Death." *JTS* 2 (1900–1901): 207–23.
Thackeray, H. St. John. "On Josephus's Statement of the Pharisees' Doctrine of Fate (Antiq. xviii. 1, 3)." *HTR* 25 (1932): 93.
Theissen, G. *Psychological Aspects of Pauline Theology*. Translated by J.P. Galvin. Philadelphia: Fortress Press, 1987.
Theobald, Michael. "*Concupiscentia* im Römerbrief." Pages 250–76 in idem, *Studien zum Römerbrief*. WUNT 1/136. Tübingen: Mohr Siebeck, 2001.
Thielman, Frank. *From Plight to Solution: A Jewish Framework for Understanding Paul's View of the Law in Galatians and Romans*. NovTSup 61. Leiden: Brill, 1989.

–. *Paul and the Law: A Contextual Approach.* Downers Grove: InterVarsity, 1994.
Thurén, Lauri. *Derhetorizing Paul: A Dynamic Perspective on Pauline Theology and the Law.* WUNT 1/124; Tübingen: Mohr Siebeck, 2000.
–. "Romans 7 Derhetorized." Pages 420–40 in *Rhetorical Criticism and the Bible.* Edited by Stanley E. Porter and Dennis L. Stamps. JSNTSup 195. Sheffield: Sheffield Academic Press, 2002.
Thyen, Hartwig. *Studien zur Sündenvergebung im Neuen Testament und seinen alttestamentlichen und jüdischen Voraussetzungen.* FRLANT 96. Göttingen: Vandenhoeck & Ruprecht, 1970.
Tobin, Thomas H., SJ. *Paul's Rhetoric in Its Contexts: The Argument of Romans.* Peabody: Hendrickson Publishers, 2004.
VanGemeren, W.A., ed. *New International Dictionary of Old Testament Theology and Exegesis.* 5 vols. Grand Rapids: Zondervan, 1997.
VanLandingham, Chris. *Judgment and Justification in Early Judaism and the Apostle Paul.* Peabody: Hendrickson, 2006.
von Rad, Gerhard. *Wisdom in Israel.* London: SCM, 1972.
Wasserman, Emma. "The Death of the Soul in Romans 7: Revisiting Paul's Anthropology in Light of Hellenistic Moral Psychology." *JBL* 126 (2007): 793–816.
–. *The Death of the Soul in Romans 7: Sin, Death, and the Law in Light of Hellenistic Moral Psychology.* WUNT 2/256. Tübingen: Mohr Siebeck, 2008.
–. "Paul among the Philosophers: The Case of Sin in Romans 6–8." *JSNT* 30 (2008): 387–415.
Watson, Francis. "Constructing an Antithesis: Pauline and Other Jewish Perspectives on Divine and Human Agency." Pages 99–116 in *Divine and Human Agency in Paul and His Cultural Environment.* Edited by John M.G. Barclay and Simon J. Gathercole.
–. *Paul and the Hermeneutics of Faith.* London: T&T Clark, 2004.
–. *Paul, Judaism and the Gentiles: Beyond the New Perspective.* Rev. and exp. edition. Grand Rapids: Eerdmans, 2007.
–. "The Triune Divine Identity: Reflections on Pauline God-Language, in Disagreement with J.D.G. Dunn." *JSNT* 80 (2000): 99–124.
Weber, Reinhard. "Die Geschichte des Gesetzes und des Ich in Römer 7:7–8:4." *NZSth* 29 (1987): 147–79.
Webster, Jane S. "Sophia: Engendering Wisdom in Proverbs, Ben Sira and the Wisdom of Solomon." *JSOT* 78 (1998): 63–79.
Weissenberger, Michael. "Die jüdischen ‚Philosophenschulen' bei Josephus: Variationen eines Themas." Pages 521–25 in *Josephus und das Neue Testament: Wechselseitige Wahrnehmungen – II. Internationales Symposium zum Corpus Judaeo-Hellenisticum 25.–28. Mai 2006, Greifswald.* Edited by Christfried Böttrich und Jens Herzer. WUNT 1/209. Tübingen: Mohr Siebeck, 2007.
Wells, Kyle B. "Grace, Obedience, and the Hermeneutics of Agency: Paul and His Jewish Contemporaries on the Transformation of the Heart." PhD Thesis, Durham University, 2010.
Wernberg-Moeller, Preben. "Reconsideration of the Two Spirits in the Rule of the Community (1QSerek III, 13–IV, 26)." *RQ* 3/3 (1961): 413–441.
Westerholm, Stephen. *Perspectives Old and New on Paul: The "Lutheran" Paul and His Critics.* Grand Rapids: Eerdmans, 2004.
Whybray, R.N. "Ben Sira and History." Pages 137–45 in *Treasures of Wisdom.* Edited by Núria Calduch-Benages and J. Vermeylen.
Wicke-Reuter, Ursel. "Ben Sira und die frühe Stoa: Zum Zusammenhang von Ethik und dem Glauben an eine göttliche Providenz." Pages 268–81 in *Ben Sira's God.* Edited by Renate Egger-Wenzel.

–. *Göttliche Providenz und menschliche Verantwortung bei Ben Sira und in der frühen Stoa.* BZAW 298. Berlin: de Gruyter, 2000.
Wilckens, Ulrich. *Der Brief an die Römer.* EKKNT 6/2. Zurich: Benziger, 1980.
Winger, Michael. *By What Law? The Meaning of Νόμος in the Letters of Paul.* SBLDS 128. Atlanta: Scholars Press, 1992.
Winston, David. "Theodicy in Ben Sira and Stoic Philosophy." Pages 239–49 in *Of Scholars, Savants, and their Texts: Essays in Honor of Arthur Hyman.* Edited by R. Link-Salinger. New York: Lang, 1989.
–. *The Wisdom of Solomon.* AB. Garden City: Doubleday, 1979.
Winter, Paul. "Ben Sira and the Teaching of 'Two Ways'." *VT* 5 (1955): 315–18.
Wischmeyer, Oda."Gut und Böse: Antithetisches Denken im Neuen Testament und bei Jesus Sirach." Pages 129–36 in *Treasures of Wisdom.* Edited by Núria Calduch-Benages and J. Vermeylen.
–. "Theologie und Anthropologie im Sirachbuch." Pages 18–32 in *Ben Sira's God.* Edited by Renate Egger-Wenzel.
Wise, Michael O. "The Concept of a New Covenant in the Teacher Hymns from Qumran (1QHa X-XVII)." Pages 99–128 in *Concept of the Covenant in the Second Temple Period.* Edited by Stanley E. Porter and Jacqueline C.R. de Roo.
–. "Dating the Teacher of Righteousness and the Floruit of His Movement." *JBL* 122 (2003): 53–87.
Wise, Michael, Martin Abegg, Jr., and Edward Cook. *The Dead Sea Scrolls: A New Translation.* San Francisco: Harper Collins, 1996.
Witherington, Ben, III, and Darlene Hyatt. *Paul's Letter to the Romans: A Socio-Rhetorical Commentary.* Grand Rapids: Eerdmans, 2004.
Wright, Benjamin G. "'Fear the Lord and Honor the Priest': Ben Sira as Defender of the Jerusalem Priesthood." Pages 189–222 in *The Book of Ben Sira in Modern Research.* Edited by Pancratius C. Beentjes.
Wright, N.T. *The Climax of the Covenant: Christ and the Law in Pauline Theology.* Minneapolis: Fortress Press, 1992.
–. *The New Testament and the People of God.* London: SPCK, 1992.
–. "The Letter to the Romans." In Leander K. Keck, ed. *The New Interpreter's Bible.* Vol. 10, *The Acts of the Apostles – The First Letter to the Corinthians,* 393–770. Nashville: Abingdon Press, 2002.
–. "The Paul of History and the Apostle of Faith." *TynBul* 29 (1978): 61–88.
–. *What St. Paul Really Said.* Oxford: Lion Hudson, 1997.
Yates, John W. *The Spirit and Creation in Paul.* WUNT 2/251. Tübingen: Mohr Siebeck, 2008.
Yinger, Kent L. *Paul, Judaism, and Judgment according to Deeds.* SNTSMS 105. Cambridge: Cambridge University Press, 1999.
Zeller, Dieter. *Der Brief an die Römer.* RNT. Regensbrug: Pustet, 1985.
Ziesler, John A. *Paul's Letter to the Romans.* TPINTC. Philadelphia: Trinity Press International, 1989.
–. "The Role of the Tenth Commandment in Romans 7." *JSNT* 33 (1988): 41–56.
Zimmerli, Walter. "The Place and Limit of the Wisdom in the Framework of the Old Testament Theology." Pages 314–26 in *Studies in Ancient Israelite Wisdom,* comp. James L. Crenshaw. New York: KTAV Publishing House, 1976. Reprint of *Scottish Journal of Theology* 17 (1964): 146–58.

Index of Ancient Sources

Old Testament

Genesis
1.27–28	45
2–3	46, 92
2.7	28, 83, 91, 92–93, 109, 142, 178
2.8	28
2.17	46
2.19	28
3.1–13	46
3.1–19	93
3.5	86
3.7	88
3.13	26, 46
3.19	83, 86, 93, 178
4.7	143, 150
5.24	30
6.5	28, 92, 142
8.21	28, 92, 142
12.1–3	38–39
12.1–6	39
15.1–6	39
15.1–17	38
15.1–21	38–39
15.6	7, 39, 42
15.9–21	39
17	41
17.1–2	37
17.1–14	38
17.3–14	37–38
22.1–19	38–39
22.1	38, 39
22.1–14	39
22.16	38
27.23	59
31.29	23

Exodus
14.21–30	44
17.8–17	52
18.20	99
19.16–19	34, 41
20.7	33
20.12	32, 55
20.17	126
21.9	164
34.5–8	117
34.6	67

Leviticus
12.5	84
18.5	7, 43, 133, 134, 166
18.6–19	84
20.10	33

Numbers
25.6–13	40
25.12	40
31.21	164

Deuteronomy
1.8	42
4.10	52
4.20	42
5.11	33
5.16	32, 55
5.21	126
5.29	52
6.2	52
6.5	142
6.24	52
7.10	142
8.2–3	59
8.6	52
9.27	42
10.12	99

10.12–13	52	14.5–6	59–60
11.22	99	15.26	99
11.28	98	15.34	99
13.5	165	16.2	99
13.14	52	16.19	99
17.7	165	16.26	99
17.18–19	52	22.43	99
19.9	99		
19.19	165	*2 Kings*	
21.21	165	2.3	99
22.21	165	2.4	99
22.22–24	33	8.18	99
23.1	165		
24.7	165	*2 Chronicles*	
25.4	164	32.8	85
25.18	52		
26.17	99	*Job*	67
27.20	165	4.19	83
28.1–14	28	6.12	85
28.9	98, 99	10.4	85
28.15–68	28	10.9	83
30.11–14	42	15.14	90
30.15	46, 133, 146	20.11	86
30.15–20	19, 27, 42, 73, 131, 134, 140, 169, 178	21.26	86
		30.19	83
30.16	28, 99	33.6	83, 91
30.16–18	131	34.15	85, 86
30.17–18	28		
30.18	28	*Psalms*	
30.19	131	2.12	59
30.19–20	28	7.5	86
31.12–13	52	8	92, 178
31.21	142	8.4	90
32.8–9	34	8.5	90
		8.7–8	90
Joshua		10	26
22.5	99	22.16	86
24.14–28	131	22.29	86
		30.9	86
Ruth		37.23	99
4.7	164	51.5	92
		78.39	85
2 Samuel		103	92, 178
12.13–14	40	103.10–14	93
22.33	99	104.29	86
		106.28–31	40
1 Kings		144.3–4	90, 92
3.14	99		
8.25	99		

Index of Ancient Sources

Proverbs	
1.7	32, 52
1.29	52
2.16	60
3.6	99
3.7	52
4.26–27	98
5.20	60
6.24	60
7.5	60
8.13	52
9.10	52
13.14	52
14.2	52
14.27	52
15.3	64
15.27	56
15.33	52
16.1	65
16.4	64
16.5	64
16.6	52, 56
16.9	99
16.33	64
20.22	22
20.24	98
21.1	64
21.23	65
23.17	52
24.21	52
24.29	23

Qoheleth	67
3.20	86
7.10	23
7.13	25
12.7	86
12.13	32, 52

Isaiah	
26.19	86
31.3	85
40.3	85
40.6	92

Jeremiah	
10.23	98
17.5	85
17.9	92
18.1–11	65
21.8	131
31.31–34	160–61

Lamentations	
1.17	84
4.8	59

Ezekiel	
11	178
11.16–17	107
11.18	107
11.19	106, 107, 160
11.19–20	159
11.20	107, 160
11.21	107
23.19	84
36–37	109, 161, 178
36.24	107
36.25	107
36.26	106, 107, 160
36.26–27	159
36.27	107, 160
36.28–30	107
36.31	107
36.33–38	107
37.1–14	35, 159
37.6	109
37.14	107, 109, 160

Daniel	
2.11	85
4.27	56
10.21	95
12.2	86

Hosea	
2.19–20	34

Jonah	
4.1–11	26

Micah	
2.1	23

Habakkuk	26
2.4	7, 42, 173

New Testament

Mark		6	139, 144, 161
10.33	155	6–8	132
		6.1–8.13	153, 163
Romans		6.1–23	130
1.3	159	6.1–8.13	129
1.3–4	158, 159	6.3–7	155
1.4	157	6.5	155
1.5	130, 163, 174	6.6	167
1.16	130	6.12	144, 149, 150
1.17	42, 173	6.14	127
1.18	154	6.14–15	129
1.18–32	137	6.15–18	145
1.23	155	6.18	161
1.32	155, 163	6.19	144
2.1	155	6.22	145, 161
2.12	137	7–8	21
2.26	163–64	7.1	132, 137
2.28	159	7.1–6	130, 161
2.28–29	159	7.3	127
2.29	159	7.4	155, 163
3.8	129, 163	7.5	127, 149, 154, 159, 163
3.9–18	137		
3.9	137	7.5–6	139, 158–59
3.20	127, 129, 136	7.6	163, 164
3.20–24	164	7.7	126, 136–37, 149
3.20–26	124	7.7–11	145, 149
3.22	125, 129	7.7–12	129
3.26	125	7.7–13	128, 141
4	42	7.7–25	20, 126–153, 159, 163, 167, 168, 171–72, 176, 178
4.15	127		
4.24	157		
5–7	141	7.7–8.13	20, 154, 163, 170–74, 176–79
5–8	140		
5.1–11	127	7.8	137, 145, 150
5.5–8	166	7.9	134, 136, 137
5.12	144	7.9–10	144
5.12–21	129, 141, 143	7.10	133–35, 147
5.12–6.23	144	7.11	145, 146, 149, 150, 155
5.13–14	137, 145		
5.14	155	7.12	127, 145
5.16	163	7.13	127, 145
5.17	155	7.14	128, 138–39, 144, 145, 147, 155, 159
5.18	127, 155, 163		
5.20	127, 143	7.14–20	139
5.20–21	129	7.14–21	129
5.21	144	7.14–25	128, 133

Index of Ancient Sources

7.15	126, 149	9.30–10.4	139
7.15–19	145	9.31	138
7.15–20	134, 136, 138–40, 144, 147–150	9.32	138
		10.2–4	2
7.16	126, 145	10.4	166
7.17	145–46, 147, 149, 150, 159	10.5	43, 133, 134
		10.5–8	42
7.18	126, 138, 145, 155	11.6	164
7.18–19	135	13.8–10	165–66
7.19	126	14.1–15.13	166
7.20	126, 145–46, 147, 149, 150, 159	14.12	127
		14.19	127
7.21	126, 130, 139, 147–48	15.18	163
7.22	150	16.26	130, 174
7.23	144, 145, 150, 159		
7.24	135, 146, 167, 171	*1 Corinthians*	
7.25	127, 135, 172	5–7	165
8.1	137, 154, 162	5.1–13	164, 165
8.1–4	127, 130, 163	5.13	165
8.1–13	6, 20, 126, 130, 153–170, 172, 176	9.8–10	164
		9.20	133
8.2	155–56, 160–61, 168	10.1–13	167
8.3	145, 154–58, 162	10.1–14	164
8.3–4	163–64	11.32	155
8.4	130, 160–67, 169	12.4–6	157
8.4–11	127	14.34	164
8.4–13	158–59, 174	15.9	146
8.5–6	159	15.56	145
8.5–13	130, 139		
8.6	126, 160, 168	*2 Corinthians*	
8.8	126, 130, 161, 166	3.1–6	161
8.9	157–58	3.3–6	159
8.9–11	159	3.7	126
8.10	157–60, 167–68	3.17	157
8.11	126, 157, 160, 168	10.6	162
8.11–12	127	11.14	141
8.12–13	127	13.5	167
8.13	126, 137, 160, 166–69, 173–74	13.14	157
8.14	127	*Galatians*	
8.14–17	127	1.4	158
8.15	158	1.13	146
8.17	127	2.15–16	4, 164
8.27	154	2.16	124, 125
8.29	154	2.20	125, 179
8.31–39	127	3	42
9–11	177	3.11	42, 173
9.1–29	154	3.11–12	166
9.16	127	3.12	43, 133, 134, 166
9.18	127		

204   *Index of Ancient Sources*

3.21	133, 134	2.7	155
3.22	125	2.12–13	163, 179
4.4	165	3.2–6	139
4.4–6	158	3.4–6	133
4.6	157	3.4–11	177
5.6	174	3.5	20
5.13	165	3.6	146
5.14	165	3.9	2, 124, 125, 164
5.22	165		
6.7–9	167	*Colossians*	
6.10	127	1.9	162
Ephesians		*1 Thessalonians*	
2.19	127	5.6	127
4.4–6	157		
5.18	162	*2 Thessalonians*	
		2.15	127
Philippians			
1.11	162	*2 Peter*	
1.19	157	2.6	155

Apocrypha and Pseudepigrapha

Apocalypse of Abraham		7.127–29	131, 179
8.1–6	39	14.29–30	136
Baruch		*Jubilees*	
3.33–35	45	11.5	142
		15.31	34
2 Baruch	137	17.17	38
24.4–9	45	19.8	38
24.15–16	45		
24.19	45	*Letter of Jeremiah*	
48.1–24	45	60–65	45
54.3	45		
		Liber Antiquitatum Biblicarum	
1 Enoch		6.11	39
5	45		
94–104	179	*1 Maccabees*	
94.1–5	131	2.52	39
4 Ezra	137, 176	*4 Maccabees*	
3.20–22	142	1.1	151
7.3–24	131, 179	1.12–13	151
7.92	142	2.5	151
7.116–131	128		

Index of Ancient Sources

Prayer of Manasseh
  139

Psalms of Solomon
  19
9.1–5 131, 179
14.2 136
18.10–12 44–45

Sirach
Prologue 31, 34
1.11–30 31, 51
1.14 49
1.26 31, 32
1.26–27 49, 50
1.26–28 51
1.30 70
2.1–6 53
2.2–3 30
2.3 30
2.6 30, 49, 52, 53
2.7–9 71
2.8 30, 53
2.10 53, 67
2.12–14 71
2.13 53
2.15–16 50
2.16 72
3.1–16 30, 32, 55
3.3 54, 55
3.6 32
3.14 71
3.14–15 54, 55
3.30 54, 56
4.10 30, 71
4.11–20 58–60, 62, 65, 138–39
4.15–16 50
4.15 59
4.17 60
4.17–18 31
4.17–19 59–60
4.18–19 60
4.19 31
5.1–6 23
5.1–8 24, 26
5.1 24
5.3 24
5.4 24, 67
5.6 25, 66, 68
5.7 67
6.18–37 58, 60–62, 65, 138–39
6.32–35 34
6.34–37 34
6.37 34, 49, 61–62
7.1–3 71
7.8 71
7.8–9 24, 54
7.8–10 54
7.9 23, 25, 71
7.10 54
7.16 67
7.17 31
7.29–31 33
7.31 31, 51
8.5 54
8.8–9 34
9.3–9 71
9.11 31
9.12 67
9.15 34, 61
9.15–16 49, 50
8.8 30
10.4–5 64
11.17–19 24
11.18–19 23, 67
11.19 24
11.21 53, 67
11.21–22 23, 70
11.23–24 23, 70
11.24 24
11.26 23, 70
12.2 70
12.3 54, 56
13.1 71
14.20–27 50
14.20–15.10 58, 62–63, 66, 138–39
15.1 49, 50, 63
15.11–12 23, 25, 28, 151
15.11–20 24, 27–30, 138–40, 152
15.13 49, 51
15.14 28, 46, 58, 131, 139, 142, 151
15.14–17 28, 58, 65, 73, 94, 113, 135, 140, 175, 178
15.14–20 27, 58
15.15 58, 131, 140, 151
15.15–17 131
15.17 28, 48, 57, 58
15.18–19 64

15.18–20	58	19.24	32, 49
16.5–10	70	20.16	24
16.6–10	67	21.1	54
16.11	68	21.6	51
16.11–12	68	21.11	32, 49, 128
16.12–13	69	22.23	53
16.12–14	70	22.27–23.6	32
16.17	23, 64, 70	23.2–6	33, 50
16.17–22	24	23.7	33
16.17–23	46	23.9–10	33
16.17–17.24	27	23.16–27	33
16.20–22	64	23.17–18	23
16.26–27	44	23.17–21	24
16.26–28	45	23.18	24
16.26–17.14	45	23.19	50, 51, 64
16.26–17.32	41	23.20	64
16.28	44	23.21–27	31
17.1–4	46	23.23	32, 33, 50
17.1–10	45	23.27	33, 49, 50
17.1–14	34, 38, 46–47, 58, 178	24.1–23	37, 38, 41
17.1–24	46	24.3–7	43
17.3	45	24.8	44
17.6	46	24.9–10	44
17.6–7	113	24.22	63
17.6–10	46	24.23	32, 35, 41, 47
17.7	28, 46, 146	24.25–29	32
17.11	41, 45, 48, 57, 136	24.34	31
17.11–12	46	27.25–29	71
17.11–14	34, 41–42, 47	27.28	68
17.12	41, 45	27.30–28.7	46
17.13	41	28.1	71
17.14	46, 146	28.2	54
17.15	64	28.6	31, 32
17.15–29	67, 70	28.6–7	32
17.15–22	46	28.7	32
17.17	34, 41	29.1–20	56
17.19–20	64	29.1	32, 54
17.20	45, 46, 56	29.9	32
17.21	56	29.11	32, 71
17.22	45, 46, 5670	29.12	71
17.23	46–47, 70	31.16	33
17.24	56, 70	32.1	33
17.25	54	32.14–16	49
17.29	69	32.14–33.6	32
18.11	68	32.24–33.1	49
18.11–12	67	32.24–33.3	50–51
18.14	69	32.24	53
19.16	54	33.3	51
19.17	32	33.7–15	64–65
19.20	32, 49	33.16–18	61

Index of Ancient Sources 207

34.21–24	54	44.18	37
34.23	69	44.20	37–39
35.1–5	56	44.20–21	37
35.1–7	32	44.21	39
35.1–12	33, 56, 69	45.5	47, 57, 136
35.4	54, 56	45.23–24	40
35.4–11	33	46.7–10	30
35.15	54	47.1–7	40
35.21–22	68	47.8–10	40
35.24	70	47.11	40
35.28–36.4	50–51	47.19–25	40
36.1–22	35	47.22	40
37.7–15	32	48.20	68
37.12	34, 49, 61	50.27–29	31
39.1	49	50.29	51
39.4	30	51.1–12	33
39.9–11	23	51.14	34
39.12–35	23, 44	51.27	61
39.17	44	51.30	68, 71
39.18	44		
39.28–29	44	*Susanna*	
39.30	44	1.53	155
39.31	44		
40.17	56	*Testament of Asher*	
40.24	56	1.3	142
41.5	32		
41.8	32, 54	*Testament of Judah*	
41.11–13	30	20.1	142
42.15	44		
42.15–43.33	44	*Tobit*	
42.24	64	4.9–10	56
43.1–26	44	4.10	56
43.5	44	4.10–11	56
43.10	44	12.8–9	56
43.13–22	44	12.9	56, 57
44–50	30, 178	14.10–11	56
44.16	30		
44.17	37		

Dead Sea Scrolls

1QS	111	3.19	101
2.5–9	142	3.24	101
3–4	19, 64, 104, 105, 107, 179	4.16	101
		4.20–23	101
3.13–15	102	4.25	101
3.13–4.26	101, 141	5.7–11	114
3.15–21	45	5.20–22	114

Index of Ancient Sources

6.18	114	7	105, 107
10–11	80	7.19	84
10.21	142	7.23	101
		7.25	84, 85, 92, 116
CD	111	7.25–26	98
2.14–16	142	7.25–27	100, 108
		7.26	102
1QM		7.26–27	97
1.1	142	7.26–31	97
13–14	80	7.27–28	98, 112
13.2–4	142	7.27–30	85, 108
		7.27–32	110, 111
Hodayot	19, 137, 176	7.28	99
		7.29–30	98
1QH^a	76, 79	7.30	85, 112
4	107	7.30–31	98, 100, 112
4.27	82, 85	7.31	99
4.29	107	7.34	84, 85, 92, 98, 100
4.31	87	7.35	98, 100, 104, 112, 116
4.32	87	7.37	87, 112
4.23–27	117	7.37–38	87
4.33	99	8.18	106
4.35	104, 119	8.24–25	116
4.35–37	119	8.26–33	95–97
4.37	84	8.27	87
5.3–35	117	8.28	95, 96, 116, 118, 120
5.18	87	8.29	87, 95, 106
5.21	84	8.30	96, 107, 118
5.30	105	8.30–31	96
5.30–31	84, 89	8.31	97
5.30–33	91	8.32–33	96
5.31	84	8.35	97
5.32	84, 88, 90	9	100–02
5.32–33	90, 105	9.9–10	97
5.33	84, 85	9.9–22	115
5.35–36	115	9.10–11	100–02
5.36	106	9.11	104
6.15	108	9.11–15	101
6.19–21	116	9.11–17	97
6.22–23	98, 102–105	9.15–22	101
6.23–24	116	9.17	100
6.23–25	115	9.17–21	97
6.24	100, 163	9.21	84
6.26	87, 114, 115	9.21–22	97
6.28–29	116	9.23	108, 115
6.29–30	114	9.23–25	88, 115
6.30	111	9.24	84, 106
6.33	114	9.25	88
6.36	107	9.26–27	97
		9.27–28	87

9.28	87, 115	15.14	84
9.29	84, 89	15.15	104
9.34	119	15.16	97
9.34–35	118	15.17	99
9.36	84	15.20	92
10	78	15.30	118
10–17	78	15.31–32	87
10.18	104	15.32	121
10.24	104, 142	15.32–34	117
11.10–24	89	15.37	103
11.11–15	118	16.32	92
11.20–24	82	16.34	84, 92
11.20–26	89	17.9	116
11.22–23	118	17.13	93
11.22–25	86	17.14–17	87
11.22	106	17.16	92
11.23	103	17.17	87
11.24	84	17.29–30	108
11.26	87	18.3–9	83, 85
11.29	104	18.5–6	83
11.30	104	18.5–7	86
11.33	104	18.5–14	86
12	78	18.7	86
12.6	114	18.24	102
12.6–13.6	92	18.25	84
12.11	104, 117	18.29	113
12.14	104	19.6	84
12.18	99	19.10	116
12.18–28	99	19.13–14	118
12.29–30	89	19.14–17	118
12.30–31	87, 90, 91	19.15	106
12.30	84, 86, 89, 92	19.19	113
12.31	84, 87, 89, 90, 98, 116	19.30–31	113
12.31–33	89	20.4–14	114
12.32–33	98	20.6–14	45
12.32	87, 106	20.14	116
12.34–36	87	20.14–15	106, 115, 116
12.36	87	20.14–16	116
12.39	97, 106	20.25	84
12.41	87	20.22	87
13.28	104	20.22–23	114
13.41	104	20.27–34	114
14.1	84	20.27–38	97
14.4	104	20.28	84
14.7	115	20.28–29	86
14.10	116	20.29	86
14.11	117	20.33–34	115
14.22–24	99, 120	20.34	87
15.6	104	20.36–37	108
15.9–12	119	20.36–38	114

20.37–38	98		4Q403–07	
21.2	84		Songs of the Sabbath	
21.5–6	114, 115			80
21.6	108, 115			
21.7	92		4Q418	
21.9	84, 92		126.1–10	28
21.10	115			
21.34	106, 115		4QH^a (4Q427)	76, 78
22.8	87		8.i.11	84
22.26	108		8.i.13–21	76
22.27	120		8.ii.8–9	76
22.29	87			
22.31	108, 115		4QH^b (4Q428)	76
23.13	84			
23.24	86		4QH^c (4Q429)	76, 78
23.33	118			
24.29–30	116		4QH^d (4Q430)	76
25.4	84			
25.12	108		4QH^e (4Q431)	76
26.35	84			
			4QH^f (4Q432)	76, 78
1QH^b (1Q35)	76			
			4Q502	80
4QMMT				
C 27–30	117		4Q503	80
4Q186	105		4Q504–06	
			Words of the Luminaries	
4Q286				80
7 ii	142			
			4Q504	80
4Q392	80		8.4–5	46
4Q393	80		4Q507	80
4Q398			4Q509	80
14–17 ii	117			
			4Q511	
4Q400			28	80
2.7	80		29	80
			30	80

Josephus

Antiquities		Jewish War	
1.60	137	2.117–66	16
13.171–173	10–16, 175	2.119–66	10, 12, 16, 175
13.172	14	2.162	14
13.173	10	2.162–65	12–16
16.398	15	2.165	12
18.1–25	16		
18.11	10, 16		
18.11–25	10, 15–16, 175		

Other Jewish Literature

Avodah Zarah		b. Sukkah	
5b	128	52b	128, 142

b. Baba Batra		Sanhedrin	
16a	128, 143	10.1	1

b. Berakhot		b. Shabbat	
61a	142	105b	142

m. Bekhorot		Genesis Rabbah	
2.2	37	22.6	143
9.5	142		

b. Qiddushin		Philo *Decalogue*	
30b	128	142–153	151
		173–74	151

m. Mishle			
12	142	Special Laws	
		4.79–131	151

Mekilta Bahodesh	
5.6	37

Sifre Deuteronomy	
33	142
45	128, 142

Greco-Roman Literature

Aristole
Poetics
13.5 [1453a 6–10]   149

Euripides
Medea
1077–1080   139, 148

Epictetus
Discourses
1.28.6–8   149
2.17.18–19   149
2.17.21   149
2.26.1–7   149

Galen
On the Doctrines of Hippocrates and Plato
4.2.27   149
4.6.19–22   149

Ovid
Metamorphores
7.20–21   148, 150
7.92–93   149

Plato
Republic
8.563d–e   137

Polybius
Histories
1.81   137

Seneca
De clementia
1.23   137

Index of Modern Authors

Abegg, M. 77, 87, 91, 103, 114, 116
Achtemeier, P.J. 147
Aitken, J.K. 28, 35, 65
Alexander, P.S. 48
Aletti, J.-N. 151
Argall, R.A. 24, 35, 61,

Barclay, J.M.G. 9, 17, 156, 165, 177, 179
Barker, P.A. 43
Barnick, V.P. 156
Barrett, C.K. 156, 157, 160
Barth, M. 125
Baumbach, G. 13
Baumgarten, J. 76
Bayes, J.F 164
Beall, T.S. 16
Becker, J. 92
Beentjes, P.C. 23, 68
Beker, J. C. 127, 146
Beld, A. van den 148
Bell, R.H. 124, 155, 156, 173
Bergmeier, R. 146, 151
Berkouwer, G.C. 170
Bertone, J.A. 168
Bird, M.F. 125
Blackwell, B.C. 168
Blenkinsopp, J. 35
Block, D.I. 43
Boccaccini, G. 11, 16, 32, 35, 51, 54–55, 61, 62, 77
Bockmuehl, M. 110
Borgen, P. 140
Bornkamm, G. 127, 128, 133, 146
Box, G.H. 55, 56, 71
Braun, H. 88
Brown, T.R. 37
Brownlee, W.H. 93, 106, 111–112
Bruce, F.F. 160, 166
Büchler, A. 54
Bultmann, R. 127, 133, 146–147
Burkes, S. 34, 67
Burnett, G.W. 137
Busch, A. 137

Byrne, B. 8, 127, 128, 129, 130, 137, 156, 162

Calduch-Benages, N. 59–60
Calvin, J. 157, 162
Campbell, D.H. 139
Campbell, D.A. 173
Campbell, W.S. 129
Carson, D.A. 4, 21, 80, 120
Carter, T.L. 148, 156
Catchpole, D. 129
Chang, H.-K. 148
Charlesworth, J.H. 77, 101
Chazon, E.G. 80
Chester, S.J. 146, 150
Collins, J.J. 29, 33, 34–35, 64–65, 67, 77
Condra, E. 80, 87, 109
Cranfield, C.E.B. 136–137, 139, 148, 157, 160–162, 166, 173
Crenshaw, J.L. 22–23, 25–26, 34, 54

Danby, H. 1
Das, A.A. 20, 132, 137, 147–148, 157
Davies, W.D. 1, 137, 143
de Roo, J.C.R. 38, 125
deSilva, D.A. 35
Di Lella, A.A. 24, 29, 31, 33, 34–35, 59–62, 65, 70–71
Dillon, R.J. 129
Dodson, J.R. 144
Douglas, M.C. 78
Dunn, J.D.G. 3–4, 7, 16, 124, 125, 127, 134, 136–137, 139, 147–148, 153, 155–156, 157, 160, 164, 169, 173, 177
Dupont-Sommer, A. 93, 103–104

Elliott, M.A. 171
Elliott, N. 155
Engberg-Pedersen, T. 5–10, 16–17, 148–150, 163, 166, 168, 179
Enns, P. 135
Eshel, H. 77
Esler, P.F. 28

Epsy, J.M. 148
Evans, C.A. 39

Falk, D. 118
Fay, R.C. 158
Fee, G.D. 127-128, 156-157, 160, 162, 166, 169
Fitzmyer, J.A. 56, 156, 160, 162
Fletcher-Louis, C.H.T. 82, 85, 92
Flint, P.W. 80
Forbes, C. 141
Freedman, D.N. 42
Frey, J. 87, 91, 92, 97, 102, 105-106
Furnish, V.P. 133

Gabriel, A.K. 157
Gammie, J.G. 33
García Martínez, F. 77, 83, 87, 91, 99, 103, 116
Garlington, D.B. 4-5, 35, 40, 44, 49-50, 52, 59, 63, 74, 127, 139, 145, 169, 174
Garnet, P. 78
Gaster, T.H. 95, 103
Gathercole, S.J. 9, 20, 68, 120-121, 143, 146, 155
Gilbert, M. 24-25
Gill, C. 148
Gillman, F.M. 156
Goldstein, J. 35
Gorman, M.J. 169
Gowan, D.E. 53, 63
Greenfield, J.C. 84
Gundry, R.H. 137

Haacker, K. 147
Hagner, D.A. 1, 177
Harrington, D.J. 28
Hays, R.B. 8, 125, 173
Headlam, A.C. 157
Hengel, M. 31, 34, 70
Hermisson, H.-J. 47
Hofius, O. 137, 145
Holland, G.S. 133
Holm-Nielsen, S. 78, 84, 85, 87, 91, 93, 99, 101, 103, 104, 110, 111, 118-19
Hooker, M.D. 4, 169
Hopkins, D.D. 79, 111, 119
Horst, P.W. van der 128
Hübner, H. 101-102, 146
Huggins, R.V. 149, 151

Huttunen, N. 149
Hyatt, J.P. 81, 93, 104

Jacob, E. 31
Jeremias, G. 78
Jervis, L.A. 134
Jewett, R. 125, 128-29, 132, 136, 146-47, 156-57
Johnson, L.T. 125

Kaiser, O. 46
Kamell, M.J. 67
Käsemann, E.
Kaye, B.N. 141, 143
Keck, L.E. 138, 147, 149-50, 157, 161-62
Kim, S. 124
Knibb, M.A. 77
Kooten, G.H. van. 158-59
Kraft, R.A. 27, 41
Kruse, C.G. 127-28, 166
Kuhn, K.G. 87
Kuula, K. 128
Kümmel, W.G. 127

Laato, T. 139
Lambrecht, J. 128, 166
Lange, A. 98, 101
Leenhardt, F.J. 157
Levison, J.R. 28, 46,
Licht, J. 79-81, 84, 92-93, 100, 104-05, 107, 110, 112
Lichtenberger, H. 81-82, 84, 86, 128, 137, 148, 161
Liesen, J. 27, 51
Lohse, E. 91, 103, 116
Longenecker, B.W. 172
Lowe, C. 155
Luck, U. 133
Lyonnet, S. 160

Mack, B.L. 30
Magness, J. 77
Maier, G. 11, 19, 64
Maier, J. 91, 103, 116
Mansoor, M. 76, 87, 91, 93, 103, 106-07, 112
Marcus, J. 142, 143,
Marshall, I.H. 6
Martin, J.D. 35

Index of Modern Authors

Martin, L.H. 11
Martyn, J. L. 8–9, 29, 63, 143, 151–52, 154, 157
Mason, S. 11, 13–16
Matlock, R.B. 8, 173
Mattila, S.L. 33, 64
McFadden, K.W. 155
Melanchthon, P. 161
Merrill, E.H. 79, 87, 98, 99, 104, 108–09, 111–12
Meyer, P.W. 133, 147, 150, 157,
Miano, D. 42
Middendorf, M.P. 128, 137–38,
Moo, D.J. 125, 127–28, 134, 136–37, 147, 155–57, 160, 162, 165–67, 172
Moore, C.A. 57
Moore, G.F. 1, 11, 142
Mowinckel, S. 76
Murphy, R.E. 28, 31, 53

Newsom, C. 100
Nickelsburg, G.W.E. 27, 33, 37, 41, 70, 140
Nitzan, B. 94, 118
Nygren, A. 150

O'Brien, P.T. 169
Oesterley, W.O.E. 55–56, 71

Packer, J.I. 139, 150
Pate, M.C. 161
Perdue, L.G. 33, 35, 43, 54, 65
Pinnock, C.H. 17
Porter, F.C. 128, 142
Porter, S.E. 143
Prockter, L.J. 35

Räisänen, H. 124, 128–29, 146–47
Rapa, R.K. 125
Reiterer, F.V. 27, 41
Rickert, G. 148
Ridderbos, H.N. 139
Ringgren, H. 81, 104
Romanello, S. 128
Rosner, B. 165

Saldarini, A.J. 11
Sanday, W. 157
Sanders, E.P. 1–7, 20–21, 31, 34–37, 43, 47–49, 53–57, 63, 65, 69, 72–74, 80–81, 87, 92, 110, 113–14, 119–21, 124, 129, 134–35, 153, 159, 171–72, 176, 179
Sanders, J.T. 32, 66
Sauer, G. 65
Schechter, S. 1, 56, 142
Schmithals, W. 156
Schnabel, E.J. 24, 32, 48–50, 108
Schnackenburg, R. 129
Shogren, G.S. 143
Schökel, L.A. 46
Schreiner, T.R. 124, 127–28, 136, 147, 155, 157, 160, 162, 164, 167, 174
Schubert, K. 91, 103, 116
Schuller, E.M. 76, 78, 83–84, 87, 91, 96, 99–100, 102–103, 114, 116, 119
Schwemer, A.M. 40
Scott, J.M. 171
Seifrid, M.A. 4, 69, 127–28, 132–33, 171
Sekki, A.E. 95, 100–02, 105–07
Sheppard, G.T. 32, 46
Siebeneck, R.T. 35
Sievers, J. 10
Silberman, L.H. 76
Silva, M. 173
Skehan, P.W. 24, 29–30, 33–34, 40, 51, 59–62, 65, 68, 70–71
Smith, B.D. 88, 124
Snaith, J.G. 57
Southall, D.J. 143–44
Sprinkle, P.M. 20, 125, 134
Starnitzke, D. 147, 157
Stegemann, H. 77–78, 83–84, 87, 91, 96, 99–100, 102–103, 114, 116, 119
Stendahl, K. 128
Stone, M.E. 142
Stowers, S.K. 125, 132, 137, 148–50
Stuhlmacher, P. 127
Sukenik, E.L. 76, 103

Taylor, C. 56
Talmon, S. 77
Tcherikover, V. 35
Tennant, F.R. 35
Thackeray, H. St. J. 14–15
Theissen, G. 145, 148
Theobald, M. 129
Thielman, F. 148, 157, 171
Thurén, L. 132, 135
Thyen, H. 78
Tobin, T.H. 127, 137, 147–49, 151

VanLandingham, C. 18, 20, 37, 39–40,
    79–81, 87, 92, 99–100, 104, 110, 112,
    117, 119, 125, 162, 167–69,
Vermes, G. 103
von Rad, G. 49, 52, 65, 67

Wasserman, E. 136, 141, 143, 145, 148–49
Watson, F. 7–9, 20, 36, 38, 41–42, 48,
    125, 132–33, 137, 147, 148, 157, 164,
    169, 173–74, 178
Weber, R. 129
Webster, J.S. 63
Weissenberger, M. 16
Wells, K.B. 166
Wernberg–Moeller, P. 98, 101
Westerholm, S. 6, 124, 135, 165
Whybray, R.N. 31
Wicke–Reuter, U. 64
Wilckens, U. 128, 137

Winger, M. 147
Winston, D. 11, 64
Winter, P. 64
Wischmeyer, O. 34, 47, 64
Wise, M.O. 77–78
Witherington, B. 132, 147, 155
Woude, A.S. van der 77
Wright, B.G. 35
Wright, N.T. 4, 7, 16, 124–25, 147, 155–
    56, 160–61, 171, 177

Yates, J.W. 93, 106, 109, 160,
Yinger, K.L. 4–5, 69, 72, 74, 169

Zeller, D. 160, 163
Ziegler, J. 23
Ziesler, J.A. 133, 145, 161, 164, 166
Zimmerli, W. 81

Index of Subjects

Adam 46, 83, 84, 86, 88, 93, 129, 137, 144–45, 178
– glory of 81, 82, 85, 117
akrasia 148–151
Almsgiving 56–57
Antithesis 126
Atonement 53–57

Belial 18, 104, 142

Christology 154–58
Covenant 34–37, 48
– Mosaic 41–42
– with Abraham 37–40
– with David 40–41
– with Moses 37
– with Noah 37
– with Phinehas 40
Covenantal Nomism 1, 124, 176
– in Ben Sira 34–37, 43
– in *Hodayot* 119–21
– in Paul 4–5
Creation 83–86, 88–94
– obedience of 43–48, 175

Determinism 25, 64–65
Divine/human agency
–models of 16–18
Dualism 97

Election 135, 153 (*see also* predestination)
– of Israel 34–36
Essenes 10–17, 75
Ethnocentrism 2, 4, 6–8
Ezekiel 36–37
– in *Hodayot* 106–07, 109
– in Paul 160–161

Faith 1–10
– in/of Christ 7, 125, 173
– justification by 124, 173–74
– and works/obedience 48–49, 52–53, 174
Fear of God 48–52

Flesh
– in *Hodayot* 89, 91–92, 105–06
– in Paul 158–59
Free will 63–65, 100, 110–13, 151 (*see also* determinism)

Genre 79–80
Grace 1–10, 36, 43, 47, 54, 65, 81, 88, 107, 108, 120, 170, 174, 176

Hermeneutics 42–43
Hodayot 153–54, 158, 163, 169, 175–76

Inclination(s) 28
– evil 142–43

Judaism
– diversity of 176
Judgment 24, 26, 29–30, 46–47, 66–73

Law (*see also* Torah)
Love command 165–66

Mercy 42, 48, 53–55, 66–70, 106, 119–22, 135, 169–170 (*see also* grace)
– and judgment 25–26, 72–73
Moral ability 28–29, 46
Moral inability 87–88, 140, 144–152

New Perspective on Paul 3–10, 124, 134, 153, 172, 176

Obedience 25
– as condition for life/salvation 27–28, 45, 47–48, 54, 57, 65, 72, 121, 135, 173–74, 178
– and intention 135
– and knowledge 116–17
– perfect 71–72

Paul
– and Judaism 153, 171–72, 177–78
– persecution of church 146

Pharisees 10–17
Predestination 95, 175–76
– and knowledge 113–14
– and obedience 99–100 (*see also* Spirit)
Prosopopoiia 132–33
Purify/purification 95–96, 118–19

Repent/repentance 54, 57

Sadducees 10–17
Scripture 178
Sin
– knowledge of 146–47
– power of 141–44
Sirach 81, 94, 113, 122–23, 131, 138–40, 146, 151–52, 162–63, 175
Spirit 107, 158–59
– and knowledge 115–16
– identification of Christ with 157–58
– and obedience 5, 121, 161, 166–67, 169–70

– and predestination 100–08, 154
– and purification 118
– as empowering agent 161, 166–67

Teacher of Righteousness 76–79
Theodicy 25–26
Torah 127–32
– and Christ 2, 124, 171–72, 177
– and death 134–35, 137
– and life 27–28, 31–34, 134–35
– and wisdom 31–34, 61–62
– Paul's defence of
– obedience to 27–28
– and sin 127–29
Two Ways
– in Sirach 19, 26, 131
– in Paul 20, 131, 146, 151, 169
Two spirits 101–02, 104, 179

Wisdom 59–63
Works of the law 3, 7, 124–25

Wissenschaftliche Untersuchungen zum Neuen Testament
Alphabetical Index of the First and Second Series

Ådna, Jostein: Jesu Stellung zum Tempel. 2000. Vol. II/119.
Ådna, Jostein (Ed.): The Formation of the Early Church. 2005. Vol. 183.
– and *Kvalbein, Hans* (Ed.): The Mission of the Early Church to Jews and Gentiles. 2000. Vol. 127.
Ahearne-Kroll, Stephen P., Paul A. Holloway, and James A. Kelhoffer (Ed.): Women and Gender in Ancient Religions. 2010. Vol. 263.
Aland, Barbara: Was ist Gnosis? 2009. Vol. 239.
Alexeev, Anatoly A., Christos Karakolis and *Ulrich Luz* (Ed.): Einheit der Kirche im Neuen Testament. Dritte europäische orthodox-westliche Exegetenkonferenz in Sankt Petersburg, 24.–31. August 2005. 2008. Vol. 218.
Alkier, Stefan: Wunder und Wirklichkeit in den Briefen des Apostels Paulus. 2001. Vol. 134.
Allen, David M.: Deuteronomy and Exhortation in Hebrews. 2008. Vol. II/238.
Anderson, Paul N.: The Christology of the Fourth Gospel. 1996. Vol. II/78.
Appold, Mark L.: The Oneness Motif in the Fourth Gospel. 1976. Vol. II/1.
Arnold, Clinton E.: The Colossian Syncretism. 1995. Vol. II/77.
Ascough, Richard S.: Paul's Macedonian Associations. 2003. Vol. II/161.
Asiedu-Peprah, Martin: Johannine Sabbath Conflicts As Juridical Controversy. 2001. Vol. II/132.
Attridge, Harold W.: Essays on John and Hebrews. 2010. Bd. 264.
– see *Zangenberg, Jürgen.*
Aune, David E.: Apocalypticism, Prophecy and Magic in Early Christianity. 2006. Vol. 199.
Avemarie, Friedrich: Die Tauferzählungen der Apostelgeschichte. 2002. Vol. 139.
Avemarie, Friedrich and *Hermann Lichtenberger* (Ed.): Auferstehung – Ressurection. 2001. Vol. 135.
– Bund und Tora. 1996. Vol. 92.
Baarlink, Heinrich: Verkündigtes Heil. 2004. Vol. 168.
Bachmann, Michael: Sünder oder Übertreter. 1992. Vol. 59.

Bachmann, Michael (Ed.): Lutherische und Neue Paulusperspektive. 2005. Vol. 182.
Back, Frances: Verwandlung durch Offenbarung bei Paulus. 2002. Vol. II/153.
Backhaus, Knut: Der sprechende Gott. 2009. Vol. 240.
Baker, William R.: Personal Speech-Ethics in the Epistle of James. 1995. Vol. II/68.
Bakke, Odd Magne: 'Concord and Peace'. 2001. Vol. II/143.
Balch, David L.: Roman Domestic Art and Early House Churches. 2008. Vol. 228.
Baldwin, Matthew C.: Whose Acts of Peter? 2005. Vol. II/196.
Balla, Peter: Challenges to New Testament Theology. 1997. Vol. II/95.
– The Child-Parent Relationship in the New Testament and its Environment. 2003. Vol. 155.
Bammel, Ernst: Judaica. Vol. I 1986. Vol. 37.
– Vol. II 1997. Vol. 91.
Barreto, Eric D.: Ethnic Negotiations. 2010. Vol. II/294.
Barrier, Jeremy W.: The Acts of Paul and Thecla. 2009. Vol. II/270.
Barton, Stephen C.: see *Stuckenbruck, Loren T.*
Bash, Anthony: Ambassadors for Christ. 1997. Vol. II/92.
Bauckham, Richard: The Jewish World around the New Testament. Collected Essays Volume I. 2008. Vol. 233.
Bauernfeind, Otto: Kommentar und Studien zur Apostelgeschichte. 1980. Vol. 22.
Baum, Armin Daniel: Pseudepigraphie und literarische Fälschung im frühen Christentum. 2001. Vol. II/138.
Bayer, Hans Friedrich: Jesus' Predictions of Vindication and Resurrection. 1986. Vol. II/20.
Becker, Eve-Marie: Das Markus-Evangelium im Rahmen antiker Historiographie. 2006. Vol. 194.
Becker, Eve-Marie and *Peter Pilhofer* (Ed.): Biographie und Persönlichkeit des Paulus. 2005. Vol. 187.
Becker, Michael: Wunder und Wundertäter im frührabbinischen Judentum. 2002. Vol. II/144.

Becker, Michael and *Markus Öhler* (Ed.): Apokalyptik als Herausforderung neutestamentlicher Theologie. 2006. *Vol. II/214.*
Bell, Richard H.: Deliver Us from Evil. 2007. *Vol. 216.*
- The Irrevocable Call of God. 2005. *Vol. 184.*
- No One Seeks for God. 1998. *Vol. 106.*
- Provoked to Jealousy. 1994. *Vol. II/63.*

Bennema, Cornelis: The Power of Saving Wisdom. 2002. *Vol. II/148.*
Bergman, Jan: see *Kieffer, René*
Bergmeier, Roland: Das Gesetz im Römerbrief und andere Studien zum Neuen Testament. 2000. *Vol. 121.*
Bernett, Monika: Der Kaiserkult in Judäa unter den Herodiern und Römern. 2007. *Vol. 203.*
Betz, Otto: Jesus, der Messias Israels. 1987. *Vol. 42.*
- Jesus, der Herr der Kirche. 1990. *Vol. 52.*

Beyschlag, Karlmann: Simon Magus und die christliche Gnosis. 1974. *Vol. 16.*
Bieringer, Reimund: see *Koester, Craig.*
Bittner, Wolfgang J.: Jesu Zeichen im Johannesevangelium. 1987. *Vol. II/26.*
Bjerkelund, Carl J.: Tauta Egeneto. 1987. *Vol. 40.*
Blackburn, Barry Lee: Theios Aner and the Markan Miracle Traditions. 1991. *Vol. II/40.*
Blanton IV, Thomas R.: Constructing a New Covenant. 2007. *Vol. II/233.*
Bock, Darrell L.: Blasphemy and Exaltation in Judaism and the Final Examination of Jesus. 1998. *Vol. II/106.*
- and *Robert L. Webb* (Ed.): Key Events in the Life of the Historical Jesus. 2009. *Vol. 247.*

Bockmuehl, Markus: The Remembered Peter. 2010. *Vol. 262.*
- Revelation and Mystery in Ancient Judaism and Pauline Christianity. 1990. *Vol. II/36.*

Bøe, Sverre: Cross-Bearing in Luke. 2010. *Vol. II/278.*
- Gog and Magog. 2001. *Vol. II/135.*

Böhlig, Alexander: Gnosis und Synkretismus. Vol. 1 1989. *Vol. 47* – Vol. 2 1989. *Vol. 48.*
Böhm, Martina: Samarien und die Samaritai bei Lukas. 1999. *Vol. II/111.*
Börstinghaus, Jens: Sturmfahrt und Schiffbruch. 2010. *Vol. II/274.*
Böttrich, Christfried: Weltweisheit – Menschheitsethik – Urkult. 1992. *Vol. II/50.*
- and *Herzer, Jens* (Ed.): Josephus und das Neue Testament. 2007. *Vol. 209.*

Bolyki, János: Jesu Tischgemeinschaften. 1997. *Vol. II/96.*

Bosman, Philip: Conscience in Philo and Paul. 2003. *Vol. II/166.*
Bovon, François: New Testament and Christian Apocrypha. 2009. *Vol. 237.*
- Studies in Early Christianity. 2003. *Vol. 161.*

Brändl, Martin: Der Agon bei Paulus. 2006. *Vol. II/222.*
Braun, Heike: Geschichte des Gottesvolkes und christliche Identität. 2010. *Vol. II/279.*
Breytenbach, Cilliers: see *Frey, Jörg.*
Broadhead, Edwin K.: Jewish Ways of Following Jesus Redrawing the Religious Map of Antiquity. 2010. *Vol. 266.*
Brocke, Christoph vom: Thessaloniki – Stadt des Kassander und Gemeinde des Paulus. 2001. *Vol. II/125.*
Brunson, Andrew: Psalm 118 in the Gospel of John. 2003. *Vol. II/158.*
Büchli, Jörg: Der Poimandres – ein paganisiertes Evangelium. 1987. *Vol. II/27.*
Bühner, Jan A.: Der Gesandte und sein Weg im 4. Evangelium. 1977. *Vol. II/2.*
Burchard, Christoph: Untersuchungen zu Joseph und Aseneth. 1965. *Vol. 8.*
- Studien zur Theologie, Sprache und Umwelt des Neuen Testaments. Ed. by D. Sänger. 1998. *Vol. 107.*

Burnett, Richard: Karl Barth's Theological Exegesis. 2001. *Vol. II/145.*
Byron, John: Slavery Metaphors in Early Judaism and Pauline Christianity. 2003. *Vol. II/162.*
Byrskog, Samuel: Story as History – History as Story. 2000. *Vol. 123.*
Cancik, Hubert (Ed.): Markus-Philologie. 1984. *Vol. 33.*
Capes, David B.: Old Testament Yaweh Texts in Paul's Christology. 1992. *Vol. II/47.*
Caragounis, Chrys C.: The Development of Greek and the New Testament. 2004. *Vol. 167.*
- The Son of Man. 1986. *Vol. 38.*
- see *Fridrichsen, Anton.*

Carleton Paget, James: The Epistle of Barnabas. 1994. *Vol. II/64.*
- Jews, Christians and Jewish Christians in Antiquity. 2010. *Vol. 251.*

Carson, D.A., O'Brien, Peter T. and *Mark Seifrid* (Ed.): Justification and Variegated Nomism.
Vol. 1: The Complexities of Second Temple Judaism. 2001. *Vol. II/140.*
Vol. 2: The Paradoxes of Paul. 2004. *Vol. II/181.*

Chae, Young Sam: Jesus as the Eschatological Davidic Shepherd. 2006. *Vol. II/216.*
Chapman, David W.: Ancient Jewish and Christian Perceptions of Crucifixion. 2008. *Vol. II/244.*
Chester, Andrew: Messiah and Exaltation. 2007. *Vol. 207.*
Chibici-Revneanu, Nicole: Die Herrlichkeit des Verherrlichten. 2007. *Vol. II/231.*
Ciampa, Roy E.: The Presence and Function of Scripture in Galatians 1 and 2. 1998. *Vol. II/102.*
Classen, Carl Joachim: Rhetorical Criticsm of the New Testament. 2000. *Vol. 128.*
Colpe, Carsten: Griechen – Byzantiner – Semiten – Muslime. 2008. *Vol. 221.*
– Iranier – Aramäer – Hebräer – Hellenen. 2003. *Vol. 154.*
Cook, John G.: Roman Attitudes Towards the Christians. 2010. *Vol. 261.*
Coote, Robert B. (Ed.): see *Weissenrieder, Annette.*
Coppins, Wayne: The Interpretation of Freedom in the Letters of Paul. 2009. *Vol. II/261.*
Crump, David: Jesus the Intercessor. 1992. *Vol. II/49.*
Dahl, Nils Alstrup: Studies in Ephesians. 2000. *Vol. 131.*
Daise, Michael A.: Feasts in John. 2007. *Vol. II/229.*
Deines, Roland: Die Gerechtigkeit der Tora im Reich des Messias. 2004. *Vol. 177.*
– Jüdische Steingefäße und pharisäische Frömmigkeit. 1993. *Vol. II/52.*
– Die Pharisäer. 1997. *Vol. 101.*
Deines, Roland and *Karl-Wilhelm Niebuhr* (Ed.): Philo und das Neue Testament. 2004. *Vol. 172.*
Dennis, John A.: Jesus' Death and the Gathering of True Israel. 2006. *Vol. 217.*
Dettwiler, Andreas and *Jean Zumstein* (Ed.): Kreuzestheologie im Neuen Testament. 2002. *Vol. 151.*
Dickson, John P.: Mission-Commitment in Ancient Judaism and in the Pauline Communities. 2003. *Vol. II/159.*
Dietzfelbinger, Christian: Der Abschied des Kommenden. 1997. *Vol. 95.*
Dimitrov, Ivan Z., James D.G. Dunn, Ulrich Luz and *Karl-Wilhelm Niebuhr* (Ed.): Das Alte Testament als christliche Bibel in orthodoxer und westlicher Sicht. 2004. *Vol. 174.*
Dobbeler, Axel von: Glaube als Teilhabe. 1987. *Vol. II/22.*

Docherty, Susan E.: The Use of the Old Testament in Hebrews. 2009. *Vol. II/260.*
Downs, David J.: The Offering of the Gentiles. 2008. *Vol. II/248.*
Dryden, J. de Waal: Theology and Ethics in 1 Peter. 2006. *Vol. II/209.*
Dübbers, Michael: Christologie und Existenz im Kolosserbrief. 2005. *Vol. II/191.*
Dunn, James D.G.: The New Perspective on Paul. 2005. *Vol. 185.*
Dunn, James D.G. (Ed.): Jews and Christians. 1992. *Vol. 66.*
– Paul and the Mosaic Law. 1996. *Vol. 89.*
– see *Dimitrov, Ivan Z.*
–, *Hans Klein, Ulrich Luz,* and *Vasile Mihoc* (Ed.): Auslegung der Bibel in orthodoxer und westlicher Perspektive. 2000. *Vol. 130.*
Ebel, Eva: Die Attraktivität früher christlicher Gemeinden. 2004. *Vol. II/178.*
Ebertz, Michael N.: Das Charisma des Gekreuzigten. 1987. *Vol. 45.*
Eckstein, Hans-Joachim: Der Begriff Syneidesis bei Paulus. 1983. *Vol. II/10.*
– Verheißung und Gesetz. 1996. *Vol. 86.*
Ego, Beate: Im Himmel wie auf Erden. 1989. *Vol. II/34.*
Ego, Beate, Armin Lange and *Peter Pilhofer* (Ed.): Gemeinde ohne Tempel – Community without Temple. 1999. *Vol. 118.*
– and *Helmut Merkel* (Ed.): Religiöses Lernen in der biblischen, frühjüdischen und frühchristlichen Überlieferung. 2005. *Vol. 180.*
Eisele, Wilfried: Welcher Thomas? 2010. *Vol. 259.*
Eisen, Ute E.: see *Paulsen, Henning.*
Elledge, C.D.: Life after Death in Early Judaism. 2006. *Vol. II/208.*
Ellis, E. Earle: Prophecy and Hermeneutic in Early Christianity. 1978. *Vol. 18.*
– The Old Testament in Early Christianity. 1991. *Vol. 54.*
Elmer, Ian J.: Paul, Jerusalem and the Judaisers. 2009. *Vol. II/258.*
Endo, Masanobu: Creation and Christology. 2002. *Vol. 149.*
Ennulat, Andreas: Die 'Minor Agreements'. 1994. *Vol. II/62.*
Ensor, Peter W.: Jesus and His 'Works'. 1996. *Vol. II/85.*
Eskola, Timo: Messiah and the Throne. 2001. *Vol. II/142.*
– Theodicy and Predestination in Pauline Soteriology. 1998. *Vol. II/100.*
Farelly, Nicolas: The Disciples in the Fourth Gospel. 2010. *Vol. II/290.*

Fatehi, Mehrdad: The Spirit's Relation to the Risen Lord in Paul. 2000. *Vol. II/128.*
Feldmeier, Reinhard: Die Krisis des Gottessohnes. 1987. *Vol. II/21.*
– Die Christen als Fremde. 1992. *Vol. 64.*
Feldmeier, Reinhard and *Ulrich Heckel* (Ed.): Die Heiden. 1994. *Vol. 70.*
Finnern, Sönke: Narratologie und biblische Exegese. 2010. *Vol. II/285.*
Fletcher-Louis, Crispin H.T.: Luke-Acts: Angels, Christology and Soteriology. 1997. *Vol. II/94.*
Förster, Niclas: Marcus Magus. 1999. *Vol. 114.*
Forbes, Christopher Brian: Prophecy and Inspired Speech in Early Christianity and its Hellenistic Environment. 1995. *Vol. II/75.*
Fornberg, Tord: see *Fridrichsen, Anton.*
Fossum, Jarl E.: The Name of God and the Angel of the Lord. 1985. *Vol. 36.*
Foster, Paul: Community, Law and Mission in Matthew's Gospel. *Vol. II/177.*
Fotopoulos, John: Food Offered to Idols in Roman Corinth. 2003. *Vol. II/151.*
Frank, Nicole: Der Kolosserbrief im Kontext des paulinischen Erbes. 2009. *Vol. II/271.*
Frenschkowski, Marco: Offenbarung und Epiphanie. Vol. 1 1995. *Vol. II/79* – Vol. 2 1997. *Vol. II/80.*
Frey, Jörg: Eugen Drewermann und die biblische Exegese. 1995. *Vol. II/71.*
– Die johanneische Eschatologie. Vol. I. 1997. *Vol. 96.* – Vol. II. 1998. *Vol. 110.* – Vol. III. 2000. *Vol. 117.*
Frey, Jörg and *Cilliers Breytenbach* (Ed.): Aufgabe und Durchführung einer Theologie des Neuen Testaments. 2007. *Vol. 205.*
– *Jens Herzer, Martina Janßen* and *Clare K. Rothschild* (Ed.): Pseudepigraphie und Verfasserfiktion in frühchristlichen Briefen. 2009. *Vol. 246.*
– *Stefan Krauter* and *Hermann Lichtenberger* (Ed.): Heil und Geschichte. 2009. *Vol. 248.*
– and *Udo Schnelle (Ed.):* Kontexte des Johannesevangeliums. 2004. *Vol. 175.*
– and *Jens Schröter* (Ed.): Deutungen des Todes Jesu im Neuen Testament. 2005. *Vol. 181.*
– Jesus in apokryphen Evangelienüberlieferungen. 2010. *Vol. 254.*
–, *Jan G. van der Watt,* and *Ruben Zimmermann* (Ed.): Imagery in the Gospel of John. 2006. *Vol. 200.*
Freyne, Sean: Galilee and Gospel. 2000. *Vol. 125.*

Fridrichsen, Anton: Exegetical Writings. Edited by C.C. Caragounis and T. Fornberg. 1994. *Vol. 76.*
Gadenz, Pablo T.: Called from the Jews and from the Gentiles. 2009. *Vol. II/267.*
Gäbel, Georg: Die Kulttheologie des Hebräerbriefes. 2006. *Vol. II/212.*
Gäckle, Volker: Die Starken und die Schwachen in Korinth und in Rom. 2005. *Vol. 200.*
Garlington, Don B.: 'The Obedience of Faith'. 1991. *Vol. II/38.*
– Faith, Obedience, and Perseverance. 1994. *Vol. 79.*
Garnet, Paul: Salvation and Atonement in the Qumran Scrolls. 1977. *Vol. II/3.*
Gemünden, Petra von (Ed.): see *Weissenrieder, Annette.*
Gese, Michael: Das Vermächtnis des Apostels. 1997. *Vol. II/99.*
Gheorghita, Radu: The Role of the Septuagint in Hebrews. 2003. *Vol. II/160.*
Gordley, Matthew E.: The Colossian Hymn in Context. 2007. *Vol. II/228.*
Gräbe, Petrus J.: The Power of God in Paul's Letters. 2000, ²2008. *Vol. II/123.*
Gräßer, Erich: Der Alte Bund im Neuen. 1985. *Vol. 35.*
– Forschungen zur Apostelgeschichte. 2001. *Vol. 137.*
Grappe, Christian (Ed.): Le Repas de Dieu / Das Mahl Gottes. 2004. *Vol. 169.*
Gray, Timothy C.: The Temple in the Gospel of Mark. 2008. *Vol. II/242.*
Green, Joel B.: The Death of Jesus. 1988. *Vol. II/33.*
Gregg, Brian Han: The Historical Jesus and the Final Judgment Sayings in Q. 2005. *Vol. II/207.*
Gregory, Andrew: The Reception of Luke and Acts in the Period before Irenaeus. 2003. *Vol. II/169.*
Grindheim, Sigurd: The Crux of Election. 2005. *Vol. II/202.*
Gundry, Robert H.: The Old is Better. 2005. *Vol. 178.*
Gundry Volf, Judith M.: Paul and Perseverance. 1990. *Vol. II/37.*
Häußer, Detlef: Christusbekenntnis und Jesusüberlieferung bei Paulus. 2006. *Vol. 210.*
Hafemann, Scott J.: Suffering and the Spirit. 1986. *Vol. II/19.*
– Paul, Moses, and the History of Israel. 1995. *Vol. 81.*
Hahn, Ferdinand: Studien zum Neuen Testament.

Vol. I: Grundsatzfragen, Jesusforschung, Evangelien. 2006. *Vol. 191.*
Vol. II: Bekenntnisbildung und Theologie in urchristlicher Zeit. 2006. *Vol. 192.*
Hahn, Johannes (Ed.): Zerstörungen des Jerusalemer Tempels. 2002. *Vol. 147.*
Hamid-Khani, Saeed: Relevation and Concealment of Christ. 2000. *Vol. II/120.*
Hannah, Darrel D.: Michael and Christ. 1999. *Vol. II/109.*
Hardin, Justin K.: Galatians and the Imperial Cult? 2007. *Vol. II /237.*
Harrison; James R.: Paul's Language of Grace in Its Graeco-Roman Context. 2003. *Vol. II/172.*
Hartman, Lars: Text-Centered New Testament Studies. Ed. von D. Hellholm. 1997. *Vol. 102.*
Hartog, Paul: Polycarp and the New Testament. 2001. *Vol. II/134.*
Hays, Christopher M.: Luke's Wealth Ethics. 2010. *Vol. 275.*
Heckel, Theo K.: Der Innere Mensch. 1993. *Vol. II/53.*
– Vom Evangelium des Markus zum viergestaltigen Evangelium. 1999. *Vol. 120.*
Heckel, Ulrich: Kraft in Schwachheit. 1993. *Vol. II/56.*
– Der Segen im Neuen Testament. 2002. *Vol. 150.*
– see *Feldmeier, Reinhard.*
– see *Hengel, Martin.*
Heemstra, Marius: The Fiscus Judaicus and the Parting of the Ways. 2010. *Vol. II/277.*
Heiligenthal, Roman: Werke als Zeichen. 1983. *Vol. II/9.*
Heininger, Bernhard: Die Inkulturation des Christentums. 2010. *Vol. 255.*
Heliso, Desta: Pistis and the Righteous One. 2007. *Vol. II/235.*
Hellholm, D.: see *Hartman, Lars.*
Hemer, Colin J.: The Book of Acts in the Setting of Hellenistic History. 1989. *Vol. 49.*
Hengel, Martin: Jesus und die Evangelien. Kleine Schriften V. 2007. *Vol. 211.*
– Die johanneische Frage. 1993. *Vol. 67.*
– Judaica et Hellenistica. Kleine Schriften I. 1996. *Vol. 90.*
– Judaica, Hellenistica et Christiana. Kleine Schriften II. 1999. *Vol. 109.*
– Judentum und Hellenismus. 1969, ³1988. *Vol. 10.*
– Paulus und Jakobus. Kleine Schriften III. 2002. *Vol. 141.*
– Studien zur Christologie. Kleine Schriften IV. 2006. *Vol. 201.*
– Studien zum Urchristentum. Kleine Schriften VI. 2008. *Vol. 234.*
– Theologische, historische und biographische Skizzen. Kleine Schriften VII. 2010. *Vol. 253.*
– and *Anna Maria Schwemer:* Paulus zwischen Damaskus und Antiochien. 1998. *Vol. 108.*
– Der messianische Anspruch Jesu und die Anfänge der Christologie. 2001. *Vol. 138.*
– Die vier Evangelien und das eine Evangelium von Jesus Christus. 2008. *Vol. 224.*
Hengel, Martin and *Ulrich Heckel* (Ed.): Paulus und das antike Judentum. 1991. *Vol. 58.*
– and *Hermut Löhr* (Ed.): Schriftauslegung im antiken Judentum und im Urchristentum. 1994. *Vol. 73.*
– and *Anna Maria Schwemer* (Ed.): Königsherrschaft Gottes und himmlischer Kult. 1991. *Vol. 55.*
– Die Septuaginta. 1994. *Vol. 72.*
–, *Siegfried Mittmann* and *Anna Maria Schwemer* (Ed.): La Cité de Dieu / Die Stadt Gottes. 2000. *Vol. 129.*
Hentschel, Anni: Diakonia im Neuen Testament. 2007. *Vol. 226.*
Hernández Jr., Juan: Scribal Habits and Theological Influence in the Apocalypse. 2006. *Vol. II/218.*
Herrenbrück, Fritz: Jesus und die Zöllner. 1990. *Vol. II/41.*
Herzer, Jens: Paulus oder Petrus? 1998. *Vol. 103.*
– see *Böttrich, Christfried.*
– see *Frey, Jörg.*
Hill, Charles E.: From the Lost Teaching of Polycarp. 2005. *Vol. 186.*
Hoegen-Rohls, Christina: Der nachösterliche Johannes. 1996. *Vol. II/84.*
Hoffmann, Matthias Reinhard: The Destroyer and the Lamb. 2005. *Vol. II/203.*
Hofius, Otfried: Katapausis. 1970. *Vol. 11.*
– Der Vorhang vor dem Thron Gottes. 1972. *Vol. 14.*
– Der Christushymnus Philipper 2,6–11. 1976, ²1991. *Vol. 17.*
– Paulusstudien. 1989, ²1994. *Vol. 51.*
– Neutestamentliche Studien. 2000. *Vol. 132.*
– Paulusstudien II. 2002. *Vol. 143.*
– Exegetische Studien. 2008. *Vol. 223.*
– and *Hans-Christian Kammler:* Johannesstudien. 1996. *Vol. 88.*

Holloway, Paul A.: Coping with Prejudice. 2009. *Vol. 244.*
- see *Ahearne-Kroll, Stephen P.*

Holmberg, Bengt (Ed.): Exploring Early Christian Identity. 2008. *Vol. 226.*
- and *Mikael Winninge* (Ed.): Identity Formation in the New Testament. 2008. *Vol. 227.*

Holtz, Traugott: Geschichte und Theologie des Urchristentums. 1991. *Vol. 57.*

Hommel, Hildebrecht: Sebasmata.
  Vol. 1 1983. *Vol. 31.*
  Vol. 2 1984. *Vol. 32.*

Horbury, William: Herodian Judaism and New Testament Study. 2006. *Vol. 193.*

Horn, Friedrich Wilhelm and Ruben Zimmermann (Ed.): Jenseits von Indikativ und Imperativ. Vol. 1. 2009. *Vol. 238.*

Horst, Pieter W. van der: Jews and Christians in Their Graeco-Roman Context. 2006. *Vol. 196.*

Hultgård, Anders and Stig Norin (Ed): Le Jour de Dieu / Der Tag Gottes. 2009. *Vol. 245.*

Hvalvik, Reidar: The Struggle for Scripture and Covenant. 1996. *Vol. II/82.*

Jackson, Ryan: New Creation in Paul's Letters. 2010. *Vol. II/272.*

Janßen, Martina: see *Frey, Jörg.*

Jauhiainen, Marko: The Use of Zechariah in Revelation. 2005. *Vol. II/199.*

Jensen, Morten H.: Herod Antipas in Galilee. 2006; ²2010. *Vol. II/215.*

Johns, Loren L.: The Lamb Christology of the Apocalypse of John. 2003. *Vol. II/167.*

Jossa, Giorgio: Jews or Christians? 2006. *Vol. 202.*

Joubert, Stephan: Paul as Benefactor. 2000. *Vol. II/124.*

Judge, E. A.: The First Christians in the Roman World. 2008. *Vol. 229.*
- Jerusalem and Athens. 2010. *Vol. 265.*

Jungbauer, Harry: „Ehre Vater und Mutter". 2002. *Vol. II/146.*

Kähler, Christoph: Jesu Gleichnisse als Poesie und Therapie. 1995. *Vol. 78.*

Kamlah, Ehrhard: Die Form der katalogischen Paränese im Neuen Testament. 1964. *Vol. 7.*

Kammler, Hans-Christian: Christologie und Eschatologie. 2000. *Vol. 126.*
- Kreuz und Weisheit. 2003. *Vol. 159.*
- see *Hofius, Otfried.*

Karakolis, Christos: see *Alexeev, Anatoly A.*

Karrer, Martin und Wolfgang Kraus (Ed.): Die Septuaginta – Texte, Kontexte, Lebenswelten. 2008. *Vol. 219.*
- see *Kraus, Wolfgang.*

Kelhoffer, James A.: The Diet of John the Baptist. 2005. *Vol. 176.*
- Miracle and Mission. 1999. *Vol. II/112.*
- see *Ahearne-Kroll, Stephen P.*

Kelley, Nicole: Knowledge and Religious Authority in the Pseudo-Clementines. 2006. *Vol. II/213.*

Kennedy, Joel: The Recapitulation of Israel. 2008. *Vol. II/257.*

Kensky, Meira Z.: Trying Man, Trying God. 2010. *Vol. II/289.*

Kieffer, René and Jan Bergman (Ed.): La Main de Dieu / Die Hand Gottes. 1997. *Vol. 94.*

Kierspel, Lars: The Jews and the World in the Fourth Gospel. 2006. *Vol. 220.*

Kim, Seyoon: The Origin of Paul's Gospel. 1981, ²1984. *Vol. II/4.*
- Paul and the New Perspective. 2002. *Vol. 140.*
- "The 'Son of Man'" as the Son of God. 1983. *Vol. 30.*

Klauck, Hans-Josef: Religion und Gesellschaft im frühen Christentum. 2003. *Vol. 152.*

Klein, Hans, Vasile Mihoc und Karl-Wilhelm Niebuhr (Ed.): Das Gebet im Neuen Testament. Vierte, europäische orthodox-westliche Exegetenkonferenz in Sambata de Sus, 4. – 8. August 2007. 2009. Vol. 249.
- see *Dunn, James D.G.*

Kleinknecht, Karl Th.: Der leidende Gerechtfertigte. 1984, ²1988. *Vol. II/13.*

Klinghardt, Matthias: Gesetz und Volk Gottes. 1988. *Vol. II/32.*

Kloppenborg, John S.: The Tenants in the Vineyard. 2006, student edition 2010. *Vol. 195.*

Koch, Michael: Drachenkampf und Sonnenfrau. 2004. *Vol. II/184.*

Koch, Stefan: Rechtliche Regelung von Konflikten im frühen Christentum. 2004. *Vol. II/174.*

Köhler, Wolf-Dietrich: Rezeption des Matthäusevangeliums in der Zeit vor Irenäus. 1987. *Vol. II/24.*

Köhn, Andreas: Der Neutestamentler Ernst Lohmeyer. 2004. *Vol. II/180.*

Koester, Craig and Reimund Bieringer (Ed.): The Resurrection of Jesus in the Gospel of John. 2008. *Vol. 222.*

Konradt, Matthias: Israel, Kirche und die Völker im Matthäusevangelium. 2007. *Vol. 215.*

Kooten, George H. van: Cosmic Christology in Paul and the Pauline School. 2003. *Vol. II/171.*

- Paul's Anthropology in Context. 2008. *Vol. 232.*
Korn, Manfred: Die Geschichte Jesu in veränderter Zeit. 1993. *Vol. II/51.*
Koskenniemi, Erkki: Apollonios von Tyana in der neutestamentlichen Exegese. 1994. *Vol. II/61.*
- The Old Testament Miracle-Workers in Early Judaism. 2005. *Vol. II/206.*
Kraus, Thomas J.: Sprache, Stil und historischer Ort des zweiten Petrusbriefes. 2001. *Vol. II/136.*
Kraus, Wolfgang: Das Volk Gottes. 1996. *Vol. 85.*
- see *Karrer, Martin.*
- see *Walter, Nikolaus.*
- and *Martin Karrer* (Hrsg.): Die Septuaginta – Texte, Theologien, Einflüsse. 2010. *Bd. 252.*
- and *Karl-Wilhelm Niebuhr* (Ed.): Frühjudentum und Neues Testament im Horizont Biblischer Theologie. 2003. *Vol. 162.*
Krauter, Stefan: Studien zu Röm 13,1-7. 2009. *Vol. 243.*
- see *Frey, Jörg.*
Kreplin, Matthias: Das Selbstverständnis Jesu. 2001. *Vol. II/141.*
Kuhn, Karl G.: Achtzehngebet und Vaterunser und der Reim. 1950. *Vol. 1.*
Kvalbein, Hans: see *Ådna, Jostein.*
Kwon, Yon-Gyong: Eschatology in Galatians. 2004. *Vol. II/183.*
Laansma, Jon: I Will Give You Rest. 1997. *Vol. II/98.*
Labahn, Michael: Offenbarung in Zeichen und Wort. 2000. *Vol. II/117.*
Lambers-Petry, Doris: see *Tomson, Peter J.*
Lange, Armin: see *Ego, Beate.*
Lampe, Peter: Die stadtrömischen Christen in den ersten beiden Jahrhunderten. 1987, ²1989. *Vol. II/18.*
Landmesser, Christof: Wahrheit als Grundbegriff neutestamentlicher Wissenschaft. 1999. *Vol. 113.*
- Jüngerberufung und Zuwendung zu Gott. 2000. *Vol. 133.*
Lau, Andrew: Manifest in Flesh. 1996. *Vol. II/86.*
Lawrence, Louise: An Ethnography of the Gospel of Matthew. 2003. *Vol. II/165.*
Lee, Aquila H.I.: From Messiah to Preexistent Son. 2005. *Vol. II/192.*
Lee, Pilchan: The New Jerusalem in the Book of Relevation. 2000. *Vol. II/129.*
Lee, Sang M.: The Cosmic Drama of Salvation. 2010. *Vol. II/276.*
Lee, Simon S.: Jesus' Transfiguration and the Believers' Transformation. 2009. *Vol. II/265.*
Lichtenberger, Hermann: Das Ich Adams und das Ich der Menschheit. 2004. *Vol. 164.*
- see *Avemarie, Friedrich.*
- see *Frey, Jörg.*
Lierman, John: The New Testament Moses. 2004. *Vol. II/173.*
- (Ed.): Challenging Perspectives on the Gospel of John. 2006. *Vol. II/219.*
Lieu, Samuel N.C.: Manichaeism in the Later Roman Empire and Medieval China. ²1992. *Vol. 63.*
Lindemann, Andreas: Die Evangelien und die Apostelgeschichte. 2009. *Vol. 241.*
Lincicum, David: Paul and the Early Jewish Encounter with Deuteronomy. 2010. *Vol. II/284.*
Lindgård, Fredrik: Paul's Line of Thought in 2 Corinthians 4:16–5:10. 2004. *Vol. II/189.*
Livesey, Nina E.: Circumcision as a Malleable Symbol. 2010. *Vol. II/295.*
Loader, William R.G.: Jesus' Attitude Towards the Law. 1997. *Vol. II/97.*
Löhr, Gebhard: Verherrlichung Gottes durch Philosophie. 1997. *Vol. 97.*
Löhr, Hermut: Studien zum frühchristlichen und frühjüdischen Gebet. 2003. *Vol. 160.*
- see *Hengel, Martin.*
Löhr, Winrich Alfried: Basilides und seine Schule. 1995. *Vol. 83.*
Lorenzen, Stefanie: Das paulinische Eikon-Konzept. 2008. *Vol. II/250.*
Luomanen, Petri: Entering the Kingdom of Heaven. 1998. *Vol. II/101.*
Luz, Ulrich: see *Alexeev, Anatoly A.*
- see *Dunn, James D.G.*
Mackay, Ian D.: John's Raltionship with Mark. 2004. *Vol. II/182.*
Mackie, Scott D.: Eschatology and Exhortation in the Epistle to the Hebrews. 2006. *Vol. II/223.*
Magda, Ksenija: Paul's Territoriality and Mission Strategy. 2009. *Vol. II/266.*
Maier, Gerhard: Mensch und freier Wille. 1971. *Vol. 12.*
- Die Johannesoffenbarung und die Kirche. 1981. *Vol. 25.*
Markschies, Christoph: Valentinus Gnosticus? 1992. *Vol. 65.*
Marshall, Jonathan: Jesus, Patrons, and Benefactors. 2009. *Vol. II/259.*

Marshall, Peter: Enmity in Corinth: Social Conventions in Paul's Relations with the Corinthians. 1987. *Vol. II/23.*

Martin, Dale B.: see Zangenberg, Jürgen.

Maston, Jason: Divine and Human Agency in Second Temple Judaism and Paul. 2010. *Vol. II/297.*

Mayer, Annemarie: Sprache der Einheit im Epheserbrief und in der Ökumene. 2002. *Vol. II/150.*

Mayordomo, Moisés: Argumentiert Paulus logisch? 2005. *Vol. 188.*

McDonough, Sean M.: YHWH at Patmos: Rev. 1:4 in its Hellenistic and Early Jewish Setting. 1999. *Vol. II/107.*

McDowell, Markus: Prayers of Jewish Women. 2006. *Vol. II/211.*

McGlynn, Moyna: Divine Judgement and Divine Benevolence in the Book of Wisdom. 2001. *Vol. II/139.*

Meade, David G.: Pseudonymity and Canon. 1986. *Vol. 39.*

Meadors, Edward P.: Jesus the Messianic Herald of Salvation. 1995. *Vol. II/72.*

Meißner, Stefan: Die Heimholung des Ketzers. 1996. *Vol. II/87.*

Mell, Ulrich: Die „anderen" Winzer. 1994. *Vol. 77.*

– see *Sänger, Dieter.*

Mengel, Berthold: Studien zum Philipperbrief. 1982. *Vol. II/8.*

Merkel, Helmut: Die Widersprüche zwischen den Evangelien. 1971. *Vol. 13.*

– see *Ego, Beate.*

Merklein, Helmut: Studien zu Jesus und Paulus. Vol. 1 1987. *Vol. 43.* – Vol. 2 1998. *Vol. 105.*

Merkt, Andreas: see Nicklas, Tobias

Metzdorf, Christina: Die Tempelaktion Jesu. 2003. *Vol. II/168.*

Metzler, Karin: Der griechische Begriff des Verzeihens. 1991. *Vol. II/44.*

Metzner, Rainer: Die Rezeption des Matthäusevangeliums im 1. Petrusbrief. 1995. *Vol. II/74.*

– Das Verständnis der Sünde im Johannesevangelium. 2000. *Vol. 122.*

Mihoc, Vasile: see Dunn, James D.G.

– see *Klein, Hans.*

Mineshige, Kiyoshi: Besitzverzicht und Almosen bei Lukas. 2003. *Vol. II/163.*

Mittmann, Siegfried: see Hengel, Martin.

Mittmann-Richert, Ulrike: Magnifikat und Benediktus. *1996. Vol. II/90.*

– Der Sühnetod des Gottesknechts. 2008. *Vol. 220.*

Miura, Yuzuru: David in Luke-Acts. 2007. *Vol. II/232.*

Moll, Sebastian: The Arch-Heretic Marcion. 2010. *Vol. 250.*

Morales, Rodrigo J.: The Spirit and the Restorat. 2010. *Vol. 282.*

Mournet, Terence C.: Oral Tradition and Literary Dependency. 2005. *Vol. II/195.*

Mußner, Franz: Jesus von Nazareth im Umfeld Israels und der Urkirche. Ed. von M. Theobald. 1998. *Vol. 111.*

Mutschler, Bernhard: Das Corpus Johanneum bei Irenäus von Lyon. 2005. *Vol. 189.*

– Glaube in den Pastoralbriefen. 2010. *Vol. 256.*

Myers, Susan E.: Spirit Epicleses in the Acts of Thomas. 2010. *Vol. 281.*

Nguyen, V. Henry T.: Christian Identity in Corinth. 2008. *Vol. II/243.*

Nicklas, Tobias, Andreas Merkt und *Joseph Verheyden* (Ed.): Gelitten – Gestorben – Auferstanden. 2010. *Vol. II/273.*

– see *Verheyden, Joseph*

Niebuhr, Karl-Wilhelm: Gesetz and Paränese. 1987. *Vol. II/28.*

– Heidenapostel aus Israel. 1992. *Vol. 62.*

– see *Deines, Roland.*

– see *Dimitrov, Ivan Z.*

– see *Klein, Hans.*

– see *Kraus, Wolfgang.*

Nielsen, Anders E.: "Until it is Fullfilled". 2000. *Vol. II/126.*

Nielsen, Jesper Tang: Die kognitive Dimension des Kreuzes. 2009. *Vol. II/263.*

Nissen, Andreas: Gott und der Nächste im antiken Judentum. 1974. *Vol. 15.*

Noack, Christian: Gottesbewußtsein. 2000. *Vol. II/116.*

Noormann, Rolf: Irenäus als Paulusinterpret. 1994. *Vol. II/66.*

Norin, Stig: see Hultgård, Anders.

Novakovic, Lidija: Messiah, the Healer of the Sick. 2003. *Vol. II/170.*

Obermann, Andreas: Die christologische Erfüllung der Schrift im Johannesevangelium. 1996. *Vol. II/83.*

Öhler, Markus: Barnabas. 2003. *Vol. 156.*

– see *Becker, Michael.*

Okure, Teresa: The Johannine Approach to Mission. 1988. *Vol. II/31.*

Onuki, Takashi: Heil und Erlösung. 2004. *Vol. 165.*

Oropeza, B. J.: Paul and Apostasy. 2000. *Vol. II/115.*

Ostmeyer, Karl-Heinrich: Kommunikation mit Gott und Christus. 2006. *Vol. 197.*
- Taufe und Typos. 2000. *Vol. II/118.*

Pao, David W.: Acts and the Isaianic New Exodus. 2000. *Vol. II/130.*

Park, Eung Chun: The Mission Discourse in Matthew's Interpretation. 1995. *Vol. II/81.*

Park, Joseph S.: Conceptions of Afterlife in Jewish Insriptions. 2000. *Vol. II/121.*

Parsenios, George L.: Rhetoric and Drama in the Johannine Lawsuit Motif. 2010. *Vol. 258.*

Pate, C. Marvin: The Reverse of the Curse. 2000. *Vol. II/114.*

Paulsen, Henning: Studien zur Literatur und Geschichte des frühen Christentums. Ed. von Ute E. Eisen. 1997. *Vol. 99.*

Pearce, Sarah J.K.: The Land of the Body. 2007. *Vol. 208.*

Peres, Imre: Griechische Grabinschriften und neutestamentliche Eschatologie. 2003. *Vol. 157.*

Perry, Peter S.: The Rhetoric of Digressions. 2009. *Vol. II/268.*

Philip, Finny: The Origins of Pauline Pneumatology. 2005. *Vol. II/194.*

Philonenko, Marc (Ed.): Le Trône de Dieu. 1993. *Vol. 69.*

Pilhofer, Peter: Presbyteron Kreitton. 1990. *Vol. II/39.*
- Philippi. Vol. 1 1995. *Vol. 87.* – Vol. 2 ²2009. *Vol. 119.*
- Die frühen Christen und ihre Welt. 2002. *Vol. 145.*
- see *Becker, Eve-Marie.*
- see *Ego, Beate.*

Pitre, Brant: Jesus, the Tribulation, and the End of the Exile. 2005. *Vol. II/204.*

Plümacher, Eckhard: Geschichte und Geschichten. 2004. *Vol. 170.*

Pöhlmann, Wolfgang: Der Verlorene Sohn und das Haus. 1993. *Vol. 68.*

Poirier, John C.: The Tongues of Angels. 2010. *Vol. II/287.*

Pokorný, Petr and *Josef B. Souček:* Bibelauslegung als Theologie. 1997. *Vol. 100.*
- and *Jan Roskovec* (Ed.): Philosophical Hermeneutics and Biblical Exegesis. 2002. *Vol. 153.*

Popkes, Enno Edzard: Das Menschenbild des Thomasevangeliums. 2007. *Vol. 206.*
- Die Theologie der Liebe Gottes in den johanneischen Schriften. 2005. *Vol. II/197.*

Porter, Stanley E.: The Paul of Acts. 1999. *Vol. 115.*

Prieur, Alexander: Die Verkündigung der Gottesherrschaft. 1996. *Vol. II/89.*

Probst, Hermann: Paulus und der Brief. 1991. *Vol. II/45.*

Puig i Tàrrech, Armand: Jesus: An Uncommon Journey. 2010. *Vol. II/288.*

Rabens, Volker: The Holy Spirit and Ethics in Paul. 2010. *Vol. II/283.*

Räisänen, Heikki: Paul and the Law. 1983, ²1987. *Vol. 29.*

Rehkopf, Friedrich: Die lukanische Sonderquelle. 1959. *Vol. 5.*

Rein, Matthias: Die Heilung des Blindgeborenen (Joh 9). 1995. *Vol. II/73.*

Reinmuth, Eckart: Pseudo-Philo und Lukas. 1994. *Vol. 74.*

Reiser, Marius: Bibelkritik und Auslegung der Heiligen Schrift. 2007. *Vol. 217.*
- Syntax und Stil des Markusevangeliums. 1984. *Vol. II/11.*

Reynolds, Benjamin E.: The Apocalyptic Son of Man in the Gospel of John. 2008. *Vol. II/249.*

Rhodes, James N.: The Epistle of Barnabas and the Deuteronomic Tradition. 2004. *Vol. II/188.*

Richards, E. Randolph: The Secretary in the Letters of Paul. 1991. *Vol. II/42.*

Riesner, Rainer: Jesus als Lehrer. 1981, ³1988. *Vol. II/7.*
- Die Frühzeit des Apostels Paulus. 1994. *Vol. 71.*

Rissi, Mathias: Die Theologie des Hebräerbriefs. 1987. *Vol. 41.*

Röcker, Fritz W.: Belial und Katechon. 2009. *Vol. II/262.*

Röhser, Günter: Metaphorik und Personifikation der Sünde. 1987. *Vol. II/25.*

Rose, Christian: Theologie als Erzählung im Markusevangelium. 2007. *Vol. II/236.*
- Die Wolke der Zeugen. 1994. *Vol. II/60.*

Roskovec, Jan: see *Pokorný, Petr.*

Rothschild, Clare K.: Baptist Traditions and Q. 2005. *Vol. 190.*
- Hebrews as Pseudepigraphon. 2009. *Vol. 235.*
- Luke Acts and the Rhetoric of History. 2004. *Vol. II/175.*
- see *Frey, Jörg.*

Rüegger, Hans-Ulrich: Verstehen, was Markus erzählt. 2002. *Vol. II/155.*

Rüger, Hans Peter: Die Weisheitsschrift aus der Kairoer Geniza. 1991. *Vol. 53.*

Sänger, Dieter: Antikes Judentum und die Mysterien. 1980. *Vol. II/5.*

- Die Verkündigung des Gekreuzigten und Israel. 1994. *Vol. 75.*
- see *Burchard, Christoph*
- and *Ulrich Mell* (Ed.): Paulus und Johannes. 2006. *Vol. 198.*

Salier, Willis Hedley: The Rhetorical Impact of the Semeia in the Gospel of John. 2004. *Vol. II/186.*

Salzmann, Jorg Christian: Lehren und Ermahnen. 1994. *Vol. II/59.*

Sandnes, Karl Olav: Paul – One of the Prophets? 1991. *Vol. II/43.*

Sato, Migaku: Q und Prophetie. 1988. *Vol. II/29.*

Schäfer, Ruth: Paulus bis zum Apostelkonzil. 2004. *Vol. II/179.*

Schaper, Joachim: Eschatology in the Greek Psalter. 1995. *Vol. II/76.*

Schimanowski, Gottfried: Die himmlische Liturgie in der Apokalypse des Johannes. 2002. *Vol. II/154.*
- Weisheit und Messias. 1985. *Vol. II/17.*

Schlichting, Günter: Ein jüdisches Leben Jesu. 1982. *Vol. 24.*

Schließer, Benjamin: Abraham's Faith in Romans 4. 2007. *Vol. II/224.*

Schnabel, Eckhard J.: Law and Wisdom from Ben Sira to Paul. 1985. *Vol. II/16.*

Schnelle, Udo: see *Frey, Jörg.*

Schröter, Jens: Von Jesus zum Neuen Testament. 2007. *Vol. 204.*
- see *Frey, Jörg.*

Schutter, William L.: Hermeneutic and Composition in I Peter. 1989. *Vol. II/30.*

Schwartz, Daniel R.: Studies in the Jewish Background of Christianity. 1992. *Vol. 60.*

Schwemer, Anna Maria: see *Hengel, Martin*

Scott, Ian W.: Implicit Epistemology in the Letters of Paul. 2005. *Vol. II/205.*

Scott, James M.: Adoption as Sons of God. 1992. *Vol. II/48.*
- Paul and the Nations. 1995. *Vol. 84.*

Shi, Wenhua: Paul's Message of the Cross as Body Language. 2008. *Vol. II/254.*

Shum, Shiu-Lun: Paul's Use of Isaiah in Romans. 2002. *Vol. II/156.*

Siegert, Folker: Drei hellenistisch-jüdische Predigten. Teil I 1980. *Vol. 20* – Teil II 1992. *Vol. 61.*
- Nag-Hammadi-Register. 1982. *Vol. 26.*
- Argumentation bei Paulus. 1985. *Vol. 34.*
- Philon von Alexandrien. 1988. *Vol. 46.*

Simon, Marcel: Le christianisme antique et son contexte religieux I/II. 1981. *Vol. 23.*

Smit, Peter-Ben: Fellowship and Food in the Kingdom. 2008. *Vol. II/234.*

Snodgrass, Klyne: The Parable of the Wicked Tenants. 1983. *Vol. 27.*

Söding, Thomas: Das Wort vom Kreuz. 1997. *Vol. 93.*
- see *Thüsing, Wilhelm.*

Sommer, Urs: Die Passionsgeschichte des Markusevangeliums. 1993. *Vol. II/58.*

Sorensen, Eric: Possession and Exorcism in the New Testament and Early Christianity. 2002. *Vol. II/157.*

Souček, Josef B.: see *Pokorný, Petr.*

Southall, David J.: Rediscovering Righteousness in Romans. 2008. *Vol. 240.*

Spangenberg, Volker: Herrlichkeit des Neuen Bundes. 1993. *Vol. II/55.*

Spanje, T.E. van: Inconsistency in Paul? 1999. *Vol. II/110.*

Speyer, Wolfgang: Frühes Christentum im antiken Strahlungsfeld. Vol. I: 1989. *Vol. 50.*
- Vol. II: 1999. *Vol. 116.*
- Vol. III: 2007. *Vol. 213.*

Spittler, Janet E.: Animals in the Apocryphal Acts of the Apostles. 2008. *Vol. II/247.*

Sprinkle, Preston: Law and Life. 2008. *Vol. II/241.*

Stadelmann, Helge: Ben Sira als Schriftgelehrter. 1980. *Vol. II/6.*

Stein, Hans Joachim: Frühchristliche Mahlfeiern. 2008. *Vol. II/255.*

Stenschke, Christoph W.: Luke's Portrait of Gentiles Prior to Their Coming to Faith. *Vol. II/108.*

Sterck-Degueldre, Jean-Pierre: Eine Frau namens Lydia. 2004. *Vol. II/176.*

Stettler, Christian: Der Kolosserhymnus. 2000. *Vol. II/131.*

Stettler, Hanna: Die Christologie der Pastoralbriefe. 1998. *Vol. II/105.*

Stökl Ben Ezra, Daniel: The Impact of Yom Kippur on Early Christianity. 2003. *Vol. 163.*

Strobel, August: Die Stunde der Wahrheit. 1980. *Vol. 21.*

Stroumsa, Guy G.: Barbarian Philosophy. 1999. *Vol. 112.*

Stuckenbruck, Loren T.: Angel Veneration and Christology. 1995. *Vol. II/70.*
-, *Stephen C. Barton* and *Benjamin G. Wold* (Ed.): Memory in the Bible and Antiquity. 2007. *Vol. 212.*

Stuhlmacher, Peter (Ed.): Das Evangelium und die Evangelien. 1983. *Vol. 28.*
- Biblische Theologie und Evangelium. 2002. *Vol. 146.*

Sung, Chong-Hyon: Vergebung der Sünden. 1993. *Vol. II/57.*

Svendsen, Stefan N.: Allegory Transformed. 2009. *Vol. II/269.*
Tajra, Harry W.: The Trial of St. Paul. 1989. *Vol. II/35.*
– The Martyrdom of St.Paul. 1994. *Vol. II/67.*
Tellbe, Mikael: Christ-Believers in Ephesus. 2009. *Vol. 242.*
Theißen, Gerd: Studien zur Soziologie des Urchristentums. 1979, ³1989. *Vol. 19.*
Theobald, Michael: Studien zum Römerbrief. 2001. *Vol. 136.*
Theobald, Michael: see *Mußner, Franz.*
Thornton, Claus-Jürgen: Der Zeuge des Zeugen. 1991. *Vol. 56.*
Thüsing, Wilhelm: Studien zur neutestamentlichen Theologie. Ed. von Thomas Söding. 1995. *Vol. 82.*
Thurén, Lauri: Derhethorizing Paul. 2000. *Vol. 124.*
Thyen, Hartwig: Studien zum Corpus Iohanneum. 2007. *Vol. 214.*
Tibbs, Clint: Religious Experience of the Pneuma. 2007. *Vol. II/230.*
Toit, David S. du: Theios Anthropos. 1997. *Vol. II/91.*
Tolmie, D. Francois: Persuading the Galatians. 2005. *Vol. II/190.*
Tomson, Peter J. and *Doris Lambers-Petry* (Ed.): The Image of the Judaeo-Christians in Ancient Jewish and Christian Literature. 2003. *Vol. 158.*
Toney, Carl N.: Paul's Inclusive Ethic. 2008. *Vol. II/252.*
Trebilco, Paul: The Early Christians in Ephesus from Paul to Ignatius. 2004. *Vol. 166.*
Treloar, Geoffrey R.: Lightfoot the Historian. 1998. *Vol. II/103.*
Troftgruben, Troy M.: A Conclusion Unhindered. 2010. *Vol. II/280.*
Tso, Marcus K.M.: Ethics in the Qumran Community. 2010. *Vol. II/292.*
Tsuji, Manabu: Glaube zwischen Vollkommenheit und Verweltlichung. 1997. *Vol. II/93.*
Twelftree, Graham H.: Jesus the Exorcist. 1993. *Vol. II/54.*
Ulrichs, Karl Friedrich: Christusglaube. 2007. *Vol. II/227.*
Urban, Christina: Das Menschenbild nach dem Johannesevangelium. 2001. *Vol. II/137.*
Vahrenhorst, Martin: Kultische Sprache in den Paulusbriefen. 2008. *Vol. 230.*
Vegge, Ivar: 2 Corinthians – a Letter about Reconciliation. 2008. *Vol. II/239.*
Verheyden, Joseph, Korinna Zamfir and *Tobias Nicklas* (Ed.): Prophets and Prophecy in Jewish and Early Christian Literature. 2010. *Vol. II/286.*
– see *Nicklas, Tobias*
Visotzky, Burton L.: Fathers of the World. 1995. *Vol. 80.*
Vollenweider, Samuel: Horizonte neutestamentlicher Christologie. 2002. *Vol. 144.*
Vos, Johan S.: Die Kunst der Argumentation bei Paulus. 2002. *Vol. 149.*
Waaler, Erik: The *Shema* and The First Commandment in First Corinthians. 2008. *Vol. II/253.*
Wagener, Ulrike: Die Ordnung des „Hauses Gottes". 1994. *Vol. II/65.*
Wagner, J. Ross: see *Wilk, Florian.*
Wahlen, Clinton: Jesus and the Impurity of Spirits in the Synoptic Gospels. 2004. *Vol. II/185.*
Walker, Donald D.: Paul's Offer of Leniency (2 Cor 10:1). 2002. *Vol. II/152.*
Walter, Nikolaus: Praeparatio Evangelica. Ed. von Wolfgang Kraus und Florian Wilk. 1997. *Vol. 98.*
Wander, Bernd: Gottesfürchtige und Sympathisanten. 1998. *Vol. 104.*
Wardle, Timothy: The Jerusalem Temple and Early Christian Identity. 2010. *Vol. II/291.*
Wasserman, Emma: The Death of the Soul in Romans 7. 2008. *Vol. 256.*
Waters, Guy: The End of Deuteronomy in the Epistles of Paul. 2006. *Vol. 221.*
Watt, Jan G. van der: see *Frey, Jörg*
– see *Zimmermann, Ruben*
Watts, Rikki: Isaiah's New Exodus and Mark. 1997. *Vol. II/88.*
Webb, Robert L.: see *Bock, Darrell L.*
Wedderburn, A.J.M.: Baptism and Resurrection. 1987. *Vol. 44.*
Wegner, Uwe: Der Hauptmann von Kafarnaum. 1985. *Vol. II/14.*
Weiß, Hans-Friedrich: Frühes Christentum und Gnosis. 2008. *Vol. 225.*
Weissenrieder, Annette: Images of Illness in the Gospel of Luke. 2003. Vol. II/164.
–, and *Robert B. Coote* (Ed.): The Interface of Orality and Writing. 2010. *Vol. 260.*
–, *Friederike Wendt* and *Petra von Gemünden* (Ed.): Picturing the New Testament. 2005. *Vol. II/193.*
Welck, Christian: Erzählte ‚Zeichen'. 1994. *Vol. II/69.*
Wendt, Friederike (Ed.): see *Weissenrieder, Annette.*
Wiarda, Timothy: Peter in the Gospels. 2000. *Vol. II/127.*

Wifstrand, Albert: Epochs and Styles. 2005. *Vol. 179.*

Wilk, Florian and *J. Ross Wagner* (Ed.): Between Gospel and Election. 2010. *Vol. 257.*

– see *Walter, Nikolaus.*

Williams, Catrin H.: I am He. 2000. *Vol. II/113.*

Wilson, Todd A.: The Curse of the Law and the Crisis in Galatia. 2007. *Vol. II/225.*

Wilson, Walter T.: Love without Pretense. 1991. *Vol. II/46.*

Winn, Adam: The Purpose of Mark's Gospel. 2008. *Vol. II/245.*

Winninge, Mikael: see *Holmberg, Bengt.*

Wischmeyer, Oda: Von Ben Sira zu Paulus. 2004. *Vol. 173.*

Wisdom, Jeffrey: Blessing for the Nations and the Curse of the Law. 2001. *Vol. II/133.*

Witmer, Stephen E.: Divine Instruction in Early Christianity. 2008. *Vol. II/246.*

Wold, Benjamin G.: Women, Men, and Angels. 2005. *Vol. II/2001.*

Wolter, Michael: Theologie und Ethos im frühen Christentum. 2009. *Vol. 236.*

– see *Stuckenbruck, Loren T.*

Wright, Archie T.: The Origin of Evil Spirits. 2005. *Vol. II/198.*

Wucherpfennig, Ansgar: Heracleon Philologus. 2002. *Vol. 142.*

Yates, John W.: The Spirit and Creation in Paul. 2008. *Vol. II/251.*

Yeung, Maureen: Faith in Jesus and Paul. 2002. *Vol. II/147.*

Zamfir, Corinna: see *Verheyden, Joseph*

Zangenberg, Jürgen, Harold W. Attridge and *Dale B. Martin* (Ed.): Religion, Ethnicity and Identity in Ancient Galilee. 2007. *Vol. 210.*

Zimmermann, Alfred E.: Die urchristlichen Lehrer. 1984, [2]1988. *Vol. II/12.*

Zimmermann, Johannes: Messianische Texte aus Qumran. 1998. *Vol. II/104.*

Zimmermann, Ruben: Christologie der Bilder im Johannesevangelium. 2004. *Vol. 171.*

– Geschlechtermetaphorik und Gottesverhältnis. 2001. *Vol. II/122.*

– (Ed.): Hermeneutik der Gleichnisse Jesu. 2008. *Vol. 231.*

– and *Jan G. van der Watt* (Ed.): Moral Language in the New Testament. Vol. II. 2010. *Vol. II/296.*

– see *Frey, Jörg.*

– see *Horn, Friedrich Wilhelm.*

Zugmann, Michael: „Hellenisten" in der Apostelgeschichte. 2009. *Vol. II/264.*

Zumstein, Jean: see *Dettwiler, Andreas*

Zwiep, Arie W.: Christ, the Spirit and the Community of God. 2010. *Vol. II/293.*

– Judas and the Choice of Matthias. 2004. *Vol. II/187.*

www.ingramcontent.com/pod-product-compliance
Lightning Source LLC
Chambersburg PA
CBHW070312230426
43663CB00011B/2098